My eyes were opened during the storm of freedom. When I look back in time I often think what an unparalleled experience it was to be grown up in the melting pot of emotions surrounding India's Freedom Movement.

As a child I was often bewildered at what I regarded to be two conflicting ideas, on one hand we were fighting the Sahibs, however on numerous occasions some of the Sahib friends were regular visitors to our home and had conversation with my grandfather. As I grew up, my grandfather patiently explained to me that the ongoing disagreement was not with the Sahibs themselves but with the ruling government.

One of my most memorable childhood memories was seeing Gandhiji in person. He was one of the most charismatic persons I have ever met. I remember feeling moved and awe stuck with his presence amidst us.

Delving into the faded pages of history has taken me no less than fifteen years, gathering information form every source thinkable. My journey enabled me to experience the ambience of those times and go through all the emotions associated with them.

My only regret is that Ramalingam's personal account of the freedom struggle had never been recorded by us, but on the other hand we are fortunate to have the account in his wife Pillamma's voice and words.

HE LET GANDHI INTO HIS LIFE

Dedication

My grandparents told me that no good work is done alone. The freedom of India was achieved by the struggle and sacrifices of thousands of Indians all over the country. Similarly many citizens of Berhampur sacrificed their lives to free the country from the colonial rule and in time went into oblivion and were forgotten by the people of Berhampur. I sincerely wish to dedicate this biography *"He Let Gandhi into His Life"* of Pandit W.V.V.B. Ramalingam, a freedom fighter of Berhampur to the memory of every freedom fighter of the town Berhampur, Ganjam District, Orissa.

Janaki Sastry

HE LET GANDHI INTO HIS LIFE

AUSTIN MACAULEY
PUBLISHERS LTD.

A CIP catalogue record for this title is available from the British Library.

ISBN 978 184963 597 4

www.austinmacauley.com

First Published (2014)
Austin Macauley Publishers Ltd.
25 Canada Square
Canary Wharf
London
E14 5LB

Printed and bound in Great Britain

Acknowledgments

I would like to express my gratitude towards everybody who provided support from the onset. I sincerely thank them for their contribution in giving me valuable information that's relevant to this historical biography- *"He let Gandhi into His Life"*. Their inspiration was encouraging to me. This mammoth task of collecting facts and figures of bygone days wouldn't have been possible without the combined cooperation of many people. I appreciate their immense patience to my constant queries about the missing pieces of this historic era.

There were two people without whom this project would not have been possible. Mr. Ramesh Pothapragada who gave me the initial support in this project; and Mr. Ch. Amritalingam, who sent me the first recorded information about the protagonist and encouraged me to pursue with this mammoth task of delving into the history of bygone days. This was quite a challenge as the street names of the town have been changed over time. And also the records of many freedom fighters of the town were deleted from the history of Berhampur. Berhampur was a town with amicable people of all religions and languages, who stood united to face the storm of Indian Freedom. Our present has its foundations in the past and it must be remembered with due respect.

I especially appreciate the cooperation of the following people:

Dr P. Laxman Rao, Edmund Ward of ESW Proof Reading Service, Dr. P. Mahalkshmi, Mike Trenchard of The Trenchard Partnership, Pudipeddi Venugopal Rao; Dr P. Santa Kumari; Mr. P. Satyanarayana (Babu); W. V.G. Venkata Ramana; Mr S . N. Rao Pochiraju; P. Raghuveer; Dorian Leveque of British Library; Dr W.G. Rama Rao; The National Portrait Gallery; Venkateswarlu Pothapragada (PV Swarlu); P.Ravitez; Mahita Sastry; P. Dev Kumar; P. Narasimha Rajesh; W. Renuka; P. Venkateswarlu (Bullu); Ian Barton; P. Sundereswar; family & friends. I sincerely thank those entire unknown contributors in the internet.

I sincerely thank Vinh Tran, the coordinator of the production team and all at Austin Macauley Publishers whose continuous support made it possible to bring this historical biography to light.

My deepest gratitude is to the family and friends who kindly donated photos from their family albums for this biography.

"It's easy to stand in the crowd but it takes courage to stand alone."

Mahatma Gandhi

Contents

1
The Big Move

In everybody's life, one unexpected event can turn your life into complete turmoil and shove you into a path of no return. Be it deliberate, be it planned, or be it the play of Fate, it can never be undone. As the river always flows forward, so in life there is no turning back. Often disasters enter into lives unaware, misfortunes strike without warning, and destiny plays mischief, just for its own fun. The victim helplessly watches his life drift away right from under his feet.

If you happened to be a traditional and an obedient wife in those days, there was no escape but to go along with the tide of life. Pillamma never forgot the day when her life dragged her into a completely new avenue. She became a mute spectator to the events that took shape in front of her without her prior knowledge or consent.

The family hadn't yet adjusted to the episode of Ramalingam's resignation when the master of the house, fondly known as 'Masterji' to all, made the sudden announcement that shook the entire family to its roots.

It was the second day in the month of March 1922 when Ramalingam, the eldest son of the family, the guardian of his extended family, announced in his calm and cool manner that he was leaving home. There wasn't any advance notice given or any time to prepare for the big move that involved his permanent separation from the extended family to which he was mentally, morally, and dutifully tied. He made his announcement casually in a candid manner, without exhibiting any emotions, soon after the family had their lunch.

If ever 'casual' was the apt word for his announcement that would be utterly wrong. He blasted his announcement more like a bombshell. The initial reaction from the family was of sheer shock, followed by panic and an unknown fright. Already two bullock-carts and a *Tonga* stood waiting outside the smaller of the two houses, which was attached to the big house where his whole extended family lived together. The two houses had a connecting door from the kitchen. Otherwise, the two houses of two different sizes were independent properties. But their back garden was one, with a common well. All the vendors and workers and servants used the back door and entered the main house from the garden. The smaller of the two houses was used by the eldest son, Ramalingam, and his family. He had his vast library and office in his quarters where he had conference with his staff and friends without interruption.

The whole family had a common kitchen where the meals were prepared for the whole family. Ramalingam preferred to eat his lunch separately, served by his wife, as it was the only time they had some privacy. In the evenings he had his meal with the whole family in the dining hall of the main house. In his presence the children of the family and his two younger brothers behaved immaculately. They ate their food in silence and in haste to 'escape' from the watchful eye of the Masterji.

Ramalingam insisted that the whole family should be present at evening mealtime, but such rules did not suit his youngest brother, Balaram, who was an outgoing person and spent a lot of time out with his friends. He hated discipline but all the same, like everybody else, he respected his eldest brother and followed the family rules. In view of the considerable age difference between Ramalingam and his two younger brothers, he became more of a father figure than a big brother to them.

Ramalingam realised that the females and the servants in his home worked hard. He told his brothers that they should have their dinner on time so that the servants could have theirs soon after. The men could go out after mealtime. Perhaps due to his professional character the Masterji believed in explaining his rules rather than ordering his family and as such the family followed them without any qualms. His logic was just and nobody at home could deny it. Unlike in some families, in Ramalingam's house even the servants had the same food as the family did, and in return the servants worked wholeheartedly and always showed their loyalty to the family.

Ramalingam had a habit of going on long walks after the evening meal, and returned home late at night. His walks put terror in the hearts of the youngsters and students. If any young person stood loitering after dark at the Barracks ground, Ramalingam would advise them to go home and study. Many of the young lads never waited to be told, since as soon as they saw Masterji at a distance they knew their 'playtime' was over. As a rule, the girls had no permission from their families to stay out after sunset.

Some men of the town spent a lot of time in the Park, across the Ramalingam-Tank, on the banks of the temple, listening to the radio and to the news that was broadcasted on the tannoy. The Park was a hot arena for discussions on the latest political issues. A few elderly men relaxed in one corner of the Park, musing about their lives and their families. The Park had different corners for different issues, but all the same discipline was maintained by all visitors to the Park. Most men felt it was a privilege to go there and mingle with the elite of the town. No female ever entered the Park alone or even accompanied by their men. There was a strict segregation between men and women, although women had their freedom to mingle with other females.

When Ramalingam returned from his rounds, he read for a while until his wife returned to the bedroom after completing her domestic duties. As the eldest of the three daughters-in-law of the family it was her duty to sort out all the domestic chores before she retired for the night. In an extended family women never had much rest. Although Ramalingam had separate quarters from the rest of the family, his wife and his three children spent their time with their cousins, uncles, and aunts in the big house and were thoroughly pampered by their grandmother. All in all it was a happy family, set up to the envy of many.

Recently, since Ramalingam had resigned from his job and become involved in political unrest, the tension in the family had developed gradually and the silent cracks began to show outwardly. None of them could confront the master of the family, so they took out their anger and frustration on his wife, Pillamma, who listened to their concerns, their taunting and pleading, with the serenity of a saint. Like them she, too, had no control over the present situation. Pillamma had no say in her husband's resolution and she accepted that her place was to be in his shadow.

On that fateful day, after lunch he started packing his books and the servants began to stack the boxes carefully in the bullock-carts

"Are you going somewhere, son?" asked his mother politely. She could boss anyone at home but when she was in her eldest son's presence, she was extremely polite and soft-spoken. Perhaps years of conditioning to respect the master of the house made her behave so meekly in her eldest son's presence.

Once again Ramalingam repeated his announcement that he was leaving home. The women began to wail and cry and the two brothers stood by the door with their heads hung low. They had no guts to protest openly. Ramalingam approached his brothers and handed over a legal document to both of them, in effect the ownership of the property. He had signed off the two houses to his two brothers; the family home to the second son, Jagappa, and the smaller house to his youngest brother, Balaram. Stunned and bewildered they watched him with tears in their eyes. Their mother tried to change Ramalingam's mind by saying that it wasn't an auspicious time to move house but she failed to convince him. Ramalingam had made up his mind, and no astrological calculations and no amount of tears from his beloved family could change his mind.

"Mother is going to live with me," he told the family. Once again the crying, wailing, and protesting began in earnest.

"I don't want to go anywhere. I'm staying here, right here!" Mother proclaimed and to show her protest was serious, she pulled her veil down over her shaved head she sat down on the floor with her legs and arms crossed and began to weep.

Ramalingam was not the one to get into any debate. He asked Jagappa to look after their mother and declared that Jagappa was now the head of the family. He promised to visit the family as often as he could.

As the bewildered family watched the scene with dazed eyes, Masterji got into the Tonga with his wife and three children. Apart from him, everybody was in tears. The neighbours gathered in the street and on their verandas to watch the free spectacle. Ramalingam's mother kept wailing, often adjusting her veil down her smooth shaven head and begged him not to go, and his brothers stood there like statues and wondered what had happened to their brother to make him leave home so suddenly.

The crowd began to speculate, at which they excelled. They let their imagination run wild.

"I think that old woman with her big mouth must have tortured Pillamma. How long can any husband tolerate it?"

"I don't think so, if you must know her mother-in-law is very fond of Pillamma. But it's true she didn't like her when she was barren."

Even after having three healthy children, including a son, Pillamma could never shed her tag of 'barren woman'. The women in the society never let anyone forget their past. They broached it at every available opportunity, and took pleasure in belittling their fellow females. Their approach was always cunning. Often they would visit a troubled family to sympathise with them, but soon with the slyness of a fox they stabbed them with their sharp tongues and departed with a smirk on their faces. The victimised family often felt drained out after the visits of their sympathisers.

One kind woman stood up for Pillamma and reminded them that she was now a mother of three, including a son. But on that occasion the women did not pursue the barren issue any further as men were present there. Bitching and belittling often took place behind the backs of men and most of the time men were ignorant of 'women's matters', as they coined it.

"No use blaming anyone when our Masterji makes up his mind, can anybody change it? Don't you know, even the Maharaja of the college couldn't make him withdraw his resignation," one onlooker remarked, with a smile on his face. It turned to a smirk as he lifted his collar up and glanced at the crowd, for giving them the inside information he got from his friend Balaram, the youngest son of the family.

The crowd was not ready to accept that the drama was all that simple. They speculated that something serious might have happened at home front for Ramalingam to take such a drastic step. A few of the women felt that Pillamma must have had a sneaky hand in the matter and remarked that she hid her wickedness tactfully behind her politeness and smiles. Another one pointed out that even Pillamma was in tears leaving home.

But some of them felt that Pillamma was pretending to be sorry to gain their sympathy. Their speculations and counter-speculations continued as the bullock-carts were being loaded. Finally majority of the women present there concluded that Pillamma was to be blamed for that family break-up. An odd few people felt that Ramalingam had lost his mind. He had first resigned from his plum job and now he left his ancestral home for good. The house-moving had become a hot issue of the town and an excellent topic for gossip. Suddenly, a wise cracker came out with his own theory: he declared that as Masterji was no longer the earning member, the family had thrown him and his wife and children into the street. There were as many opinions as there were mouths. The citizens' tongues wagged endlessly.

Some of their comments reached the mother's ears and saddened her more. Attacks and counter-attacks, comments and criticisms flourished in town like nobody's business. The bystanders had their fill of gossip for days to come. As always, they were united in their attacks for a while, but soon they began to quarrel among themselves about their personal virtues and faults. After every public attack of any victim, the people inevitably quarrelled among themselves, some to establish their superiority and others to show their integrity. They quibbled to show to the society that they were beyond reproach.

Pillamma and the family took their first steps in a rented house in Birakaveedhi not far away from the family home in the Temple Street. Efficiently, Pillamma arranged the house with the few belongings she had managed to bring with her. Her new neighbours dropped in one by one to welcome the new family into their street.

After dark, Balaram, the youngest brother, visited the new home, carrying a gunny bag. He entered the house from the back door as Ramalingam was in conference with some people on the veranda. As a rule, Balaram avoided his elder brother and went to Vadina, his sister-in-law for any help. She treated him like a younger brother.

"Vadina, mother has sent this for you. You forgot to carry any kitchen utensils."

"Why bother? Let your brother starve, for all I care."

"You know you don't mean that, Vadina. What about the children? Are you going to starve them too?"

She gave way to tears. "Balaram, I don't understand your brother. Here I feel like a fish out of water. How am I supposed to live here all alone?"

Balaram informed her that the situation was worse at home, and Mother never stopped crying. On top of that, women came round blaming Pillamma for all this. Mother told them to go away. He was afraid that the women would go out and bad-mouth his Mother. He fretted that from every possible angle the whole family was at a loss. Balaram promised to visit them every day and told Vadina that he would do all her errands. The Town School where he taught was just across the street. He assured Pillamma that she was not alone and how much the family loved her.

His assurance eased her troubled mind; she stopped crying and managed to bring a smile on her face.

"Vadina, did brother tell you why he moved out so suddenly?"

"No Balaram, he never gave me any opportunity to talk. You saw him ... it's not even been a few hours since we came here. Already his followers have followed him here. There is no reprieve from them."

After he left she made a quick meal with the few rations that were there in the gunny bag and fed her children. The next day Balaram had done her shopping for her. He visited her every day in the lunch break at his school or in the evenings.

It was a few days later that she picked up her courage and confronted her husband about the move.

"Sir, what happens to our house there?"

"What house? We've got no house now."

"I mean the house we lived in until now."

"That is not ours anymore. I've given the two houses to my two brothers. Jagappa will live in the house he was in and Balaram in the house where we lived."

"What about us and our children? Don't they need a roof too?"

"Is the roof all you want? Look—this house is big enough for us and our children. Soon Komalam will get married and go away with her husband, and then there will be only us two and two little ones. Surely we can cope here, can't we?"

Pillamma was not satisfied with his replies. She insisted that her own children also had a right to their grandfather's property. In his calm voice he tried to explain to her that he had made his choice not based on rights but on justice. Pillamma reminded him that as a father he was doing injustice to his only son. She felt that his two brothers should give them some money in lieu of the free property they had gained, so that they could buy a small house for themselves, and that would be some justice for her son. She made a strong emotional appeal on behalf of her three-month-old baby son and launched into tears again.

Ramalingam first comforted her and then put forward his thoughts. "My life partner, my best friend, please calm down. Our understanding goes a long way from the age of your being eight. Do you remember those golden days? Let me explain, I need your full support now. To be honest, nobody asked me for the property."

He told her that was the right thing to do under the circumstances. He told her he had taken a bold step and resigned from his job against everybody's wishes. As Gandhiji said, nobody knew how long this struggle for freedom would last. Maybe it would never end.

"Under these conditions I can't let my brothers suffer for my actions. In this path of freedom we may lose everything and our entire lives are at stake in this battle. That is my choice and you are standing by me as you always do. But do I have the right to jeopardise my brother's lives because of me or for me? They see me as their father, they give me the respect I don't deserve, they regard me immensely, and they would never go against me. If I didn't give them any property, they wouldn't grudge. I'm certain that willingly my brothers would sacrifice their lives for me."

He became emotional and tried to hide it from his wife. She was pleased to see that even the mighty Masterji had some emotions left in him. He understood her smile and told her that he was not heartless. But now he was duty-bound and took the leap into the sacrificial fire willingly.

"No, you are not heartless, just stubborn as a mule," laughed Pillamma.

He laughed with her.

"That's my girl. Calling your husband names is a sin ... do you know that?"

"It's not name-calling ... I'm merely stating the simple facts, sir."

"Agreed."

He laughed again. She insisted on knowing more facts. He put forward his thoughts that had made him give away the property to his two brothers. He talked about the privileged childhood he had and how he was raised like a prince. He was educated at the best college in the country, in Madras. He told her of the luxuries he had as a child and at Madras, with servants and a cook to look after him. He was never short of money. His father spent lavishly to make his son a real *sahib*.

Ramalingam recalled how the show was all over when his father died very young, and penniless. He told his wife the facts she already knew, that he had to pay off all his father's debts and shift from Chatrapur to Berhampur.

He told Pillamma that his two young brothers never experienced the luxuries he had. They had basic education in the town. Ramalingam as the elder brother felt it was very just to let his two younger brothers have a piece of their father's property to make their lives better. He concluded his statement saying that his brothers deserved the houses they now had not by right alone but as a gift from him and his wife.

Pillamma listened to his statement and made no comment. Her silence unbalanced him. He needed her support in all his decisions. He valued her good will and her friendship.

"My dear wife, try to understand me. There are two houses and three brothers. I had a good start in life and they needed it too. Sadly it wasn't to be."

He took a deep breath, remembering the vanity in which his father had indulged in his life time. He told her that if ever they needed help his brothers would certainly stand by them. He once again reminded his wife that his involvement in this freedom struggle could be a long journey of no return, and its effect would certainly fall on them too, for just being his brothers. He told Pillamma that one of the reasons to leave the family home was to protect his mother and brothers from the after-effects of his involvement in the freedom movement. Moreover, he wanted his brothers to make their own lives in their own way.

For a long time, quietness weighed the place. Pillamma went into deep thinking. He waited for her reaction. He was certain that she understood his logic in leaving the family home. But Pillamma listened to his logic with tears streaming down her face. It was hard to say whether the tears were of joy or of pride for her husband's justice, or tears of sadness for not possessing any property.

"Sir, as the eldest son, it's your duty to look after your mother. Go and bring her here, sir."

"No, my wife, mother would not want to leave her husband's house. Let her stay where she is happy. She feels comfortable with Jagappa. We're not far off, are we? We can meet them every day."

Pillamma never complained again about the property. And in their long life together they never purchased a house of their own, and Ramalingam never owned any property of his own.

He left home, discarding all comforts, and never tried to recoup them in his lifetime. That momentous decisiveness had sealed their fate and their unknown future forever and there was no turning back for the couple.

Ramalingam's resolution was firm. He left his past within the walls of his ancestral home and stepped onto the road to nowhere, there was no path in vicinity but in his mind his destination was towards freedom, the freedom of his country. He had already adopted a simple, ascetic way of life, wearing *Khadi* and exchanging his boots for simple sandals. He was oblivious to his surroundings, unaware of the dawn or oblivious of the setting sun. The evening sun cast long shadows behind him.

Pillamma dutifully took shelter in his shadow and took steps forward, wishing and hoping that they would eventually reach their destination.

Prof Ramalingham, 1918

2

The Police Raid

The great change in Ramalingam's life had all started in early 1921 after Gandhiji's visit to Berhampur. He addressed a large gathering at the Barracks ground about non-cooperation with the British Government. Gandhiji's ardent speech had inspired a considerable number of people in the audience:

"I have been travelling from one end of the country to the other to see whether the country has evolved the national spirit, whether at the altar of the nation it is ready to dedicate its riches, children, its all, if it was ready to make the initiatory sacrifice. Is the country ready? Are parents ready to sacrifice literary education of their children for the sake of the country? The schools and colleges are really a factory for turning out clerks for government. If the parents are not ready for the sacrifice, if the title-holders are not ready to give up their titles, *Swaraj* is very nearly impossibility. No nation being under another nation can accept gifts and kick at the responsibility attaching to those gifts, imposed by the conquering nation. Immediately the conquered country realised instinctively that any gift which might come to it is not for the benefit of the conquered, but for the benefit of the conqueror. That moment it should reject every form of voluntary assistance to it. These are the fundamental essentials of success in the struggle for the independence of the country whether within the Empire or without the Empire."

His emotional speech made his audience stop and think about the future of their country. Gandhiji continued to impress his audience with his 'boycott theory' of the non-cooperation with the government. Gandhiji felt that explaining his ideas to the public openly would be the best way to achieve his goals of freedom, the *swaraj* of the country. Gandhiji needed public support and their participation in the struggle for freedom.

Initially the public weren't all that sure about the boycott. Unperturbed, Gandhiji toured round the country addressing the public. He told the doubters of the boycott his views about it candidly:

"There are many other points about boycott, I would reiterate two things. It will mean that non-cooperation must commence at the top, and if the best minds of the country refuse to associate with that Government, I promise that the Government's eyes will be opened. The condition is that those who refrain will not go to sleep, but move from one end of the country to the other and bring every grievance to the notice not of Government but of the public and, if my programme is carried out, the Congress will be going on growing from year to year and give public expression to those grievances, so that the volume of wrong, ever increasing as it rolls, will

inflame the great nation and enable it to harbour, to conserve all its anger and its heat and transmute it into irresistible energy."

His emotional oration inspired many youngsters as well as adults from every field of life.

The programme and policies of the non-cooperation movement that was adopted at the promotion of Swadeshi and a boycott of foreign-made articles, surrender of honorary posts and titles, rejection of official Durbars, progressive rejection by lawyers of British courts, boycott of elections appointing new Councils, refusal by clerks and soldiers to serve for the Government, and boycott of Government-run and state-assisted schools began to take shape. The progress gained momentum. It taught the subdued Indians fearlessness.

Soon Gandhiji's patriotic zeal gripped the entire nation. The weapon of passive resistance, or *Satyagraha*, that Gandhiji gave to the nation, emerged as the greatest asset of the Indians. He reminded the public that **"Non-cooperation is a measure of discipline and sacrifice and it demands patience and respect for opposite views. And unless we are able to evolve a spirit of mutual toleration for diametrically opposite views, non-cooperation is impossibility."**

Although he stirred an immediate enthusiasm among the public, the inspiration Gandhiji created dwindled away soon, to his disappointment. People were reluctant to give up their titles or their luxuries. Losing a government job meant starving and their families would suffer. Already Ramalingam had given up his job, and titles he never cared or craved for. He led the movement from the front by setting fine examples. He had as many followers in this as he had an equal amount, perhaps more against him. Some people felt that it would be foolish to forego a comfortable life style for a cause that might never end successfully. Those who did not agree with Gandhiji's non-violence programme sniggered at those national songs that began to emerge everywhere in local languages. Some people ridiculed the leaders of the town who promoted them as if they were the ace war missiles. British cavalry trotted along the Barracks grounds of Berhampur town without intervening with the public. Every evening families relaxed in the open air of the Barracks ground and their children entertained them with the national songs to the amusement of some and to the ridicule of others.

Another request Gandhiji made to Indians was to boycott government schools. As a good measure, Masterji Ramalingam, who led the town's people from the front, withdrew his nine-year-old daughter, Komalam, from the Town School, ending her formal education. Pillamma objected strongly but at the same time followed her husband's wishes. For her, education was the prime priority. Pillamma compromised with the situation and sent Komalam to be educated by a private tutor, Chalmayyagaru, who lived nearby. Being very intelligent, Komalam continued her education with her tutor. She was her tutor's pride and joy.

Komalam spent her spare time learning embroidery, crochet, and sewing. She also had singing lessons from a local woman teacher and played Harmonium. She had a sweet voice to enhance her charming character. Komalam was loved by all, and she made her mark on everybody she met, not because of her father but because of her kindness and good manners and very good looks. When people complimented Komalam, her father gave all the credit to his wife, who had raised Komalam to be a delightful young girl. He was proud of his daughter, and none of his other children could ever take her place.

Gandhiji's visit and his speeches gave tremendous impetus to the freedom movement. Soon the Congress movement was popularised by his followers. It was a kind of dynamism which was not known before in the vast land of India. Some more volunteers from all professional fields joined the freedom movement. Masterji Ramalingam was an ace speaker and he inspired many of them.

The law courts began to work slowly. There wasn't a complete boycott of government institutions but there was enough to slow down the running of the Government. Gradually it turned out to be a go-slow movement.

The speeches of the Masterji did stir the conscience of many. The stream of thinking, the stream of self-realisation, and the stream of conscious awareness of the 'slavery' under British rule began to seep slowly into their hearts. The stream began to gain momentum steadily and before long it became like a river. Once a river starts flowing it never stops until it reaches its destination. The Sea of Freedom waited for the river to reach her.

It had been four months since Masterji Ramalingam's family settled at Birakaveedhi, leaving their ancestral home to his mother and the extended family

His involvement with the freedom movement became his mission, and he had no time to spend with his family. But every evening he visited his mother to ask about her welfare.

The front room and the veranda of his rented house became his office, and his followers and some eminent people of the town met there regularly to discuss the movement and strategies. In turn, all followed the strategies of their national leader from the top.

The police kept a vigil on Masterji. His mother was extremely concerned for her son and similarly she was worried about her other two sons, as they too had connection with her revolutionary son Ramalingam. Balaram, the youngest son of the family was the go-between for the two families. He visited his 'Vadina' everyday, always entering the house by the back door, like the women and servants did. His mother was torn between the two families, but she did what she thought was right to safeguard her two sons first, and prohibited them from visiting their elder brother. But Balaram had his own mind. He visited his favourite sister-in-law and spent some time with the children, doing small errands for the family.

Masterji Ramalingam along with his ardent followers marched through the town, urging people to observe non-cooperation. They distributed pamphlets of Gandhiji's speeches translated into local languages of Telugu and Oriya. Masterji promoted *Khadi*, the hand-woven cloth which he had already adopted, and *Charkas*, the spinning wheels.

Gandhiji tackled the British in the textile industry. In those days, in India it was a crime to spin cotton into yarn and to weave yarn into cloth. All cotton was exported to the mills in England. The British Government felt that Masterji

Ramalingam was instigating the people, and ordered the police to confiscate all 'illegal' literature from his office, which order they followed straight away.

The news of the police raid was spread to every corner of the town. Suddenly the most revered Masterji Ramalingam was seen as a common criminal. The very fact that the police ever knocked on his door was beyond their comprehension. They felt that a police raid was held to disgrace the honour of their Masterji. In fact, the police went to the house and talked to Masterji politely before entering his premises. Masterji realised that they were only following their orders, and without any protest left the house and stood in the street while the police conducted their duty. They ransacked his office and took some papers and books, and saluted Masterji politely before they left.

When his wife Pillamma saw the police in the house, stunned Pillamma watched them in fear and fright. She took her three children into the bedroom and shut the door behind her. After some time when her husband opened the door, she came out like a mouse from a hole. She was surprised to see him so calm.

"Are they still here?" she asked with great concern.

"No, my dear. They did their duty and left."

"Why did they come here? Why didn't you stop them?" She was enraged, but helpless tears streamed down her face.

"You are being unnecessarily emotional. There is nothing to worry about, it's all part of the game," he said, trying to make light of the matter.

"Sir, for you everything is a joke! I died of shame and fear when the police entered our home."

"Sorry, my wife, I know it's not a joke. But be prepared ... it's only the beginning. Try to understand the gravity of the situation. We may have many more raids. Nobody knows what the Government is thinking, nor are we aware of what their next move will be. But it's expected. Surely we can't expect the Government not to react, can we? Until now they ruled without any interruptions from us. This is as much a shock to them as it is to us. That's why Gandhiji asked us to be prepared for the worse reaction."

"I'm so scared."

"Don't be afraid. Now there is no turning back. Do you remember the old saying? A drowning man doesn't care about the depth of the water."

She expressed her concern for the welfare of her children. The children were bewildered and frightened to see the police raid the office.

"I assure you, nothing will happen to them. The Government is playing games with Gandhiji and his followers. But they are not going to hurt our children. They still possess their English decency. I met a lot of them at college and at work and still have some good English friends. They are just normal people like us. You too have met some sahibs, are they bad? This game of chess is going to continue as if it is played between two gentlemen. Let's see who makes the last move." He uttered those words with stern determination and walked out.

Masterji kept his inner thoughts within himself. There was no precedence in the current situation, no role models, nothing to hang on to, or anything to follow but the sheer guts of Gandhiji, who wanted to play the game without metal weaponry. He wanted to fight with his mettle, with the bullets of words encoded with his statements. Gandhiji's cunning and intelligence were unparalleled. The intellectual citizens of the country understood him and were ready to sacrifice their lives for the cause. They all believed that one day it would certainly materialise. When that glorious day would come about was beyond anybody's comprehension.

As soon as her husband went out, Pillamma took her three children and arrived at the door of Atta, her mother-in-law who lived in their ancestral home, round the corner in the adjacent street. She wanted to cry her heart out to her family to ease her troubled mind, to get some assurances from them. A shoulder to cry on was all she longed for.

Pillamma felt that her husband was taking no notice of her agony. He did not indulge in comforting her, and instead he told her to face the situation without fear and without much expectation. Pillamma felt so lonely and she needed her family to comfort her and give her some assurance of what even she had no concept. The entire situation was beyond her comprehension. Pillamma trembled with fear of the unknown ogre that lurked around the corner. Her first concern was for her children and how to protect them from the storm of this 'freedom' movement.

As she anticipated, the whole family was mourning. The children sat in a corner, like statues. There was no frolicking among them, nor could their laughter be heard. In fact, the now silent house gave the creeps to Pillamma.

It was her young girl, Komalam, who took the initiative to ease the tension, which she often did under any situation. She ran to her cousins and hugged them, and then the children started playing happily. Hearing the children's laughter, Atta and the others in the family came to the front room. Pillamma hugged her Atta and wept like a child. Atta comforted her as well as she could. Together the whole extended family cried and condemned the police raid as obnoxious. They were all charged emotionally, profuse sympathetic words were exchanged between them, and they vowed to put a stop to it all.

Atta complained that she couldn't go to the Temple as before, as all the neighbourhood did was to discuss and dissected her and her family because of the police raid. Atta complained that her eldest son had brought disgrace to the whole family. Instead of maintaining the family's prestige, he became the cause of their distress.

The humiliation of the situation, and the rebuff from the society was too much for the old lady to endure. During her husband's reign, whatever his other personal life had been, he had maintained his dignity and earned respect for his family. The family was honoured by their fellow beings, they were respected by the society, and they were invited to all social functions as chief guests. Atta reflected on her glorious past and compared it to her eldest son's reign. She couldn't accept Ramalingam's callous behaviour. If she could, she would have put a stop to all that nonsense.

"Do you know, Vadina, I had no courage to go to school today. How can I face the staff? What would they say? I won't be able to bear it if anyone talks ill of our family. I won't be able to tolerate it if they insult our big brother," the boisterous youngest brother Balaram said, blurting out his anger and agony in the same tirade with a clenched fist which he punched in the air several times as he spoke towards the unknown opponent.

"Yes, Vadina, no patients have come to me today," moaned the second brother, Jagappa, who ran his Ayurvedic clinic from home.

"There is a *Puja* at the opposite house, but nobody came to invite us! I saw the group of women go to every house to invite; as they passed our house they put their heads down and hastily walked ahead. Don't you think they have deliberately excluded us from their society?" Tears rolled down second daughter-in-law Venu's face, which she made no attempts to hide.

In those days it was customary for women to go in a group to invite guests personally to the functions held at home. Sometimes they would have a band-party to lead them, as some families showed their opulence at every stage of their life, even while inviting guests to their functions.

Pillamma had no words to console Venu, who was generally a quiet person who never exhibited her emotions to the family. Pillamma was consumed with guilt for causing so much pain to the family. She felt responsible for their worries, but made no remarks and remained silent.

"This is only the beginning! Soon we could be ostracised and they will throw us out of our town. Is this what I want to see in my last days?" cried Atta, wiping her tears with her sari and quickly adjusted her veil that slipped from her clean-shaven head. As per customs and as a widow she shaved her head and covered it with the end of her sari.

Pillamma found herself in a predicament. She knew they were not accusing her directly but they were hurt beyond any comfort. She found herself in a real pickle. She had gone there for comfort and ended up comforting them. With a positive mind Pillamma assured Atta that they would never be ostracised. But Atta felt that there was no reprieve for the whole family and told Pillamma that they were all cursed and doomed forever.

"Atta, it's not all that bad," said Pillamma. "There are many other men in town who have also joined the movement."

"What movement, Pillamma? It's no use – it's us who will be moving out soon." She found it unbearable to face the public denunciation.

"The non-cooperation march is just a one-off," Pillamma said, and told Atta that the police raids also happened in several other homes.

"That won't restore our prestige back, would it, Pillamma? Once the prestige is smeared with black tar even a complete whitewash would not remove it, it leaves its traces forever. We are doomed eternally."

"It's not all that bad Atta, the police were very clean and there were no smears. They first polite saluted Masterji and took his permission before entering the house." Pillamma tried to make the raid look decent and honourable.

"I am surprised at you. How can you support your husband, how can you be so serene? Can't you put some sense into him? If you ask me, it's all your fault. You could have stopped him from marching in town. A woman who couldn't control her husband is not worth calling a wife." Her bitter anger and frustration now turned to Pillamma.

Pillamma let her cast her frustration upon her—she was used to Atta's outbursts that flared up from time to time, but they were only like soap bubbles, either quickly blown away or burst out. When she became calm again, Atta showered profuse affection on Pillamma. Over the years Pillamma had learned not to argue with her Atta, especially when she was in such a mood. She waited for the storm to ride over which she knew would happen sooner than later. As the eldest daughter-in-law she took her duties seriously and learned to cope with everyday tiffs with a gentle smile.

Jagappa came to his Vadina's rescue, and asked his mother not to blame her. Balaram reminded his mother that she as a mother could have controlled her eldest son as she controlled the rest of the family.

"See, who is talking? If you're that brave to face society then why did you not go to school today, son?" retorted Atta angrily at her son.

"Oh, that ... just like that, today, I took a day off to be with you all crying women and support you." He tried to ease the situation in his usual jolly manner.

"Indeed, what a supporting young man you turned out to be. But let's see you face your brother and speak your mind to him directly," challenged his young wife. "Look, Balaram, your big brother is coming. Show your bravery!" taunted his mother, readjusting her veil on her shaven head. Balaram opened the door for his big brother and quietly disappeared from the family 'conference', and Jagappa followed him behind. With the two sons hiding away from their big brother, Atta resolved to silence and kept quiet. Ramalingam inquired about the welfare of each member of the family before leaving the house with his wife and children.

As usual, Komalam held her father's hand and walked proudly with him. Pillamma carried the baby in her arms and Saroja clung on to her mother's sari. The family walked with their heads held high, Komalam chatting away with her father, while Pillamma and her second daughter Saroja followed them.

Suddenly, as they entered their street Birakaveedhi, Pillamma noticed a group of people rushing towards them. She cringed in fear and clasped the baby tight in her arms. Frightened little Saroja hid behind her mother. Unaware of the crowd ahead, her husband and Komalam marched on, laughing and joking.

As they passed, people bowed their heads and greeted their leader politely. A few young men came forward and touched their Masterji's feet and took his blessings. They all talked non-stop about yesterday's march and vowed to continue it until their demands were fulfilled. As the group walked along with the family, a few women came out of their homes to wish Masterji and his family well. Pillamma watched them in dismay ... these were the same women who had made snide remarks at her the day before were now welcoming her husband as a hero. She tried to understand their mentality but was glad they had not excluded her and her children from the neighbourhood. Pillamma couldn't logically deduce the reason for their sudden change of attitude.

When they reached home they found a large gunny bag on their veranda. One of the women said a policeman had left it there. One young man opened the bag in front of all. To their surprise, it was full of Ramalingam's books and papers.

"The Sahibs could do nothing to our Masterji," remarked one.

"*Masterji ki Jai!*" (Glory to Masterji!) hailed one young man, and the slogans of national chants reached sky high- '*Jai Gandhiji!*' '*Jai Bharatmata!*', the people cried with emotion. A few young men carried the books into the house and arranged them in the shelves.

Pillamma entered the house by the back door with her children while Masterji busied himself with his followers in the front room, and their meeting carried on well into the late night. Pillamma slept rather peacefully that night, after enduring those turbulent few days earlier. There were no more repercussions of the previous day's police raid on their house.

Later on she learned that when the police returned the books, they said sorry to have raided the house, apologised, and asked for forgiveness as they had no choice but to follow the orders of their chief. Pillamma's life began to settle down to a semi-normal comfort, although from time to time she heard a woman or two snigger at her for being a criminal's wife. Normally she would tell her husband about it, but decided not to trouble him with her own worries. She decided to support him in his cause and not to burden him with her own problems. She had become accustomed to the labels that people attached to her; first she was a barren woman and now a criminal's wife! British government gave titles to their loyal subjects whereas those women dished out titles for free. Pillamma laughed at her situation!

The few hours her husband spent at home were precious for her and the children; he was a devoted father. She heard women's sniggers, listened to their gossips, and witnessed some women's misbehaviour towards her when she attended some women's functions. She took it all in her stride and gulped them without any complaint.

The women had a unique style to attack her. Whenever she attended a function one of the women would make the initial remark, saying that Pillamma had no shame to come into public. Another would say that she would rather die of shame than appear in public if the police ever raided her house. One woman told the group how her husband had prohibited her from mixing with the criminal's family. Another said that sahibs were watching everybody and there was more trouble on the horizon.

"It's best to keep out of trouble. It's no joke provoking the sahibs, they will punish and they are justified to do so," said one woman, expressing her wisdom.

"He may give any name to whatever he does, but it's simply veiling the truth. Masterji is no less than a criminal, if I dare say," one haughty woman remarked aloud, and looked at Pillamma. As Pillamma showed no reaction, their comments took a direct attack on her.

"What's your explanation, madam? Do you think your husband is a criminal?" challenged one woman, staring Pillamma in the face. Pillamma ignored her and approached the group and wished them. Her composure disquieted them. They looked at each other and smiled feebly, and then began to converse with Pillamma as if she was a long-lost friend. Pillamma learned to adjust to such farces and learned to exist in the society like a brave woman or a brave freedom fighter.

Gradually Pillamma began to understand the nature of some people, what they said to her face, and what they really felt about her, were not necessarily one and the same thing. She adopted her smile as her silent weapon to face and tolerate the society in its raw form. Strangely enough, Pillamma also had a strong following on her own merit. Her intelligence, her kindness, and her support to the destitute women earned her the respect she deserved. She took the compliments and criticisms with the same attitude, just as two phases of life, and learned to exist among both her friends and enemies without fear and concern. For every evil there is a remedy, and her good friend Mangamma stood by her like a protecting wall.

Pillamma kept her life and her troubles away from her husband. She wasn't sure if he was aware of the rebuffs she was facing in the society or not. Neither of them mentioned their worries to each other. Pillamma resigned herself to confront the insults and rejections on her own, and save her husband from her burden. When he retired at night, Ramalingam was exhausted both physically and mentally. His mind was strong and his determination was rock hard, but his body was not used to the hardships he was facing. Only Pillamma knew how tenderly he was raised and what a comfortable and luxurious life he had enjoyed until now. Now he was pursuing the movement with his strong willpower. He showed signs of tiredness when he returned home. She took care of him like a mother, and tended to him with all her love and devotion. In her heart of hearts, she began to worship him as a hero.

Gandhi, 1920

3
Non-Cooperation Movement, 1922

Initially it was hard to say whether the Non-Cooperation Movement was one hundred per cent successful or not. Some people were reluctant to give up their titles or their luxuries. Their basic needs of everyday existence compelled them to deviate from the call of Gandhiji. They felt that it would be foolish to forgo a comfortable lifestyle for a cause that might never end successfully. This pessimism of the public could not deter the aims of Gandhiji or his ardent followers. Throughout the country his principles were observed by many Indians.

The press tried hard to publicise how the Non-Cooperation Movement had failed. Gandhiji reacted to it in his own tranquil manner.

"We are spiritual beings, going through Human Experiences, and today's moment becomes tomorrow's memory."

Seeing his undeterred progress of the movement, the press took a different angle and portrayed him as a saint playing on the sentiments of the people, to which he strongly objected.

"I'm neither a Saint nor a Politician," said Gandhi, elucidating his position, "I seem to take part in politics, but this is only because politics today strangle us like the coils of a serpent out of which one cannot slip whatever one tries. I desire, therefore, to wrestle with the serpent."

The press found him dangerous when he was provoked. He replied in such a way that made the Government seem as a monster. To be on the safe side, the Government for a while banned the press, but anyhow, the information and the speeches of Gandhiji reached the public very well. The beggars, wandering *fakirs*, street singers, and travelling people became the pigeon-carriers. The banning of the press failed utterly. Throughout the country national songs echoed national feelings. In some places singing those national songs in public places was prohibited. Music is the soul of the heart. Outside in public places the songs were banned but they gained momentum in no time, and even the children began to sing them at the Barrack's ground, at homes, and in the streets without fear or care. Umpteen lyricists and then singers sprouted up everywhere. The recording companies began to promote those national songs in local languages. The songs and the singing had a medicinal effect on people and a strange lull ruled the places. People became calm as their children sang sweetly, and the adults found them soothing. The revolutionists found the songs inspiring. The same lyrics produced a different effect on different people; inspiration to some and soothing to a few, awakening in many to a strange phenomenon that had never sprouted before. The concept of 'freedom' began to sprout in their hearts without their knowledge. The seeds of freedom became established in the soil of India and they waited for the monsoon to wake them from their hibernation.

Gandhiji understood the British mechanism well, so he tactfully tackled the textile industry. At that time, since it was a crime to spin cotton into yarn and weave it into cloth in India, he popularised the *Charka*, the spinning wheel, and the public adopted it easily and thus the British relented. Suddenly, the local *Khadi Bhandar* (the Khadi shop) picked up trade and supplied the demands of the public for more *Khadi* clothes and Gandhi-caps. The young and the old cottoned on to the new fashion of sparkling white Gandhi-caps. At every meeting, at every gathering, at most functions people attended wearing this headwear, so much so that at a few weddings they were even distributed as a gift. Whether they believed in the freedom movement or not, the fashion of Gandhi-caps became the latest trend. Some of Ramalingam's European friends wore them when they met him, but Ramalingam never wore one himself. Perhaps he was not fashion-conscious! But the *Khadi* clothes did not manage to reach the top of fashion—their coarse material and the lack of colour failed to woo the fashion-conscious public.

Young Komalam had her own dreams. She listened to the stories of great women of India, like Jhaansi ki Rani, Rani Padmini, Gargi, and the great mathematician Leelavati, and wished to be clever like them. Komalam wanted to grow up and do a lot for her country. Her mother often told her how Dr Margaret Bhore had given her life, so she longed to be a doctor and serve her people. She kept her dreams within her dreams and obeyed her father's wishes, making no complaint when she was removed from the school. She kept herself occupied with learning all that was available in those days, including astronomy and astrology. Like her father, Komalam excelled in mathematics. She was loved by all, and she made a lasting impression on everybody she met—not because of her father, but on her own credit.

More volunteers from all professional fields joined the freedom movement

Gandhiji said: **"Hunger is the argument that is driving India to the spinning wheel. The attainment of the *Swaraj*, our freedom, is possible only by the revival of the spinning wheel. A plea for the spinning wheel is a plea for recognising the dignity of labour."**

The *Charka* became a popular toy for the rich and an instrument for the poor and needy. Pillamma encouraged women in the neighbourhood to spin, and they gathered on her veranda to spin the *Charkas*. Soon such group activity became popular and Komalam entertained and inspired the women singing national songs. *Charka* songs became popular. *Charkas* of all sizes flooded the market; it gave the carpenters an income that they had lacked until then. The spinning was fun. For a few it became a fashion statement and a prestige matter in high society and at the same time the *Charka* became an inducement for the ardent flowers of the 'freedom'.

On 31 July 1922, Gandhiji called the nation to start a total boycott. He asked Indians to burn all foreign clothes. Resign from Government employment! Refuse to pay taxes! Forsake British titles!

The country's response to Gandhiji's call was not unanimous or quick. The public differed from Gandhiji. Some felt it was not necessary to take such a drastic move. Gandhiji was challenged about his call by his own people and the media bombarded him with questions. The wise man answered them in simple terms.

He urged the use of *Khadi* and Indian material as an alternative to those shipped from Britain. Gandhiji asked to burn all foreign clothes, discard them for good, and replace them with *Khadi* material. Once he had made a statement, Gandhiji never wavered from it; instead he continued to promote his ideas with vigour. He was certain that the public would eventually understand his methods.

Although the moment started with some inhibition, soon the bonfires spread all over the land. Ramalingam lit a bonfire at the Barracks ground. For the first time, his wife, Pillamma, came out into the public to participate in the *Swadeshi* (domestic product) spirit. At other times she remained in his shadow and never tried to eclipse him. Pillamma carried her bundle of clothes on her head like a *Dhobi* woman, a washer woman, to the amusement of some and to the admiration of many. Her followers, carrying their bundles of clothes on their heads, marched through the streets in a procession followed by Komalam and her young friends. The children of the town sang national songs all the way to the Barracks ground. There, amidst loud cheers and some faint boos, the women tossed their clothes one by one into the bonfire. The police stood at a distance and watched them, but they did not interfere as they had no orders to do so. The active women's movement took its initial roots there and then quite voluntarily. From that day onwards women played a key role in the freedom movement in the town. It gained momentum day after day.

Masterji and his fellow freedom fighters went from village to village and promoted the idea of discarding foreign clothes, adopting *Khadi*, and promoting the spinning wheel. In the villages, the *Charka* took on without any problem.

To counteract, the Government, who knew the crux of the weakness of the villagers, distributed free liquor to them and some poor people even in towns accepted the free booze without any qualms. Now the congressmen had another problem to resolve. They sought the help of the women's brigade to raid on liquor shops and divert their men from drinking with some success.

The press challenged Gandhiji on this new revolution. They criticised him as a foolish man who burned his own home. He was beyond any criticism.

"In burning my foreign clothes I burn my shame," pronounced Gandhiji.

"Surely, sir, instead of burning the clothes, why not give them to the poor? So many Indians roam naked in the streets," sneered one European journalist.

Gandhiji was not perturbed at his comment. He replied in his cool manner, **"It would be wrong to give this material to the poor, for the poor, too, have a sense of honour."**

"Burning is a crime, a crime against the Government. Do you encourage crime, Mr Gandhi?" The journalist continued to attack him.

"The materials were not burned as an expression of hatred for England, but as a sign of India's determination to break with the past. Indians have been ruined by the English factories by taking away work from India."

"Sir, you are instigating people against the Government. Is it a deliberate plan?"

"May I remind you that the British expedition began proclaiming 'trade and not territory'? Now Britain has crippled the weaving industry in

India. It has accumulated wealth, waged wars, monopolised trade, and established their rule over India. These *Swadeshi* measures are not against the methods but against the measures," Gandhiji replied.

Gandhiji reminded Indians that 'spinning' was a national duty and asked them to adapt *Khadi* as the State dress. He reminded Indians:

"'Fire' was symbolic of transformation of impotent hatred into conscious self-pity. The pity we've been tolerating for aeons under a foreign rule." His message reached every corner of the land by his ardent supporters.

For his involvement in burning the foreign clothes and instigating the public against the Government, Ramalingam was sent to one year RI the Rigorous Imprisonment at Berhampur Central Jail in 1922. It was his first imprisonment. Along with him, Malladi Krishna Murty, V.V. Giri, and Pullela Sitaramayaa from Ichapur were also arrested.

Sometimes the social stigma was too much for Pillamma to bear. Even in later years, the memory of that fatal day of her husband's arrest haunted her from time to time. Her husband had been arrested in full view of the public. While he walked to the jail with his head held high, with shackles on his wrists, she retreated into her house with her head hung very low. The comments of the people around her echoed in her head continuously. As ever, the people—both men and women—threw vicious comments at her. They blamed her for her husband's arrest. Pillamma was disheartened by the critiques and kept her mouth shut.

One young man came forward to support his guru, Ramalingam: "What did Gandhiji say? **'Jail is not jail at all, particularly when the whole of India is a prison.'** Wow! What a statement. He knows how to defy the sahibs."

"It's alright for you men to talk big. Did any one of you foolishly act to get jailed?" challenged one woman of some considerable age.

"Madam, we are ready to fight for our freedom. That's for sure." He stood there thrusting his bulged chest forward and a few more boys imitated him.

"Boys, you haven't seen the world. Poor Pillamma has to cope with three children on her own. I feel so sorry for her."

The public's comments often became personal and cruel. They laughed hysterically, saying that perhaps Masterji preferred to be in jail than be with his wife. But a few women stood firm to support Pillamma. They debated openly on Pillamma's doorstep. Their cutting remarks did make Pillamma's heart bleed, yet she remained silent.

Pillamma heard them alright, but her senses became numb, and she failed to think of her future. Her eldest daughter, Komalam, wiped her tears and went into the kitchen to heat up some milk for her mother. By the time she returned with a glass of milk she found that her mother had fainted on the floor, and her little brother lay in her lap. She picked him up and put him in his cot. Komalam sat by her mother, wiped her face with a wet cloth, and fanned her gently. When she opened her eyes she hugged her daughter and both of them cried, sharing their sorrow and their helplessness of the situation.

To add salt to the wound, Ramalingam was also fined six hundred rupees. If he did not pay it up, his sentence would be extended. The society around Pillamma was not as broadminded as the politicians. Her husband's imprisonment itself had brought disgrace to the whole family and to their relatives. Nobody wanted to be associated with the fallen family and kept their distance.

People began to gossip. Their gossip and their sneers and sniggers were too much to tolerate for Masterji's extended family. Day and night Ramalingam's mother cursed her existence. The members of his extended family were afraid to step outside in case they got arrested or rebuked by the society. Atta kept Balaram away from Town School where he was a teacher. She was equally worried for Pillamma and her children. The two families were imprisoned in their own homes from the society. Those who wanted to support the family were afraid of the constant police vigil in front of Pillamma's house.

The two families of Ramalingam in two different streets were housebound. After ten days the police watch was lifted. Balaram went to assist his Vadina. She told him of the fine, but sadly none of them had any ready cash with them. She pawned her gold with a goldsmith in the neighbourhood to arrange the six hundred rupees, but Balaram was afraid to go to the court to pay it. Chalmayyagaru, Komalam's tutor went and fetched the police inspector who knew Masterji's family very well. After his duty, the policeman went in plain clothes to Pillamma as a family friend. She requested him to deposit the fine at the court and he paid it in full, thus not increasing the sentence. There were never any bad vibes between the police and Pillamma's family. Masterji insisted that the police should do their duty, sincerely and should put their friendships and family ties aside.

Once the police vigil was lifted, Pillamma's friends began to visit her again. Some of them showed real friendship while many taunted at her plight as if they took great delight in her tragedy. Pillamma became immune to those unwelcoming words. She listened to them with immense patience and learnt to endure their taunts without tears. She saved all her tears for her bedroom where she drenched her sorrows into her pillow after her children had gone to bed.

One kind woman suggested that now Pillamma should put a stop to all her husband's activities. Straightaway other women blamed Pillamma for escalating the situation go bad by carrying the bundle of clothes like a *Dhobi* woman to the Barracks bonfire and tossed the clothes into the bonfire.

"Consider yourself lucky, the police could have easily arrested you for burning clothes," remarked one woman, as if she was disappointed that Pillamma got free.

"Pillamma if you must know you made a spectacle of yourself carrying the bundle on your head like a washer woman."

"You are a *Brahmin* woman and you have violated your caste acting like a *Dhobi* woman. You disgraced us by your behaviour."

"It was a sure sign of doom," moaned an elderly woman. As a conclusion, the critics pronounced that Pillamma had to pay a price for her folly and took immense delight in seeing Pillamma's stooped body. Pillamma put one foot in her doorway and fainted. The elderly woman nursed her while others continued to wag their tongues. They said that by her foolish charade Pillamma had also jeopardised her daughter Komalam's future. Now, as the daughter of a jailed man, a criminal, they said that no groom would come forward to marry her and she would remain a spinster all her life. Another said that any young man would consider himself to be fortunate to marry the virtuous Komalam. As the group of women debated about the future of Komalam, Pillamma heard them all but did not react.

Komalam found the whole situation intolerable. She slipped out from the back door and fetched the family's well-wisher, Mangamma, her aunt. By the time she arrived the women had tortured Pillamma mentally to their hearts' content and left the house.

After a month Pillamma was allowed to visit her husband in jail for five minutes. He told her that from now on she was in charge of the family and he bestowed upon her all the rights to make decisions for the family, and asked her to be a father and mother for their three children. He had given her the unwritten power of attorney for the welfare of the family. He told her that the imprisonment was only a start and there would be many more. He talked and she listened and returned home with a strong determination in her mind. If nothing else, Pillamma had pride within her and she was not prepared to bow in front of anybody at any time. She took a forward step to cope without her husband for the next twelve months.

After two weeks her mother-in-law sent for her. The women hugged each other and cried, and that eased their agony to some extent. Atta told her that the police kept a vigil on them too. She asked Pillamma and the children to come and stay with them until her son returned from the jail. But Pillamma refused, saying that her presence with them might bring more trouble to her two young brothers-in-law and the family, and her eldest son had left home for their safety. She told Atta that she could never go against her husbands' wishes, not even in his absence. But as usual Balaram kept visiting the family during his lunch break. Often the visits of Pillamma's mother gave her some moral support. As per tradition, Pillamma's mother could not stay with her daughter.

The days dragged by and gradually Pillamma resumed her normal duty. In the afternoon women went to her as before to listen to her read from the Holy book Ramayana to them. When some of them tried to rake her wounds she would divert the topic to the scripture she was reading to them. Pillamma was not one to cry in front of others. What she despised most was their pity. Sometimes she opened her heart to her nine-year-old daughter Komalam and was resolved to the situation. Her husband had warned her that the fight for freedom might never end and there would be many sacrifices that he and his family had to make. Pillamma supported his mission but at the same time she wished to have had a normal life with her husband and children. Now that this was never to be, she had reconciled herself to her situation mentally. In his absence she lived with the memories of his ardent love for her and the children. Time kept moving at its own speed, and so did Pillamma's life.

Pillamma opened her heart to her best friend, Mangamma, and told her about her concern for Komalam's marriage. That evening after dark, Mangamma sent her personal *Tonga*. Pillamma took her three children and went to her in-law's house. They slipped in unnoticed by the neighbours. There was no vigilante in the street, either by the police or the neighbours. Pillamma shared her worries about Komalam's marriage with Atta. Her Atta assured her that she would find a suitable groom for Komalam. After the evening meal she returned home with her children in the same *Tonga* under the veil of darkness.

Masterji's jailing continued to have adverse effect on the whole family in two streets. They were ruthlessly ostracised and were deliberately forgotten at social functions. The two families had no invitations for any social functions; the conservative society had excluded them without any qualms. Those women whose men were employed in the Government avoided keeping any connections with Pillamma's family. They were afraid to upset the sahibs by keeping contact with Masterji's family, as they felt such connections would be an insult to the sahibs. Sahibs spelled out clearly to their loyal employees their disapproval of Pillamma's family. Like a mushroom, a cloud of fear loomed over the town. Everybody dreaded who would become the next target of the Government.

After two months Mangamma invited Pillamma and her Atta to a social function at her place. But as soon as they arrived the other guests objected and wanted to leave the function. But Mangamma put some sense into them and requested them to support their friend in her time of need. The function went off well, but with a strange strained atmosphere. Mangamma was a wealthy and prominent woman of the society and none of them had the courage to go against her. She broke the ice of the boycott amicably.

Gradually the social prohibition on Pillamma was lifted by the neighbourhood but a few stubborn and adamant women kept themselves aloof. Pillamma took it all in her own stride with a gentle smile on her face. Her life returned to the semi-normal. As the months elapsed, the fear had ebbed away.

Time kept moving at its own speed, and so did Pillamma's life, progressing slowly with the weight of social disgrace upon her head and with the absence of her beloved husband, carrying the responsibility of raising three children on her own. She waited for his release, and longed to resume a normal family as before.

Unfortunately that was never to be. We can live on our past memories but can never repeat them as before. There is only a debut appearance of the drama of life and there are no repeats and never replicates it. Life cannot be carbon copied it makes its image once and disappears in time. The tide of freedom carried her along with her children towards their unknown future. All she could do was to go along with the flow, hoping and wishing that they would all reach the shore one day. That hope alone gave her the strength to continue to live for the future, the family's glorious future that she dreamed of.

Gandhi & Charka

4.

Sixteen months before. The Curtain Rises & the Drama begins!

It was noon on that significant Monday morning in the year of 1920. A town on the eastern coast of India was quiet, the sky was clear without any clouds; the whole town of Berhampur was hiding indoors, some at workplaces, children at schools, and women in their homes to avoid the blazing sun of the midday. Unknown to the residents, a dark cloud was looming over yonder. Pillamma, the wife of Ramalingam, prepared the lunch, and adjusted the dinner seat, a mahogany wooden low stool called *Peeta* with four short legs decked with silver motifs on the edges. She placed a double-sided two-in-one silver dinner plate in front of the *Peeta* and she smiled to herself sweetly and discretely. She knew exactly how her husband liked his dinner plate to be placed, just half an inch away from the *Peeta*, to enable him to sit comfortably on it and reach the dinner plate without stretching forward.

The silver dinner plate, about fourteen inches diameter was unique, with reversible sides. It was specially made for her wedding and was a gift from her late uncle. On one side in the centre was the image of Lakshmi, the goddess of wealth, and on the other side was Saraswati, the goddess of knowledge. Her husband preferred the Lakshmi, alias Nidhi, side of his plate—in privacy he called his wife, 'My Nidhi!', or 'my wealth'—and when he finished his lunch she would turn it over and eat her food on the same plate with the Saraswati image on view. Her thirst for knowledge was never-ending.

Pillamma was a woman who believed in traditions and followed them meticulously and thus never dined with her husband. Her husband wanted her to sit next to him and eat food at the same time, but he understood and respected her sentiments. His wife was duty-bound and respected the family traditions in which a wife was never equal to her husband. He was the eldest son of the family and so Pillamma, being the eldest daughter-in-law, had to maintain the family traditions. They were aware of their responsibilities, and they both conducted them with dignity and diligence.

Pillamma became a good role model for her two younger sisters-in-law. They respected and also strangely feared her unnecessarily. They were eager to impress her. Between the three daughters-in-law there was a strange bond. There was plenty of love; there was immense affection, and also a deep understanding. The other two looked up to Pillamma. They would have loved to be as clever as she was, and they would have loved to be well educated like her. All the same, they were content with performing their womanly duties to the fullest, and efficiently. Pillamma went into her bedroom and placed the silk *dhoti* and shawl on the four-poster bed. Her husband first changed from his three-piece suit into his silk *dhoti* and shawl before dining. She placed another three-piece suit of navy-blue colour, her favourite, on the clothes stand ready for his afternoon classes. She placed the well-polished shining black boots by the clothes stand. She looked around the bedroom and began to croon a song. She was never tired of serving her husband. She loved the routine and enjoyed attending to all his needs personally. Their relationship had crossed the boundaries of a normal couple. In privacy they were lovers. He loved and respected her and in return she cherished his eternal love for her. She would not have minded giving her life for her beloved husband.

Once again, Pillamma looked at herself in the mirror. She adjusted her sari, and straightened it carefully. Her husband loved the pastel shades on her tall and slim body. That day she wore a pastel pink sari made of fine muslin cloth embroidered with small white roses. Ramalingam sent her saris to Paris to get them embroidered or decorated in fine French lace. She twisted her long luscious hair into a bun over her nape and adorned it with one pink rose. She looked stunningly beautiful in her simplicity. Except for her *mangalasutram,* the wedding chain, she had no other jewellery round her neck. Pillamma had two gold bangles on each of her wrists, which she had worn from her childhood, and she had never parted with them. To overcome the frustration of waiting for her beloved, she began to prance up and down the room, undid her hair and tossed her head in weariness. Her luscious hair covered her face, hiding tears that began to seep from her eyes. Pillamma longed for those few private moments alone with her husband and got restless when he did not show up on time.

She heard the *Tonga* stop in front of her house. Quickly she tied her hair up in a bun, replaced the pink rose, walked gracefully to the door, and opened it. In came the Master of the house, as cheerful as ever. She went into the kitchen and started serving the food. She placed the special dish she had made for him in a silver bowl on the right side of the dinner plate and covered it with a silver plate. She daily loved surprising her husband with her culinary expertise, and in return he loved and enjoyed her surprise-dish, specially made for him. The rest of the food was prepared by the cook for the whole family.

Ramalingam changed into his silk Indian clothes – a *dhoti* and a shirt and went into the kitchen to dine. He began to eat food rather silently. Somehow words failed between them. His unusual silence warned Pillamma of some oncoming disaster. She trembled slightly, but quickly composed herself and tried to make some feeble conversation. Apart from replying with a nod or a yes that day, her beloved was resolved to Silence, with a capital 'S'. She could have interrogated him with questions, but chose not to pester him with a demand for explanations of his silence. She knew he would eventually tell her of whatever was troubling him when he felt it was the right time. She was not a nagging wife; she understood her man and trusted him wholeheartedly. She held her breath and waited to face the storm that was likely to burst soon. She wondered if her youngest brother-in-law had got himself into some sort of mischief again.

Ramalingam retreated to his room after dining. Pillamma finished her food quickly, tidied up the kitchen and went into the bedroom. If ever there was something her husband wanted her to know, he told her in the bedroom, never in front of others.

But when she reached the bedroom she was surprised to see him asleep. Generally, he waited for her to return to the bedroom where he hugged her and talked sweet nothings before he indulged in a brief afternoon nap. But now his eyes were shut and he was fast asleep. She could not disturb him, so she settled down on the rocking chair in the corner of the room, just looking at him. After half an hour or so, he woke up and passed by her, ignoring her presence there. His odd behaviour disturbed her, yet she waited patiently, though for what, even she was not sure.

He went into the bathroom and returned wearing a *Khadi-dhoti* and a *Khadi* shirt and stood in front of her like a child showing off his fancy dress. She exhibited no reaction, but instead smiled softly at him. She put his new attire down to the sort of mischief which he often performed in her presence.

"Sir, aren't you going to change into your suit? The *Tonga* will be here soon," she said, reminding him of the time.

"There is no need for it, my dear, I've resigned from my job," he announced with the calmness of a tempest cloud, which often appeared coolly before erupting. He expected her to burst out with anger, and he had mentally prepared himself to face her rage in his own way and calm her down with a big hug.

"Why, sir?" she asked, ever so tenderly. Her tenderness eased his worry a bit.

"My lovely wife, Gandhiji has called the educated youth to join the struggle for freedom," he said–a brief statement which meant nothing to her.

She remained silent.

"My dear, do you think I have made a mistake?"

She did not reply.

"My good wife, you know I can't do anything without your support. You're half of me. Are you with me on this, my sweet, better half?" he pleaded with her like a boy would plead with his mother to let him go out to play.

"Always, sir. I am always with you. You do know that, don't you?" she assured him with a sweet smile.

"Do you really mean it?"

"Yes, sir. Whatever you do I'm with you."

"Thank you, thank you very much. Now I have the strength of a thousand elephants in my heart ... Look at this leaflet from Gandhiji. Life is not worth living under slavery, is it my wife? I wonder why we didn't think of our freedom decades ago."

She took the leaflet in her hands and held it tight.

"Do you remember Gandhiji came to our town a couple of weeks before?"

"Vaguely, yes, I do remember. Now, you told me he gave an emotional talk to the public. What was it all about – The freedom of India from slavery under British rule?"

"Gandhiji began a nationwide campaign to enlist support for the non-cooperation movement. Here read the leaflet."

She read it aloud. **"If Indian people showed discipline, self-denial, readiness to sacrifice, capacity for order, confidence and courage, then *Swaraj*-Indian independence would be attained in a year."**

He took a deep breath and looked at her reaction, but Pillamma exhibited no emotions or reaction.

"With his speech he pointed out the injustice of Punjab to us. The massacre at Jallianwala Bagh has angered the Indians."

"Yes, it was barbarous. I read about it in the newspaper."

"Now Gandhiji made a programme for all us Indians, with these points: boycott of law courts, educational institutions, council elections, foreign cloth, and government functions, picketing of liquor shops and refusal to get recruited in the army. But my dear wife, the programme was not just negative. It included the building of new institutions. National Education was encouraged. Stress was laid on *Khadi* home-spun cloth. *Charka* is to be the symbol of freedom."

Pillamma listened to each word carefully and tried to digest them.

"Hundreds of National schools were already established all over India. Gandhiji wanted us to show great unity, determination, and courage," he continued as if he was lecturing his pupils at the college.

"So have you become a soldier, sir?" She tried to make light of the whole issue.

"Not any soldier, the one who 'covets nothing for himself'," he remarked, observing her face. Her face was blank.

"Again, as Gandhiji said, '**Science of non-violence can alone lead one to pure democracy**.' So I am a soldier without a gun, ready to sacrifice my life for the cause I believe. My fight is without arms. Already thirty thousand Indians have joined the movement, and I'm one among them."

"Do you really think you can be so selfless, sir?"

"Not just me, we both have to be. I will take you along with me."

"And you want me to resign from my job?" She burst out laughing.

"Perhaps not, you and I have other responsibilities. You cannot resign from your domestic duties."

"That's exactly what you are doing, if I may say so, sir."

"Agreed ... whoever can argue with you and win? I'm serious. I shall try my best to continue to conduct my responsibilities dutifully, but I need your support. When I fail I want you to be there to pick up the pieces."

"Sir, you're frightening me! You know I cannot do anything without you. Please don't leave me alone."

"Silly child, when did I say I'm leaving you?"

"I told you many times not to call me a child. I was a child when we got married, but not now, sir." Since their marriage he had called her a child to tease her, which she resented, even then.

"So sorry, my good wife. A bad habit I cannot get rid of," he apologised sincerely.

"Even your father told you many times not to call me a child. I wish he was here to chastise you."

"Sorry, my dear."

"I'm a mother of your three children, if I may remind you." She pretended to be angry.

"I am genuinely sorry, please forgive me." He knelt down and begged her with folded hands.

"Alright sir, just this time." She laughed hysterically for reasons even she did not know.

"But my dear, grown up wife, this is no laughing matter. Right now I'm standing knee-deep in the river of this freedom movement. Nobody knows when this river will turn into a spate and wash everything out to sea. Be prepared for the worst, my love. Let's see where the stream is going to drag us."

You should know, sir. You've got the oars in your hand."

"Seriously, are you with me?' he asked. "I need your support."

"Be assured, sir, I am always with you."

"Thank you; in that case I have crossed the first hurdle. The rest I can jump over in time," he muttered to himself, under his breath.

Pillamma heard him clearly, but made no comment. She sat there in silence trying to absorb the situation and the predicament her husband's decision had got her into. He went and fetched the chessboard. They played chess silently, slowly moving the pawns on the board. They were both lost in their own thoughts. Generally, Pillamma was very competitive when she played chess or bridge. She was an ace player of cards and chess and many board games. She often played *chintapikkalu* (tamarind seeds) with the women of the house, a game of skill and patience. The player had to hold as many seeds as she could in one hand and slowly drop them on the floor in multiples of fours, called '*punji*', without dropping any other seed in her hand. If you drop a seed your turn is over. The more fours you drop on the floor they can be arranged in the counts of horses and elephants. With the rest of them left in her palm, the player had to flick them and catch them on the other side of the hand. With her large palms she could hold several tamarind seeds in one hand and win the game. But at that moment, she had lost all her appetite to defeat her husband, although she often did so, and he loved to be defeated by her.

Theirs was a unique bond. Pillamma had known him since she was eight and hence they fought and argued like two children before they realised they were husband and wife. Her father-in-law had taught little Pillamma to play chess and card games. In his father's presence Ramalingam dared not say a word against his little wife. Yes, she was eight when she got married and he was just thirteen. Their friendship became stronger when his little wife Pillamma began to be educated under the supervision of his father. She showed good progress. When her husband returned home from Madras for summer holidays, he was surprised to see her read and write. His father also made the two children play chess and watched with glee when his pupil, little Pillamma, defeated his son. For him, she was his pride and joy.

The young Ramalingam often talked to her about his college and how girls of sahibs and some Indian girls who attended the same college were smart and clever. He taught Pillamma new tricks and games with numbers, and from that time she began to call him Sir, ignoring his real name, Ramalingam. On every visit he brought some good books for her, and her father-in-law encouraged her to write letters to his son, which he monitored at all times. The two young people became good friends before they started their marital life and their friendship and trust continued even in their married life. Their union was unique.

Its foundation was based on deep understanding and a complete faith in each other.

The other females of the house were appalled at their Master's generosity towards his little daughter-in-law, Pillamma. As the head of the family, he had always kept them in their place and never gave them a voice of their own. Not that he was a dictator, but he merely followed the traditions of those days. He looked after the women of the house and provided them with a comfortable life style, giving them rich jewellery and clothes to fit his status. They were never short of anything, nor did they aim for anything different, whereas the spirited little girl, Pillamma, was different to them all. The Master, Rangam Pantulu, had seen the girls of sahibs active and smart and now that Pillamma showed the same spark in her, he wanted her to be smart like a *memsahib*.

The memories of those glorious days flashed in front of her like a picture show. It all came to an abrupt end when her father-in-law died and her education came to a standstill. She jerked herself out of her melancholy when Ramalingam gave her a gentle nudge.

"It's your turn," he prompted her, to make the next move. She moved a pawn aimlessly. The pawns of their life were scattered here on the chessboard of their future.

"I know, dear, you still are in a shock, aren't you?"

"No sir no shock ... but I'm trying to comprehend the situation. You dumped the news of your resignation on me without any warning. How do you expect me to react?"

"Agreed. I had no time to plan and execute my decision. Perhaps you may think it is a hasty decision on my part?"

"No sir, you never make any hasty decisions. Your moves are always calculated and to the point that much I'm certain."

"Thank you, my love. I know you understand me and don't form rash opinions of me."

Pillamma looked at him tenderly.

"Gandhiji, as the leader of the National Congress, has to increase the reach of the party among the masses who reside in the remote corners of the country in order to eradicate its elitist status. He repeatedly said, **'No movement can be truly successful unless wholeheartedly supported by the inhabitants of the Indian villages.'**"

"I agree," she said. "Freedom of mind and body is what we all need."

"How true you are. But dear, I must warn you, we don't know how this is all going to end. Perhaps it may never end at all. The whole freedom fight might go against us all and we might continue to be slaves to the rulers. We must be prepared for the worst. I need your full support, my sweet wife."

Pillamma listened to him silently without showing any expression on her face.

"Once again I must warn you. This struggle may not see the light in our lifetime, but, as Gandhiji says, it's a beginning. All beginnings must start somewhere and we are making that start. Perhaps our next generation may enjoy the fruits of our struggle. It's not an easy road, so are you with me? I need your support. Without you I'm not capable of doing anything." He began to plead with her like a child who wanted to get his own way.

"Sir, I've dedicated my life to you from the age of eight. I'm with you till the end. Come what may don't turn your back on freedom now. Nobody appreciates a wavering mind. Good or bad, you made a choice. Now it's up to you to go with the tide."

"We may have to make many sacrifices, my better-half!" His voice quivered as he uttered those few words.

Pillamma noticed a hint of doubt in his tone and reacted with emotion. "Life is short. We must make our existence worthy. But don't worry. We will fight this battle together, sir. I will go with you."

"I'm the most fortunate man to have you as my wife. That's why I call you *Nidhi*, my fortune. Thank you, Nidhi, now I can get involved without feeling guilty. I thought if you objected I wouldn't be able to carry on my work sincerely."

"I know you, sir. Once you make a decision, you never turn your back on it. I have full confidence in you."

"From now on, these *Khadi* clothes are my wardrobe. I shall be eating only one meal a day. As Gandhiji said, *'We must experience the hunger and poverty of our own people to understand their needs.'* One meal is more than enough to sustain my life. I hope you understand it, my dear wife. Don't force me to eat at night. You know mother will be upset, so I shall leave it to you to explain to her and the rest of the family. Whatever happens, never leave me, my fortune, my Nidhi. I need you. I depend on your support in this gigantic cause, which may never come to anything in the end."

"No sir, I have promised to be by your side. I shall also wear *Khadi* clothes and have one meal a day like you.'

"As Gandhiji said, he wants us to switch to *Khadi* home-spun cloth so that it uplifts the nation that is under the heel of foreign power, England. I switched to *Khadi* to show my determination to follow him and his principles."

"So do I, sir. I want to follow you."

"No, there is no need for that. I would hate it if you followed me blindly. Make changes when you are ready for them, not a moment before. You're free to live as you were before. Anyway, you are still breast feeding your infant son, so promise me you will not resolve to eat only one meal a day."

"Alright sir, I shall obey you. But allow me to follow in your footsteps and switch to *Khadi* clothes. This decision is not negotiable," she pronounced with a cheeky smile on her beautiful face.

"I'm not negotiating, but I beg you not to make any hasty changes in your life style. Perhaps Mother will not take it kindly. She has got enough on her plate to cope with her 'vagabond' son, don't you think?" He laughed uncontrollably.

"Vagabond? That's a bit drastic, if you must know."

"Perhaps a drifter? I'm drifting from my path."

"Don't label yourself, sir. Leave that to the public, they are more inventive," she teased him cheekily.

He looked at her briefly and knelt down on the floor. He shut his eyes and silently prayed to God Almighty, thanking Him for giving him a life partner like Pillamma. Now he had the hard task of revealing the news to the rest of the family. They played cards for a while and waited for the gathering of the family on the back veranda facing the garden for their evening tea and tiffin. As they gathered there they heard a commotion in the front of their house.

5
The Aftermath

Already a large group of men had gathered on his doorstep and waited on the front veranda. Masterji, as he was fondly addressed by the people, went to the front door and stepped onto the veranda in his sandals, *Khadi dhoti,* and a *Khadi,* long shirt, and stood in front of them. At once people stood up in reverence. Without any hesitation they broached the topic of his resignation, and they discussed and condemned his resignation at the college as if it was their right to do so. There was no such thing as a personal matter in that town. All affairs were everybody's affairs. A lot of love and affection was hidden behind their interference and in their deep involvement with other people's lives. The arguments and counter-arguments echoed on the veranda. Masterji replied to each and every one of them in his enchanting voice and convinced them that his decision was final and there was no turning back on it. It was not negotiable. His talk had inspired some young men of the town and they vowed to follow in his footsteps. When the deflated well-wishers left the place in dribs and drabs, moaning and grumbling at Masterji, an elderly relative arrived to chastise him.

He came straight to the point. "Ramalingam, have you got any sense, son?" His age gave him the indisputable authority in the society to put the naughty ones in order. Masterji stood still with folded hands showing his reverence to the elderly man.

"What a foolish thing to do! Didn't you think it was necessary to discuss with your elders before resigning from your job?" He reached the armchair on the veranda and settled down comfortably. He placed his walking stick on the arm of the chair and waited for an answer, but there was no reply from Masterji, who remained in his standing position.

"Have you forgotten you've got three little children? What about their future?"

Masterji remained silent.

"Does Pillamma know about this? Poor girl must be devastated."

Masterji maintained his silence.

"As the eldest son of your father you've got many responsibilities on your shoulders. Have you forgotten them, son?" He continued to show his authority, mingled with deep disgust.

Masterji did not even look at him he cast his eyes to the floor and stood still.

"It's no use! I'm wasting my breath! I have failed to put any sense into you. We all know what a stubborn man you are, but now you're proving to be foolish too."

Masterji said nothing in his defence.

"If you ask me, you've taken after your father. He squandered all the wealth and left you three boys with nothing. Are you going to do the same to your brothers and your children?"

Any son would defend his father even when he was wrong, but right then Masterji found it to be wise not to utter a word in defence or in anger. He followed the rule that silence was golden.

"I see you've no shame. Are you prepared to give a begging bowl to your family? Are you able to envisage the seriousness of the situation, my son?"

There was no reaction from Masterji.

The old man shook his fist at Masterji. "Whoever heard of that puny man Gandhi? It's alright for him to sit there in Delhi and make declarations. If you ask me, Gandhi is corrupting our brains and misleading the young." His rage erupted – he stood up and stamped his walking stick on the floor, his body shivering like a dry leaf.

"Sir, please take the chair," Masterji pleaded with the elderly man, who looked as if he could collapse at any minute.

"I haven't come here to sit and praise you, son. Take my advice, and don't be foolish to resign from a well-paid job with the Maharaja. If you must know it's a crime to deny our Maharaja – he might even whip you in public."

Masterji watched the elderly man silently.

"You're supposed to guide your students through their lives, but now, sadly, you're guiding them to the sea of disaster to drown? What an example you're setting for your students, to disobey elders, to discard responsibilities, and to be selfish and foolish?" He raised his voice and slowly people began to gather on the road across the street. They dared not face the angry elderly man.

Masterji slightly shook his head to say no. His reaction and the presence of public across the street gave the old man more strength to speak his mind.

"I predict one day you and your Gandhi will all end up in the ocean. No sahibs will come to your rescue."

Masterji looked across the street where people began to gather and sighed.

"The sahibs must be laughing at your Gandhi and his foolish followers," he eyed the public to see how they reacted to his seniority. They dared not cross the elderly man who was scrupulous in attacking people – it could be their turn next. Seeing the frightened public stand in silence, the old man changed his attitude from counselling to challenges and threats. To maintain his status as the elder of the town he had to change the mind of Masterji from his resignation. His prestige would be at stake if he failed in this mission. But Masterji did not react in any way.

"Son, listen to me! I worked with the sahibs and you can never win them. They have got an army – what army has your Gandhi got, I ask you?" To be true, nobody knew what work the old man did, he changed his story frequently and claimed that he was in an important position with the sahibs, he was their right-hand man. When it came to discussing sahibs in public generally the public opted out. They believed in letting the sleeping dogs lie, afraid that the sahibs had eyes on their back...

Masterji looked at him with pity. The elderly man ignored his look and continued, "Yes son, sahibs are strong and clever, and also cunning, so nobody can win them."

Masterji began to show his restlessness by slightly moving his standing position from one foot to the other. The elderly man noticed it and decided to conclude his advice.

"Son, people in the town respects you. Keep their respect alive, son. I'll go and talk to the Principal and he will withdraw your resignation. Tomorrow, go back to work and forget all this nonsense."

After his final warning and advice, the elderly man walked out with his head held high, while the public watched him in awe and respect. They were certain that he had managed to change Masterji's mind. Then a few more elderly people came along trying to change Masterji's mind. They talked until they got tired, but not a word came out of Masterji's mouth in defence or support of his 'act'. Masterji took public advices and abuses with reverence and remained silent.

They all left, cursing Gandhi and feeling sorry for the so-called Masterji who had failed to make the right choices in his life. As elders of the town, they felt that it was their duty to put some sense into the fatherless young man, and they left morally deflated. They took his stubbornness personally. So far, nobody had ever refused their advice with such stubbornness. They cursed these changing times when people did not respect the elders anymore. They found it hard to accept such a denial from the man they all had respected earnestly.

Balaram, the youngest son of the family, carried the news of his brother's resignation to the rest of the family, gathered in the rear quarters. The family was speechless and they huddled together with some unknown fear. Their mother broke the silence with her wailing and crying and none could stop her. Her cries reached the people on the veranda and slowly her agony spread out in the street. Women of the town began to gather in the back garden, thinking that there was a death in the family. Pillamma quietly retreated to her bedroom and shut the doors behind her. She anticipated that their anger and frustration with her husbands' resignation would certainly turn on her. She was aware that there was no escape from the family's wrath, but for the time being she sought for some peace and hid in her bedroom. When the visitors ebbed away she returned to the kitchen to prepare the evening meal for the family as she always loved to do. The elderly cook made meals for the family in the daytime, but in the evenings his failing eyesight gave him trouble and Pillamma took charge of the kitchen.

Evening meals in that house were a special time. The whole family ate together and the three daughters-in-law served the food. Children and men had their food first. It was the prime time to broach any topic fearlessly in that dining hall. Masterji would find out the welfare of each member of the family in the open discussions.

"Brother, why aren't you joining us? Are you on hunger strike?' asked Jagappa, the second son of the family.

"Brother, is it true you've resigned from your job?" The youngest brother, Balaram, broached the topic boldly and put his head down quickly as such boldness was not much appreciated by his mother.

"No, I'm not eating," said Masterji. "Let the women also finish their meal and we shall gather in the courtyard. I need to speak to you all." He walked out of the door and sat on an easy chair on the back veranda of the courtyard. The hub of the crowd had eased and the cool breeze of the evening soothed his aching soul.

Suddenly there was a knock on the door. Masterji went to the door, and a messenger from the Maharaja of Khallikote stood there with folded arms. He stepped in and placed a tray full of sweets draped in a red silk cloth on the table in the entrance hall and put a purple velvet roll of parchment by it. He stood there politely with folded hands. Masterji took the message and sent him away.

"Brother, a message from the Maharaja, it must be important," remarked the nosy youngest brother, Balaram. He was impulsive and his brother never chastised him for his curiousness.

"Let's meet in the courtyard in an hour," said Masterji, and he went to his room. Pillamma looked at her husband with some fear. She was mentally preparing herself to face the storm that would soon burst out there. As soon as he was out, Balaram started his interrogation.

"Vadina, what is the matter? Tell us please, I can't wait. This suspense is killing me."

"Balaram, you're still a child. Your son is more matured than you," laughed Pillamma, trying to ease the situation. The servants took the children out to play in the hall, others gathered in the courtyard. Rugs and bolsters were arranged in a circle to seat every member of the family. Both women and men had equal place in that household. Masterji came out of his room and took his seat with his family. They waited for the oncoming disaster, such gatherings always spelled danger. They sat there slightly trembling within.

"I've got an announcement to make," Ramalingam the head of the family said, and paused, looking straight into their eyes. As the Master of the house it was his duty to comfort them first and make them feel at ease.

"There is nothing to fear. Nobody is in trouble. The only woman in trouble is our Bharatmata," he orated, a well-rehearsed prologue to his audience.

"Bharatmata? You mean Mother India?" exclaimed Balaram. The youngest brother of the trio had no patience for anything.

"Yes, my brother Balaram, our Bharatmata is tied in the shackles of slavery."

"So?" he interrupted bluntly, and others were frightened for him.

"So, I have decided to join the freedom fighters to release our motherland, our Bharatmata, from her shackles."

"How?" asked Balaram, with some sort of childish curiosity.

"I want to inform you all that I've resigned from my job and from now on I shall do my best for the freedom fight. Gandhiji has called the youth to support him."

"No job? No money?" asked his mother, with some disgust and some concern.

"I shall make some changes to my life, but that should not affect anyone of you. You are free to live your lives as you do now."

There was a long pause. He waited for few minutes for them to respond or to react in any way they chose, but they remained seated in utter silence. Masterji stood up and returned to his room quietly. He knew they needed some time to digest the news. As soon as he walked out, the gathering woke up from their trance. They bombarded Pillamma with umpteen questions, for which she had no answers to give.

"When did you know about this, Pillamma?" demanded Atta, her mother-in-law.

"Why didn't you warn us before, Vadina? What are we supposed to do now?" asked Jagappa with great concern.

"Nothing, you heard your brother. Nothing will change. All changes relate to him alone and nobody else," Pillamma replied softly.

"Look at those clothes. Your father would have died of shame. They are so undignified, don't you think so?" demanded Atta, her mother-in-law. She held Pillamma responsible for her son's drastic decision.

"They are called *Khadi* clothes, Atta," said Pillamma. She chose to say as little as possible. Even she needed time to digest the situation.

"So rough, how could anyone wear them?"

"None of you need to change into *Khadi*. If you remember all changes apply only to your brother and none else." She reiterated her previous statement.

"I don't know, somehow I feel soon we'll become the laughing stock of the town," the mother of Masterji cringed in shame.

"Vadina, surely you can change his mind, can't you? For our sake?" pleaded Balaram with childish innocence, although he knew his brother's stubbornness. None could ever change him once he made up his mind.

"Vadina, we know he never says no to you," pleaded Jagappa.

"You know your brother, once he makes up his mind there is no turning back. It's best we let him follow his principles."

"Principles? What principles, I ask you? Soon he was to be the Principal of the college and suddenly he throws it away for some principles? I can't understand ... I must be stupid," Balaram burst his anger towards his favourite, Vadina.

"That doesn't matter now, Balaram. That chapter is closed for good. No point in arguing about it. Your brother has taken the decision and we must accept it if we can't respect it."

"You're supporting him? Are you also in this, Pillamma? Hope it's not your brilliant idea?" her mother-in-law accused her.

"Atta, I have no say in it. Like you, I too was just informed of his decision. I'm as helpless as we all are."

"But you talk as if you agree with him?"

"Atta, as his wife I obey him. There is nothing I can do more than anyone of you can do." Her reply left them in more puzzlement. They dispersed slowly with umpteen doubts, worries, and a sort of shame in their hearts. They were not sure how his decision was going to affect the whole family.

They dispersed and re-gathered in the kitchen garden far away from the Master's bedroom. They argued about their family prestige, and how the society might look down on them. Pillamma sat there silently and let them fume out their anger, mostly at her. She knew it was the natural reaction to a bombshell that the Master of the house had blasted in front of them.

"You know what, Vadina, more than anything it's his clothes that would bring disgrace to us all. Did you see how rough they are?" moaned Balaram, the fashion-conscious young man. "We've seen some politicians wear fine clothes and they enhance it with a Gandhi-cap. They look ever so smart. Surely our brother can be like them can't he, Vadina?'

In reply Pillamma dispensed a feeble smile.

"You must stop him from this madness. If you want you can. You must, for our sake, I order you to stop his madness, do you understand girl?" the frustrated Atta spoke in anger. Pillamma just listened and said nothing in reply. "Did you ever see him in creased clothes? He is known for his immaculate attire," the mother-in-law added, with some pride.

"He looks so dignified in his suit and polished shoes. When he enters the college even the Principal stands up and greets him respectfully," Jagappa moaned to his family.

"I know son, I heard it too. It's all because he looks like a Maharaja. Nobody has got his dignity, or his calibre. Maharaja of Khallikote is so fond of him. He respects him immensely," Masterji's mother moaned to her children.

"Now we all are going to be the laughing stock in the community," said Balaram, nearly in tears.

"Vadina, we beg you, don't let him go astray. Our family's prestige is at stake. He has to think of us too. It's his responsibility to keep the honour of our family," Jagappa pleaded with folded hands.

"Surely you heard the story of a king and the poor Brahmin. When they refused to let him sit with them to dine, he changed into rich clothes and sat down to eat. Instead of eating food he feeds it to his rich clothes," she said, trying to make the matter light.

"Vadina, life is not a fairy tale. It's easy to tell moral stories but not so easy to follow them," his agony reflected in his voice.

"Maybe not for all, but your brother follows what he preaches. That's what makes him so special. You must all respect your brother's decision, like I do. He never does anything without thinking clearly. As for the clothes, it doesn't matter. If you ask me, his dignity is enhanced by his sincere following of Gandhiji. Not that I'm saying Gandhiji has chosen the right path. Nobody knows, only time will tell. Until then I am hundred per cent with your brother. For us he is the same man. He loves us all as before," she cried, and surprised herself at her speech, and how she ended up justifying for her husband.

Nothing more was said as their last hope had vanished in front of them. The only person Pillamma who could have changed Masterji's mind had sadly chosen to stand by him. They dispersed quietly.

Pillamma sat there all alone thinking of her husband's decision. She had her own doubts and worries, and she wasn't sure what the future held for them. She went into her room, and found her husband sitting in the rocking chair, and rocking gently. As soon as she went in he stood up and gave her the parchment he had received that evening. She read it and re-read it—it was a simple message, more like a telegram: **Don't be in haste, please wait until I return from Madras. Your friend, Gajapati.**

"Sir it's clear what Maharaja wants you to do."

"Yes. I read it too."

"So, what is your next step? He is a good friend of yours, isn't he?"

"A very good friend indeed, and friends understand each other."

"How did he become your friend?"

"Perhaps we both have the same interest in education."

"The college is named after his ancestors, isn't it?"

"Yes, that's true. The name of Khallikote College was conferred on it in the year after he was born in 1893. His ancestor, Raja of Khallikote, donated 16.5 acres of land for it. When the college faced an acute financial crisis around 1893, then the district Magistrate A. W. B. Higgins approached the Raja Sahib Harhar Mardaraj Deo of Khallikote who generously donated liberal amounts and later created an endowment with a lakh of rupees. Since then it has become Khallikote College."

"That's so interesting. Do you think he will be annoyed with you?"

"Certainly not, he is a friend and friends respect each other. I have no worry on that score."

"I think it's very nice of him to send you the message."

"Indeed. He always cared for me."

"Are you going to tell mother about this message?"

"Do you think I should?"

"Yes I do. Atta is worried. She thinks Raja Sahib might punish you."

"In that case, you tell her not to worry. And tell her that Raja is a good friend of mine. Assure her that I will not be whipped in public, as people say," he burst out laughing.

"Sir, Atta is really upset."

"I know, and I understand her concern. It's all part of the sacrifices we all have to make. It's not the time for soft touches, nor is it the time for sentiments and emotions. I leave it to you to make the family realise that I have made up my mind and there is no turning back."

Pillamma ended the topic and they both retired to sleep away the night. They shut their eyes but they couldn't shut down the turmoil that was brewing in the hearts of every member of the family. They waited for the sun to rise, hoping that would bring some light into their lives and sooth their aching souls.

Maharaja K. C. Gajapati Dev, 1920

6
The Strict Regime

Pillamma's troubles had just begun. The women from the neighbourhood gathered in the back yard and settled on the mats that were spread out for the visitors and Pillamma sat amidst them like a sacrificial goat. Their pressure began in earnest. It would have been easier to face cannon than the daggers of their words. They gathered there to pressurise Pillamma to change her husband's decision and withdraw his resignation. In that small town anybody's business was everybody's concern.

One woman made her opening remark to the delight of others.

"Pillamma, how could you sit so meekly and do nothing?"

At once the others took turns to taunt their victim. They proceeded with full force as if they had rehearsed the whole scenario earlier.

Pillamma had no other option but to listen to them with her mouth shut and head hung low. It was the protocol of the day for such public interference and she had to obey the social rules, which she did ever so politely. Then she remembered her mother's words: *'My dear daughter Pillamma, learn to endure. That's the best thing to do when you cannot fight them.'*

One sympathised with Atta, Pillamma's mother-in-law, and pointed to Pillamma how upset she was. Another commented that Pillamma never cared for Atta's feelings. Shrewdly they tried to create a rift between the mother-in-law and her daughter-in-law. At such moments it was profitable to compliment one that was in 'power' and ridicule the other. Although their comments were addressed to Pillamma, their whole intention was to gain the support of Atta so that they could freely tear Pillamma to pieces

"Who knows, it could have been her idea in the first place. Who knows what ideas Pillamma puts in his mind behind shut doors?"

"Look at her how demure she looks! It's all an act, if you ask me. I've seen many such women. They appear as if butter won't melt in their mouth. They exhibit kindness from outside and within are hard as rock."

"You mean like an elephant's teeth – one set to show to outside and another set of teeth hidden inside to chew and swallow?" laughed another woman, sniggering at Pillamma. Her envy towards the literate woman who stood out in a crowd spilled like venom from a cobra.

Another kind woman, who admired Pillamma, came to her rescue and snubbed the badly mouthed group. But it had no effect on that highly provocative crowd. Arguments and counter-arguments, accusations and counter-accusations, spread like wildfire at that place. A couple of them punched each other, but at once an elderly woman separated them by force. But in no time the place became an arena for a war of words. Atta intervened in the flow of free brawl and requested them not to blame her Pillamma and upset her unnecessarily.

The other two daughters-in-law remained safe in their rooms, not wanting the attention of the crowd to turn on them. When a storm comes it sweeps everything in its path, and they were afraid that those women would easily turn on them. Even though they had no role to play in the drama that was taking place, those interfering women were quite capable of slinging some dirt onto anybody. The two young daughters-in-law observed that the best policy was to keep their distance in such situations. 'Do not trouble trouble until trouble troubles you.' was their motto.

"I don't agree with you, sister," one woman orated, slowly scanning the group watching her with intent. The word 'sister' has immense strength in such situations. It gives the speaker the familiarity she never had before. It makes the receiver succumb meekly to the speaker. It drags the listener into the speaker's trap unwittingly. It makes the receiver numb to reaction. All in all, the word 'sister' makes the receiver a puppet in the hands of the speaker. It is a potent word in the hands of a speaker, but a kind word in the hands of real brethren.

The women continued to empathise with Atta. They told her what a noble mother-in-law she was and how fortunate Pillamma was to have her support in spite of her cunningness. They chose each word with calculation. As a final statement the supporting woman extolled Atta by saying how much she wished to have had a mother-in-law like her. That woman had successfully added fuel to the bonfire started by her with a bit of compliment to the listener and a bit of fuel to the victim, Pillamma. It was all a cunning display of venom, with a capital V, in front of the society.

Fake compliments were the ammunition to the word 'sister'. Atta became mute for a while as the compliments had their effect on her. For a moment she was engulfed with the euphoria of fame. The speaker noticed Atta's reaction and smiled to herself. It is said: 'Hit the iron when it is hot', so she at once added some more oil to the fire. She told Atta that if Pillamma genuinely wanted to stop her husband from the nonsense of resignation from the college she could easily put a full stop to it. She added that it was a wife's duty to put her husband in order.

The woman made her concluding speech and looked around at her comrades as such! Maybe a moment late, but Atta woke up from her euphoria. She told the woman that she knew her son and what a stubborn man he was. She told them that even she couldn't have made him budge an inch from his staunch decision. Atta dabbed her tears with the end of her sari and sighed. The gathering watched Atta silently.

Contrary to their expectation and disappointment, Atta's reaction was rather mild and bland.

Atta told them that it was her fate to have witnessed such a miserable day in her life and moaned that she shouldn't have lived after her husband's death to witness this family tragedy. Then she wept bitterly. It was hard to say whether she wept for her husband or for her stubborn son. Her tears and her agony impressed few and delighted some women. There were very few genuine sympathisers present there. One elderly woman tried to console Atta, in her philosophical way. She told Atta that like everybody else even she had to face her fate and pay up for her last birth's sins.

The atmosphere became strained and they pondered about their own fates in their present lives. One young woman woke the crowd with a jolt by saying that she did not believe in fate. She declared that any wife could get anything she wanted from her husband in her bedroom. She assured them that any husband would become a puppet in his wife's hand in the bedroom. With a big grin on her face she divulged her wisdom to her fellow sisters. Some younger women at the gathering looked at each other and giggled, whereas others put their heads down and shivered gently; perhaps they remembered unsavoury experiences in their bedrooms.

Generally women suffered in silence and accepted their fate if their married life was not pleasant. Once a young girl became married she had no choice but to tolerate her married life with silent endurance. Endurance, yes endurance was what all married women learnt to accept in their lives.

Once again Atta asked the women not to blame her Pillamma. She looked tenderly at her daughter-in-law, who sat there with tears in her eyes and her mouth shut. But the women were not willing to give up. One of them pronounced that if Pillamma had been womanly enough, she could have stopped her husband's madness even before it started. She sneered wickedly at her victim, Pillamma, and smirked. Now their discussion and comments became wars of words between two sections of the group, one for and one against the family, especially the literate and smart Pillamma.

"There is no need to be so rude," protested one kind woman. She reminded them that Pillamma was as much of a woman as anyone present there and added that Pillamma was much prettier than all of them. The opposition was not ready to be defeated. One of them commented that if Pillamma was woman enough she could have had a baby earlier. Atta became furious at that, and challenged the critic. She reminded her that now Pillamma had three lovely children that the family loved.

"Well at last, the cockerel crowed after dawn," sniggered one. Her aim was to belittle Pillamma, forgetting that she had come to sympathise with the family

"What's so great about it? It was the younger daughter-in-law who first gave a child to the family, didn't she?" She reminded Atta how she pined to see the child of her first son. She told her how Atta often felt humiliated to see her Pillamma barren.

Atta realised that the crowd was turning nasty; she had to protect her Pillamma. It was no use trying to reason with those women. For them, having a child a bit late in a married life was as much of a sin as being barren. Atta remembered how she herself had put her Pillamma down in public when she had late conception. At the same time, she despised it if an outsider pointed a finger at her family. She protected them like a mother hen. She turned to Pillamma and asked her to go and get afternoon tea ready for her eldest son. Pillamma took her hint and went into the kitchen and hid there like a scared fawn.

Atta managed to save her Pillamma from the fangs of those evil women who had come to pay their sympathy but tore the young woman to pieces like vultures. Pillamma began to make tea. Black tea with lemon was what her husband loved. As the water was boiling in the pan, her thoughts began to bubble in her mind.

Those were the days when she had already had two miscarriages. She was going through severe depression and her emotions were haywire. All the same, she prepared everything for her younger sister-in-law, Venu, and her new baby's naming ceremony. She decorated the crib with fine silk flowers which she had made from silk cloth. Gold chains were hung from the four posts of the crib. Streamers of silver bells were draped all around the crib. The string to rock the crib was made of twisted gold threads. As per custom, each guest would go to the crib and bless the baby and gently rock it. The crib for the baby was rich and comfortable. Pillamma was very artistic in everything she did. She made it ready to receive the guests.

It was the second daughter-in-law's firstborn, a beautiful baby girl, who cheered everybody in the family. Pillamma took comfort in holding the baby in her arms. Fortunately her sister-in-law Venu had no qualms about it. Gladly she let Pillamma, the eldest daughter-in-law, take care of her baby. Venu loved Pillamma and respected her a lot. The guests, all adorned in their fineries, arrived for the naming ceremony. At such gatherings they freely exhibited their wealth to the other women in the society.

"Don't let Pillamma hold your baby, Venu! She's a *godraulu* (barren), she'll bring bad luck to your baby," one woman blurted out viciously as soon as she entered the hall.

Straight away Atta snatched the baby from Pillamma's arms. Strangely it was the same woman who loved and protected Pillamma whenever anybody pointed a finger at her. But she, too, was a slave to sentiments. Atta succumbed to society's common beliefs and superstitions. Suddenly Pillamma slipped from her favour like sand from a fist. Atta snatched the baby from Pillamma's arms and handed her to Venu.

"She's not a *godraulu*, the poor girl had two miscarriages, didn't she?' an elderly woman remarked, showing great sympathy to Pillamma. Now the attention turned towards the sympathiser, and they pointed out to her how her own daughter-in-law had three miscarriages and told her that she would never give an heir to her family fortune. One even suggested that she should get another healthy bride for her only son. That woman was stunned by their wickedness. She stood up and walked out of the function. The only support Pillamma had disappeared like a summer cloud.

Not knowing how to face the women, Pillamma went into to the kitchen and cried silently. She remained there on one pretext or another until the function was over and the guests had left. After the function, Atta took the baby and went to her room, and Venu followed her. First of all she took the *disti*, a ritual to cast off evil eyes from the baby, and then handed the baby over to Venu.

Pillamma wiped her tears and began to prepare the evening meal. In spite of her trying hard not to weep, she failed to control her tears. They found a way to drip out of her eyes and into the cooking pot.

"There is no need to cry your heart out! God has answers for everything and He shows a path for every soul." A kind hand tapped her on her shoulder.

Pillamma turned around and saw an elderly woman standing behind her. She was dressed in a cotton sari wrapped around her like a shawl and without wearing a blouse. She had a few colourful beaded chains round her neck and no other ornaments. Her kind words and her soothing voice trembled Pillamma from within, and she hugged the woman, and wept uncontrollably. The tribal woman let Pillamma shed all her tears and held her in her arms, giving her the warmth and assurance she had longed for since the function commenced. For a few moments, utter silence reigned between them. The tribal woman had a habit of appearing suddenly at functions uninvited, but the women of the town regarded her as a bearer of good fortune, because whenever she attended a function invariably something good happened there. Thus the women of the town welcomed her presence at any gathering. She would come at her own will and leave abruptly at her own will. Seldom did she speak to the women nor did she accept any food or gift from the people. All they knew about her was her name Narasamma. Her age remained a debatable issue, and it stretched from eighty to one hundred years. The people let their imagination go wild when guessing about her. The woman never agreed or disagreed with her abode, it remained a mystery to people. They assumed that as a tribal woman she lived in the forest or on the hills.

Pillamma apologised to the elderly woman and dabbed her tears with her sari. She touched the elderly woman's feet with reverence. The woman watched the agony of the young woman and assured Pillamma that there was a cure for her pregnancy and miscarriages problem and she could treat her, but it would be difficult and the treatment could be a bit severe to bear. Pillamma said that she would do anything to be a mother and her husband would pay her as much as she demanded. The woman laughed and told Pillamma that the treatment wouldn't cost her a single *paisa*. She reminded her that the treatment was not going to be hard on her husband but it would be difficult for her. She had to follow a strict regime. Pillamma was prepared to do anything. She felt that her life was worthless without having children. In spite of all her efforts to not cry, she wept pitiably.

"It's not all that hard," she assured Pillamma. All she had to do was to control her food habits. Her assurance had eased Pillamma's troubled mind. Pillamma had to give up salt, sweets, and fried food, and follow the food regime very strictly. She vowed to follow it. The woman told her that the treatment was not for a day or two, not for a week or a month, but it was for one whole year. Pillamma assured her that she had a staunch determination and begged her to treat her and get her out of her barrenness.

Suddenly Atta entered the kitchen and was not pleased to find the old woman there. A tribal woman was not allowed to enter a Brahmin kitchen. She accused the tribal woman for plotting against her and misleading Pillamma. She demanded to know what the old woman, Narasamma, was doing in her kitchen. Narasamma was not perturbed and instead wanted to know how Atta could have let the crowd tear Pillamma to pieces.

Atta felt guilty at that and told Narasamma that she was helpless and the fact was that Pillamma had failed to be a mother. She added that she couldn't hide the fact that Pillamma was barren and she could not stop the women talking.

Atta wept and told the old woman how she had to face their insults on a regular basis for having her first daughter-in-law Pillamma being barren.

Narasamma assured Atta that there was no need to despair and Pillamma could have a baby too after one year of her treatment. Her words refreshed Atta's mind she found a ray of hope for Pillamma and their family prestige. Atta gave permission to let Narasamma treat Pillamma with some herbal medicine. The old woman told her that it was a boon given to her by a wandering saint forty years ago, which she could use only once. She looked deep into Atta's eyes, which flustered her momentarily. Quickly Atta composed herself and replied that she was prepared to do anything for an heir. Atta reminded the old woman how people say that Pillamma had a curse on her head.

Narasamma told Atta that there was no curse on Pillamma's head. Even God couldn't curse a good woman like Pillamma. She told her of the strict food regime Pillamma had to follow, and asked her to support Pillamma. Atta promised to do everything to hold the child of her eldest son in her arms. Atta told her that Pillamma was a fatherless child, born with bad luck. They both touched the elderly woman's feet and Atta gave her a basketful of fruit, but the woman took just one orange from it and walked out with a gentle smile on her face. She was a godsend to Pillamma, they thought.

Immediately Pillamma began to follow the strict regime. She had her husband's full support behind closed doors. There were some protocols of the family which even Ramalingam couldn't ignore, one of which was not to interfere in the female quarters routine. His mother was in charge and he respected her regime. Generally she was efficient and just towards her daughters-in-law. Now with the new baby in the house the second daughter-in-law was indeed in her favour. Whenever Pillamma tried to pick up the baby, Atta would snatch it away from her hands. Somehow she believed a barren woman might hurt the baby. Whereas Venu, the baby's mother, trusted Pillamma completely and let her cradle the baby willingly. She had adored Pillamma and wanted her little girl to be smart like her aunt. Pillamma had learnt to grin and bear it whenever her mother-in-law taunted her, which she did mostly when there were visitors.

The women in the neighbourhood encouraged her to throw daggers at Pillamma. But as soon as they left she was kind to Pillamma. Pillamma had learnt to cope with two sides of her mother-in-law; she knew Atta still loved her in her own way. She endured Atta with respect. Pillamma always remembered her mother's advice: 'Don't be a pond – if you do, then your life will become stagnated and without destination. Daughter, always live like a river flowing forward. You may come across stones and sticks but still the river flows over them towards its destination. Don't live like a pond.'

Ramalingam noticed the new routine of his wife; he gave her full sympathy but advised her to tolerate the routine. He assured her that his mother's attitude towards her was a passing phase. Once she had a child the matters would resolve themselves. Pillamma had endless patience and she understood her husband's helplessness in the matter. It was a standard routine in many families, where the mother-in-law never missed a chance to put down their son's wife.

Pillamma was determined to go through the strict routine that the elderly Narasamma gave her. She had to eat food without salt, sugar, or any oil, just some plain bland or boiled food of rice and vegetables of a certain kind. All root vegetables were to be avoided. The worst of it all was that she could have only one meal a day, in the morning. At night she was allowed to eat a fruit: a banana, or a guava, none of the oranges that she loved to eat. She could have green coconut water once a day, which was not so easily available. The groceries were the same for the whole family, and no special purchases were made for Pillamma.

Pillamma started her diet earnestly. She wanted to have a baby, and a baby she craved at any cost. Her two previous miscarriages had drained her emotionally. Now she put all her trust in the elderly Narasamma. With all her deep faith in the Almighty she took her first dose of the herbal medicine.

Before the sunrise she bathed by the well, and stood there in her wet clothes, when Narasamma entered the house from the back garden gate and gave her a little parcel of powder wrapped in a Neem leaf, which Pillamma swallowed dutifully. She reminded her that she had to observe celibacy for twelve months until her treatment ended. Pillamma told her that her husband was very cooperative and there wouldn't be any problem. Then Pillamma returned to their temple at home, and said her prayers before entering the kitchen. Ramalingam watched her with admiration. To give her full support he too opted out from the evening meal and began to take only fruit.

His mother resented her son's gesture but dared not tell him how she felt. She often moaned to the other women. She told them that it was not her son's fault in making babies and there was no need for him to starve. She condemned Pillamma for letting her son suffer for her misfortunes. She often declared that Pillamma was born unlucky, as she had lost her father as soon as she opened her eyes in her mother's arms. Now she had lost two babies even before they were born. She said that Pillamma was born with bad Karma.

Sometimes she complained to her second and third sons about Pillamma and told the two sons how their father had pampered Pillamma when he was alive. It was his pampering that had made Pillamma bold and shameless.

Atta added, "Anybody would have died of shame for being unable to be a mother, but not Pillamma. She dresses up like a queen and wanders about happily. Do you know what? The women laugh behind her back, does it matter to her? No, she goes everywhere and attends all functions. Why not? She is the Master's wife, she speaks well, and she can read and write unlike us ordinary women. See our Venu, nice and strong, and what a beautiful baby she produced."

Her two sons were more tolerant towards their Vadina. Sometimes men have more kindness in them than women. The youngest son Balaram resented his mother picking on his Vadina. But her taunting from time to time was blurted out in dribs and drabs when she knew her eldest son, the breadwinner, was out of the house or not around, but she would put a stop to it as soon as she saw the master come in.

Atta had a strange relationship with her eldest son, Ramalingam. She respected him and in a strange way she gave him the place of her husband in the household with whom she had had a delicate relationship. She had spoken only when she was spoken to, and she feared him. She had never questioned her husband's decisions, nor dared to argue with him. Not that he ever mistreated her, but she accepted that he was the boss, the master, and she was his obedient wife.

He gave her full freedom to deal with the house matters, and make decisions about the welfare of his daughters. As far as his eldest son was concerned, he was protective towards him. He had high ambitions for his first son. He wanted him to be equal to his sahib friends. He sent his son to be educated in Madras. Perhaps that had created an abyss between the mother and son. Even when he was at home he spent a lot of time in his library and never spoke unnecessarily. The mother never could be close to her son.

To be true, Atta was not a bad woman at all. In fact she did love Pillamma more than her other two daughters-in-law and even her two daughters. But Pillamma's barrenness created a rift between her affection towards Pillamma and her own social status in the society. Wherever she went out the women showered her with their pity and constantly reminded her that her eldest son hadn't got any children. Neighbours encouraged her to blow her top and blame Pillamma. For them, the act between the angry and frustrated Atta and the obedient and helpless Pillamma was all just a free entertainment. But Pillamma kept her thoughts to herself. Endurance was her strength. She never complained, nor did she lose faith in the treatment that Narasamma was giving her.

When her mother-in-law was in good mood she would boil some vegetables and feed Pillamma. Other times she would roast an aubergine and even without peeling it dumped it on her plate and walked out. Pillamma was at her mercy while Atta's affections fluctuated like a pendulum. Pillamma always remembered what her mother told her from her childhood: *'Talli,'* her pet name for her daughter – *'a woman's life is like a thorn on a banana leaf. Pull it out, it rips the leaf. Leave it there it keeps hurting. Just bear it, my Talli. Hope the thorn never strikes your life.'* Sometimes she used to say: *'Talli, married life can be like a knock on the elbow, no wound to show but the pain is unbearable. See that you don't get knocks, but if you do, you've no other option but to endure it. '*

Pillamma's mother had bleak views of her life, but she always said her husband treated her well when he was alive. All in all, she taught her daughter to endure, and endure they both did, her mother as a widow and she as a childless woman. The society never excused a married woman without a child. Some unfortunate women committed suicide, unable to bear both the vicious treatment at home and the wicked taunting by the society. Some women watched helplessly when their husbands found another wife to have an heir to their family. Pillamma knew she was not in fact barren, as she had two miscarriages. She lived in hope, and hope is the sustenance of life!

Pillamma's mother lived at the other end of the town. She was deeply concerned about her daughter's health and diet. Often, she secretly sent a tumbler of milk with full cream to Pillamma through a vegetable vendor. Often vegetable vendors became go between for many daughters-in-law and their mothers in town. They trusted the vendor and often he or she acted as the guardian angel, carrying messages and food for their daughters. It was Pillamma who made the purchases from the vegetable vendor every day in the back yard of their house. Pillamma drank the milk and it was a good sustenance to her bland diet. Her mother was not allowed to visit her often, because being a widow she had not shaved her head and kept her hair long hair and tied it in a bundle over her nape. If she came Atta wouldn't allow her to dine with the family, and she was served on the veranda, like an untouchable. Atta followed Hindu Brahmin traditions to the word and she couldn't excuse anyone who disobeyed them.

Sometimes Atta and Pillamma's mother met at some female functions in the town. The town always had something to celebrate. There were several festivals, weddings, nuptial parties, pregnant women's blessing parties (baby-shower parties), naming ceremonies, new mothers' blessing parties, annual festivals, special female pujas like Varalakshmi puja, children's birthdays, especially the child's first year birthday party, the girl's 'adulthood' party (the start of their first menstruation), then seasonal religious parties. Almost every week there was a function at somebody's house or at the Temple. The women loved to attend the functions and exchanged news and gossip of the town, and compared their saris and jewels invariably.

Until recently, whenever Atta attended the functions, some of which were exempt for her because she was a widow, she would take her two daughters-in-law and exhibit them proudly. The third son was still a bachelor. Wherever she went Pillamma was treated with regard as the wife of Masterji Ramalingam, the Professor of Khallikote College who had gained immense respect and the love of the town's people because of his sincerity and integrity. Pillamma also made her own mark on the society with her dignity and intelligence and good manners in the community.

Recently her status had diminished considerably. Pillamma had to face the ridicule of the women when she attended some functions, especially if it was a function for a child. The women attacked Pillamma with words that could shred her heart to rags. She cried inwardly and opted out from attending such functions to avoid embarrassment to her family. That did not stop them. The agony for the family continued as they teased her mother-in-law for having a barren wife to her eldest son. When she returned home, Atta would take out her anger on Pillamma. She understood Atta's distress and endured it.

Venu often asked Pillamma to look after her baby. Venu was a kind woman and she understood Pillamma's agony. She wondered how she could tolerate all those rebuffs from everybody who took pleasure in making her feel worthless. However, Pillamma always maintained her calm and never dropped the gentle smile off her face. Venu admired Pillamma's tenacity. She loved Pillamma more than words could say. While Atta was having a nap she took the baby and placed it on Pillamma's lap. The warmth of the baby on her lap jostled her out of her musing over her past. Pillamma cuddled the baby and rocked her gently in her arms, singing a lullaby, and slowly the baby dozed off.

Knowing her society Pillamma, was determined to become a mother at any pain. She continued to have her weekly dose of herbs from Narasamma. As per her instructions, the couple conformed to celibacy. Weeks became months, and months gradually turned to a year. On the final day, Narasamma gave her the last dose, blessed young Pillamma, and walked out with a gentle smile on her face. Pillamma watched her with awe. She felt elated, she felt fulfilled, she twirled round and round like a little girl. Pillamma felt emotional, and then she wept loudly, shaking all over. Her mother-in-law watched her from the kitchen window. When she began to weep, Atta ran to her and held Pillamma in her arms and neither of them uttered a word. As a woman, as a mother, Atta felt the agony of her young Pillamma deeply.

That day she prepared a feast for the family and fed Pillamma with her own hand. Venu decorated Pillamma's bedroom like a new bride's room, with jasmines and incense sticks. With all her hopes and carrying all her dreams she walked into her bedroom like a new bride and collapsed in her husband's arms.

Call it a miracle or the magic of the herbal remedy, but Pillamma became pregnant within three months. She waited for Narasamma to visit her. Her mother-in-law sent for her but she was nowhere to be found. Pillamma conceived after a year and had a son, but her joy did not last long. In his third month the baby boy died of an unknown illness in his sleep.

7
The Tragedy

Of all his children, Masterji had a soft corner for his firstborn daughter Komalam. She was his life, she was his love, and she was his reason to exist. She stood up to his expectations. At seven she was well versed in Ramayana and excelled in her musical talent. It was her mother who taught her Ramayana, and the music teacher loved and valued her gifted student. She sang Kirtanalu, Jayadeva Geetalu, and many other devotional songs in her sweet melodious voice. Every evening Komalam waited to show her father her latest achievements. Her greatest asset was her charming smile.

For Komalam, her father was her hero, her father was her guide, and her father stood above all and above everything. Komalam loved and cherished her little brother too, as a special gift bestowed upon her by God the Almighty. Her older cousin, Peddapilla, Jagappa's firstborn, often teased Komalam for not having a brother like she had. From that day onwards Komalam prayed for a brother, and on her way to school she stopped by the Temple and prayed for a brother. Komalam had a younger sister called Saroja, four years younger than her, but she longed for a brother. There wasn't much emotional involvement between the two sisters. Saroja spent a lot of time with her mother or at her neighbour Chalmayyagaru's house, where she became their foster daughter.

Masterji also loved Saroja, who appeared like a china doll, small and dainty. But Komalam occupied his free time. She was his companion at home, and she was his everything—there was no parallel to his firstborn. Literally, she was the second born as the first son had died in his infancy, and thus Komalam, in fact, was his first surviving child.

That ominous night, Saroja had high fever and Chalmayyagaru fetched a local doctor, as Masterji was out of town. Chalmayyagaru, the doctor, and Pillamma sat all night with Saroja, tending to her. By the next morning before dawn she breathed her last; she died in her sleep. Masterji returned the next day to hear the demise of his daughter Saroja.

The whole extended family stood by and comforted the bereaved parents, and as a father, Masterji performed the last rites for his second daughter. Another phase of their life took a tragic turn. Masterji recovered after a few days, and resumed his work, but it was Pillamma who went into depression.

Her past kept appearing in front of her, taunting her of her misfortunes. Pillamma was a most unfortunate woman to have had two miscarriages and her infant son's death, and now also losing her Saroja. Pillamma loved children. She longed for them, and she went through a rigorous regime of diet to conceive. Finally, she was happy to have had three lovely children.

But Pillamma felt that Fate had once again laughed at her, and she failed to accept the demise of her second daughter. There, her neighbour Chalmayyagaru family also mourned for their foster child. For one whole year they mourned for her Saroja and abolished all celebrations at their home.

Pillamma resumed her normal duties, but at every waking minute she pondered over the death of Saroja. In every lonesome moment she retreated into her past and cursed her own existence. She considered herself to be the most misfortunate person ever born. She accepted that she was not born with a silver spoon but with ill luck and an iron spatula that kept digging at her with its wide blade. She became despondent, and cursed herself constantly. She recalled how her miseries had begun even before her life came to surface. As soon as she was born her father had died suddenly. As a widow, her mother had to face many troubles, and she faced social isolation as a doomed widow and was considered as bad luck to other women and remained in seclusion. Fortunately her own brother took his widowed sister, the new born baby, and her son into his care. He was a wealthy man and gave them a very comfortable life.

As a fatherless infant they did not have any naming ceremony for her, hence they began to call her Pillamma, literally meaning 'a little girl', the name that stuck with her all her life. After her marriage her father-in-law gave her the name Mahalakshmi, which only appeared in official records; to the world she remained simply 'Pillamma'. She longed to make a mark in this world, she was intelligent, courageous and full of energy, yet she remained just Pillamma.

Pillamma's childhood was nothing noteworthy but was comfortable. Her brother, who was fourteen years older than her, was sent away to Madras and received good education and hence she had no close contact with him. Pillamma missed out on her childhood and sibling attachments, and grew up as a lonely child at her maternal uncle's family whose own daughters were grown up and were at their in-laws. People labelled Pillamma from her birth as 'the girl of misfortune'. As she grew up she became aware of her place in the society, she was perceptive of her surroundings, and she noticed and realised the hardships her mother had to face in society as a widow, but fortunately her own brother protected his widowed sister from the society, so much so he protected her from shaving off her head as widows of the day did. It was considered a sin for a Hindu widow to keep her hair.

As Pillamma was growing up, they lived in a total social isolation. This kind of social rejection bothered young Pillamma. They seldom went out, and most of her childhood was spent at home, but in comfort. Young Pillamma longed to spread her wings and fly high. Her mother often reminded her that she should be grateful to her uncle and not to demand for anything more. From a very young age Pillamma learned to be accommodative. She had learned to obey and she had learned to endure things and take her life as it was. Her ambition to go to school like her brother faded away as she grew up.

Her father-in-law, known as Rangampantulu, took a liking to the fatherless baby Pillamma, when he first saw her at his eldest son six year old Ramalingam's 'Upanayanam', the thread ceremony function. Then and there he picked up the six-month-old baby in his arms and declared that she would be the bride for his son.

Rangampantulu was a bodybuilder and always carried a knife with him. Pillamma's mother was frightened for her baby but nobody had the courage to say no to the bodybuilder gentleman. Silently the mother of the baby Pillamma prayed for her infant's safety.

Rangampantulu carried the baby all through the ceremony and bestowed upon her many rich gifts. There at that auspicious thread ceremony function of her future husband, the infant Pillamma's future had been written and sealed for good. While growing up, Pillamma often visited Rangampantulu's house on his request. She wasn't scared of him as other people were, and instead she saw him like a father figure. All she knew about her own father was his name, Venkatarao, and nothing more. Her mother, Aaadilakshmi, was a woman of few words. Whenever she went to Rangampantulu's house he sent her home laden with gifts, to the annoyance of the women in his own house, but none of them had the courage to go against the wishes of their master.

Rangampantulu was a colourful character. He was known for his indulgence in drinks and women. He had thirty-two hunting dogs and often went on hunting expeditions with his Sahib friends. He entertained the Sahibs in his private bungalow outside the village of Chatrapur. His private life and his domestic life were quite a contrast and separate. He wanted to raise his eldest son as a prince to be equal to the Sahibs. He sent his son to the best college in the country, The Presidency College in Madras, where he lived like a prince, with three servants, one valet, one errand boy, and a cook. He had his own house to reside in, and owned a private *Tonga*.

Whatever private life he had, Rangampantulu was just at home. He got his two daughters married very young, as per tradition. He kept the family traditions alive, but at the same time adopted the Western ways of drinking and entertained females in his private bungalow. His good looks and his handsome personality gained him popularity among the socialite women. It was said that whenever he walked majestically down the main street some women would throw *chits* at his feet, inviting him to their homes, which he graciously obliged.

Rangampantulu indulged in all the luxuries money could buy. He imported gin from England, and his clothes and perfumes from Paris. But his princely style of living began to drain out the vast family inheritance. He died at the age of thirty-four with liver failure, as the drinking had taken its toll on him. He left a widow and three sons, and now his eldest son, still in education, had to take their responsibility.

Rangampantulu's ancestors had also had an interesting life themselves. Four generations before him, the seven brothers had left their village, Wunnava Gramam, with five rupees between them and went in search of a livelihood. Their father, being a teacher and a priest, had given them a good education before he died. The family was poor and their mother sent them into the wide world to make their own lives. The seven of them became separated and chose different paths.

The eldest son, senior Ramalingam, became a Dewanji (chief minister) to a Raja of a small kingdom. He married a Mahrastrian, the daughter of a priest, the royal Purohit, and settled down. He was intelligent but unscrupulous. He went to any extent to show his loyalty to the Raja.

Once there was a dispute between the farmers and the Raja about a mango orchard in the kingdom. They all claimed the mango orchard. The Raja invited the Governor Sahib of the district to come down to his kingdom to sort out the dispute. Dewanji Ramalingam was well aware that the farmers had the rights over the mango orchard. But he couldn't let the Raja lose his prestige in front of the British Governor Sahib. That night, as the Governor was resting in his camp, Dewanji Ramalingam ordered his men to clear out the entire mango orchard and level it to the ground. It was all done secretly in the darkness of the night.

The next day the Governor dismissed the complaint of the farmers invalid as the argued land was bare and gave the judgement in favour of the Rajah. The helpless farmers waited for a chance to take revenge on Dewanji. After a few weeks, when Dewanji was returning home in his palanquin after collecting taxes from the neighbouring villages, the angry farmers ambushed him, killed him, and cut him into pieces as he had done to their mango trees and put the body pieces in the palanquin and returned it to his family. For days his family lived in fear, but the farmers assured them that they would never harm any of them, as they were not guilty of the crime.

The late Dewanji Ramalingam had two sons: Rangarao, known as Rangampantulu, whose daughter-in-law was Pillamma, and Narasimha Swamy, who lived at Chatrapur with his large family to the ripe age of ninety.

Rangarao, nee Rangam Pantulu, first had two daughters. After a long time, having no sons he planned to adopt his cousin's son, the seven-year-old W. V. B. Ramalingam, but changed his mind when he did have his own son, whom he named as W. V. V. B. Ramalingam, distinguishing him with an extra initial V which was to represent 'Varaha'. In the future, the two cousins adopted two entirely different paths—one adopted the Ruler's lifestyle, took a contracting job, and was known as contractor Raosahib (a title bestowed by the rulers) Ramalingam. His namesake, Pillamma's would-be husband, stood against the rulers and adapted the lifestyle of Gandhi and was known as Pandit Ramalingam. Often their names being so similar with the exception of one initial 'V' and their wives' names being the same, Mahalakshmi, caused some confusion in town. Much wasn't known about the rest of their other ancestors.

When Pillamma was married at the age of eight, she resigned her life to being an illiterate wife. Fortunately, her father-in-law came into her life as a godsend. When he asked her what she would really want as a gift from him she expressed her wish to go to school. At first he was livid with anger but immediately appointed two tutors to teach his young daughter-in-law, against the wishes of the women of the family.

Pillamma adored and respected her father-in-law like a father. There again, destiny snatched away that favour from her early in her life. Her father-in-law died there years after her marriage, bringing a full stop to her education. After his demise, the real situation of his financial status came to light. Rangampantulu had lived in luxury on borrowed money. His eldest son-in-law took charge of his estate, sold off the remaining property, and paid off the pending debts. He settled the wife of the deceased and her two young sons into a more modest accommodation at a nearby house at Chatrapur. With the remaining money, he let young Ramalingam continue his studies at Madras.

Now Ramalingam had to change his plans of further education in London and become a lawyer instead he joined the college at Rajamundry to complete his B. Ed. His young wife Pillamma was sent to live with her eldest sister-in-law, who gave rigorous training to Pillamma to befit into their family traditions. There the regime was strict to the point of back-breaking. Pillamma had no one to turn to. Her husband, young Ramalingam, was still at Madras, but occasionally when he came over for holidays he brought her some books which she read secretly in their bedroom. Those few days when he was at home, her husband discussed his life at the college and often told her how some Indian women classmates competed with the boys equally in studies and sports. She noticed his admiration for those intelligent women, and longed to be in a college too, a dream she very well knew would never be realised in her life. But he, with his modern views, encouraged his young wife to read more and be knowledgeable of the world around her. At that time he was equally helpless to get her out of the house. There were traditions to be followed and responsibilities she had to take up as a good wife.

He was aware of the sweet talk his eldest sister bestowed upon his wife in his presence, which veiled the reality of the truth. He often wrote letters to his wife which none of the women at home could read. Sometimes they gave her the letters and other times they destroyed them right in front of her eyes. Pillamma was just eleven, and watched their atrocities helplessly. Pillamma's mother lived in the same town but was not allowed to visit her only daughter. She got the news of her daughter's welfare from the vegetable vendor who went from house to house to sell her goods. The vendor became a go-between for quite a few families where the daughters-in-law had restrictions imposed on them. During his holidays, Ramalingam spent a few days with his young wife and a few days with his mother at Chatrapur. He was always duty-bound.

On her thirteenth birthday when she was matured, the nuptials were arranged at Chatrapur. Ramalingam had completed his teacher-training at Rajamundry and returned home to take up his responsibilities. Now at the young age of nineteen, being the eldest son of the family he became the new master of the house. He took the reins of the household into his capable hands. Very efficiently he sold away their modest property at Chatrapur. He shifted with his mother, his wife and two brothers to Berhampur into their own modest home that his father had purchased just before he died.

Berhampur had good schools, and at once he enrolled his two young brothers into high school. Pillamma embraced the new responsibilities with open arms. She loved to hear the school stories her two young brothers-in-law told her every evening. She could discuss things on an equal level with the two boys, and they adored their intelligent sister-in-law. So far, they had seen women restricted to household duties and nothing more. They had the familiar notion that women were lesser beings, which Pillamma condemned vigorously. Soon they became close to their Vadina and revered their well-learned big brother from a distance.

The adjoining house, the smaller of the two, became the residence of Ramalingam. In time, the two younger brothers were married to suitable brides, and now the extended family lived in comfort and in harmony. But nothing ever runs smoothly at all times. Life has its own ripples. The troubles began to brew for Pillamma when the second daughter-in-law of the family, much younger than her, had a baby first. They called her Peddapilla. By that time Pillamma had already suffered two miscarriages. She cursed her fate once again. Fortunately all the three daughters-in-law got on very well, and the younger two looked up to their literate sister Pillamma and took her advice on every matter.

Pillamma's thoughts always halted at the onset of the events that followed. Pillamma unable to recover from the loss of her second daughter, Saroja, remembered and recalled the tragic day when she lost her infant son a decade before. She tried to hide her agony from her children. Young Komalam was her soul mate, and she envisaged her mother's trouble. But whenever Komalam saw her mother shedding tears silently she went and sat with her. No words were exchanged between them but their thoughts gelled with each other. Young Komalam consoled her mother as if their roles were reversed. After a while, Pillamma woke up from her tragic trance and resumed to her domestic duties skilfully and Komalam took care of her little brother. Together the two females supported each other like two good friends, both hiding their emotions tactfully from each other. Pillamma's grief took its own course in its own time.

Now a few months passed by, and Pillamma maintained her 'normality', but her husband Masterji noticed her anxiety and restlessness in her daily life. He tried to reason with her, reminded her about the essence of *Bhagwat Gita*, which she often read, and failed to make her understand the essence of karma yoga. Generally, the death of a loved one often creates guilty feelings in many victims and Pillamma felt that she was responsible for Saroja's death. The child died of some viral fever which was prevalent in those days, and many more children in town succumbed to the virus. Every tragedy is unique. No amount of consoling, no amount of reasoning, and no amount of guilt feelings could alleviate someone's sadness. Only time had the knack of healing it, but some permanent scars remained.

Pillamma had tremendous maternal feelings in her. Although she had two children, she longed to replace Saroja. She wanted to have another daughter. Masterji was not all that keen about another child; he was more concerned for Pillamma's health, as each conception had drained her physically and emotionally.

He discussed the matter with Dr Margaret Bhore, their family friend and physician at the local Janana Hospital. She assured him that the bouts of depression that Pillamma was going through were a normal process of healing. She promised to give her a good pre-natal care and would supervise the delivery. After one year Pillamma gave birth to a healthy girl at the women's hospital under the care of Dr Bhore.

Perhaps the trauma of the family had an adverse effect on the toddler, Ramam, who had reached three but had not yet learned to speak. Dr Bhore assured the family that Ramam's milestones were normal and that generally boys tend to speak a bit late. Komalam took good care of her brother and waited upon him day and night.

Now Pillamma had recovered from her loss and got busy looking after her baby daughter, Subbulu, a charming bouncy baby. Laughter and happiness had once again re-entered the family.

8
A Year of Bliss

1924 was an eventful year in Pillamma's family. For one year the domestic bliss continued. The birth of another girl had eased her mourning for Saroja. They named the baby Subhadra but called her Subbulu.

After his return from jail, Ramalingam was unanimously elected as the Chairman of the Municipality. The family recovered financially. But Pillamma's three-year-old son gave her cause for concern as he had not yet learned to speak. He mimed for his needs and promptly his doting sister Komalam attended to him. Although Dr Margaret Bhore assured Pillamma that physically everything was alright with her son, for a second opinion Pillamma took Ramam to his uncle Jagappa, their family doctor. Pillamma had immense trust in her brother-in-law's diagnosis. After examining the boy he declared that nothing was wrong with the boy except that he was lazy. He asked her not to respond when he mimed for his needs. In his father's absence, her maternal affection consumed all her common sense and she waited upon her son tenderly. Likewise, because Komalam also doted on her precious brother, the two indulged in spoiling the lazy boy. Ramam meant everything to them, most of all for Pillamma, in being her only surviving son.

Masterji was aware of his wife's blind affection for her son; she was clinging on to him with the fear of losing him. She had yet to overcome the trauma of losing Saroja. Although the boy occupied most of her time, Pillamma could never forget the memories of Saroja and her deceased infant son. Bereavement has no time scale. It is manifested in each person in a different form. Pillamma's constant fears and anxiety for the safety of her children was exhibited in her tolerance of the laziness of her son. She almost neglected to discipline her son as she did with her daughters.

Masterji patiently waited for the day when his wife would get over her anxiety and resume normal care of her son. He waited for his wife to get over her insecurity and raise her son the same way she raised her Komalam.

In 1924, Masterji became more and more involved with his work at the Municipality and the Congress. He took it upon himself to organise the 38th National Session of the Congress at Kakinada (then known as Coconanda) whose president was the eminent congress worker, Maulana Mohammed Ali. As ever, in his prolonged absences from home, Pillamma managed her three children on her own.

At the Municipality, Ramalingam personally supervised public health and sanitation. Already the country was in a semi-epidemic state of malaria. The biggest problem was how to control mosquito-breeding. Ramalingam surveyed the conditions of the town and found there were 250 water tanks, called *cheruvulu,* in Berhampur, and they were holding stagnant water. Their natural drainage was blocked and the stagnant water became home for the mosquito-breeding.

As the Chairman of the Municipality, he with his excellent team of engineers provided adequate drainage to all the tanks in the town. With his team he travelled to the surrounding villages and helped to eradicate the problem of stagnant water. It worked for a while, but then slowly the villagers slipped back into their habits and let the stagnant water accumulate on road sides, bazaars, at home, and everywhere. Regularly the teams of people visited the surrounding villages spraying DDT on open stagnant water sources, which reduced the problem of mosquitoes temporarily.

The Government declared that local bodies were to be responsible for health administration, including the control of epidemic disease. The epidemic of cholera threatened all around the country. As a preventive method, Masterji promoted giving the cholera vaccine to the people of Berhampur and the villages around. Masterji's health regime had become popular with the public, although a nightmare for most children who feared the needle. He supervised the cholera vaccine programme personally with a list of all the citizens of the town in his hand. He, with his brigade of doctors and volunteers, went from street to street vaccinating every person, and ticked them off his list. Hence there was no escape for cowards and nobody could hide or run away from the needle. As a result the cholera epidemic that had gripped the country had not yet reached his town. The governor of the Ganjam District personally congratulated Masterji for his preventive methods. Mr Joseph Bhore, secretary of public health, also extolled Masterji's work in the public health.

Ramalingam paid great attention to all aspects of public health. He supervised the work personally on a regular basis. Every morning before dawn he walked in the streets to see if they had been swept by the sweepers and sprinkled with water to reduce the dust. It was said that he walked with a *Neem* stick toothbrush in his mouth and went for a stroll every morning. The town was praised for its neatness and sanity by the then governor.

Masterji took each task one by one, concentrating on it with complete commitment. Then he concentrated on roads. He was the first municipal leader to have introduced tar-roads and pavements for pedestrians. The road-roller making pukka roads thrilled children of the town. They used to run after it and watched the miracle of levelling the road. While the workmen worked, Masterji would sit on the veranda of a house in the street and supervised the road-making. He left nothing to chance. Once the roads were made, they were pukka and withstood all weathers.

The three-year-old Subbulu was very talkative, and often amused her six-year-old brother Ramam. Sometimes she copied his miming and then teased him when he failed to speak like her. The two siblings began to form a strange bond with deep rivalry with each other, which Pillamma noticed but did not interfere with their sibling jealousy. Ramam tried to control his little sister the same way he did his older sister Komalam.

One day when Komalam was at her tuition, Pillamma brought a bowlful of sweets for the two children and left it on the table. Subbulu ran to it and ate the sweets one by one to the annoyance of her brother. Without stirring from his chair Ramam mimed for a sweet, which little Subbulu simply ignored and continued to consume the sweets in the bowl. He cried, fussed, and stretched his arms out, begging for the sweets, but his little sister took no notice of him. If Komalam were there, she would have fetched the sweets and fed her brother. Subbulu was not yet aware of this strange protocol of sisterhood. For her, Ramam was no more than just another child, a competitor to her existence and she tried to establish her position in the family in her own way, with her cute talk and pleasant personality. He cried again to see if his mother would come to his rescue.

As long as the two children were not at each other's throat Pillamma let them play in their own way. Subbulu was cheeky but never hurt her brother. The frustrated boy stood up and ran to the table and tried to snatch the bowl from his little sister. She ran around the room with the bowl, teasing her brother. Ramam chased her, and Pillamma was delighted to see her son run around. When he failed to catch his sister he yelled, "Me sweet! Me sweet!" uttering the first 'golden words' of his life. Pillamma came out of the kitchen to look at him. He ran to his mother now, crying, "Me sweet! Me sweet!" Perhaps his words scared Subbulu – she dropped the bowl on the floor and hid behind the door. Pillamma gave Subbulu a big kiss and hugged her son. The baffled little girl looked at her mother and smiled sweetly.

Within weeks, Ramam improved his vocabulary and to the delight of his parents the two siblings argued, fought, and played as normal children do. Their sibling jealousy also grew with their friendship. The two active children competed with each other for everything, for toys, for food, for their mother's affection, and Komalam's attention on a daily basis. Now Ramam had found out that his little sister was clever and he learned to be her equal. Masterji noticed that his wife's affection always tilted a bit more towards her son. He smiled to himself and made no remarks.

Now Pillamma was concerned about her son's education. He was six and had not yet gone to school. Compared to his age group he was far behind. Since Masterji had withdrawn Komalam from the Town School she dared not send her son to school. She sent him to Chalamayyagaru along with Komalam who continued her education there. To her delight, her son began to make good progress at the tuition.

In 1926, Masterji was elected as the Vice-president of Nagpur Railway Union. He travelled to and fro to attend meetings at Nagpur, Khargpur, and sometimes at Calcutta. His presence became a rare sight at home. Of all in the family, Komalam missed her father most and waited eagerly for his return. When he was at home he was a devoted father and spent all his time playing and talking with his children, but somehow Ramam shied away from his father and hid behind his mother. When approached by his father he was timid. He replied with a simple 'yes' or 'no' to his father's questions, still holding his mother's hand.

Little Subbulu amused her parents and siblings with her antics. The little time they were together with their father became the most precious for the family. Amidst his busy schedule, Masterji had never forgotten to visit his mother when he was in town, to ask about her welfare. Komalam always accompanied him to her grandmother's house. She loved her cousins and they waited for her visits.

Masterji never took a *Tonga* to travel in town. He walked everywhere and regularly visited one street at a time to enquire about the welfare of the people. He was their councillor, well-wisher, and for those who couldn't go to the municipality with their queries he was their mobile office. He listened to their problems both of domestic and personal nature and often they sought for his advice on their children's education.

When the families offered him a seat he preferred to stand and talk to them and never accepted any refreshments anywhere. Some people found it hard to stand and talk but at the same time found it impolite to sit while Masterji stood in front of them. Gradually he convinced people that it was alright for them to sit in his presence. His evening rounds were well appreciated by the public.

On his way home from his rounds he made it a point to stop by the Barracks grounds where some youngsters still loitered after dark. When they saw him approach the Barracks they scurried away and went home, and buried their heads in books. Masterji encouraged the boys to play and also insisted that they did not neglect their studies. Play and studies were well balanced by youth in his presence in the town. During his teaching career, he established a new style of student-counselling and used to give feedback to their guardians or parents individually. This endeared him as one of the best teachers of the town. He found his responsibilities were laid towards all people of the town.

He earned respect from students and their parents by his sincerity. During his time at Khallikote College, the Standard 7th English teacher was ailing. The Principal, Ganapati Iyyer, asked Ramalingam to take up classes and later conduct the examination. When the regular teacher returned and saw the mark-sheet of his class, he was not at all pleased, and complained to the Principal that a mathematics teacher had marked an English paper as if it was mathematics, because a student was given 98%. The Principal made the English teacher comfortable and sent for Ramalingam, who was asked to explain himself to the English teacher. Ramalingam took out a model answer which he wrote as a 7th Standard student would possibly produce. Compared to the model answer, Ramalingam explained that the student had made only two mistakes—hence he gave him 98%. The student was Bachu Jagannath Das, who later became the Chief Justice of Orissa High Court and further a judge at the Supreme Court of India. His students also included some eminent citizens of free India, such as V. V. Giri, the future president of India, and Lingaraj Panigrahi, the Chief Justice of Orissa High Court. All his students had great reverence for their guru, Pandit Ramalingam.

Ramalingam was not a sportsman. He played chess and bridge, at which his wife Pillamma also excelled. Once Ganapati Iyyer, the Principal of the College, pined over why his Khallikote College never won the Inter-College Football Tournament of the district. Ramalingam promised to try to make the college win the tournament. Ramalingam studied the game, and drew out a strategic plan. He made the team practise the planned game repeatedly under the supervision of their game's master. With their hard and dedicated practice the College football team had won the cup the very next year. The college continued to follow

Masterji's master plan in the football game, which he never played. Masterji could resolve any problem by his logical and methodical approach to it. He took up each problem as a personal challenge.

Similarly he often went to the *'bastis'* where poor people dwelled and looked after their welfare. As the leader of the municipality, Ramalingam gradually cleared the waste land at one end of the town and gave it free to the poor to develop the Victoria Market, which still thrives. The market had created a living for many and in time it had extended vastly. The governor of the district appreciated Ramalingam's dedication to the welfare of the town and congratulated him personally. Later in Free India, one young IAS officer wrote in his memoirs that Pandit Ramalingam, as the Municipality Leader, was his inspiration in his work.

9

The 1927 and 1928 Civil Disobedience Movement

The man who most clearly formulated the concept of Civil Disobedience for the modern world was Gandhiji. Drawing from Eastern and Western thoughts, Gandhi developed the philosophy of *Satyagraha*, the non-violent resistance, or civil resistance.

In 1927, Gandhiji visited Berhampur to detail further reforms in the structure of Indian Government. On 5 December 1927 he reached Berhampur, but that day being his 'silent day', he spoke to nobody. On the next day, 6 December, Gandhiji addressed the public at the Barracks ground. He asked the women to fight against the evils of liquor and to boycott foreign clothes. The movement started well but slowly relapsed. Gandhiji also asked people to discard feelings of aversion towards 'the untouchables' (people of low caste), a vision close to Gandhiji's heart.

Later he met Ramalingam and other leaders to discuss further plans. Komalam also accompanied her father to meet Gandhiji. All her life she cherished that experience of meeting the great man in person. As ever, she had even charmed Gandhiji and he blessed her for a great future. He asked her about her schooling and she replied that she had come out of the Government School but was getting education from her guru, Chalmayyagaru, privately. Gandhiji was impressed that some people had responded to his call of boycott of Government schools. He asked young Komalam never to stop learning and told her that India had very talented gurus who could educate pupils with knowledge that was unparalleled to any British education, which tended to be one-sided, promoting English values, and ignoring Indian spiritualism and Indian values. Komalam had a thirst for knowledge and learnt all she could from her tutor. She profitably utilised the vast library her father had at home.

Gandhiji's main aim of visiting Berhampur was to promote his strategic plan of complete disobedience to the orders of the British Government. Gandhiji said:

"It's contrary to national dignity for any Indian to serve under a government which has brought about India's economic, moral, and political degradation."

Soon after his return to Sabarmati Ashram, Gandhiji wrote to Ramalingam and others about some mismanagement at the *Khadi Board* (the *Khadi* shop). Until then, Ramalingam believed in delegating work among his workmates and relied on them. Now seeing some misappropriation by his fellow workers he decided to personally supervise all matters that were concerned with finances.

Gandhiji spared no one when misappropriation was found. He dealt with it straightaway.

35. LETTER TO I. SANYASA RAZU AND OTHERS AS AT THE ASHRAM, SABARAMATI

December 15, 1927

DEAR FRIEND,

I have secured from Deshbhakta Venkatappayya the names of these Andhra friends who gave proper legal guarantees for the moneys advanced by the Khadi Board, now Charka Sangh, for Khadi work. I understand that you are one of these guarantors and that there is difficulty in securing payment from you. I would make a fervent appeal to you to discharge your obligation, which is not merely legal but also moral. And we who profess to serve the country are in my opinion more bound by moral obligations even than by those that are merely legal. I therefore hope that you will discharge this obligation as if it was a first charge upon all your assets and induce other friends to discharge their responsibility.

Yours sincerely,
Gandhi M.K.

(1) IVVATURI SANYASA RAZU, DEVADI
(2) GADEY RAJAMANNAR, BERHAMPUR
*(3) UNNAVA RAMALINGAM PANTULU, MUNICIPAL CHAIRMAN, BERHAMPUR
4) MALLADI KRISHNAMOORTHY PANTULU, VAKIL, BERHAMPUR
(5)THAKUR RAMAKRISHNARAO (Now gone to Kashi)

(Ref: THE COLLECTED WORKS OF MAHATMA GANDHI, from a microfilm: S.N. 12649)

Straight away, Ramalingam, the Municipal Chairman intervened in the matter and repaid the money from the funds to the *Khadi* Board. Sanyasi Razu, who dealt with finances of *Khadi* Board explained that the matter was nothing more than a simple neglect on his part, since he was otherwise occupied. Ramalingam repaid the loan with an apology to the *Khadi*-Bhandar, all the guarantors signed it, and a copy was duly sent to Gandhiji's office at Sabarmati Ashram. With the consent of all the members, Sanyasi Razu's work load was reduced and an assistant was appointed to him.

Gandhiji had a tremendous memory for details, he never forgot anyone he met, and he cared for them like a father, true to his public's affectionate name to him as 'Pitaji'. On his visit to Berhampur, Gandhiji wrote a letter to Ashram Women:

6. LETTER TO ASHRAM WOMEN, BERHAMPUR.

Silence Day [December 5, 1927]

SISTERS,

I got your letter written by Manibehn. I have very little time to write today. I am convinced that we should not permit jewels in the Ashram. As long as there is terrible starvation in our land it is a sin for us to keep or to put on a ring weighing even a grain. Our clothes must be just sufficient to cover our nakedness and to protect us against heat and cold. All of you should try to reach this ideal.

I shall not write today about how the desire for ornaments arises. It looks as though you have also not understood my question properly.

How is it that Lakshmibehn is ill? She never used to fall ill.

Blessings from

BAPU

(Sometimes Gandhi was called Bapu, meaning 'father'.)

(Ref: THE COLLECTED WORKS OF MAHATMA GANDHI)

When Gandhiji appealed for funds the women of the Berhampur town stripped off their jewellery and placed them at his feet. Gandhiji thanked the generosity of the women of Berhampur. Even in the villages the women donated their meagre jewellery to Gandhiji.

On the morning of 21 September, Gandhiji shaved his head and wrapped a piece of *Khaddar* around his loins. Thus he resolutely took to the loin-cloth. Inspired by his speeches and his visit to the town, Ramalingam began to grow his beard, which enhanced his personality. He did not need to shave his head, as he was already balding! He discarded his shirt and covered his broad chest with a *Khadi* shawl. Unlike Gandhiji, Ramalingam had a good physique, inherited from his father.

Now Ramalingam was resolute to the life of a *sanyasi*, a hermit continuing to have one meal a day, which he had already adapted from the day he had joined the freedom movement, and now he was vowed to celibacy. This was a big decision to make. He consulted his wife Pillamma, his life partner, and with her agreement they both agreed to celibacy. He was forty-two and his wife was five years younger than him. Their youngest child was just three years old. When it came to sacrificing for the cause, Pillamma never divulged from it, and wholeheartedly supported her husband in all his decisions. She accepted that his life was dedicated to the town and the freedom of the country and there was no place for him to indulge in family life.

Once again Gandhiji stressed the importance of *Charka*, the spinning wheel:

"When all about me are dying for want of food, the only occupation permissible to me is to feed the hungry and hunger is drawing them to the spinning wheel," orated Gandhiji, with immense emotion to his public. Whenever he spoke, wherever he addressed the public, Gandhiji invariably inspired the people around him, as if they were hypnotised by him. Ramalingam and his colleagues extended more *Charka*-centres in town, and that promoted the sale of *Khadi* and helped to solve the problem of unemployment to some extent.

Gandhiji's struggle to wipe out the flight of the 'untouchables' was recognised at the town. Ramalingam and his colleagues had adopted the policy of equality, but their attempts to make the untouchables enter the Temples had really become a struggle. Just two Temples in town agreed to allow the untouchables enter temples and the leaders accompanied the untouchables to the Temple where they worshipped with the town's people. The majority of people strongly objected to Masterji's act and pronounced it as blasphemy. The magnanimity of the temple trustees, who were an independent body, failed to keep up their promise for a long time. Within weeks they had again banned the untouchables from entering the temples. The news had reached Gandhiji and he strongly objected, saying it was a break of faith. He wrote an open letter to the leaders of the town:

BREACH OF PROMISE?

When I was in Berhampur, Ganjam District, last year, I was taken to a temple which I was told was open to all, including the so-called untouchables. I was accompanied by some untouchable friends. A few weeks after, I received a letter that the trustees had declared prohibition against the entry of untouchables. I was loath to believe the statement.

If the information is correct, it is clear breach of promise by the trustees—a promise that was publicly made not merely to me but to the public of Berhampur through me. I wonder whether the trustees have any defence of explanation to offer. The untouchables have undoubtedly a clear case for offering *Satyagraha* in this case. I do hope however that the public of Berhampur will redeem their self-respect by insisting on removal of the bar, if the bar does as a matter of fact exist.

(Ref: From a photostat S. N. 13182)

Once again the leaders of the town led by the Chairman of the municipality, Masterji Ramalingam, appealed to the trustees of the temple, and reluctantly they agreed to let the untouchables enter the temples at certain times of the day. Those promises were more often broken than honoured. The town was very conservative and it wasn't easy to change their minds. They swayed to and fro and the entrance of the Harijans, (Gandhiji had named the untouchables as *Harijans*, 'the children of God') to temples was never resolved satisfactorily. There was a constant tug of war between the temple trustees and the town's reformists. Meanwhile, Ramalingam and other broadminded citizens of the town welcomed the untouchables and non-Brahmins to their homes. One such emerging young congress worker was Goutu Lachanna, and Ramalingam with his wife attended the young man's wedding, and blessed the couple.

To carry out the task to follow Gandhiji's boycott policy appeared to be impossible. Ramalingam and his colleagues managed to influence a few more people, but at the same time equal if not more numbers of people resumed their duties at work as before, defying the leaders of the town. The people's economic situation wiped out their resolution to follow Gandhian principles to the word.

All the same, the undeterred Ramalingam along with his colleagues promoted the disobedience movement at Berhampur. It was active and almost revolutionary. Its main aim was to paralyse the Government by mass support and by understanding the acts which the British Government considered as illegal. The people's demands were against repressive laws:

To reduce land revenue
Abolition of salt tax
Levying duty on foreign clothes
And to reduce Military Expenditure.

The British Government refused outright to agree to any of those proposals.

Thus the Congress proclaimed its faith in Civil Disobedience as a weapon, which was equally effective and more humane than armed rebellion. The war of 'words' between the rulers and the ruled, attacks and counter-attacks, continued nationwide. Now the spark of the flint was ignited, waiting to set alight the whole nation. The sparks spread slowly and gradually around the country. At the same time, life continued for many people as before, unaware of the under current flowing under their feet. Masterji kept his wife informed of the situation whenever he could. Now the family depended entirely on Pillamma. He also relied on her integrity and never questioned her about family matters as he had handed over the family responsibilities into her care. Pillamma maintained the harmony of her family to her best ability.

Now her main concern was about her daughter Komalam's marriage. Komalam was growing, and many girls of her age were already married. Those women's threats constantly worried her –'Who would marry the daughter of a criminal?' echoed in her heart and frightened her. Masterji had spent time in jail and hence was viewed as no less than a common criminal by some sects of the society

Ramalingam was beyond people's criticism. Undeterred, he continued to remain involved in his work. Ramalingam was always inventive. Although he followed Gandhiji, he often initiated other projects on his own steam. He realised that none of the reforms were tailor-made; the cloth had to be cut and shaped and then stitched, all in a specific order. To obtain a piece of cloth requires finances. Thus he decided on a savings project, to improve the common man's income by his savings.

To start with, the major Imperial Bank at Berhampur was an institution of the Government which mainly served the elite and wealthy. Masterji aimed to improve the economies of the common man. He took the movement further by starting a mobile bank. At the onset, he collected the savings, however small they were, by visiting the people in person and he gave them their pass books. The concept of savings was novel to them, but they had faith in Masterji. He made the commoner realise that he too could have a nest egg for the future. But it wasn't all that easy as it had sounded.

In the beginning, Masterji and his volunteers went from village to village, from house to house, first convincing the people about saving, and then collecting their meagre savings. Well-maintained records were kept by Masterji, and he personally supervised the daily intake and issued the savings-books to each saver. Where public finances were concerned, Masterji supervised personally. He never wanted another mishap like the one with *Khadi-Bhandar* to happen again. For the first time, the commoner felt that he had a small fund to rely upon.

Most English-educated Indians looked upon anything Indian as barbarous. Some people looked down on Ramalingam and ridiculed him, saying that he was begging for money from door to door. That did not stop his pursuit. Masterji's aim was to have a 'people's bank' in which they could save their money in safety and also allow them to borrow from the bank.

In Berhampur, there was no shortage of critics to his new venture. People made snide remarks and Pillamma had to listen to their remarks constantly, and at the local Venkateswara Temple his mother had to face the women who ridiculed her eldest son Ramalingam without any qualms. The old lady found it hard to swallow their taunts. Some women went to Pillamma's house and attacked her with stinging words.

"What is this world coming to? It's all going wrong," said one woman as a prelude.

"Nothing strange! After all, he is a Brahmin—it's his trade," another woman sniped at Pillamma.

The women pointed out that it was a common practice of Brahmins to beg. In town the poor Brahmins went on their daily rounds reciting *slokas* on the doorsteps and received alms from the households, on which they survived. There was another age-old Vedic custom that still remains in vogue, though it has changed somewhat in form to suit modern requirements. It was a system by which the charitably disposed assist the poor Brahmin boys in their education, and in providing meals for them. One family will agree to give one or two meals a day to a certain student for a certain day in the week, and others will do the same until the whole week's maintenance of the poor student is provided for. The poor student will sometimes say that he lives 'by weeks', i.e. each day of the week he gets his food at a different house.

The laws of hospitality in India are very real, and it is imperatively binding upon those who can do so to give food to needy travellers, regardless of caste or condition. It's believed that to send a hungry suppliant away empty-handed is not only unkind, it is a positive sin. Whatever the original theory may have been, it is far from being the case that all Brahmins live in these modern days by gifts and alms. The learned professions and other walks of life are crowded with Brahmins, who labour for their subsistence as others.

There is another kind of Brahmin, called the Panchangam Brahmin, who recites a daily almanac. He begins by repeating it in a sing-song manner and at a very rapid rate, showing the benefits to be derived from hearing the almanac. He then goes on, in a more deliberate manner, to state the details of the day. People give alms to those Panchangam Brahmins who went to their doorstep. This practice was well in use in those days at Berhampur.

"Don't be ridiculous! Our Masterji is from a well-to-do family. His father was a *Zamindar* (a landlord). Even if he is a Brahmin and even though it is his tradition, there is no need for him to go begging. He comes from a rich family." The woman appeared to be pro-Masterji, but in fact she was stabbing him in the back, a knack few women exercised tactfully.

"That was their past glory, sister. Don't you remember his father left his sons as paupers? Everybody knows that, that's no secret."

"Are you blind, woman? Masterji is not a pauper."

"Well, I don't have to say anything. Just look at him. His *Dhoti, Chappals*, and those thick and rough *Khadi* they all wear—it's such a disgusting sight. I would rather die than be seen in those rough clothes," said a snob expressing her contempt at Pillamma. Since burning foreign clothes, even Pillamma had adopted to wearing *Khadi* saris.

"Sister, have you forgotten his *Khadi* shoulder-bag he carries everywhere? I wonder, what does he carry in that? Perhaps his Brahmanism?" The woman burst out laughing at her cracking joke.

"Laugh as much as you wish. You are as stupid as you look. Masterji and many men of our town are followers of Gandhiji. Maybe you haven't even heard of his name!" ridiculed a pro-Gandhi admirer.

"Soon we're going to be free from slavery," emoted a young woman with glee. She waited to see if anybody had any positive attitude for Masterji's family, before she showed her loyalty to the family. Until then she had found it wise to sit on the wall and not to take sides. She silently admired Pillamma, and for her she was her role-model. But she kept her thoughts to herself lest she be ridiculed in public.

"Rubbish! Nothing of the sort. At least now we can wear decent clothes and eat decent food. Once we are free we've to look like them," she said, pointing at Pillamma. Pillamma began to avoid temple visits and social functions, not for the fear of the women's 'attacks' but to protect her daughter Komalam from hearing such remarks about her father, whom she adored unconditionally.

Once after returning from an errand found Komalam sitting on the parapet of the well, crying bitterly. Pillamma realised that the little girl had heard the snide remarks about her father. Pillamma felt like requesting her husband to give up his urban-bank project but she couldn't do so. He had already discussed the matter with her before he commenced the project. He complimented her on how prudently she managed the family budget but reminded her that not all could do so. But the needs of people were similar and hence he felt he should encourage the poor and average citizen about saving for a rainy day. His intentions were worthy and she couldn't stop him now.

Once Masterji took up a task there was no turning back. He was like a flowing river always going forward, crossing obstacles on the way, or by-passing them tactfully to reach the destination. Often she wondered what their destination was and when it would be in sight. Pillamma sighed and accepted the events as they took place in their lives, and let them continue to flow at their own pace. In such dire situations, Pillamma invariably recollected her husband's opulent lifestyle before, and sighed at that.

The opinion of the public about the mobile bank was divided equally between its supporters and opponents. The critics felt that a bank should have an impressive building and not work with a begging-bowl. But, the mobile bank began to grow in strength day by day.

Ramalingam laid the foundations of this Urban Cooperative Bank for a steady growth with the aim of raising the economic conditions of the people of Berhampur. The bank at Berhampur was set up with donations and public support. He personally supervised the construction of the building from its start. Bricks were brought from Khargpur, which was known for its strong bricks. The bank building was constructed under Ramalingam's direct supervision with his accustomed meticulousness, keeping an eye on strength and beauty. Ramalingam spared no pains to build the bank with a sound footing through his untiring zeal and sincere efforts. Masterji's vision of a people's-bank for ordinary people was realised. It was an important means of promoting the economic prosperity of the people and is still functioning with full capacity. The all-round success of the bank was mainly due to the efforts of Ramalingam, the Masterji.

"Pandit W.V.V.B. Ramalingam who has given the lead in many political, social and cultural activities of the Ganjam District during the hard Regimentations of the British Government has also laid the foundation of this Institute for a steady growth with the aim of raising the economic conditions of the people of Berhampur City."

Sri Adikanda Sahu – President, the
Aska Cooperative Central Bank Ltd,
and The Vice-President, State Cooperative
Union, Cuttack.

(Ref: Golden Jubilee Souvenir of the Bank)

"To have been able to serve sixty per cent of the population of a town is a unique achievement in itself. Because of the tradition of single-minded devotion to the institution by the successive office-bearers, among whom I have the privilege of knowing Master W.V.V.B. Ramalingam, the famous non-co-operator who has made a success of Cooperation."

Nityananda Kanungo – Minister
for Consumer Industries.

(Ref: Golden Jubilee Souvenir of the Bank)

"The all-round success of the Bank is mainly due to the early efforts of its former secretary Pandit W.V.V.B. Ramalingam who is a veteran Co-operator of the State and who spared no pains to put the Banking sound-footed through his untiring zeal and sincere efforts."

Sri A. P. Panda – Joint Registrar
of Cooperative Societies, Orissa.

(Ref: Golden Jubilee Souvenir of the Bank)

"11 July 1924 was a lucky day in the life of this Bank, when Pandit W.V.V.B. Ramalingam was elected as Secretary of the Bank. As a member of the committee that framed new bye-laws in 1917–18 and as a director from 26-2-1919 it was but just that he should have been chosen to guide the destinies of this Bank. From that day to 14-7-1930, he continued as Secretary, when the Civil Disobedience Movement called his services and sent him to jail. He took charge again on 1-12-1930 and served the Bank as Secretary till 18-7-1932 when he offered Individual Civil Disobedience and again went to jail. During these terms of his absence, his disciple and the oldest Director of the Bank today, Sri R. Suryanarayanamurty was elected and was in charge as Secretary. Pandit Ramalingam took over again on 10-4-1933 and continued till 24-7-1938 when he voluntarily relinquished his office.

"The Bank building situated in one of the most prominent localities of Berhampur was constructed under Pandit Ramalingam's supervision, with his accustomed meticulousness with an eye on strength and beauty"

Sri Mocharla Sitaramayya, Advocate
and Honorary Secretary.

(Ref: Diamond Jubilee Souvenir of the Bank)

"The reason for the success so far achieved by the Urban Bank is the soundness of its management on scrupulous business lines and the extraordinary self-less interest evinced by a succession of influential directors, among whom Pandit W.V.V.B. Ramalingam, who has devoted his energies for a pretty long period to put the Bank in the right lines. It is a matter of great pleasure that he has left charge of the affairs of the bank in the hands of his worthy disciple Sri Mocherla Sitaramayya who is still continuing as the Chief Executive Officer of the Urban Bank."

Sri L. Dandapat, Deputy Registrar, Cooperative
Societies, Southern Division, Orissa.

(Ref: Diamond Jubilee Souvenir of the Bank)

PANDIT W.V.V.B. Ramalingam
Secretary, Berhampur Co-op Urban Bank Ltd.
Hazra Bhanvan, Cuttack-1
Ranihat.

30 November, 1956.

The Berhampur Cooperative Urban Bank Ltd. has, during these fifty years, weathered many storms and withstood a few cyclones. All the same, being carefully nursed after every damage, it has been growing from strength to strength. It is being realised now that the way of strengthening the financial position of the country is mostly through cooperatives. Hence greater responsibility lies hereafter on the members and directors of the Bank. Let it not be presumed that in future there will not be any difficulties. They always crop up, on and off. The members will have to elect as directors only such as are imbued with the spirit of cooperation, have a growing sense of responsibility in public activities, and are willing to learn patiently the working of the Bank. They should not be swayed in the election by any extraneous considerations. The Directors have to study fully the details of the financial position and vigilantly watch the progress of the Bank. If they cannot spare the necessary time they should never get into the management of any financial concern. For there is no honour nowadays in being a director; on the other hand there are many risks. If members and directors behave with such realisation of responsibility, the Bank will go on thriving as far as human effort is concerned.

The fifty years is but the childhood of an institution. I wish the Bank all success and steady growth in strength.

(Ref: The Berhampur Cooperative Bank Ltd – Golden Jubilee Souvenir 1956)

Reminiscences of Sri R Suryanarayanmurty, director since 1924 till today continuously for over 32 years (the oldest sitting director):

"The Berhampur Cooperative Educational Employees' society was started and I acted as Secretary of the same society. During the first non-cooperation days, my Guru Sri W.V.V.B. Ramalingam resigned from his job and joined the first Non-cooperative Movement. From the years 1924 to 1938 Pandit Ramalingam was the Secretary and any attempt at enumerating his real zeal and enthusiasm for the improvement of the Bank would be inadequate in my hands. I was only a helping hand and followed his footsteps. In the years 1930 and 1932 when Master Ramalingam was in jail, he was elected as Director and during his absence, I was elected as the Secretary.

"After the Bank was housed in a most modern building of its own and the administration of the bank was put in order, Master Ramalingam resigned. After him Mocherla Sitaramayya was the Secretary and Master Ramalingam was consulted in all important matters of policies."

(Ref: Golden Jubilee Souvenir 1906–1956)

"The Bank had developed considerably during the time of Pandit W.V.V.B. Ramalingam, who has in fact laid the foundations for the steady progress of the Bank. He has under his personal supervision constructed an imposing building for the Bank."

(Ref: Diamond Jubilee Souvenir, 1906–1966: The President's Report.)

Once the building was complete Ramalingam handed it over to the elected committee and trained bankers. He remained its unanimously elected honorary secretary for many years to come. The salient feature of the bank was that every decision of the bank on every matter, however important or trivial, was always decided unanimously or not at all, the system continues to date. Thus the bank gained the trust of the people and began to prosper. It had created a healthy convention that can be followed by any financial institution and earned the reputation and faith of the people.

Masterji's aim to educate the common men and encourage them to save for their future had been realised within two years. The same people who ridiculed and laughed behind his back now slowly began to use the Co-op bank.

Ramalingam never looked for glory; when his project came to be successful he passed it on to the capable people to run it and moved on to the next project. He was inventive and always sought for improvement in people's lives.

The Berhampur Co-operative Urban Bank Ltd, 2010

10
Simon Effect

As Gandhiji often said, the cities were not India. India lived in her seven *Lakhs* (100,000) villages and the cities lived upon them.

Ramalingam took charge of village development with his gang of volunteers. A lot of women of the town took an active part in it. They approached Pillamma to join them and lead them as her husband did. This put Pillamma in a dilemma. She was also inspired by all the revolution that was taking place in front of her and was led by her husband. But the motherly instinct within her eclipsed her desire to follow them and join the female brigade of freedom fighters. She refused to join the women's league, saying that her first duty was towards her young children whose father was always away. They pleaded with her to change her mind but she gently refused, which angered some of them. Then her best friend, Mangamma, stood by her and supported her choice. Pillamma realised that it was her sole responsibility to raise her three young children. Although Komalam stood by her, she would be getting married and would leave home to join her husband, whereas Ramam her only son and Subbulu her little girl were at home.

As it was, the upheavals at home and his father's frequent absence took their toll on the little boy, and even at six he was still unable to speak, and he mimed to communicate. Pillamma was concerned about it, but there was nothing she could do about the present situation. Although Subbulu, a good three years younger than her brother, became talkative and received all the attention from the neighbours and family, Ramam remained hidden in his shell.

The women's brigade reluctantly left Pillamma to her choice while a few criticised her for being selfish and not supporting her famous husband, who had become a valuable supporter of the freedom movement in town. Some suggested she leave the children with their grandmother and join them. Pillamma couldn't shirk her responsibility and instead burden her aging mother-in-law. Ramalingam had left his ancestral home in order not to burden his brothers and mother with his work and with his involvement in the freedom movement. He did not want them to be affected by the challenges he undertook. He loved them and he wanted to protect them by being away from home. To some extent he was right, but his every action indirectly had an effect on them too. His mother and brothers often had to face the taunts and the criticisms from the public, but the extended family remained united in his absence.

Pillamma had already become an exponent of tolerance. She endured all that she came across in her life and accepted the public opinions of both the positive and the negative with the same spirit, and never wavered from her dedication to her husband and her children. Theirs was a unique friendship that was uncommon in those days. The couple trusted each other without any provisional clauses. They relied on each other for their mental and moral support and they depended on each other for their salvation from the stresses of the life they were both going through. They were each other's soul mates. The couple, both Ramalingam and Pillamma, were both dedicated to their duties, one to the public and the other to their family. They were resolved to their life as it struck them, yet they remained good friends more than ever. From time to time, Pillamma expressed her dislike of the never-ending movement, but then Masterji would gently remind her of his duties which he could not shun. She accepted it, and led her life to the best of her ability.

Gandhiji continued his travels throughout the country. Often he reiterated his mission to the diminishing enthusiasts. He said:

"Hunger is the argument that is driving India to the spinning wheel. The attainment of the *Swaraj* is possible only by the revival of the spinning wheel. A plea for the spinning wheel is a plea for recognising the dignity of labour."

Once the initial fad of the spinning wheel had slowly dissipated, Gandhiji once again reminded Indians of the importance of the *Charka*. Once again it became popular with the public. The waves of revolution were like waves in the sea; they had their ebbs and flows, their tides.

Now Gandhiji coined another word: *Swaraj* (freedom) to enhance the importance of the spinning wheel. He was criticised for instigating the public against the Government, to which he replied:

"Our non-cooperation is neither with the English nor with the West. Our non-cooperation is with the system the English established. It is a refusal to cooperate with the English administrators on their own terms."

The British Government tried to pacify Gandhiji by appointing the Simon Commission, without a single Indian member, to investigate India's constitutional problems and to make recommendations. Congress boycotted the Simon Commission.

Gandhiji told them clearly:

"We know what we want. We do not need British reforms. England is indebted to India."

Soon, 'Simon-go-home' slogans and demonstrations spread all over the country to the annoyance of the Government. They declared such demonstrations as illegal. Immediately Gandhiji declared that:

"The British Government deprived the Indians of their freedom but has based itself on the exploitation of the masses, and has ruined India economically, politically, culturally and spiritually. We must sever the British connection and attain Purna *Swaraj*."

The first cry for *Purna Swaraj*, complete freedom, began to echo through the country. A new revolution took birth there and then, but the Government failed to take it seriously. But the ripples of tsunami began to develop in the ocean of freedom.

Gandhiji asked people not to participate in elections to the legislative assembly and once again asked Indians to resign from it. He also declared that 26 January should be observed as the Independence Day all over India. Later, after attaining the independence, 26 January had officially become the Republic

Day of India and is celebrated annually with vigour and pomp and every year the elite of the world's nations attends the Republic Day Parade At Delhi.

Gandhiji's speeches stirred the conscience of many Indians, and many more followers joined his flight. But undeterred, the Simon Commission went from town to town hoping to gain support. When they visited Berhampur, Ramalingam dined with them along with his colleagues, amidst the people of different castes and religions. How Ramalingam and the leaders of the town mingled with the Simon delegation and had dined with them became the news of the town and was well publicised in the local newspapers. Joseph Bhore, the joint secretary of the Simon Commission, and his wife, Dr Margaret Stott Bhore, were Ramalingam's family friends and had dined in his house many times before. But now the news of his dining with these Christians, and people of other religions and sects, became a big issue in town. The public condemned Ramalingam and considered his act as sacrilege to his Brahmanism and they duly outcast him and his whole family from the society. He accepted it with a smile, but his mother found it hard to accept this kind of social denunciation. She feared and dreaded its consequences on the whole family. Their children would not get any marriage alliances, they would be outcast at all functions, and people would refuse to dine with them.

The consequences of dining with other castes are varied and strictly forbidden for a Brahmin. Society then was very conservative and was reluctant to make any amends even to their leader, Ramalingam. Ramalingam was a Brahmin by birth and they expected him to obey the traditions and all the customs and set a good example for the younger generations. Ramalingam's father regularly entertained his European friends and Sahibs in his bungalow away from home. He dined and wined with his Christian friends, and nobody ever dared to raise a complaint. He was a Brahmin at home and performed all his duties dutifully. Ramalingam's father maintained two different lifestyles, one at home and one with Sahibs, whereas his son Ramalingam was more open in his life and never hid his views of life from anyone. He was like an open book. He followed what he preached, even if it went against public opinion. Ramalingam had more liberal views. He respected his responsibilities as a Brahmin, but at the same time he was not conservative. From his college days, he had friends of all faiths and some Europeans bereft of their wealth and prestige, who remained friends even when he joined the freedom movement. As ever, Pillamma remained unperturbed. For Ramalingam the caste system was caused by social prejudice rather than religious beliefs.

But Ramalingam's mother insisted that he should go through the purification procedure in front of the public. She was concerned about the future of all her grandchildren, including Komalam, the daughter of Ramalingam. She was of marriageable age and Atta was afraid that she may not get a suitable proposal from a good Brahmin family. She wanted her son to perform *Prayaschittam.*

Prayaschittam is a Sanskrit word and is the Hindu term for 'atonement'. It is the word used for the portion of Hindu law and the *Dharmasastra*, the moral code that has to do with the expiation of sins. It is an Introspection of Human values laid by the society. Faith is a bridge between evidence and belief. His mother felt that *Prayaschittam* would help the whole family to regain their place in the society. They could not exist without the society. By dining with people of other casts and religions Ramalingam had become impure in the eyes of the society and his mother was determined to restore her family prestige and their place in the society as before. Ramalingam was then in a dilemma: he believed in equality and not in rituals. He knew that rituals are not religion. Religion brings about rituals as tools to maintain the religion. But his mother, belonging to a previous generation, held on to her beliefs. He agreed to go through *Prayaschittam* to please his mother and his extended family and his conservative friends. The caste regulations for the avoidance of contact with people of other religions and non-Brhamins were strict enough in those days. Caste is very rigid and any breach of it was considered as a most serious offence. One of the penalties for such an offence was an expulsion from the community. The three-day *Prayaschittam* ceremony began at his ancestral home that he had left.

The religious ceremony was held in full view of the public. The Brahmin families sat inside the house and non-Brahmins settled on the verandas and witnessed the holy ceremony. It is a measure of removing sins for violating moral and ethical codes of the society. To overcome their sins, *Yagna* and *Homam* are performed. *Yagna* is a combination of rituals recommended by Vedic Scriptures. *Homam* is a fire ritual recited by scared chants. Most Brahmins are engaged in other secular activities. Only qualified Brahmin can conduct the religious ceremonies. Ramalingam, having a photographic memory, had learnt all scriptures as a priest does. The *Yagna*, his purification ceremony, began in earnest. *Yagna* is a very powerful Vedic procedure to remove negative Karma. Yagna helps to neutralise difficulties. *Yagna* is specifically for the attainment of particular obstacles or challenges that a person or family has at that time.

Yagna is the combination of *Karma* (the ritual), *Gnana* (the inner significance of every ritual) and the underlying current for both these is *Bhakti* (devotion). The three-day religious ceremony was held with satisfaction to all concerned, and to conclude the ceremony a grand feast was given to all who attended the ceremony. To Ramalingam's dissatisfaction, food was served to the non-Brahmins on the verandas and the Brahmins in the house, and all the food was prepared and served by Brahmins. Helplessly he watched the injustice being done to fellow human beings in the name of religion and caste, which he abhorred. Ramalingam could not change the attitudes of the society, nor was he agreeable with their narrow-mindedness.

After the feast, Ramalingam took a vow in front of his guests with the boldness of a tiger. He counter-attacked the society by announcing that he had vowed not to dine anywhere else except at his home and to eat the food that was cooked by his wife. From that time onwards, he had not dined even at his brother's house and to his mother's despair. He visited them regularly as before but never took any food there. His announcement had surprised many, and a few felt that it was just a gimmick to cover his sin to dine with 'the untouchables' and people of other religions. Once Ramalingam made a decision, he never wavered from it. Until his last day on earth, he never dined outside his home. He had not imposed any restrictions on his wife and children.

As before, he continued to entertain others in his kitchen and Pillamma had no qualms about it. Now Masterji was labelled as a reformist and a danger to the traditions of Hinduism, but he was beyond any labelling. He acted on his beliefs and nobody or nothing could change his mind from his principles. He believed in the equality of all humans and he followed his principles to the last. Fortunately, he had his wife's full cooperation in all he did.

Now the town's people were in a dilemma. His thirst for knowledge made Masterji learn all Vedic Hymns like a professional priest. When he attended a function the priests dreaded his presence—if they missed a line or if they tried to skip the procedure Ramalingam would correct them. Thus people loved to have Ramalingam at their functions to supervise the completeness of the religious ceremony. Besides their selfish motives, as the most important personality of the town they could not exclude him from social functions at which they offered food to the guests. Ramalingam put their minds at rest by attending all functions, but never even took a glass of water there so that they had not to go against their religious beliefs. Gradually people became used to his ways and accepted him amidst them, on his terms.

Masterji strived to bring drastic changes to the society—one of which was the parasite of the society where people were measured by the gifts they took to a function. He tried to abolish gifting altogether. He announced that invitees to his house should not bring any gifts to the function. People found it a bit strange, but gradually they got accustomed to it.

He told his wife to neither take nor give gifts at social functions. Many people followed his principles when they attended the functions at his place, but at the same time they looked down on Pillamma if she attended their functions without bringing any gifts. Secretly Pillamma took appropriate gifts to the functions she attended. She managed to deal tactfully with both her husband's reforms and the traditions of the society in which she lived. She had learnt to cope with the situation and became balanced between the principles of her husband and the protocols of society. They often did not agree, but she managed well with all disagreements, bearing a smile on her face.

Now Ramalingam was completely immersed in his work. He wanted his six-year-old son to join the youth congress, to which Pillamma protested vehemently. She did not want her only son also to be dragged into the storm of freedom; she refused to pack his bag for the camp. So his father folded his own shirt and packed it in a bag and then took the boy with him to the youth congress. As a protest, Pillamma took her little girls and went to Chatrapur, to her great-uncle's house. The first rift of their life came to surface. It was a battle between her maternal instinct and the keen involvement of a father to make his son his follower. At the camp, some children were imprisoned for a night and the next morning Ramam was released along with fellow youths. The father and son returned to an empty house.

Masterji realised that he had upset his wife. He couldn't carry on his work without his wife's support. Ramalingam went to collect his family, but no words were exchanged between them. Pillamma returned home with her husband and peace was restored in the family. Masterji promised never to go against her wishes again, and bestowed upon her complete freedom to make all decisions regarding their children. No more was said about their tiff. Hence his six year old son became a prisoner for only one night and perhaps made a token gesture in the freedom struggle!

First Republic Day

11
Komalam's Marriage

That day a strong argument broke out between mother and daughter, mother being the grandmother of Komalam, and the daughter being Komalam's paternal aunt, the eldest sister of her father Ramalingam, known as Pedatta to all. As Komalam had reached the marriageable age, rigorous search for a suitable boy began in earnest. Pillamma, her mother, was married at the age of eight, which Komalam had already crossed by five years.

Komalam's grandmother felt that she should marry in the family to a cousin so that she would have a peaceful married life. After all, the family would be kinder to the daughter-in-law than to a complete stranger from another family. Those were the attitudes of Komalam's grandmother, known as Nanamma to all her grandchildren, as Atta to her daughters-in-law, and *Amma*, mother, to her three sons and two daughters.

As the elder of the family and moreover the grandmother of the bride, it was her duty to approach the boy's mother. She broached the topic with her eldest widowed daughter about the marriage alliance of her son Rangam with Komalam, to which she agreed straight away. As the mother of the groom Pedatta took all the decisions of her family, she couldn't see any objection to the proposal. While the young Pillamma had been in her care all those years ago, she had domesticated her into her ways. The widow had taught Pillamma how to be a good wife to her husband, and thus she was certain that Pillamma in turn had taught her daughter Komalam all those good traits that she had acquired from her. The widow was content that Komalam would be a good wife to her son and an excellent daughter-in-law to her. When the old lady was about to leave carrying the good news of this alliance, her daughter, the mother of the groom, broached the topic of dowry and explicitly told her all she wanted for the groom and what more she expected to be given to her as a gift at the wedding. The widow boasted to her mother that her son had received many offers from wealthy parents, willing to give a handsome dowry and all other extras as gifts and also agreed to conduct a lavish wedding to suit her status.

Status was a strange phenomenon; invariably the status of a mother of a groom was raised to the heights of Himalayas in front of a girl's parents. It was as if the girl's parents went to her with a begging bowl and she reserves the right to donate her son or not. The groom's mother invariably had an upper hand in the negotiations of any marriage proposals. Often would be mother-in-law utilised all her rights without any qualms. Her bachelor son was her property and she has the privilege to sell him to the highest bidder in the marriage-market. The groom's mother Pedatta told her mother that she anticipated a rich dowry from Komalam's parents. Her own daughter's demand for dowry had surprised the old lady, as she was aware of her son Ramalingam's principles, big or small as he was against dowry he abhorred such practices. Her own daughter's demand made her very angry. Although she knew that her son Ramalingam was absolutely against giving any dowry and despised its practice, as she was the mediator in this alliance she carried the demands of her daughter to Ramalingam.

He was livid. He refused the alliance blatantly and vowed rather to keep his daughter at home forever than sell her as a commodity, the old lady was in a fix. She couldn't convince her son to accede to the dowry-demands of his own eldest sister nor could she convince her widowed daughter to change her mind. The mother and daughter's arguments continued endlessly for weeks, until eventually the mother gave up on the marriage proposal and cursed her daughter for being so stupid and stubborn, and losing the beautiful and lovely Komalam for her son. But the adamant woman, counting on a big dowry, refused the proposal outright.

Now the old lady renewed her search to find a suitable boy for her granddaughter Komalam. She approached the marriage-broker who brought the proposal of the son of a renowned wealthy advocate, P. Venketsawrlu. He provided the bio data of the groom and his family. The advocate had two sons—both eligible bachelors. It sounded good, but she, who was wise and protective of her granddaughter Komalam, made her own enquiries about the two suitors. The women who gathered at the Temple often exchanged news and views of each other regularly. There was nothing personal or any matter a secret in the town. All businesses were everybody's business—call it care, call it concern, call it interfering or by any other name, but it was the norm of the day in the town. None were exempt from it.

The old lady brought home the news of the two eligible bachelors in dribs and drabs every evening. When Pillamma went there she shared the news with her, and together they rated and evaluated the suitability of those two bachelors.

She gathered that the younger son was good looking and was studying at the prestigious Viswabharati University of Santiniketan in Calcutta. He had no bad habits like smoking and drinking, not even chewing *paan* (Betel nut). Because of his good looks and his fair skin he was fondly called *Errababu* and his brother *Nallababu,* who had rather a shade darker skin. They were named according to their skin shades, like the Sahibs did. Above all, the second son was closer to Komalam's age by twelve years than his brother Nallababu. Accordingly the family opted for Errababu and asked the broker to approach the groom's father.

The groom's family felt honoured to receive the proposal, and gladly agreed to the proposal of their second son and demanded no dowry. When the alliance was progressing well, Mr. P. Venkateswarulu, the eminent and wealthy advocate of the town, raised his objection to the bride's family as she was the daughter of a poor jobless teacher called Ramalingam. The advocate felt that the bride's family was below his status, but the rest of the family wanted Komalam to be their daughter-in-law. The advocate also objected to the genealogy of Ramalingam's father who had had to sell the '*Roundmeda*', the circular house, his residence at the time, to him to pay off his debts. The roundmeda originally belonged to a Nawab in the 19th century. Gradually it came into the possession of Rangampantulu, father of Ramalingam, and after his death it was sold to the advocate P.Venkateswarlu. The circular house had a vast circular veranda with adjacent cells. It was said the Nawab kept his elephants there.

But the rest of the family had fallen in love with Komalam, a beautiful, intelligent girl of immaculate manners and good upbringing. Any bachelor in town would have loved to marry her. Her good looks, her manners, her charm, and her intelligence also impressed Errababu's family too. They did not want to lose that alliance with Komalam, and hence they did not say an outright 'no' to the proposal. The marriage was put on hold with the pretext of waiting until their eldest son, Nallababu, got married. Meanwhile, the second son continued his studies at Viswabharati University at Shantiniketan in Calcutta.

When P. Venkateswarulu, the eminent advocate, died at the age of 75 and once again the marriage proposal of Errabbau was resumed, and this time, against the traditions, it was broached by the groom's family to Masterji. As per tradition, Masterji's family had formally invited the would-be groom to come and meet the girl, to which Errababu refused politely saying that there was no need for it and he would be honoured to marry the daughter of Masterji.

The marriage of Errababu and Komalam took place in 1928. The ten-day marriage ceremony was held with all traditions in vogue at the Holy Shrine of Sukonda. Komalam was officially named as Taratarini Rama Subbamma, with the name of the goddess Taratarini and her great grandmother Rama Subbamma, hence Masterji got the wedding invitations printed with the bride's official name. But people of the town did not know who the bride was. Tired of explaining to each and every person that Komalam's real name was Taratarini Rama Subbamma, Ramalingam reprinted the invitation cards with the bride's name as Komalam. The people recognised the bride and accepted the wedding invitations.

Then, Ramalingam being the chairman of the municipality, there were umpteen volunteers who came forward to make all the wedding arrangements. The petromax lights were placed all the way from Beerkaveedhi to Lakshmi Nrusimha Temple at Sukonda, a distance of a good two to three kilometres. The roads were lit with petromax lights and floral decorations on either side of the street, flourished in their bright colours. The floral *shamiana* of fragrant jasmines spread its perfume all around. The floral arrangements were arranged to the taste of the groom, who was artistic and a naturalist. The sweet girl of Berhampur, everybody's favourite girl—Komalma's marriage became the marriage of the season. All participated and extended their helping hands in preparations. The arrangements were made to fit the status of the late advocate P. Venkateswarulu and the groom's party. The whole town turned up at the wedding. The caravan of bullock-carts, Tongas, and a few cars travelled to the marriage venue. Along the way several resting places were erected where people rested and had their refreshments specially prepared by several cooks.

Komalam the bride was carried in a decorated palanquin to the mandapam, the marriage venue. It was hard to say whether it was due to the popularity of the bride, Komalam, or her father that made the occasion so successful.

The wedding was enhanced by the attendance of the lady doctor, Dr Margaret Bhore (née Margaret Stott) who had delivered Komalam at her hospital in 1913. The doctor being Komalam's idol, the bride was thrilled to see her at her wedding.

Ramalingam gave his young son-in-law the Holy Books, Ramayanam, in Sanskrit and Bhagvat Geeta as a gift at the wedding, which the groom cherished heartily.

The ceremony continued for ten days in a very traditional way to the delight of all the people. Eminent musicians entertained the guests. The bride wore a white *Khadi* sari for the main ceremony, and then for the other ceremonies that followed, as per tradition she wore the silks her in-laws gave her. Whether in silks or *Khadi* the bride looked stunning in their attire. It was said that she had enhanced the quality of the wedding saris by her own beauty.

After the initial wedding ceremony, the fun and frolics began at home where women took the main role and men retired to the *shamiana* in front of the house and the groom remained in the custody of the women for the following ceremony. They teased the bride and the groom, sang traditional wedding songs, and entertained the newly-wed pair to their delight. The groom sat there helplessly while the bride endured the women's frolics with a smile. Her calmness surprised the groom. So far, he had not yet spoken to her, but both of them performed the rites and traditions as expected of them.

The crowd of women amused themselves by playing tricks on the newlyweds. They made them play with a floral ball and the gallant groom let his bride win every time, to the annoyance of his sisters. Then, finally the newlyweds had to pick the diamond ring from a pot full of milk three times. Both of them immersed their hands and searched for the ring. It was said that whoever found the ring and won would have the upper hand in their marriage. Once again the groom willingly lost the contest, to the delight of the bride's party and to the annoyance of groom's family.

All the fun and games were over amicably. Now the last, the final ceremony remained to be carried out. It was an important ceremony, which more often distressed the bride's father than pleased him, a ceremony Masterji despised, in which the groom often blackmailed the bride's father by making unreasonable demands which became a burden to the bride's father. The demands varied from gold, cash, or property to any other expensive items. The already burdened father had to oblige and give the demanded gift to the groom. On failure, sometimes the marriage was dissolved on the spot. Often the bride's family dreaded that *Alakapanupu* ceremony.

As per tradition, the groom's sisters urged Errababu to demand for a rich gift before he could attend the ultimate family reception feast. As per tradition, the groom sits on a bed known as *Alakapanupu*, literally meaning, 'I'm on strike.' 'Until you give me what I demand I'm not going to come to the feast and shall amicably conclude the wedding ceremony.'

Masterji despised such traditions that taxed the bride's family and many a time he had intervened and saved the marriage of many young brides in the town. In Masterji's presence at any wedding the groom's party restrained themselves from making unreasonable demands. They respected Masterji and at the same time feared him, knowing that he was absolutely against such taxing social customs. Now the women waited to see how Masterji would solve the demands of his own son-in-law. They were certain that as the father of the bride he would succumb to the demands of the groom. After all, no father wants to see his daughter's marriage dissolved on the spot. The women were determined to make demands to suit the status of the late father-in-law of the bride who loved riches and pomp. They tried to brainwash the groom, asking him to make a demand to suit his late father's status. Some women waited to see the groom bring Masterji to his knees by his demand. They waited gleefully to see the 'fun' begin.

The groom, Errababu, didn't want to make any demands but being the youngest of his siblings, he had to obey his sisters and sat nervously on the bed and waited for the bride's party to approach him. He was aware that Masterji disapproved of such traditions which taxed the bride's family continuously on the pretext of customs and traditions.

The news of his *Alakapanupu* reached Masterji, but he was not perturbed. He walked into the room where Errababu sat on the floral decorated bed and waited nervously. As soon as he saw Masterji approaching him, Errababu jumped off the bed and stood in front of him like a naughty school boy. Slowly Masterji went up to him and handed over a large box and asked him to open it. At once the groom obeyed him and ripped it open as fast as he could and there he found a brand new *Charka* to the delight of many and to the disappointment of the groom's sisters and some other women. The groom thanked Masterji for the gift and the *Alakapanupu* ceremony was concluded affably. There were no more demands from the groom's side. They all feasted on the lavish food served for them and completed the marriage ceremony.

The time had come to bid farewell to Komalam. Amidst tears and happiness the new bride went to her in-laws in a brand new Rolls-Royce. She carried with her the fine crocheted door and window curtains, the embroidered bed-sheets, table covers, and handkerchiefs she had made as her trousseau. Her husband Errababu who himself was an artist admired her skill and appreciated the gifts she brought for him.

On their very first night, Errababu told her how he had longed to marry her from the day he had seen her at a function when she was ten. He adored Komalam with all his love, and their marriage stood the challenges and tides of time and they faced the ups and downs together. There never was any misunderstanding between the two. He loved her deeply and she cherished his love. For him she was his life. There was no equal to her.

Errababu was wealthy and in his house Komalam was treated like a queen. She had umpteen servants to attend to her and all the comforts one can ask for were there ready for her. To go along with her husband's life-style, Komalam discarded her *Khadi* clothes and wore fine silks and a lot of jewellery. She looked as pretty as ever in her new rich attire as she did in her plain *Khadi* clothes. Her natural beauty pleased her husband, and he adored her with all his mind and soul. Theirs was a match made in heaven. For Errababu, Komalam was his wife, his lover, and his sweetheart; he relished the warmth of her love.

When he was four years old he had lost his mother and in no time at all his father had married again, to a girl who was very young. His father was a prudent man. He provided his two sons from his first wife with good properties and lands and settled them well financially, but then sent them away from home and washed his hands of them. Errababu had everything, except maternal love. His older sisters had their own families to take care of. The two brothers became close. As Errababu showed interest in education, he was sent to study at Santiniketan in Calcutta to study under the guidance of Rabindranath Tagore. With his natural flair for arts and fine things Errababu flourished at Calcutta. He adored the beauty of his wife and treated her like a precious gem. They had a beautiful relationship like true lovers and their love strengthened with time. Their first son, Raghuveer, was born when Komalam was just sixteen.

Errababu's brother was more interested in the stock market and investments. He had a comfortable life with his wife and children. Errababu had given the power of attorney to his older brother Nallababu, who managed their joint business empire.

Raghuveer, fondly called *Veeradhi*, the firstborn, was everybody's darling, mostly to his maternal grandparents. Every day he was sent to spend some time with them, accompanied by a servant in a chauffeur-driven car. The infant became more attached to his grandfather, who hardly had any time for the grandson. The boy had a luxurious life as a child.

Errababu was an artist in mind and body; he was a great singer and was well known for his folk songs, called *Enkipaatalu*. After his first son was born, he and his older brother Nallababu started an automobile-trading concern, called Ganjam Automobiles at Berhampur. Everybody said that the firstborn son had brought him good luck. Errababu was its General Manager with his 50% hold, but his elder brother managed the company as per his wishes. Thus Komalam's married life ran smoothly without any hitches.

Her little sister Subbulu now was the baby of the family. She was pampered by her mother and her brother. She was not close to her father who was always away on his mission. By four years of age she also went to Chalmayyagaru with her brother. She showed excellence in studies to the delight of her mother.

Taratarini Temple

99

12
The Railway Strike: 1928–1929

1928 It was historically a significant year in India. Once the celebrations of Komalam's wedding were over, Pandit Ramalingam had unrest at hand. As the President of the Bengal Nagpur Railway Union, he had a delicate situation to handle.

Employees of various railway systems in India (the North-Western Railway, Bengal Nagpur Railway, and The East Indian Railway) decided to strike, demanding better working conditions and better treatment by the management.

The major concerns for their agitation were that the management should respect their choice of leaders, to refrain from the use of direct or indirect intimidation, and that working conditions should be altered. Underlying all the unrest was the rejection of colonial, capitalist, and racial domination. The workers had to contend with the often invisible forms of manipulation and connivance between leaders, officials, and management of the railways.

The workers wanted the rights of workers: to be considered as partners in the production process and not mere servants of the management. These issues were of paramount importance during the 1928 strike. It showed the capacity of workers to organise themselves and pledge solidarity with each end of the class spectrum, from sweepers to white-collar workers. Strikers' meetings protested against wage differentials and the abusive conduct of some European staff, who ridiculed the workers as being incapable of working for more than two hours in the heat.

In 1926 Ramalingam became the elected President of the Bengal Nagpur Railway Labour Union. In 1927, railway companies all over India took a unanimous decision to reduce their railway workforce in order to cut costs. In response to this decision, strikes were called by the workers of the Bengal Nagpur Railway at Khargpur in February 1927.

During that period, there was general discontent among the workers of the Indian Railway's company over the long working hours, low wages, and racial discrimination against native Indians in the railway. At about the same time, the management of the Southern Railway Company decided to lay off over 3,000 workers to compensate for the purchase of costly machinery in the workshops. Supporters of the strike had, however, claimed that the cost-cutting was mainly an excuse and that the real reason for the layoffs was to get rid of extremist elements in the Railway Union. Already there was severe unrest for several reasons, which spread all over the country:

1. Railway carriages, restrooms were marked 'For Europeans only'. This segregation annoyed many Indians.

2. Secondly, there was grievance about the two-tier wages. Anglo-Indian Ticket Collectors received 32 Rupees per month, while an English ex-soldier, as

a guard got 125 Rupees. Such plum jobs of railway guard were allotted to Europeans only.

3. The Anglo-Indians had a rough deal; although they could speak fluent English, plum jobs did not come their way. The Europeans nicknamed them as 'che-che' (Perhaps from the Hindi word which literally means dirt; or perhaps imitative of their supposed singsong speech) while their own countrymen named the Anglo-Indians as 'Kutcha-Butcha'. Kutcha-Butcha is a Hindi phrase that means 'half-baked bread', and is used to refer to biracial people of (East) Indian and (white) British.

At both ends, the Anglo-Indians were the losers and were deprived of promotions and good jobs.

4. The Indian Railway took steps to retrench workers and decided on a formulated test to help retrenchment. The labourer's leader strongly objected to this kind of testing as the work force was not literate in English and some not even in their own language.

The Union members demanded that such testing should be abolished. The bosses decided to teach the menials a lesson. It sent all the workers out of the workshop and affected a closure. News of this event spread all over India, particularly in South India where it had severe effect.

Strikes took place from 14 July 1928 and continued for ten days. It was a historic strike that shook the whole of India. All the railway employees of both the highest and lowest cadre joined the strike. The management was forced to cancel all the trains.

They arrested innumerable workers. The labour union offices were raided. At first the bosses played their own strategies. They wanted to break the unity of the strikers. It was said that they shunted the same train to and fro to dupe the strikers.

Ramalingam led the strike at Berhampur. He had his own strategies, employing his own method to uncover the truth of the shunted trains. He asked the young volunteers to go to the railway station and note down the engine number that went to and fro, which they did with immense enthusiasm. There was no shortage of young volunteers to visit the railway station, as it was the youths' favourite pastime. The male youths spent a lot of time on the platform observing the trains go to and fro. Most trains stopped at Berhampur for half an hour or so, as it was a junction for many commuter trains going from north to south regions and other lines.

Often well-clad young men stood on the platform eyeing pretty girls travelling in the trains. Other times they stood by the Higginbotham's book stall, flicking through the pages of the magazines but their eyes firmly set on the female passengers on the train. Higginbotham's book stalls were to be found at many railway stations. C. H. Higginbotham was an English Librarian who came to India and established bookstalls at railway stations from 1904.

The young volunteers handed their report to Masterji, which showed the same train was shunted up and down on the tracks. Soon the news of the tricks of the railway bosses came to the public's attention; it was published in the local papers. The games of the bosses were exposed in total to the strikers. As a result the strike was intensified with more vigour. Now the bosses stooped very low, they approached Ramalingam with a bribe of one *Lakh*, one hundred thousand rupees, to stop the strike. But they failed to corrupt this decent citizen and the leader of the town, who had surrendered his everything to the causes he believed in and set an implicit example to his followers. Disappointed they engaged the help of some Anglo-Indians to break the strike, but even that attempt also utterly failed.

Eventually both parties negotiated and compromised and the workshop began to work. The salaries were amended, although not completely on equal terms.

In a strange way the unrest of the railway employees had sufficient effect in other fields. People began to think that it was alright to speak their mind, and gradually the fear of the sahibs began to ebb away. Until then the Indians had been accustomed to obeying Maharajas and Rajas, of which some were praiseworthy and few rotten rulers existed, and people often obeyed them unconditionally. Few people revolted against the tyrants, but the consequences they paid were their lives. In general, people became accommodative to their conditions and accepted the ruler's ruling as final.

But now, Gandhiji had woken up the sleepy citizens from their moronic mind set, their submissive and compliance state. Gandhiji roused a feeling of self-respect and sacrifice for the rights they deserved so much. The word 'rights' became a buzz word for the general public. The leaders, commoners, and Gandhiji's followers woke up from the trance of slavery and began to think about and question their status in their own country under a foreign rule. This awakening began to grow in strength day by day. At work, in the fields, and in the streets, wherever some people gathered and interacted with each other, the discussion of 'foreign rule' became a hot topic. Yet some of them were cautious about expressing their views openly. They were afraid of any consequences from the sahibs. Fear was the weapon of the rulers and they used it discretely.

Some old loyal servants of the sahibs remained loyal to their masters, but the idea against a foreign rule had demonstrated its effect on the youth of both the literate and illiterate equally. Thinking was not anyone's personal property; all living beings tend to think in their own way. While the illiterate thought of their rights in simple terms the literate exploded their views in bombastic language. The affect was the same on all the public. In every corner of the country a new revolution had sprouted and they carried on discussing it openly. Added to that, Gandhiji's speeches began to make some sense for them. The situation was quite magical, as if some sleeping lions were woken up with a jolt.

The words of the great man continued to be heard in every town.

"It was our love of foreign cloth that ousted the wheel from its position of dignity. Therefore I considered it a sin to wear foreign clothes."

Gandhiji repeated his statements again and again until it reached every Indian's ears.

"Thus the economics that permit one country to prey upon another are immoral," Gandhiji added to his statement.

People in general were like children cottoning on to any new fad quickly and dropping it with the same speed. Thus Gandhiji and his supporters often reminded people of their duty. Ramalingam orated, emotionally touching the hub of people's souls. Once again Ramalingam and his colleagues revived the spinning wheel in the town. Some people took up spinning for fun and some took it as a cause. Pillamma and Komalam began to spin regularly as before. Komalam continued to spin even at her husband's home. The spun yarn was taken to *Khadi Bhandar*, the shop where it was exchanged to cloth of equal weight with an extra nominal fee.

At the end of the year, Pillamma had a personal tragedy in her life. Her mother died.

Her only brother, Lingam Pantulu, was employed by the British Navy and worked as a clerk and interpreter, living at Chatrapur. He was a scholar and could speak and write in several European languages besides many Indian languages. It was said that he had brains similar to his late scholarly second maternal uncle, Lingam Lakshmaji Pantulu, who wrote several books in French and German, some of which are still available.

After their mother's bereavement, Lingam Pantulu shifted to Berhampur, and took residence in Pillamma's house, which she inherited as Streedhanam from her mother. She also inherited all her gold and jewellery, which included her mother's *eduvarala nagalu* (edu meaning 'seven'– the seven-day-jewellery), which was unique. It is a belief that mainly seven planets rule the seven days of a week. Women of wealthy families wore specific jewellery made of a special gem for each day of the week. The planets to represent each day were:

Sunday – The ruler is Sun; its gem is Ruby.

Monday – The ruler is Moon; its gem is Pearl.

Tuesday – The ruler is Mars; its gem is Coral.

Wednesday – The ruler is Mercury; its gem is Emerald.

Thursday – The ruler is Jupiter; its gem is Yellow Sapphire.

Friday – The ruler is Venus; its gem is Diamond.

Saturday – The ruler is Saturn; its gem is Blue Sapphire.

Women had their jewellery sets made of those precious stones. Each set often had a necklace, earrings, nose rings, finger and toe rings, bangles, waist-belt, plait ornaments, head ornaments, and anklets.

The *Streedhanam* was security for a girl in her life. It was her insurance to fall back on in times of need and was only inherited by the female offspring and was protected by law. As Pillamma was the only daughter, she inherited all her mother's gold and a small house at Berhampur.

Now, Pillamma had her only brother nearby to console her and share their loss. Her brother, fondly known as Lingammamma to all, was fourteen years older than Pillamma. It was said he was married when he was young but soon the marriage was dissolved and he remained a bachelor. He spent his life surrounded by books.

Lingammama had an interesting lifestyle. A very old woman called 'Buddi' was his housekeeper. She lived in the anteroom attached to the kitchen with her little orphaned granddaughter. The kitchen was also unique. It had only two earthen pots, one to boil milk and one for her to cook food for her and her granddaughter. In the back yard there was a small cowshed for two cows.

Buddi looked after the cowshed and milked the cows. The cowherd took them out daily to the nearby forest to graze and brought them back in the evening. Buddi took care of the young boy's food too.

Lingammama never ate any solids. Twice a day he drank milk freshly milked by Buddi. He spent the rest of the time in his library. His front room had one wooden easy-chair without any cushions, where he sat and read, and the surrounding walls had bookshelves reaching the ceiling full of many bound books.

Upstairs in his bed room there was one wooden bed and a pillow and one blanket. In the wardrobe he had a pair of white *lungis* (like sarongs) to wrap around his waist and two white shirts. The open yard that connected the front room and the kitchen had a shower unit, which the residents used.

In appearance Lingammama looked like Rabindranath Tagore, the poet and the first Non-European to win a noble prize for Literature, with his long white beard, long curly hair, tall and slim body. Lingammama had a charisma that made everybody bow in front of him. His hobbies were walking and writing.

In spite of Ramalingam's active involvement in the freedom movement, some of his sahib friends still kept their friendship with him, and their friendship withstood the storm of time and tide. Some such good friends were the Bhore couple, Dr Margaret Stott and Joseph William Bhore – later he was knighted – and the two families interacted socially.

Pillamma supported her husband's 'work' wholeheartedly but she remained in his shadow and never tried to eclipse him. She loved him and she trusted him and valued his decisions. She never forgot how he respected her first as a friend, and then as a lover before they lived together, a privilege that very few women of her time had. Even now he always put her in the picture of his activities. He never held any secrets and their trust with each other grew with time. He never imposed his views upon her. He gave her the freedom to make her own choices and often he asked for her opinion on political matters.

She recalled how he weaned her from being the typical obedient Indian wife. When they began to live together, she sought his permission to attend a women's function to which he promptly replied with a big 'no' and refused flatly. He never allowed her to discuss or debate the matter, which left her in sheer frustration. The regular lame excuses she gave the women for not attending social functions earned her the titles of 'snob' and 'unsociable'. She heard their criticism and wept inwardly about her situation. She couldn't go against her husband's wishes and at the same time she became tired of inventing excuses for her absence at the functions.

On one occasion she picked up her courage and attended a function without telling her husband and without taking his permission. She returned home trembling to the bone, because as yet they had never had any major disputes as such. She was certain that the consequences of her so-called 'bravery' would certainly have adverse effects on her family life. At the same time her inner free soul revolted. All the way home she rehearsed how to react to his anger and how to support her action.

When she saw him waiting for her on the doorstep, all her courage drained away like quicksilver, and meekly she climbed the steps with her head hung low, he stepped aside and let her enter the house. She stood in front of him like a naughty child. For few moments complete silence ruled the place. Tears began to fill her eyes, and she had no intention of shedding tears in front of him as that would be a sure sign of her defeat, her weakness. She had taken the bold step to fight for her rights and now she was not prepared to give in. She held her tears back and waited. Those few moments were the longest wait she ever had to endure, but then suddenly her husband burst out laughing.

She just stared at him, since that wasn't the reaction she anticipated. Again he laughed and took her in his arms, which led the flood gates burst open. She wept uncontrollably. When she finally calmed down he told her not to behave like an ordinary woman asking his permission for her every movement. He asked her not to be so fragile like a woman who could not make her own decisions. He reminded her that she was not his slave but his life partner, and they trusted each other. He assured her that she was his equal and not his subordinate needing his approval for every step she took. Once again, he ascertained her position in his life as his friend, lover, and an equal to him, if not greater, and he told her that he had complete faith in her and in her choices. She always cherished his love for her and relied on it in hard times, while it worked like a rewarding elixir to her.

Now, after the general strike of the Railways, in which Masterji took the lead role, the women's group became more active. Once again they approached Pillamma to be their leader. She thought about it with an open mind. She had to make choices, knowing that whatever she decided would also affect the life of her children. They were very young, and besides being a mother she had to be also their father, due to his frequent absence in their lives. She weighed the pros and cons of the situation, and decided that her first responsibility was towards her children.

She recalled her childhood as a fatherless girl with a helpless widowed mother; she had been sheltered in her maternal uncle's home. Her uncle was more than a father to her but her aunt kept her at a distance and her mother remained obedient to her sister-in-law. Her past flashed in front of her eyes. She feared for the welfare of her three children. The motherly instinct within her dominated her desire to follow the women's group. She refused to join the women's league, saying that her first duty was towards her children in their father's absence.

The reputation of a person is like a piece of string that can be stretched or shred into pieces. They pleaded with her to change her mind and her polite refusal angered them. They called her a coward and a selfish woman, and some went to the extent of saying that she had no guts, unlike her husband who sacrificed his life for the cause. She was labelled a selfish narrow-minded woman who thought only about her own children when the whole country could be her children. Some said she was not a worthy wife to their Masterji. There was no stopping them – they chose choicest words to insult her and put her down. She stood there in silence and let them spume their steam of anger at her. Disappointed and angered, they finally left her alone and went away. But her best friend, Mangamma, stood by her and supported her choice, as the three children were her priority and her responsibility.

Until now Ramam hid in his shell, but thanks to his little sister he began to talk, although lacking confidence. The young boy needed her more than her country did. Her husband often used to say that only a mother could make or mar a child's life, and she had no intention of ruining her son's future.

She never disagreed with her husband and she maintained a simple lifestyle as her husband preferred. Masterji made proclamations for the family and she followed them meticulously. But when her children were involved she was protective towards them. They didn't have the luxuries that their father had enjoyed, but she compensated for that with her love and discipline. She never had to shout at them, because they behaved well and if they were naughty she could control them with her 'look' alone. They were well brought up in her care.

13

1930 Salt March

By 1930 the people of India were growing restless under the yoke of British rule. On 12 March 1939, Gandhi wrote to Viceroy Lord Irwin complaining about the salt tax:

Dear Friend,

God willing, it is my intention to set out for Dharasana and reach there with my companions and demand possession of the Salt Works. The public have been told that Dharasana is a private property. This is mere camouflage. It is as effectively under government control as the Viceroy's house. Not a pinch of salt can be removed without the previous sanction of the authorities.

It is possible for you to prevent this raid, by removing the Salt Tax.

I had hoped that the Government would fight the civil resisters in a civilized manner but the lord ignored and laughed at Gandhi's salt movement. Instead he said, "At present the prospect of a salt campaign does not keep me awake at night."

Violation of the Salt Act was a criminal offense. Even though salt was freely available to those living on the coast (by evaporation of sea water) Indians were forced to purchase it from the colonial government.

Gandhi declared a Salt March as a protest against the salt tax. Gandhiji declared:

'At present Indian self-respect is symbolised, as it were, in a handful of salt in any Satyagrahi's hand. Let the fist be broken, but let there be no surrender of the salt.'

Gandhiji led the Dandi march from his base, Sabarmati Ashram near Ahmedabad, to the sea coast near the village of Dandi. As he continued on this 24 day, 240 mile (390 km) march to produce salt without paying the tax, growing numbers of Indians followed him. The Dandi March was a remarkable event in the history of the Indian freedom movement as it was an undetermined protest by Gandhiji and his followers to end the British domination forever. A reporter observed that "As people followed the fortunes of this marching column of pilgrims from day to day, the temperature of the country went up."

The march was to signal a non-violent uprising against all governmental power to achieve full publicity and educate the masses against the British Raj injustices, as a means to trigger off a broader movement against the British power.

The Salt March started on 12 March 1930 and reached the village Dandi on April 5 1930. Mahatma Gandhi made a clarion call for action, and set forth from

Sabarmati Ashram on 12 March to Dandi, with the slogan: "Our cause is just, and our means are strong, and God is with us."

Ramalingam along with his colleagues began touring their district's entire sea coast to find a spot where salt could be securely prepared. The leaders and volunteers met at Berhampur and held discussions at Varadaji Samajam Hall (now known as Andhra Bhasbhivardini Samajam) to locate likely venues for salt preparation and they discussed methods to intensify the movement.

Both the Ganjam Utkal and Andhra Congress committees met and elected Ramalingam, then Municipal Chairman of Berhampur, as director to lead the Salt Satyagraha movement in the Ganjam district. Konda Venkatappayya from Andhra arrived at Berhampur, as the first point of his itinerary, to supervise how Salt Satyagraha was progressing along the entire east coast. Naupada was finally chosen as the venue for the preparation of salt. On 6 April two batches proceeded towards the sea simultaneously, one led by Masterji Ramalingam from Berhampur and another under the leadership of N. Naryana Murthy from Srikakulam.

Once the salt laws were broken, every day it became a usual feature for people to make salt by boiling water in Naupada at the sea coast or by bringing the salt water home and making salt. Even children at schools began to make salt with the sea water from Gopalpur. Salt-making became a national 'hobby'.

On 13 April, the last day of the National Week of Protest against salt tax, the violation of salt laws rose to a high pitch. A band of nearly 1,000 volunteers under the leadership of Masterji Ramalingam set out on foot towards Naupada. Early in the morning they marched from the house of Emmidesetty Sriramamurthy, and then reached the Narasimha Temple to perform Puja to show reverence to God and then they all arrived at Bezzipuram toll gate. From there they next proceeded to Gollaturu village, as if they were on some sacred mission. The distance from Berhampur to Naupada was about 75 miles. All the marchers wore white *Khadi* and it was named as 'White flowing river'. On the way more volunteers joined the procession and showed their solidarity with the satyagarahis and they received resignations from village officials who chose to end cooperation with British rule. As they entered each village, crowds greeted the marchers beating drums and singing traditional folk songs as if they were guests at a wedding. Each night all the marchers slept in the open. The villagers provided them with food and water, which the marchers accepted with gratitude.

Every day, more and more people joined the march. To keep up their spirits, the marchers sang the famous ballad, 'Ragupati Raghava Rajaram', Gandhiji's favourite prayer song, and many national songs while walking to the sea. Along the march people from the villages joined them and the march gathered momentum as it advanced towards the sea. Cast, creed, and sex were forgotten. Hundreds of women also took part in it and they joined their hands together and followed the Salt March.

Along the way one villager seeing the marcher's missionary work was so moved that he took clumps of earth from under the feet of Ramalingam and put them on his head. Later, when he auctioned the soil, it fetched him 5 Rupees. The Andhra Patrika Daily reported on 15 April 1930 how soil under the feet of the leader Ramalingam was put to sale.

This event reflected how emotionally even in a backward area people reacted to the movement. The people came completely under the spell of Salt Satyagraha. When the procession reached Ichapuram, women enthusiastically received them with *aarati,* a religious ritual in which persons are greeted with oil-lamps and flowers. Inspired by their reception the marchers went on to the sea cost and broke the salt laws successfully. They collected salt in any container they could find and on the beach itself made the salt. The salient feature in this respect was what Gandhi wished for. He wanted the masses to be sufficiently enlightened by wide propaganda which was amply fulfilled. As a result, the Ganjam District rose to great heights with some adroitness.

In return Gandhiji also reciprocally used to show his trepid affection for the notable leaders on every convenient occasion; few times he visited Ramalingam at his house and accepted his hospitality, and discussed political matters with him.

Ramalingam, the eminent Ganjam leader, held a lot of respect from both Oriya- and Telugu-speaking people of the district and integrated them into one entity, showing that they were a power to be reckoned with. Satyagraha of the 1930s also forced the British to recognize that their control of India depended entirely on the consent of the Indians.

On 19 April 1930, Ramalingam was arrested by Mr Austin, the governor of the area, and was sent to Vellore Jail for two years. The prominent freedom fighters of Madras Presidency, N. C. Ranga, V. V. Giri, and Tenneti Viswanathan were his jail mates. The captives never wasted their time in the jail; they exchanged their language skills, and Ramalingam learnt Urdu and Tamil from his fellows. He and his prison mates taught the other prisoners to read and write. He believed that education was the only weapon a poor man could carry with him. There, in the jail, he earned a new identity for himself. They began to address him as '*Panditji*', his title of Masterji was dropped, and he began to fit into his new title Pandit Ramalingam with ease.

For Pillamma, the two years were a long time in which to maintain the family all by herself. Due to the long distance of about 600 miles from Berhampur to Vellore Pillamma's prison visits were sparse. She felt lonely, and thus asked Errababu and Komalam to come and live with her for a while, which they obliged without any problem. The toddler grandson Veeradhi cheered up the family. For the first time in his life, Errababu experienced a mother's affection with Pillamma , he regarded her as his mother and found her to be his mother substitute. Errababu being sensitive and an emotionally deprived person longed for some maternal affection. Pillamma became his mother, and he began to call her 'Amma'. She looked after him as if he were her son. Errababu was not a big eater and he ate like a bird, but she made the dishes he liked and served them tenderly. They had a good rapport, and for a few months Errababu and his family lived at Birakaveedhi and enjoyed the hospitality of Pillamma. Her friends were glad that she had some moral support from her daughter and son-in-law while her husband was at Vellore Jail.

One afternoon Errababu suddenly changed his mind at midday, just before lunch, he collected his wife and son and moved out of Amma's house while some curious and a few aghast neighbours watched the scenario with glee.

Those who envied Pillamma for having such a good son-in-law rejoiced at his exodus with her daughter and child. But her well-wishers felt sorry for Pillamma. Her son-in-law's sudden departure gave scope for people to gossip about her without any inhibitions to her face.

"She must have upset her son-in-law, otherwise why would he leave the house at midday?"

"He may be a good man but we all know the status of a son-in-law: he is no less than a God but she treated him like a son. Whoever heard of a son-in-law ever become a son?" jeered another woman.

"Don't you know, our Panditji is a reformer? He gave Errababu a *charka* at an *Alakapanupu* ritual. Do you think the son-in-law forgot that insult?"

"He may appear to be calm and sedate but he is a man. He is no ordinary man – he is a son-in-law. He should have been treated with the upmost respect."

"Pillamma always treats everyone with respect and she considered him to be her son. She really treats him like a son."

"That is the problem, sister ... She is an intelligent woman, isn't she? There is no need to mention any names, but some of us go to her for advice, don't they? Then this wise woman, Pillamma, should know that a son-in-law can never be equal to a son. She certainly got her equation wrong. Every son-in-law knows his position in a family. No fool would let his status go down the drain and take the role of a son."

"Respect, woman, respect! That's what the son-in-law lacked in that house. Pillamma must have treated him with disrespect."

"I don't agree. There must be another reason for his sudden departure. After all, he is a businessman. Perhaps he had to attend to it."

The women argued among themselves about the virtues of Pillamma and her faults with the same vigour in front of her as if she was not there. Varied individuals and varied opinions floated around and there was no stopping them. In the town, anybody's business was everybody's business and that was the unwritten law of those days!

"Just wait and see. I'll find out who instigated Errababu to this hideous behaviour. He should have stayed with Pillamma in her time of need – poor woman – trying hard to cope with the situation. It's not easy to manage your home without a man around. Ramam is still a child. It's Errababu's duty to support Pillamma," said a staunch supporter of Pillamma, vowing to get to the bottom of the incident.

After a couple of days Pillamma stopped feeling sorry for herself, and concentrated on an important issue with which she was deeply concerned. She was glad Komalam was happy with Errababu. On that score she had no worries. Her concern was for her son. After debating about the pros and cons of her thoughts she had come to a definite conclusion. Now she had decided to make her son's future safe. He was nine and yet had no formal education. She remembered how Komalam was removed from the Government School when she was nearly nine.

Knowing very well that her husband was against the Government Schools, she decided to go with her heart. She approached Balaram, her youngest brother-in-law who was a teacher at the Town School, and requested him to admit

Ramam in the school. Balaram was afraid to go against his brother's wishes. He worked there to earn for his family, and fortunately Ramalingam did not impose his views and principles on his brothers. When he moved out of the family home with his wife and children, he vowed never to interfere in his brothers' lifestyles. All the same, those two brothers always respected their elder brother and were ready to give their lives for him. There was a strong bondage between the three brothers.

Pillamma understood her youngest brother-in-law Balaram's predicament. She requested Chalmayyagaru, her children's home tutor, to admit her nine year old son Ramam at the Town School. As a woman she couldn't go to school directly; that would be seen as an insult to her husband. There were some unwritten protocols for a wife in society and she obeyed them at all times. Maintaining the honour of her husband always remained her priority under any circumstances.

She wrote a letter to the Headmaster of the Town School and sent it through Chalmayyagaru. The Headmaster, Rayaprolu Subbaraogaru, took the boy in. In the admission register he enrolled his name as W. Gandhi Rama Rao and Chalmayyagaru signed the admission form as his guardian in absentia, since Pillamma, being a woman, could not sign it on her husband's behalf. The Headmaster added the name of Gandhi to the boy's name with tact so that it might appeal to Pandit Ramalingam, the ardent follower of Gandhiji and thus W. Rama Rao became W. Gandhi Rama Rao.

Balaram watched the admission procedure in tears. He was torn between his love for his nephew and respect for the wishes of his older brother, Pandit Ramalingam.

At school they put the young boy in Class Four, according to his age. Ramam began to bloom at school to the delight of his mother. She sent Subbullu to the Municipality Elementary school near Barracks ground. She secured their education in her own way. Now regularly she pawned her gold to support the family and every time she thanked her late uncle and her late mother who had given her the gold and a house as *Streedhanam.*

Pillamma had become an ace to camouflage her own troubles and endure the separation from her husband and had to stand like a guardian angel to her own children, securing their future with some good education. Her husband wrote to her when he could, but those letters were censored and hence they couldn't be of much comfort to her. She recalled the lengthy letters she used to write to her husband when he was at the college in Madras, and his interesting and inspiring replies. Now she relied upon her pleasant memories for her moral strength.

For a few weeks Pillamma fretted about the sudden departure of Errababu. On the grapevine some neighbours found out the real reason for his sudden departure. Errababu's eldest sister who lived in the same town objected to her 'little' brother going to live in his in-law's home. She told him that it would be below their prestige and their alt father would not have accepted it and warned Errababu that he would lose all his respect in society. She, as his eldest sister had tremendous influence on Errababu. Although there wasn't much interaction between them, she managed to keep an eye on her brother and his wife. She made it her affair to interfere in their life and control them from a distance. In spite of her living in the same town, when young Errababu was raised by the servant his sister kept her distance on the pretext that she had her own family to look after. Errababu loved and respected his sister, and found it hard to disobey her as a younger brother. In those days, they respected their elders and he was no exception to it.

Pillamma decided to resolve the problem in her own way. At first she made a social call to a family in the same street where Errababu lived, and returned home in a Tonga. Errababu noticed Amma's visit to the neighbour and told his wife that her mother had been in the street but had not called upon them.

Their common family friend informed Pillamma that Errababu wanted her to visit them. After a fortnight she went to Errababu's house. He did not know how to receive her. He regretted having left her house so rudely and leaving her alone when she needed their help most. For few minutes the atmosphere was strained. Then Pillamma picked up Veeradhi and cuddled him and asked him to come with his parents on *Sankranti,* a festival day for a meal. Errababu told his son to tell his grandmother that they would all come on *Sankranti* day. Briefly little Veeradhi became the mediator for his father and grandmother. They continued to make conversation indirectly through the little boy. Komalam found the whole charade so funny she burst out laughing, and Errababu joined her. Their laughter had lifted the mist that hung over the two families. Pillamma returned home in Errababu's car driven by a chauffeur while the astonished neighbours watched her with open mouths. As before, daily Veeradhi visited his grandmother and spent a lot of time with her. And every evening Komalam and Errababu went to collect their son and had a meal with their Amma.

The two years dragged on for Pillamma. The two years of separation from her husband were like aeons to her. Undeterred, Pillamma managed the family, and continued to educate her two children. Education always remained her priority.

After his release from jail, Ramalingam, now known as Pandit Ramalingam, returned home. He was received by the citizens as a hero. For days he was occupied with Congress matters, meeting people, and discussing further plans for *Purna Swaraj*. He had no time for his wife or children. Pillamma was kept busy providing food and refreshments to umpteen Congress Workers who visited Panditji.

Every night she worried about Ramam's education. She feared that her husband might not take her decision to put the boy at school with an open mind. Her husband was a man of principles and he never compromised under any circumstances.

After two weeks, when the ebb of 'followers' had eased a bit, Ramalingam asked his wife where the children were. She mumbled that they were at school and slowly informed that Ramam was attending the Town School. He said not a word to her as she expected. He did not flare in his anger nor did he chastise her in any way. He went straight to school, which was close by, and showed his disapproval in no uncertain terms for his son being admitted to the school. The Headmaster hung his head low and made no reply, and stood in front of Pandit Ramalingam like a naughty school boy. Ramalingam demanded to know who had given him permission to admit his son to school. The Headmaster politely informed him that Mrs Pillamma had requested him to admit him.

Ramalingam was speechless to know that Pillamma had gone against his views. He composed himself, stood still, and pondered about the situation. He remembered that he had given his wife full freedom to make any decisions of the family. He had given her unwritten power of attorney when he was first sent to Jail.

The Headmaster stood nervously and wondered if Pandit Ramalingam might remove his son from school as he had with Komalam some years before. To his surprise Pandit Ramalingam, who respected his wife's wishes, returned home silently. He was a just man and man of principles. Once he had given his word he never retreated from it. He returned home and no more was said about the matter, and Ramam continued his education at the Town School without any hitches.

Town School, 2010

Ramam, 1929

14
Equal Status for Women

In 1931, Motilal Nehru passed a "Resolution of Remembrance" to honour the women of India. The Government was wary of any resolutions by the political leaders, so as a precautionary measure it banned the press. But the travelling *Sadhus, Fakirs,* singers, beggars, and nomads who went on foot from place to place secretly carried messages from the leaders of the freedom movement to the public. They made it possible to defy the press ban by the Government successfully. In each town and village the flag-bearers promoted the ideas of freedom regularly. On the same day, all over India, even in remote villages, the 'Resolution of Remembrance' was read out in their local languages. It was an emotional pledge to give equal status to the women of India and they had equal voting power like the men, a system that continued even after Independence.

"We record our homage and deep admiration for the womanhood of India. They shared equally with their men, the sacrifices and triumphs of the struggle for freedom," said Motilal Nehru.

Once again the women of Berhampur asked Pillamma to lead them in the freedom movement but she gently turned down their request saying that she was most needed at home for her young children and her priority was to raise her children as good citizens. With all her personal problems at home, she had opted out of active politics and refused to join the Women's League, which was not short of volunteers. Perhaps they felt that having the wife of the eminent citizen, Panditji Ramalingam, would enhance their group. The women already had some opposition from their men and many ridiculed them behind their backs. Those were the times when women were confined to domestic duties. They wanted the wife of Masterji to be their leader, because she had gained respect and was revered by men as the perfect supporter of their Masterji, and they would perhaps have less conflict with the men of the town. Moreover, many women secretly admired the brave Pillamma who stood against the tides of family upheaval and raised her children single-handed and never let the smile on her face melt away. For some people she was their heroine while for some she was merely the wife of a famous man and few envied her for all that she stood for.

Undeterred, the women of the town took active part in the movement. Their thoughts clashed with the determination in the maternal feelings of Pillamma.

Some of them took her blatant refusal personally and felt that Pillamma had insulted them. When it came to exist with her individuality in the society for Pillamma it was like walking on a tight rope. The women's group acted rather strangely with Pillamma. Most of them boycotted her and stopped inviting her to their social functions. The rejections and abuses were nothing new to Pillamma. Over the ten or so years from the day her husband had resigned from his job at the college, she faced them in small doses and they reached their peak when, at the first time he got arrested, the society's affection towards her and her family was like the tides of a sea; they ebbed and they receded with time. She had learnt to accept everything that Fate tossed upon her, and their rejection of her from time to time had also become a norm for the women of the town and Pillamma learnt to endure it all as before. Many a time she felt anxious, empty, helpless, worthless, guilty, and sometimes she became irritable with herself. Whatever her inner feelings were she managed to hide them from her children and never shed tears in public.

Already her husband was in jail and if she were to desert her children they would become orphans. She wouldn't and couldn't let it happen. Those two children, her nine-year-old son and her six-year-old daughter were her life, her responsibility. As their father Masterji Ramalingam told his students at the college that their education should take priority in their life and they should be well educated so that they could take care of their motherland after India gained Freedom, she concentrated on her children's education. She remembered how her husband was often telling the youth that India needed well-educated children to take care of it.

As ever her best friend Mangamma stood by her. She was there for her at all times. Without her friend saying anything, Mangamma envisaged Pillamma's agony. Once again Mangamma stood by her when society boycotted Pillamma. Mangamma was one of the wealthy women of the town, but she was known for her generosity and discipline. She was well balanced in her views regarding kindness and justice and she couldn't tolerate any injustice, however small the matter might be. She was the prominent guest at any function. Now she stood by her friend and refused to attend any functions without Pillamma. The women gave in to her demands, mainly for three reasons: she often took rich gifts to the functions, many felt honoured to be visited by her, and some of them—but not all—realised that they had been unfair to the lone woman who was maintaining her family alone. Mangamma took her friend, Pillamma, in her *Tonga* to attend the functions. Gradually she was accepted back into the female world of the town.

Meanwhile Pillamma began her Literacy Classes for women at her home. She continued to give matinee readings of epics to the women. With her sweet melodic voice Pillamma recited the verses from the epics and explained them to the women. They were captivated by her readings.

It was popularly known that Pillamma had healing hands for minor ailments. She often treated women and children with her herbal remedies, which she had learned from her mother. Her mother received the healing mantras and remedies from a wandering *Fakir,* saying that the remedies would work only when they were used for the benefit of people and not for any remuneration. It was said that wandering *Sadhus* and *Fakirs* sometimes came down from the Himalayas and mingled with the people. When they found the right, suitable person, they passed on their mantras and healing remedies to the right person and returned to Himalayas.

It had been three years since her mother's demise. Now Pillamma carried on utilising her late mother's remedies to help the people around her; mostly poor women, although a few of the rich approached her at her home. Soon she gained the name of being 'a lucky hand'. Belief and faith is stronger than any other remedy. In the days when the doctors were not available to all, Pillamma's free help was much appreciated by the people in pain.

On one occasion a tribal woman went to her with a strange request. Her daughter had become pregnant after fifteen years of praying and pilgrimage to all holy places and taking several quack remedies. Pillamma's past flashed in front of her—how she had longed to have children—so she understood the women's feelings.

"That's good! All will be well, but do take her to the hospital," Pillamma advised, remembering how Dr Bhore had helped her during her own pregnancies.

"Amma, will you please bless my daughter. We've come for your blessings," she said, beckoning her daughter, and the shy young woman emerged from behind the gates. Pillamma blessed her and once again asked them to go to the women's hospital for check-ups.

"No, Amma. If I take her to the hospital her mother-in-law will never take her back, and nobody from our community goes to hospital and shamelessly gives birth in front of all people."

Pillamma's past flashed in front of her again. She tried to reason with the woman about hospital care.

"Amma, it's alright for rich, clever people like you. We are simple and stupid people and we cannot cross the steps into a hospital. Our village head will banish us from the clan. He will slaughter the whole clan. My daughter's in-laws will kill her and the baby."

Pillamma recalled how her own family refused to visit her at the hospital when she had Komalam. She sighed. *Rich or poor ... the prejudices are the same*, she thought, and remained silent.

"Amma, you are like God to us! Don't be angry with us. Bless my daughter."

"No, I'm not angry. Go and take good care of her. Everything will be alright."

"Amma, I want to ask you something. Don't get angry."

"Ask—do you want some clothes or money?"

"No, Amma. You have healing hands, and you are blessed by God. I want my daughter to give a safe delivery, so until then; can she wear something you have worn? She will wear it until the baby is delivered and then she will return it."

Pillamma was amazed at her request. The tribal woman had perfect speech and was very articulated. At the same time she appeared humble and innocent. Pillamma was in a dilemma. She couldn't give the woman her *Khadi* clothes. They were heavy and the dainty pregnant girl would find them difficult to manage.

"Amma, don't be angry. I'm not begging. I ask for a good luck charm from you. Give us anything you have used that will bring good fortune to my daughter so that she can have an easy delivery and go back to her husband with her child. Amma, I promise I will return the item as soon as the baby is delivered."

Pillamma realised that the tribal woman wanted an item, not clothes. Pillamma went in and thought about the request. 'They have faith in me. Faith surpasses all known remedies. The mind does play according to our thought processes. The concept of fear of the unknown stems from the depths of our brain and similarly the concept of faith also emerges from our brain and gives moral strength. The pregnant woman is weak and fragile. She needs all the help. The woman believes in me—perhaps that would give her the strength to give birth to her baby easily. It's not up to me to analyse whether their faith is valid or not. That is immaterial now. For the young woman, the birth of her child is more important than her own life. I must help her and I will.'

Pillamma emerged from the house and stood on the veranda holding a *kante,* a gold choker, in her hand. The tribal woman watched her in surprise. She wondered what Pillamma was doing with the shiny gold choker. Pillamma climbed down the four steps slowly one at a time as if she was counting them and reached the young woman and put the *kante* around the pregnant girl's neck. She deliberately had given her the gold choker so that she could sell it and pay the local midwife for delivery and the mother could send her daughter and the baby to her husband with plenty of gifts. The speechless women, the tribal mother and daughter, left with tears streaming down their faces. No more words were said by either of them. The tribal woman thanked Pillamma for her generosity with her eyes and escorted her daughter home.

For the first time Mangamma disagreed with Pillamma. She felt that Pillamma had acted rather foolishly, as she was overcome by her own emotions concerning her own pregnancies. Memories of her pregnancies— the ups and downs, the delights and tragedies—always remained in the forefront of Pillamma's memory. Mangamma thought that her friend had fallen for a scam from two cunning tribal women and undoubtedly had become a victim on her own doorstep. She warned Pillamma that she would never see the choker again, but Pillamma did not tell her that she had gifted the choker to the pregnant young woman and she did not expect it be returned.

Now at the hospital Komalam gave birth to another son whom they named Lakshman, after the historical brother of Rama. So Komalam's two sons had the names of the two brothers in Ramayana, her favourite epic story.

Panditji was still in jail and had not yet met his second grandson. Veeradhi was more attached to his grandfather, and pined for him. So a couple of times the family took him and his new brother on their brief visits to Vellore Jail. When he saw the new baby he thought that he was Errababu's nephew. He was delighted to meet his new grandson, and the baby's first encounter with his famous grandfather was in jail.

Eight months later, Pillamma heard drums played in front of her house. A large group of tribal people in their colourful gear danced and sang songs and the whole street came out to watch the display. When they saw the young boy, Ramam, on the veranda they picked him up and put a peacock-feathered cap on his head and danced with him, but Subbulu hid behind her mother. A group of women gyrated slowly, singing songs to the slow drum beat. Then one elderly woman came forward and placed a colourful cane basket lined with tender banana leaves and placed it at Pillamma's feet, at once all the tribal women yodelled in their traditional manner. The bewildered Pillamma picked up the basket with both hands and was delighted to see a beautiful baby boy all wrapped in a colourful shawl.

"Amma, he is your gift to my daughter, now that she is a mother. With your blessings she has become a mother, a mother of a bouncy baby boy. Bless my grandson, Amma, and with your blessings he will grow into a strong man," said the tribal woman. Then she beckoned baby's father, parents, and the rest of the tribe. One by one they came forward and touched Amma's feet in reverence. Then the tribal woman placed a banana-leaf parcel at her feet. Pillamma picked it up and found her *kante*, the gold choker, inside it. Her eyes filled up with tears.

"Amma, with your blessings my daughter gave birth to her son. She wore the *kante* every day until the boy was delivered. You have magic in your hands Amma, and now we have come to return your *kante*." She laid her head on Pillamma's feet and wept uncontrollably. Pillamma picked up the tribal grandmother and made her sit on the veranda.

Pillamma went inside and fetched a new *Khadi* sari, turmeric and kumkum packets, and fistfuls of rice and lentils, some sweets, and a coconut on a bamboo tray and gave them to the new mother. Then she picked up the baby in her arms and placed the *kante* on his neck, at which the baby smiled as if he understood her love and her kindness.

"Keep it with you and may you have many more healthy children," Pillamma said, blessing the mother and baby. The tribal head came forward and placed a bamboo stem full of honey on the veranda and the group left, singing and dancing to the beat of loud drums.

Her neighbours watched the tribal dance with delight and soon they spread the news of the *kante* to all. Some felt that Pillamma was foolish to give away a gold choker to a tribal woman and others extolled her generosity, and few thought Pillamma should have known that charity begins at home. Only Mangamma understood her friend's emotions. Pillamma gave the choker willingly to help a young mother and as a reward for her honesty. Moreover Pillamma was not bound by wealth but by sincerity in anybody. Mangamma felt that Pillamma rewarded the gold choker to one honest woman.

In reality nobody knew what exactly Pillamma felt, perhaps not even Pillamma herself, she often did what she thought was the right thing to do. Mangamma was glad that her friend's faith in the tribal woman was worth it.

Pandit Ramalingam was a father figure to the Bengal Nagpur Railway Workers Union. He was elected unanimously as the Union's vice-president, in absentia while he was still in jail. Even from the jail he used to advise the office-bearers how to act and keep good relations with the employers. The Bengal-Nagpur Railway's bigwigs—all Europeans—took heed of Ramalingam's advice and maintained a very good relationship under his tenure of vice-presidency and later after his release from jail Ramalingam became BN Railway Union's President. The workers adored their Panditji and they kept his photo along with the images of gods and worshipped him in their homes. For Indians, goodness was godliness and they revered the person who stood by them in their need as if he was a God. When the workers were on strike Pandit Ramalingam's photos were given to each donor as a gift and those donated amounts were used for their maintenance during the strike period.

In 1932, once again Gandhiji appealed to the nation to fight for *Purna Swaraj*, the complete freedom of the country. Panditji, who had just been released from jail, took charge of this movement at Berhampur. He instigated civil disobedience against foreign clothing and the picketers picketed shops that sold them. The trade had come to a standstill and some picketers burnt a few shops against the wishes of their leaders. The crowds of protesters got carried away with their emotions and the chaos spread to too many places. Once again, Panditji was arrested for instigating the public against the Government and causing civil disobedience. He was arrested and was sentenced for one year Rigorous Imprisonment at Vellore Jail, along with eminent freedom fighter C. Rajagopalachari and other leaders of the Madras Presidency.

Pillamma's joy of having her husband at home resulted as something like a mirage in the desert; he came and went like a flash of lightning and once again she remained alone. The loneliness began to take its toll on her. She began to suffer from high fever frequently and the doctor declared that it was malaria and the fever (the ague) attacked her on a regular basis. Its symptoms were strange. She would suddenly receive a high temperature and yet shivered as if she was in the arctic without any protection. No amount of blankets could keep her from shivering. She was truly overpowered by the symptoms of malaria: high fever, shaking chills, amnesia, muscle pains, and nausea. Once the fever receded she would wake up as if she were out of a trance, and immediately resumed her domestic duties.

The doctors from the hospital and their family doctor Jagappa declared that it was a mild form of malaria, and she had received it from a mosquito bite. Pillamma was known for hygiene and cleanliness. The whole family slept under mosquito nets and yet she was suffering with malaria. That bothered her a lot and she took extra care to see that her children were safe and obtained new mosquito nets for them. At first the two children were scared of the ague, but became accustomed to its seasonal attacks on their mother. Her maidservant stood by her, comforted the children, and looked after them until Pillamma was well again. When she recovered from the bout of malaria she became weak, as if all the energy was drained out of her and she looked ashen. Fortunately those ague attacks were rare.

But another problem came to surface her feet began to show some swelling. At first they were painful. The doctor told her not to worry too much about it since it was another symptom of malaria. But Jagappa, who always was frank with diagnosis, told her that she had filarial infection, often carried by mosquitoes, which deposit the eggs of roundworms in a person's body. He told her that the swelling could come anywhere in the body, mostly in the lower limbs. The doctor from the hospital treated her with a quinine solution and Jagappa treated her with his herbal medicines. The malaria drained a great deal of strength from her body, but she refused to inform her husband about it. She did not want to disturb him on her account when he was in jail and there was nothing he could have done except pine for her. Pillamma, who herself was a grandmother, missed her own mother. Like most humans she longed to rest in her mother's arms and be comforted by her. Sadly that was never to be; she had passed away soon after Komalam's marriage.

Pillamma often sat alone by the well, her favourite place where she found peace and quiet and shut her weary eyes. One day while she sat there, tears began to stream down her face. Suddenly she felt two gentle arms cuddle her and she opened her eyes to see Komalam in front of her. Her daughter dried her mother's tears and led her into the house. They walked in silence and no words were exchanged between them. When she entered the house she found Errababu and his two sons there.

"Amma, we've all come to be with you," he announced in his soft voice, and looked at his servant who fetched their luggage into the house and stood outside.

"Amma, why didn't you tell us about your illness? Are we strangers to you? Do we have to hear about your illness from outsiders? Never mind. Now we are here and we will be here with you," said Errababu, with emotion. To hide his tears he then quickly went outside and drove away.

Pillamma was overwhelmed with excitement and she felt light like a feather, her loneliness was lifted for the time being. She had not forgotten how Errababu had left her house abruptly when he came to live with her family before. She decided to cherish their company as long as it lasted.

Now Errababu took a firm decision. He told his older sister that he had moved to his father-in-law's house and that he would be there as long as he was needed. The children loved having their little nephews with them, and once again the laughter of the children echoed around the house. The sceptical neighbours expected that this bliss wouldn't last long. Errababu's sister could do nothing to instigate her brother to leave them, as he had pre-informed her of his decision before the meddling woman created trouble. Komalam took care of her mother like a mother.

Even after Panditji's return from the jail they all lived together in his rented house for another three years.

Veeradhi, Komalam, Lakshman, 1932

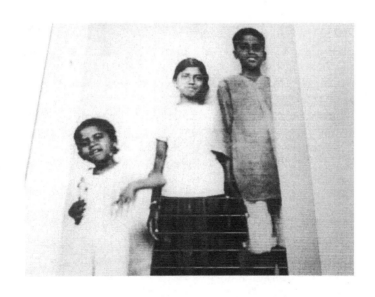

Veeradhi, Subbulu & Ramam, 1930

15
Blessed

1933 was a most notable year for Panditji's family. After two sons a girl was born to Komalam and Errababu, and the parents and grandparents were thrilled when Lakshmi was born into the family. Her birth was most memorable. Komalam longed to have a daughter and her dream daughter made a dramatic appearance in the family. That day while her mother was making *garelu*, lentil fritters, Komalam, who had just finished gardening, went to the well to wash her feet. Suddenly she had pains and the baby girl was delivered there, by the well. Komalam, it seemed, always had easy deliveries. Pillamma shouted to her husband to fetch Ranga the midwife, but Panditji who misheard his wife went to fetch his nephew, Rangam. But fortunately, the delivery was easy and the baby was born by the time the midwife arrived.

Naming a baby is considered to be a sacred matter, and therefore it is an important Hindu tradition. It involves the immediate families and also close relatives and friends. Traditionally known as *Namkaranam*, this naming ceremony is conducted in an elaborate manner. On the eleventh day of the baby's birth the house is cleaned and sanctified for the ceremony. The mother and the infant are bathed traditionally with a massage of sesame oil and turmeric paste and shampooed with shampoo seeds called *kunkudukayalu* and are prepared for the ceremony. Relatives and close friends are invited to be a part of this occasion and to bless the child.

Priests arrived to conduct the most elaborate Namakaranam ritual. A grand feast was prepared for all, to suit the status of Errababu's family. When it came to celebrations he was particular to maintain the standard and prestige of his late father, P. Venkteswarlu.

The eldest of the family, Naanamma, the grandmother of Komalam and great-grandmother of the baby, decided to name the baby girl Santa, the sister of the legendary Rama. The family agreed as it was the appropriate name for the sister of two boys who were named after the legendary Lord nee Raghuveer and Lakshman.

Sadly, in the early morning of that special day on 2 December 1933, Panditji's elderly mother, the great-grandmother of the new baby girl, expired, and all the celebrations were cancelled. At such times superstitions overrule logic. The family was advised by the well-wishers never to hold any *Namakaranam* function for the baby girls as it brought tragedy to the family. Panditji tried to reason with his family, saying that his mother had died of old age and she wouldn't have wanted the family to abandon the naming ceremony, but their personal sentiments and superstitions overpowered the women of the family. From then onwards it became the family's tradition not to have any *Namakaranam* ceremony for their daughters.

Of all the family it was Komalam who was most disappointed since she wanted to do everything for her little girl but was wary of crossing fate and facing any more tragedies. They called the baby girl Santa Kumari as her great-grandmother had suggested. Komalam showed more interest in her daughter than her two sons. Komalam had dreams for her baby. She visualised a glorious future for her and wished to educate her to be a doctor. For Komalam, the role model was Dr Bhore who had given her life. Dr Margaret Bhore had played an important role in Komalam's life in person and in her absence

When Pillamma had been pregnant again in 1913 after her the death of her three months old son, Ramalingam had decided to give her all the support. He had consulted Dr Margaret Bhore and had taken his wife to the hospital for prenatal care. Joseph Bhore and Dr Bhore were Ramalingam's friends for a long time. Her visits to the local Janana Hospital had been kept a secret from the family, as women of decent families never visited hospitals. But at Berhampur nothing remained a secret for a long time. Soon Atta had found out about the visits and had protested strongly. She had told her son that all the women in the family over several generations had delivered babies at home and she considered it to be rude and ill-mannered to deliver a baby in front of all. Ramalingam had paid no heed to his mother's pleas and objections. Pillamma had already had a few miscarriages and her son had died in his infancy at three months, and considering her health Ramalingam was not prepared to take any chances with her next pregnancy. Atta had been unable to do anything to her adamant son, so she had shown her disapproval of Pillamma. By this time Pillamma had learnt to endure her Atta's love-and-hate relationship with the same spirit.

At first Pillamma had been afraid to go to the hospital, but Dr Bhore had received her personally at the Tonga and had escorted her to her rooms, and she had continued to do so on her every visit. Slowly they had become bound in friendship and Pillamma had begun to trust the doctor.

On the due date Pillamma had given birth to a healthy baby. The family had refused to see the baby at the hospital, but the baby had not been short of visitors. The baby had created commotion before her birth and even after her birth she had created havoc in town.

The baby had been a 'caul baby', born in its 'sack and veil' as some people called it, and she had become the talk of the town. To be born in the 'caul' means that a baby is born with an intact amniotic sac with some of the amnion (membrane) covering the baby, and are generally called 'caulbearers'. Caulbearers can be male or female, and may come from any social class, and any racial or religious group. There are no geographical boundaries to this phenomenon. There are several omens and superstitions attached to caul babies: that these babies will grow up strong, healthy, intelligent, and prosperous. It is considered as good luck to be born with a caul. Being born with a caul is an extremely rare situation, probably occurring at one in a million births. A legend developed suggesting that possession of a baby's caul would give its bearer good luck and protect that person from death by drowning. Hence cauls were highly prized by sailors and they were often sold to sailors for large sums of money since the caul was regarded as a valuable talisman. There were many notable people born in cauls: Lord Byron and Sigmund Freud, to name but a few.

Pillamma had been devastated to see her caul baby; she had been covered over head and torso, and only tiny feet had been visible. Dr Bhore had told her that the baby was lucky to be born in a caul but that had not eased Pillamma's mind. She had prayed to the Almighty to save her baby. But the rumours in town were spreading wild. Some had predicted that the new baby would bring disaster to all and that the town was doomed. And a few had even suggested that the baby should be killed to safeguard the town.

Visitors from near and far had flocked to the hospital to witness the strange baby. The phenomenon of the caul had never been heard of in that area. Some had said it was a punishment to Pillamma for violating the traditions and delivering the baby in the hospital. Dr Bhore, with immense patience, had explained to one and all that a caul baby was a lucky one and that only blessed babies were born with a caul. Dr Bhore could speak the local language, Telugu, and she had understood the culture of the people and was aware of their beliefs. She had told them that a caul baby might have been a queen or have had a regal birth in her previous birth. As people often believed in rebirth, the doctor's theory had appealed to them, and gradually they had turned around in thought and began to see the baby as good fortune to her parents and to the town.

The doctor had convinced the public but Pillamma had been devastated and constantly worried about her baby. Their family doctor and her brother-in-law, Jagappa, against his mother's wishes had gone to see her as a doctor—not as a relative. The whole family had valued Jagappa as their doctor. He had assured the worried mother that the baby's caul would naturally peel off and all would be well. Dr Bhore and Jagappa had continued to take care of the baby at the hospital. After a fortnight the peeling had been complete and a beautiful baby had emerged out of it like a butterfly from a cocoon.

Dr Bhore had placed the baby in Pillamma's arms and commented, '*Mee papa enta komalamga undi*' in Telugu, meaning: 'How tender and beautiful is your baby'. Thus Pillamma had held her baby close to her heart and had called her Komalam, and thus she remained Komalam to all. But she had had the proper *Namakaranam* naming ceremony at home, which Atta had arranged. Once she had seen the baby, all her anger with the baby's parents had vanished into thin air. Dr Bhore had attended the naming ceremony to the delight of all, and the baby had been duly named Taratarini Ramasubbamma, adding the names of the Goddess Taratarini and Panditji's grandmother's name, but the name of Komalam became hers. Once again Dr Bhore had praised the fortunate baby and had assured a few sceptics that the baby would be most fortunate and would spread happiness and cheer to all she would meet. Nobody had the courage to disagree with a memsahib. Komalam had become the dearest child of all. True to predictions Komalam had easily made friends with everybody and people had loved her for her charm and kindness. She had been considered the most beautiful girl in town.

While growing up Komalam had heard of her birth story in episodes, in small instalments, and as an epic story from her mother and other people. She had developed an unknown admiration for Dr Bhore, who was clever, kind, and her parent's friend.

Komalam had her own ambitions in her life—she had wanted to be a doctor and to help people—but she had never expressed them to anyone and went along with the family decisions. When she had been removed from school at the age of nine her dream had come to a halt. Her mother Pillamma had understood her daughter's ambitions but had been helpless, as the tide of the freedom movement engulfed Komalam's future. Komalam had never complained about anything, but now she wanted to fulfil her dreams through her lovely daughter, Santa Kumari. Santa was also her aunt Subbulu's favourite. Komalam waited for the day when her dream daughter would become a doctor. Only time would tell if her dream would materialise or remain a shattered dream like hers.

Now with this third child born, the rented house of Panditji at Birkaveedhi was somewhat crammed, and so Errababu suggested that they all move to his residence in R.C. Church Road, a vast bungalow with umpteen rooms and much space. Panditji considered that it would be helpful to Komalam to manage her three children, and his wife Pillamma would not be living alone if he went to jail again. His life was most unpredictable and both Pillamma and he accepted their life as it was. As Panditji had no objection they all shifted to their new abode. The large hall of the bungalow became his office, and soon it was known as Panditji's house.

The house was a beehive of activity of the Congress Party and many noted Congress leaders visiting Pandit Ramalingam there, including Gandhiji. On 7 November 1933, Gandhiji started from Wardha on an all-India tour for the uplifting of the downtrodden *'Harijans'*—literally meaning 'the children of God'—to restore equality between man and man. *Harijan* is a word coined by Gandhiji to address people of low caste.

Gandhiji's plea to people was:

"The inner oneness pervades all life. God is one and all life is from Him and in Him. Untouchability is the very negation of this magnificent truth."

Gandhiji was on the move, addressing meetings, and opening wells and temples for the Harijans, which was often forbidden for them. Gandhiji auctioned articles presented to him and collected funds for their cause. People loosened their fists. Coins and jewellery were poured in for them in abundance. Gandhiji's reaction to public generosity was:

"I want your hearts, along with your money."

Gandhiji had a particular mission before him: the eradication of 'untouchability'. He often challenged the public with sensational statements:

"If we believe that we are all children of one and the same God, how can there be untouchability amongst us, His children?"

He organised village sanitation on a rational basis and exhorted the *Harijans* to give up eating carrion and drinking liquor. To some extent he lightened their miseries and restored their self-respect.

At Berhampur, Gandhiji visited Pandit Ramalingam and his colleagues at his residence in R.C. Church Road to discuss the matter of 'untouchablility'. He was aware that Panditji had been socially denunciated when he had dined with the members of Simon Commission and people of all castes and religions.

Gandhiji renounced the use of any conveyance for the Harijan tour in Orissa, and toured by foot. He wanted to cultivate more intimate contact with the villagers. He wanted them to "Awake, arise, and realise the sin they had inherited and harboured."

Gandhiji's visit to Pandit Ramalingam's residence had become the talk of the town. Some were afraid that Panditji might burden them with his views and reforms. Most people liked the tone of the reforms but were hesitant to incorporate them in their lives. The men of the town met at the park, in Park Street, (now known as Gandhi Park) which played an important role in the freedom movement. It was maintained well with manicured lawn and well laid garden. Mostly the educated men gathered there every evening to discuss politics. Every evening the all-India Radio news was broadcast on the tannoy from the central room to the people. Radio was not all that common in homes, but through the radio Gandhiji's messages often reached them promptly, unless it was banned. Newspapers were controlled by the Government and free speech was discouraged during the freedom movement. All the same, the free press had their own means of promoting their views to the public, and one such way was through the tannoy at the main park of the town.

In the evenings the park was busy with the people. They talked in whispers about politics and had several views and several political groups, each with their own agenda. All the same, none of them interfered with the other groups. It was a most civilised gathering at the park. Children and women never went there.

The fight for freedom was a spate of movement that affected young and old, women and children, and the educated and the illiterate in the same way, and that was the charisma of Gandhiji. He had awoken the conscience of the masses. The men discussed and argued about the reforms the leaders might impose on them after Gandhiji's visit to the town. They debated how to stop the reforms and argued relentlessly but failed to come to any conclusions.

The town's people could not do anything about the reforms that Pandit Ramalingam and other eminent leaders tried to introduce to the town. Some of them agreed to reforms and accepted Harijans amidst them, whereas a majority of them ignored the reforms. Once again the leaders of the town tried to negotiate with the Temple authorities and allowed Harijans to enter the temples.

At Ramalingam's bungalow, the well was opened to all. It was a sound drinking source for all the people in the neighbouring area and even in midsummer the well never dried up. Errababu built a small gate at the side entrance of the bungalow through which all the people could easily have access to the well. The family also used the same water from the well and all the family's cooking was done with it. These kinds of gestures by quite a few leaders remained a token gesture. But the majority of the high-caste people maintained their traditions. Some did so openly and some secretly. Thus Gandhiji's dream of giving *Harijans* an equal status never became a complete success.

Santa & Subbulu

Dr. Margaret Bhore (nee Stott) & Joseph Bhore,

16
The Miracle Doctor

The country witnessed drastic changes in all fields. It was in turmoil. New laws were made and new legislations were formed to control the uprising in the country. Slowly and steadily, it began to seep in like water under a mat. The non-violence movement had reached its peak, since the majority of the country had become aware of the struggle for freedom and the slogans of *Purna Swaraj*. The complete freedom of the country echoed all over the nation.

By 1931 the Government declared the All India Congress as being an unlawful association. The provincial governments were ordered to take action against provincial and district Congress Committees and as a result a succession of Congress Presidents was arrested. Some more changes took place. The Reserve Bank was to be the currency authority of India, independent of the Government, and was established by an Act in 1934.

By 1935, elections were held for the provincial legislatures. The results gave a shock to the Government—the Congress commanded a majority in Uttar Pradesh, Bihar, Orissa, Central Provinces, Bombay, and Madras. Maharaja Krishna Chandra Gajapati took oath on 1 April 1936 when the state of Orissa was formed. It was a historical moment for all. Ganjam District was severed from the Madras Presidency and became a part of Orissa, making Berhampur an important town of Orissa. The second PM, Biswanath Das, became the leader of Orissa on 1 July 1937. (In those days the State leaders were called Prime Ministers instead of Chief Ministers as we address now.) He appointed Pandit Ramalingam as his advisor on Cooperation and Local Self-Government. Panditji fixed his own salary at 300 rupees when he could have earned 2000. When he was appointed as the advisor he asked his wife how much she was spending on housekeeping. She replied that it was about 300 rupees, and hence he fixed his salary at exactly that. He never used his status to make money.

1937 was a memorable year for Pillamma. Pillamma took the two little granddaughters with her and shifted to Cuttack into the house allotted to Panditji. That was the first time she had left her home town and had gone to live in a city where the lifestyle was all very different. Their house was in Pension Lane at Cuttack. It was a three-storied house that belonged to a Muslim family, Asif Ali, a well-known businessman, who lived on the top floor. They drew water from the well by a bucket attached to a rope from their top floor. It was an amusing sight for the children to see.

Pillamma first concentrated on education. She admitted the four-year-old Santa into the Convent School Nursery, but the little girl did not take to its regime and had to be withdrawn. Komalam, who dreamt for her daughter to have a good English education, was disappointed. Her toddler sister kept the neighbourhood amused with her antics. The landlady, Mrs Begum, fell in love with the toddler and spent a lot of time with the little girl and pampered her thoroughly. She loved the child so much she wanted to adopt her but Pillamma refused gently.

After a long time Pillamma got closer to her husband at Cuttack. The pressures of the Congress work eased a little. Panditji returned home every evening after his official work and they dined together, the luxury of which she had been deprived over the last decade and a half. Panditji commuted between Cuttack and Berhampur frequently to continue his Congress work there. Komalam and the rest of the family spent the school holidays at Cuttack. Those visits were a relief to the whole family. After ten months they returned to Berhampur.

By 1938 a third son was born to Komalam. He topped his siblings in weight, born at eleven pounds, and he earned the nickname 'Bhima', the legendary strong brother of Pandavas in Mahabharata. He began to grow up in the household with his special space amidst his four siblings.

With his good looks and charming personality he became the most favoured nephew of his only uncle, Ramam, who did not hesitate to show his favouritism to his bonny nephew, ignoring the other children. He would take him out for walks and pamper him a lot. Every household had its favourites. Santa always remained Komalam's second favourite as Ramam, being her only brother, was her most loved—there was no equal to him. The sibling bondage between the two was unparalleled. Ramam would do anything for his sister Komalam and she would give her life for her brother Ramam. She had loved him from the day he was born. The joy of having her own brother stayed with her until her last breath.

Veeradhi, as the first grandchild, was favoured by his grandparents. Lakshman was his father's pride. Jani, the second granddaughter, a tomboy, was a true admirer of her grandfather. She followed him so much like a true disciple from an early age that she became his shadow. To top them all, Komalam remained the most favourite child of Panditji and Pillamma. Komalam was loved and admired by her husband Errababu. He cherished her and took great care of his wife.

The household became active with all the children mingling, Pillamma's two children and her five grandchildren appearing almost as siblings. Subbulu, her second daughter, and her first grandson, Veeradhi, with the age gap of only five years between them, were especially very close. Strangers often mistook them all as Pillamma's children.

During his Orissa tour in March 1938, Gandhiji met Panditji at Cuttack and again they discussed *Purna Swaraj*. He stressed how provincial autonomy had become a reality when elections were held and Congress had won with a majority. Gandhiji felt that it was a strong indication of the Indian people's support for *Purna Swaraj*.

Perhaps as the result of Gandhiji's meeting with him, Panditji returned from Cuttack to Berhampur, and led the *Purna Swaraj* movement along with many supporters. They were all duly arrested, and Panditji was sentenced to one year Rigorous Imprisonment at Berhampur jail, where the prisoner was engaged in hard labour. Pillamma was devastated. Her blissful good life at Cuttack had vanished into thin air as soon as they had returned to Berhampur. Her husband had been arrested and the fate of her situation had resumed as before.

By 1939, Komalam's health took a bad turn. She had developed an abscess in her stomach. She was first treated by the family doctor, Dr Venkata Rao, and her own uncle, Jagappa, but the pain was not reduced. Although women patients were welcome in government and municipal hospitals, they never attended the out-patients and were rarely admitted. It was due largely to the efforts of Christian women doctors and nurses that this prejudice against modern medicine was broken down.

Already their family friend and trusted doctor, Dr Bhore, had been transferred to another state in India. Panditji, against his extended family's wishes, admitted Komalam to the hospital, where the treatment was severe; they drained the puss from her stomach at regular intervals. Komalam couldn't withstand the treatment and they had to bring her back home. The European doctor visited her at home and checked on her health, but she had made no improvement. Finally, the doctor from the hospital gave up with her and asked the family to say their last prayers for Komalam and left. But the family continued with the treatment, hoping she would never die, and they prayed for a miracle to occur. Meanwhile, the puss in Komalam's stomach seemed to grow day by day, and the nurse continued to visit her patient and administered the treatment, draining the puss off and disposing of it. The doctors did not name her condition. They simply referred to it as a 'burst stomach ulcer'.

Finally, Jagappa, who also adored his niece, Komalam, took charge of her treatment and began to treat her with his medicines, a system he had developed on his own. He was not a trained medical doctor, but had worked with a doctor and had read all the books on medicine and had developed his own method of treatment, which was a boon to many patients that visited him regularly at home. He visited Komalam three times a day to administer the medicine with his own hands. When it came to treatment of anybody he administered the dose with his own hands. He was a meticulous physician and never took any chances with patients.

Meanwhile Pillamma took charge of all the children and the household. Her responsibilities multiplied day by day and she took them in her own stride. She spent every spare minute with her daughter and prayed to the Almighty. Panditji remained calm and often sat beside his Komalam. He talked to her softly and she listened to him quietly. What he said and what she heard remained their affair. Perhaps he gave her courage and hope for the future. A devastated Errababu watched helplessly as his love and his life suffered in front of his eyes and gradually deteriorated. The whole family was perturbed by Komalam's illness. The stream of visitors who came to see Komalam disturbed her. Errababu stood guard and kept the visitors away from her. Some of them took objection to this, but Pillamma soothed the situation by saying that Errababu was only following the doctor's orders, as they did not know if Komalam's condition was infectious or not. The fear of an unknown illness reduced the flow of visitors, but some close friends continued to visit. Although they were not allowed into Komalam's room, they asked about her and some of them gave a helping hand with the housekeeping.

After a month's treatment by Jagappa the puss disappeared, gradually her pain reduced, and after three months Komalam recovered fully. Now that Komalam had recovered but still remained frail, Pillamma became a mother to all at home. Komalam, who was not the one to sit idle, gave her a helping hand in simple household duties. It took a good few months before Komalam recovered completely. Jagappa visited her daily until she was completely healthy.

The European doctor at the hospital was impressed with the 'treatment' Jagappa had given Komalam. He became Jagappa's apprentice for a few months and learned the skills from the native doctor. Even among the sahibs there were some who respected his knowledge and bowed in front of him. As Panditji used to say, "There are rulers and there are scholars." Scholars are always pursuing knowledge without prejudice, whereas the rulers concentrate on ruling by any means and often by putting down the natives and their wisdom. Komalam's abscess never returned to trouble her again. Jagappa's medical skills became a hot topic among sahibs. He was often consulted whenever some patients arrived at the hospital with some strange symptoms. They began to address him as Dr Jagappa, which tickled him.

Biswanath Das

Chief Minister of Orissa, 1937

17
Transformation of the Town in 1940

By 1940 many changes began to take shape in town. One night children and adults gathered in the streets to witness a miracle beam of light that floated in the sky for a few seconds and then suddenly disappeared. Astrological predictions and the forthcoming doom and superstition flourished freely. Everybody had their own theory about the strange phenomenon in the sky. People talked about it in awe and fear. There was fear in the unknown that frightened people and it stood to no reason or logic. One day the miracle beam would travel cross the sky and disappear, and another day it travelled from east to west and disappeared. Another day it went vertically into the sky. The beam created havoc in town. Its magic continued for few more nights until a reporter traced it down to being the sign of Gemini Circus coming to town and the beam of light was their gimmick to attract people.

The Gemini Circus pitched its tents in the Barracks grounds. The town buzzed in excitement. The clowns paraded through the town on open carts drawn by bullocks, and twirling and jumping girls led the parade and distributed the pamphlets. Children ran after the carts floating pamphlets. On another day the circus paraded their animals in cages through the town. Later the elephants carried clowns who did daring gymnastics upon their backs. The Gemini Circus wooed the public, exhibiting bit by bit of their acts. After a weak their first debut was made to the public. People from near and far flocked to see the circus.

Gemini Circus was well received at Berhampur, and it was a welcoming relief from the upheaval of the *Purna Swaraj* movement. Pillamma, Komalam, and the children also went to see the circus. In the evenings and after school children wandered around the circus tents on the Barracks grounds to have a glimpse of the crew. The circus kept their cages in public view which delighted the children. Seeing the tigers, elephants, monkeys, and bears was a delight to young and old. The circus stayed in town for eight weeks before moving to another place, which definitely left a void in the entertainment of the town.

Despite the amount of followers of Gandhiji's methods of freedom fighting with non-violence there was an equal amount of people who despised it. At Berhampur, Ramalingam was seen as pro-Gandhi and some quarters decided to bring him down from popularity.

As Chairman of the Municipality he supervised the welfare of the citizens personally. Health was his greatest concern. He supervised an annual inoculations programme.

Ramalingam had a strange sleeping routine. He worked all day without rest and at night he read until two in the morning and then took his sleep. He would wake by five, having slept for just three hours. He had one meal only a day, and he also rationed his sleep to the three hours.

Ramalingam's second concern was the daily cleaning of the town. Early in the morning, with a Neem toothbrush in his mouth Ramalingam walked around the streets to supervise if they had been swept and sprinkled with water.

On that eventful morning the sweepers of the Town went on strike without warning and the streets remained upswept. Ramalingam realised who could have been behind this unexpected strike. He returned home and again went out, this time with a broom, and he began to sweep the road himself. In no time at all many volunteers of all ages came out with their brooms and joined him in the cleaning process. The news had spread around the town. Many came to stand by their Panditji while a few stood on their doorsteps to watch the fun. The reporters arrived with their notepads and cameras. Within half an hour the sweepers went running to Panditji and fell at his feet to beg his forgiveness for their folly. They grabbed the broom from Panditji's hand and got back to their jobs. He asked them all to come to his house after they had finished their work.

A few curious people stood outside the gates of his house to see what would happen and how he would pacify the sweepers. One among them was a man locally known as Johnny, with his receding red hair, a lanky man in his forties. He was unemployed and always wore a three-piece suit that was threadbare, even in midsummer. His appearance was unkempt and he was pro-British government. He had instigated the sweepers to go on strike and ask for more salary. People said that in spite of his European looks he was discarded by the sahibs and the Anglo-Indians in town disowned him. Thus Johnny remained a loner, not belonging to any community.

By midday all the sweepers gathered in the backyard of Panditji's house. The workers' anxious families, women, and children stood at a distance by the well and watched in fear of what Panditji would do to their men.

To their surprise Pillamma had arranged a sumptuous meal for all of them. The servants laid out the banana leaves on the veranda and asked the sweepers to freshen up by the well, which they obeyed as if they were in a school. Then the delicious food was served by Pillamma, Komalam, and Subbulu. As soon as the food was dished out the sweepers' children standing by the well ran to their fathers to share the food. Pillamma also served food for their families.

When the eating session was over, Panditji came out into the backyard and asked all the sweepers to meet him at the Town Hall that evening. They left, wondering what would happen to them at the Town Hall and were concerned about losing their jobs.

At the open meeting at the Town Hall Panditji listened to their grievances and promised to look into them. In return he asked them never ever to jeopardise their own families and families of other people in town by going on strike. He explained why it was essential to keep the town clean every day. And he requested them in future to come to him directly if they had any grievances. He emphasised that the hygiene of the town was most essential and, no matter what, they should never repeat such an action again. After discussing their problems with the committee he increased their salaries and he also opened a school in their area so that their children could be literate too. Education was always his priority. The European officer praised Berhampur as being the neatest town in the Ganjam District while Ramalingam was the Chairman of the Municipality.

Pillamma often suffered with malaria fever; the ague was severe. To avoid malaria attacks in town Panditji arranged for a team of doctors to go into the workers' locality and give free medical help to the residents, which revolutionised the welfare of common men.

Life never runs smooth. It's like a neap tide with ripples and with ups and downs. The two eldest grandsons of Panditji had typhoid at the same time. The two teenage brothers were laid down in bed for one and a half months. They lay in adjacent beds in the anteroom of the dining hall. Mother and grandmother kept a constant vigil on them. The stress of their illness affected all the family, as the other children were neglected.

Subbulu was kept in charge of them. She believed in a strict regime and the children resented it, creating more stress in the family. To top it all the two brothers took advantage of their illness and continually made demands. Only in the presence of their father or Jagappa the two boys became mute and ideal patients. The stream of visitors who went to see the patients created more problems by giving free advice of their own concerning medicines and sometimes warning Komalam that typhoid was a killer. Eventually Jagappa took charge of the situation and banned all visitors to the patients.

Komalam was a very practical person who found her own inner peace. She spent her spare time translating Hindi Tulasi Ramayanam into Telugu. She wrote on small pieces of scrap paper with an ink pen and stacked them away above a beam in the storeroom. She never showed this to anyone, but Pillamma noticed her writing and encouraged her to carry on writing.

Subbulu's education at college had pleased both her mother and Komalam. Education had been their dream and had never materialised. Subbulu took up science subjects at college, with Physics, Chemistry, and Mathematics. She was the first girl in the family to have had Higher Education. In a way, she had set a new trend for all the girls in the family. Pillamma always felt that removing a bright girl like Komalam from school was not fair to the girl, but she could not go against the tide of the 'movement'.

Now the two sons recovered from their typhoid and resumed their schooling. In 1941 the political situation of the country was not running smoothly. An Indian National Army was established by Subash Chandra Bose, who believed that no freedom could be achieved by the strategy of Gandhiji, with non-violence alone. By 1941 it was an offence to make speeches against war and as a result 20,000 were jailed. Meetings were banned and were forcefully broken up by the police.

Recently the children of the town were excited about a new drill class that started in the grounds of an office by the Raghunathaswamy Temple. Children of all ages from six to sixteen were recruited. Jani and her friend Gunnu joined the drill class. They were each given a red-coloured bandana to tie round their necks, and a stick to carry while marching. The drill classes thrilled the children and they were asked to keep it as secret. The children failed to understand why they should have to keep the evening drill classes a secret and form whom it should be hidden. But the very word 'secret' excited them and they felt that they were on a special mission and secretly whispered to each other about the new drill classes at school and playground and Barracks ground. The secret was secretly passed on form one child to another.

After a fortnight, Pillamma found Jani flashing her bandana to her younger brother and boasting about her secret. Pillamma was furious that Jani had violated her advice not to accept any gifts from others. The little girl confessed about the drill class and told Pillamma that it was a secret. Immediately alarm bells rang in Pillamma's mind and she informed Panditji about the secret drill classes that were held every evening near the Temple and she was more worried about its secrecy. The police were quick to act and they curbed any general unrest immediately. At once the police got involved and found out that it was an organisation training the children to fight. It was an unofficial organisation in support of Azad Hind Fouz. It was abolished straight away. There ended the drill classes, and the children lost their scarves. Their secret mission came to an abrupt end. For a few days they blamed each other for letting their secret out. Strangely enough, nobody owned up to having violated the secret, not even Jani or Gunnu. The secret of their violation remained a secret between the two good friends.

Errababu, 1933

18
Gurudev

1941 was the year in which Rabindranath Tagore, along with many other famous persons such as James Joyce and Virginia Woolf, bade goodbye to this world. The atmosphere of the Ashram at Santiniketan was profoundly embalmed with the fresh memories of Tagore. The Santiniketan Ashram, also known as Tagore's Ashram is located in Santiniketan, West Bengal. Its foundation was laid by Maharishi Debenture Tagore, father of Rabindranath Tagore, in the year 1863. In 1901, with the efforts of Nobel Laureate Rabindranath Tagore, the ashram was converted into an open air school that was eventually recognised as the Viswa Bharati University in 1921.

Even his recent death seemed tantalising, intriguing, and yet invoking to all who gathered there to be in utter unison with the all-embracing spirit of Tagore.

Errababu was a pupil of Viswa Bharati University at Santiniketan. The motto of the Viswa Bharati was *Where the World Becomes One Single Nest*. The aim of this educational institute was the quest for truth, blending the methods of learning of the East and West.

The ambience of the Santiniketan was calm and tranquil and it created a relieving space in the complex density of human experience. Errababu travelled to Calcutta to pay his homage to his Guru Rabindranath Tagore, who was fondly called 'Gurudev'. Rabindranath Tagore (1861–1941), a poet, philosopher, composer, playwright, painter, dramatist, and controversial essayist was one of the strong personalities who shaped the cultural life of India at the turn of the 20th century, when the country was struggling for its independence and searching for its identity in the international community.

Tagore was born into an influential Bengali Brahman family of several generations of intellectuals. He briefly studied in England in 1878–80, exploring the works of Shakespeare. In 1901 he moved to Santiniketan in eastern India, and established there an institution that was to become his own Santiniketan University, alias Viswa Bharati University. He received the Nobel Prize for Literature in 1913. *Santiniketan* means 'abode (*niketan*) of peace (*santi*)'. Santiniketan became a spiritual centre where people from all religions were invited to join in meditation and prayers. It was here that Rabindranath Tagore created the school of his ideals, with the central premise that learning in a natural environment would be more enjoyable and fruitful.

Tagore travelled widely around the world. His visit to Southeast Asia in 1927, in particular, opened his eyes to the role of Indian culture in a wider Asian framework. He was particularly interested in what he called the "operatic" Southeast Asian theatre forms. He exclaimed that India had lost this kind of form and he dedicated much energy to creating his own theatrical style, also combined with dance.

He was the first non-European to win the Nobel Prize for Literature, and it was for Gitanjali, a collection of poems.

The school was expanded into Viswa Bharati University in 1921. Many world famous teachers came to be associated with it, including C. F. Andrews and Alex Aronson. Some of its illustrious students were Rani Gayatri Devi, Indira Gandhi, Satyajit Ray (film producer), Abdul Ghani Khan (noted Pashto language poet) and Nobel Laureate Amartya Sen (in Economics, 1998).

For Errababu, the memories of his stay at Santiniketan were immense and most memorable. It was the place that moulded him into a sensitive and artistic person and helped him to discover himself and his intellect. He recalled the days when one could notice the nuances of seasonal changes in Santiniketan. The monsoon would arrive with a special appeal. The singing of cuckoos would declare the onset of spring while one could feel a hint of autumn in the cool air. Various festivals revolved around the seasons in which he took an active part, both in drama and singing. There he learned music, dance, acting, and crafts at which he excelled. The teacher-student relationship was very unique in Santiniketan. If a student aspires to learn many things at Santiniketan, they have the ideal environment in which to do so.

Errababu was himself an intelligent man, mastered in languages along with law and arts. There the subjects were not limited for a student. He could learn science or arts or both, as he chose. Errababu's ambition was to be a lawyer like his father. There at Santiniketan the uniqueness was a blending of the ancient with the modern in India. Santiniketan maintained creative links with the West, with the unity of music, art, and education, with freedom of thought and discussion, secularism, and a sense of Indian-ness, without being narrowly national. All these were in the air to breathe and make one's own. Errababu relished it all as a student.

When Tagore was awarded the Nobel Prize, W. B. Yeats in particular was deeply impressed with his work and wrote an introduction to Gitanjali. The publication of the English edition of Gitanjali in 1911 earned Rabindranath Tagore the Nobel Prize in literature. A collection of over one hundred inspirational poems, Gitanjali covers the breadth of life's experiences, from the quiet pleasure of observing children at play to a man's struggle with his god. These are poems that transcend time and place. With this honour Tagore became famous in both India and the West. In 1915 Tagore was knighted by King George V. However, Tagore renounced his knighthood in protest of the Jallianwala Bagh, or Amritsar Massacre in 1919. In a repudiation letter to the Viceroy, Lord Chelmsford, he wrote:

"The time has come when badges of honour make our shame glaring in the incongruous context of humiliation, and I for my part, wish to stand shorn of all special distinctions, by the side of those of my countrymen who, for their so-called insignificance, are liable to suffer degradation not fit for human beings."

At that time Errababu was studying at Santiniketan and joined the uproar and protests of the massacre, hailing Tagore's renunciation of his knighthood. In a sense, that was his initiation into the idea of freedom for the country.

Errababu attended the funeral procession along with thousands of Tagore's fans.

The Tagore euphoria, European or otherwise, tore up everyone and they hailed the death of a poet.

Gurudev nee Rabindranath Tagore
(From Errababu's album)

Although the world mourned for Tagore, for Errababu it was no less than a personal loss. Errababu mourned as if his own father had died. He adored Gurudev as a child would adore his father. Errabbu became an orphan at a very young age, first losing his mother, and also distanced from his father, who had remarried soon after Errababu's birth and had to release his two young sons to please his second wife. In spite of all the financial comfort his wealthy father had provided him, Errababu felt like an orphan and longed for parental love. His schooling came to a halt, and he was raised by servants. By the time he was an adult his brother had started a motor business at Berhampur. Errababu had no interest in business and he gave the power of attorney to his brother while he ventured to find his own path and obtain more knowledge. He was a thinker and he wanted more out of life. The inherited wealth alone did not satisfy him. He made his own decision and went to Santiniketan to continue his education. By twenty-four he had passed his Matriculation in the first division, and then continued his degree there.

When he went to Santiniketan, Errababu saw a father figure in Gurudev. His stay there was the most memorable and enjoyable one of his life. It had made him tender, loving, and caring. It moulded his character into that of a fine young man, sensitive and artistic. Now with the demise of Gurudev, Errababu felt that everything of his existence had been wiped away, and once again he felt like an orphan. He recalled the ambience of Santiniketan, which had given him security and safety. Now with so many doubts and fears of the future, he returned home after attending Tagore's funeral. There remained a void of parental love that made him withdraw from further pursuits and ambitions he had had. Added to that, the loss of property in the business ran by his older brother collapsed his dreamland. His dreams of going to London and obtaining a study in law like his father came to an abrupt halt. After completing his degree at Santiniketan he returned to an empty nest. But when married with his love, Komalam, together they built their own nest, which gave him some stability in his life. For Errababu, Komalam was his love, his wife, and his inspiration to exist.

On his return from Calcutta, his wife Komalam stood by him like a dear friend. He spent most of his time in music and singing and he developed his own unique way of singing the folk songs, *Enki Paatalu*. Like his Gurudev who had connected with village life through songs and poems, with *Enki Paatalu* Errababu came into close contact with the common village folk. *Enki Paatalu* was written by the famous Telugu poet, Nanduri Venkata Subbarao (1895–1957). *Enki Paatalu* was an anthology of songs on and by a woman called Enki.

Enki and Naidu Bava are the main characters of the *Enki Paatalu*. Enki is a washer-woman who is in deep love with Naidu Bava. The central theme of poems is the love and romance between them.

These songs strangely coincided with his own silent love story and reflected his own feelings for love. He had admired a nine-year-old girl, Komalam, when he first saw her at a wedding. He had been smitten by her beauty and charm. She had looked different from all others at the wedding, even in a simple *Khadi* skirt and a blouse and without any jewellery she had still looked like a princess. She was wearing a bunch of jasmines in her two long plaits. She had stood out from the crowd like a diamond in a crown. She had sung some traditional wedding songs at the function and he had listened to her closely, mesmerised by her voice. Her appearance, her beauty, her long luscious hair and most of all her sweet enchanting smile had enveloped him in a new euphoria; strange feelings had engulfed him and he had failed to understand them. He had been young then and she had been a little and Errababu could not put a name to his admiration or his attraction to her. She had made a deep impression on his mind.

He had never spoken to her but he came to know that she was called Komalam. He had seen her only once, and that had been from a distance, before he had left to study at Santiniketan, but Komalam remained his dream girl. He never told anyone about that admiration. He never dreamt that one day she would become his life partner. But Time plays its own tricks unaware to humans. To fathom the mysteries and magic of Time is beyond human capability, which can only analyse and discuss the ramifications on hindsight. Perhaps Errababu's deep love for an unknown girl was sincere and true. In spite of his father's objection to the marriage, Time brought them together, in the name of an arranged marriage. On his return home from Santiniketan after completing his degree, his eldest sister broached the subject of marriage and told him about the marriage proposal to Komalam. Even without seeing his bride-to-be as per tradition, he agreed to the marriage proposal. On their nuptial night he told Komalam of his silent love for her for over five years. She cherished her husband's love all her life.

The folk songs became Errababu's trademark. He became well known for his singing of *Enki Paatalu* in Town and elsewhere and he was even offered a recording deal. Time heals all wounds both physically and mentally. Gradually Errababu recovered from the loss of his Gurudev and began to concentrate upon the freedom movement at Berhampur.

He found comfort in developing his own private flower garden adjacent to his quarters, which always looked spectacular. He took up photography and often Komalam was his subject. Music, books, and garden became his solace. Often he recalled the good times he had enjoyed at Santiniketan and still revered his Gurudev. His and Komalam's married life rose above the normal life when they were together like true lovers, singing for each other, respecting one another, and cherishing the time they had together. In the freedom struggle and among the constant visitors and domestic work, Komalam and Errababu had few moments together and those few moments became their lifeline in the toils and turbulence of those days.

VISVA-BHARATI

Founder-President
RABINDRANATH TAGORE

Ref. No _____

SANTINIKETAN,
BENGAL, INDIA.

August 17,   193 5

Mr. P. L. Narasimha Rao was a student of the Visva-Bharati. He was active and well behaved during his career here. He is an Andhra coming from a respectable family, knows Telegu, Oriya and understands Bengali and Hindi. He used to take keen interest in various activities of the Asrama and I wish him every success.

(Errababu at Santiniketan)   Librarian & Lecturer,

140

19
Do or Die: 1942

The Quit India Movement was popularly known as 'Do or Die'. The Quit India Movement (*Bharat Chodo Andolan*) was a civil disobedience movement launched in India in August 1942 in response to Mohandas Gandhi's call for '*Satyagraha*' (independence). The All-India Congress Committee proclaimed a mass protest demanding what Gandhi called "an orderly British withdrawal" from India. The call for determined, but passive resistance appears in his call to Do or Die, issued on 8 August at the Gowalia Tank Maidan in Mumbai on year 1942.

The Working Committee, the All India Congress Committee and the four Provincial Congress Committees were declared unlawful associations under the Criminal Law Amendment Act of 1908. The assembly of public meetings were prohibited under rule 56 of the Defence of India Rules. The arrest of Gandhi and the Congress leaders led to mass demonstrations throughout India. Thousands were killed and injured in the wake of the 'Quit India' movement. Strikes were called in many places. The British swiftly suppressed many of these demonstrations by mass detentions; more than 100,000 people were imprisoned.

The 'Quit India' movement, more than anything, united the Indian people against British rule. Although most demonstrations had been suppressed by 1944, upon his release in 1944 Gandhi continued his resistance and went on a 21-day fast. By the end of the Second World War, Britain's place in the world had changed dramatically and the demand for independence could no longer be ignored.

The evening after the Quit India Resolution was passed Gandhiji addressed some memorable words to the Indian people. The very electrifying words were:

"Every one of you should from this moment onwards consider yourself a free man or woman and act as if you are free. I am not going to be satisfied with anything short of complete freedom. We shall do or die. We shall either free India or die in the attempt."

The next morning Gandhiji and all other important Congress leaders were arrested. The Government hoped that this would stifle the movement. But the rulers had not correctly gauged the changed mood of the people. There were spontaneous acts of hartals, strikes, and processions following the arrests. Students played a major role in organising those demonstrations, which at first were mostly non-violent. The police replied with more arrests, *lathi* charges (with heavy iron-bound bamboo sticks), and firing. In widespread areas of the country such as in Bihar, Bombay, the United Provinces, the Central Provinces, and Madras people began attacking symbols of the oppressive foreign government. Post Offices were burned, trains were derailed, and telegraph lines were severed. Factories were closed and the production of war materials was suspended. The 'Do or Die' slogans came to an abrupt halt. Meanwhile famine spread all over the country. The public protested against the Government's mismanagement.

At Berhampur, Ramalingam led the protest march and was duly arrested and sentenced to six months Rigorous Imprisonment at Berhampur jail. At that time he was the elected Chairman of the Municipality. Because their Chairman was in jail, the committee unanimously agreed to elect his wife Pillamma in his place. She became the Chairperson of the Municipality of Berhampur. She was well read and well informed regularly by her husband of the politics of local and central government. That was a turning point for the family. Pillamma who until then resisted taking any active part in the freedom movement followed her husband's path willingly. Komalam encouraged her to accept the position at the municipality and as the second in command Komalam took charge of the family.

As the acting Chairperson of the Municipality, Pillamma, née W. Mahalakshmi, took up her duties seriously, at the same time not forgetting that she was the wife of Pandit Ramalingam. Every day when the *Tonga* from the Town- Hall came to pick her up from home to maintain the honour of her husband, and not to overpower him Pillamma would leave home from the backdoor entrance and walk round to the front of the house, so as not to undermine her husband's status. She observed meticulously the unwritten protocols of the day at all times. She was dutiful at the Town Hall, conducted affairs with diligence, and on her return every day she resumed her domestic duties at home. Komalam stood by her and maintained the family in her absence so as not to cause any imbalance on the home front.

The family was allowed to visit Ramalingam in jail just once a month for five minutes. When Pillamma tried to discuss Municipality matters with him, Panditji merely said, "I have full faith in your capacity do what you think is right and you will never go wrong." The mutual respect and trust they had for each other was solid. Openly in public the couple never disputed with each other but in private Pillamma expressed her views and opinions frankly, while he listened to her with respect as if she was a colleague not a menial to him. But when it came to his work, he always followed his heart and performed his tasks dutifully.

She never said, 'I told you so', neither did he ever mention her mistakes if she ever erred and they both had deep understanding and were duty-bound, one to the country and the other to the family. Ramalingam respected Pillamma as an equal partner in his life, if not a superior. He was always appreciative of Pillamma, who managed the family well in difficult situations and crossed the hurdles single-handed with any complaints to him. She had accepted that her husband was totally committed to the cause he believed in and would sacrifice his life for it. She cherished the few moments she had with him at home.

One evening, Pillamma had to go to a meeting at the Town Hall where they showed a documentary about mosquitoes and their harm. She took her two granddaughters with her for two reasons. To start with a woman from a respectful family never went out on her own after dark without an escort or a family member with her. Even as an acting Chairperson she could not break society's unwritten law. Then Pillamma felt like treating the two girls to a picture show. At the meeting it was decided that a film was to be shown at different villages to educate them about sanitation, health etc. It was a black and white film with narration. The sound and moving pictures captured the attention of viewers. The work was delegated to capable members of the committee.

The two girls were thrilled at the privilege they had over their brothers which seldom happened in the family. By the time they returned home with their grandmother after the meeting it was past nine o'clock in the night. Errababu waited on the main entrance veranda restlessly. As usual, Pillamma and the girls entered the house by the back door. Errababu, the girl's father, was furious. It was hard to say whether he was angrier with his daughters for staying out till late or with Pillamma who, he felt, held Ramalingam's responsibility in his absence. Pillamma was about to tell him that the girls were with her and were safe. But Errababu waited for no explanations and declared that the two girls should go without food for the night and sleep on the floor in the enclosed veranda.

Pillamma was in a dilemma. As the elder of the family she could overrule his decision but considering that Errababu was the son-in-law she decided not to react and make matters worse, and besides, she was also aware that Errababu's anger was like a soap bubble that would burst soon, as it never lasted for long. Silently Pillamma retreated to her room. Komalam made no remark as she knew that it would escalate the matter and moreover she could not go against her husband in front of her children. The mother and the grandmother accepted that Errababu's anger was justified in the circumstances and made no protest on behalf of the two little girls. They had no wish to magnify the situation. The women were certain that all would be alright by the morning.

The two little girls who came home to brag about their special treat to their brothers were stunned to see their father so angry. They even forgot to cry and quickly stepped into the veranda and crouched on the floor, gently shivering. That veranda was clearly visible from Errababu's room. He watched the two terrified girls for a while and shut his bedroom door.

Pillamma sat on the kitchen veranda and felt sorry for her two granddaughters. She waited until everybody was asleep, and then she took some food on a tray for the girls and pushed it under the door without switching on the lights. Then she pushed through a blanket for them and left. The two sisters ate the food in silence and then huddled together under one blanket without any quibbles. Perhaps that was the only time the two sisters were close to each other. Pillamma sat outside the enclosed veranda and kept an eye on the girls. Her all-night vigil did not go unobserved by Errababu.

It was Pillamma who was the disciplinarian at home, yet she loved all the children more than her life. Errababu understood her concern for the two girls sleeping in the dark veranda. He respected Pillamma a lot and if she had chosen to overrule his punishment he would have ceded to it. They had mutual respect for each other. For him Pillamma was like a mother and he would never go against her wishes.

Before dawn Pillamma woke up the girls, got them ready for school, and sent them out of the house.

Errababu came out of his room and no more was said about the previous night's drama. At home even the girl's brothers dared not tease them, which they would have done if the sisters had been told off by Pillamma or their teachers. But when the matter was involved with their father it was a serious matter, and all the children kept their mouths shut. The girls were disappointed that they could not boast to their brothers about their visit to the Town Hall and this made them feel jealous.

But once they were at school they narrated to their friends about the documentary they had seen the night before and never mentioned the punishment they had been given. Fortunately for the girls their older brothers went to a high school and were not in their path. Seeing a real movie with sound was a novelty for many children, and a few envied the sisters' privilege, thanks to their grandmother, and no doubt some of them challenged their mothers as to why could they could not be like Pillamma. For a couple of days the two sisters became the heroines at the school.

The older teenage boys of Errababu became a problem at home as they spent most of their time on their bikes than anywhere else. Errababu came to realise that the two boys were neglecting their studies, and hence confiscated their bikes and put them away in the attic. The two brothers, Veeradhi and Lakshman, were almost like twins, being always together in everything and in every mischief. They were the apple of their Gran's eyes. For her, they could do nothing wrong. All the same, the discipline at home was strict and she also maintained it regularly.

The two brothers felt cheated when their bikes were stored away in the attic. One Sunday when grandfather was in conference with his committee in the hall, the two boys came up with a brilliant idea. Just outside the gates in the street, several bikes stood leaning to the wall. They could not resist the temptation. They knew those meetings of their grandfather ran well into the afternoon, so they decided to take two bikes for a ride and put them back before the meeting was over. They put their plan into action, and almost before they realised it, they cycled all the way to the seaside town of Gopalpur, a good fifteen miles away, and when they returned home there was dead silence at home. The meeting was over.

When it had finished, all the people had been leaving, but the cycles had gone. The owners of the two bikes raised the alarm. The servant boy disclosed the boys' secret. Their father apologised to the owners and promised to return the bikes soon. Some of them remarked about the boy's upbringing and a couple of men said they would grow into thieves one day. Errababu heard it all with immense humiliation.

The whole household came to a standstill when the two brothers returned home triumphantly. The boys were starving and crept into the house from the back door. Gran took them into kitchen. She was about to feed them when Errababu entered the kitchen and dragged the two boys by their scuffs into his room, and drew the curtains. The boys stood still and admitted to having taken the bikes without permission. He told them that their action was nothing less than thieving. Remembering the committee members' remarks about his sons, Errababu lost his temper, picked up a cane, and began to thrash the boys. Pillamma stood outside the room and shivered at the cruelty upon the two young boys, while Komalam sat in the kitchen and wept bitterly. The thrashing continued, but when she could not bear it anymore Pillamma ran to her husband and cried that Errababu was killing his two sons and asked him to help.

As a rule Ramalingam never interfered in such family matters and moreover he felt that Errababu had the right to discipline his own children as he chose. But Pillamma kept crying, and begged her husband to save the two boys. Ramalingam seeing her agony walked to Errababu's room and picked up the two boys by their arms, bringing them out. Errababu said nothing. He never disobeyed his father-in-law. There was a revered relationship between the father-in-law and the son-in-law, and each treated the other with deep respect. In spite of living under the same roof the two men never had any misunderstandings or tiffs. Errababu looked up to his father-in-law as his guru and treated him with reverence, a trait he had learnt at Santiniketan from his Gurudev Tagore. And Ramalingam gave his son-in-law his respectful place in the family.

Once they were out of the punishment room, Gran took the boys into the kitchen and the two women tended the wounds of the wounded boys. In the evening grandfather took the two boys and the bikes to their owners and made them apologise; the matter ended amicably. Those who made snide remarks about the boys and their upbringing never opened their mouths in front of Pandit Ramalingam and forgave the boys. They could not go to school for ten days until their physical wounds were healed. As ever, Jagappa treated them with his special ointment and tonic. Their physical wounds healed faster than their emotional wounds and they never forgot their punishment and humiliation. It kept them distanced from their father. They never touched another bike again and their own bikes rusted in the attic.

20
Refugees: 1943

The nation was in turmoil. **"Keep the nation alive, even at the risk of death,"** declared Gandhiji. His slogan was still 'Do or die'.

The country was caught in the fever of free India and complete freedom, *Purna Swaraj*. Subhas Chandra Bose, another leader, had coined the two words *Jai Hind* (India Forever) as the greeting of Indian nationality, which caught on quickly and people began to greet each other with a *Jai Hind*. In a way, it replaced the English 'Good Morning', and the Indian greeting, '*Namaste*'. The authorities remarked that Indian nationalism was a sign of Indian's backwardness, and even the Indian demand for independence indicated their narrow-mindedness.

There was an acute shortage of food in India, and famine spread all over the country. In response to an urgent request by the Secretary of State of India and Archibald Wavell Viceroy of India to release food stocks for India, Winston Churchill as Prime Minister of that time responded with a telegram to Wavell asking if food was so scarce, why Gandhi hadn't died yet. It appeared that during the famine Churchill was more concerned with the civilians of Greece (who were also suffering from a famine) than the Indians.

Refugees poured in from Burma, the sedate town of Berhampur woke up with a shock. Panditji, who had just returned from jail once again, took charge of the activities. He and his colleagues organised fund-raising for the famine victims. For weeks they went around the town collecting food, clothes, and medicines for famine relief and people gave generously. Immediately Panditji's office became a storage place for the collection. He cleared out of the hall and shifted to a back room which had been mainly a store room with cupboards, one iron safe, old wooden chests, and a spare large four-poster bed. The volunteers sorted out the food and clothes in the hall and distributed them to the famine victims. His office became a refugee-relief centre for months.

Pillamma's house became a safe place for distant relatives from other neighbouring states who arrived in batches seeking help. Their children were weak and hungry. With tremendous care she looked after them. The house was full of people. Children spent a lot of time playing in the garden. The famine victims stayed between six to eight weeks and some for six months. Under Pillamma's care they began to revive from hunger and as soon as they picked up their health they returned to their homes.

The work load on Pillamma and Komalam multiplied day by day yet neither of them ever grumbled. Patience was their virtue. But now the funds were drying up. Already Panditji had donated the farmland to the tillers when the Government tried to confiscate his lands, which in reality belonged to Pillamma since she had inherited them as Streedhanam from her late mother. The police never distinguished about such nitty-gritty or minor matters. For the authorities, with Panditji being the head of the family, everything belonged to him, and therefore they could confiscate anything without any hesitation.

The farmers in the early years of owning the farms showed their gratitude and their loyalty to the family and gave a couple of bags of pulses and rice to them. But soon their good will dwindled away and the product from the farms stopped coming. Now the family had to buy everything from the shops. The burden of feeding the multiple groups of families that came to the house for shelter became difficult. Pillamma's jewellery began to be pawned to feed the families.

There was no relief from the continued freedom struggle. Instead the pressures from everywhere began to tighten their grip on the family. There was no regular income from either of the men, Panditji or Errababu. The conditions at home fell to poverty level. Large brass vessels and some silverware were sold away to maintain the family. It was hard to say how much Panditji was aware of the financial situation at home. Pillamma had neither discussed it with him nor troubled him with the facts.

Subbulu was still at college. She needed to be married, and that was Pillamma's worry. Her son Ramam was at Patna studying medicine. His boarding and lodging had to be provided for. Her grandsons Veeradhi and Lakshman were still at high school and they needed their school fees. Education for girls was free, so the two granddaughters had no expenses. Pillamma constantly worried about pending expenses.

One day the silver dinner plates of the family were sold away and were replaced by brass plates. Pillamma was most upset to sell the dinner plates. They had more sentimental value for her. On each child's first birthday she had bought them a full dinner set with a silver tumbler, dinner plate, sweet bowl, and a soup bowl, and two spoons etched with their names and their date of birth. Each set had its own logo of a goddess or a god carved on the set. From brass plates the family wares were reduced to natural products, mostly found in the garden. Food was served on banana leaves, or *vistrakulu* plates, made of dry leaves. Their servant gathered large dry leaves from the garden and in the afternoons the servant and the women of the house made those leaf-plates by stitching them together with fine needles of a reed. It was an art, and Pillamma and Komalam both excelled in it.

The work load multiplied day by day and the two women had to constantly economise with everything. In the process they could hardly take any rest from dawn to midnight. The mother and daughter worked to keep the family going, while gradually their health began to dwindle.

Sometimes, tribal women brought their wares from the forest to sell in town and they bartered others for rice, lentils, or cloth. Pillamma, who knew how hard it was to look after a family and the hardships of surviving in the forest, often purchased from the tribal women and never let them go empty-handed.

Occasionally the tribal women brought fresh large lotus leaves that they collected from lakes or ponds to sell, a dangerous task since the lakes were infested with crocodiles and hidden whirlpools. Pillamma bought them to use as dinner plates. Children loved to eat in them, because when hot soup was served, on the porous stem at the centre of the lotus leaf, it erupted like a small volcano and the bubbles soared up dramatically and burst out, a delightful sight for them. Pillamma watched the children's excitement and sighed heavily. They were not aware of their declining economic status. She felt helpless to stop the receding fortunes and the destiny gripped her family in its iron hands.

The mother and daughter silently carried on with their duties, and neither of them moaned about their finances. They accepted the situation, while in their minds they longed to get relief from the never-ending freedom struggle to resume a normal life. Komalam stitched all clothes for the family by hand. She was an expert seamstress, but the older boy's trousers and shirts were given to a tailor to be stitched, although she stitched all the underwear by hand.

After the domestic work, the women got themselves busy spinning cotton. The thread was taken to *Khadi Bhandar* where one could exchange the yarn for the same weight of cloth, also paying minor transaction fees. Pillamma's granddaughter Jani loved taking the yarn to *Khadi Bhandar*, which was situated behind the Post Office. She spent a few minutes watching the Post Office at work. She was fascinated by the hustle and bustle there, and everybody looked so important. She watched the people at the counter, the noise of the stamping impressed her, and she decided that she would become a Postmistress one day. She watched heaps of mail being sorted; she also wanted to be a Postwoman. Her wish list increased day by day. The little girl was beginning to explore the world around her.

Komalam took special care of the cows in the barn, and when they returned home after grazing in the forest she fed and washed them with her own hands. Then she fed the cowherd, a young boy of eight, some food and sent him home. Komalam and the servants made cow-dung cakes and dried them on the barn wall. The cow-dung cakes became fuel to heat the water for bathing and washing.

The loyal servants worked with integrity. Pillamma never ate her food until all the servants had eaten theirs first. Her kindness was extended to servants and visitors alike. She felt that the servants worked hard for two meals a day, so it was her duty to see that they were fed well and ate the same food as the family did. She treated them as a part of the family. But there was one old servant who had been in the family for a long time and he was much older than everybody at home. He came with Pillamma as a part of her dowry when she got married and stayed loyal to the family, witnessing their ups and downs. He would wait until Pillamma had her food first and then would have his. Sometimes with extra unexpected guests there wasn't enough food left over for them. Then the women drank a glass of diluted yoghurt called *majjiga* with a pinch of salt and finished their meal and so did the old servant. Because of the cows at home there was never a shortage of milk or milk products.

It became a regular event to pawn or sell away any valuables. Pillamma became used to losing everything. Once it was gone it was gone forever. She became accustomed to the situation and accepted that it was a one-way street, and the lost goods would never return to the family.

The refugee's problem was not solved entirely. The streets of Berhampur were full of beggars or refugees with mutilated bodies. People said they were war victims. Petty thieving became a big problem in town. Relief efforts never seemed to be enough. The more they helped, the more refugees entered the town. Nothing was safe nor was anybody secure. People lived in an unknown terror. One day Errababu caught a thief stealing the clothes from the clothes line. He seized the thief and thrashed him thoroughly, throwing him into the street. Komalam felt sorry for the thief. She packed some food in a banana leaf and handed it to the beggar as he was limping down the street. Perhaps Errababu had seen what his wife did but he understood her kindness and pretended not to have noticed it.

Now the servants kept a close eye on the open gates of the house and everybody felt they had to secure their homes and property and all strangers were watched with suspicion. Even the regular beggars and vendors were also affected. An eerie atmosphere strangled the town. The Government and voluntary organisations tried to sort out the refugee problem.

After six months the town returned to some sort of normality. Most of the refugees were replaced into organised camps all over the country. A few talented people settled down in the town and began to make a decent living among the considerate people of Berhampur who respected honesty and hard work. They stood by them and helped them to settle down in their town.

One among them was an old man who made beautiful leather sandals and slippers. He set up his shop by the roadside on the pavement opposite to the Barracks, which was the main road for offices and other institutions. Panditji purchased a pair of handmade leather slippers from the old man first. Soon others followed him, and as a result the shoemaker became a regular sight across the Barracks ground. Talent was always welcomed anywhere and everywhere by all. Another woman opened a small canteen to sell cold drinks that she made from lemons and berries she had collected from the edge of the forest. Another local vendor placed his ice-cart next to the cold-drink stall and together they made a good living. Soon some small-scale businesses sprouted in town. Berhampur welcomed them all.

Pillamma told her granddaughter Jani, who was a little less serious about everything than her studious sister Santa, how important it was to have a skill to survive. Pillamma always educated Jani with a free spirit and with good examples, which the little girl absorbed easily.

As the hub of famine relief and refugees ceased and the family returned to some normality, suddenly another problem cropped up in the family. It was early in the year of 1946, when Komalam's cousin Bucchi, an ex-soldier, arrived in the darkness on Pillamma's doorstep. Komalam opened the door and found her cousin standing in front of her. As soon as he saw her he burst out crying. She took him into the kitchen and called her mother. Bucchi looked worn and withered in his tatty uniform. His haggard appearance and his weeping eyes spelt disaster to Pillamma. He collapsed in her arms and wept like a child. Ever since their mother had died the two boys, Bucchi and his younger brother, often spent a lot of time with their aunt Pillamma who became their unofficial foster mother and Komalam their beloved cousin sister who loved them a lot and pampered them, treating them as she treated her own brother Ramam.

Pillamma calmed him down first and shut the middle door that led to the front rooms where the men were asleep. Bucchi told her that he had deserted the army and escaped from Burma, as he could not take the torture any longer. Pillamma knew that a deserted soldier could be shot dead and she had to protect him at home. Komalam boiled some water and arranged a bath for her cousin and then they put him in fresh clothes and fed him. The loyal servant of the family, Dhano, assisted the weak Bucchi to climb up to the attic where he slept for the night. Now the two women vowed to keep his presence at home a secret from the rest of the family, because Panditji, if he knew of Bucchi's desertion would personally be handing him over to the police. Pillamma wrote a note to Balaram the teacher, Bucchi's father, and sent it with Jani. Although the girl was very young, Pillamma trusted her to carry important messages. Jani would do anything for her grandmother. Next morning at school the little girl handed over the *chit* to Balaram.

That evening Balaram visited Pillamma as he often did. He met his son Bucchi in the storeroom. They all decided to keep his presence a secret. He couldn't take him to his own house as the police would be searching there first.

Now like a lost kitten Bucchi was moved from one house to another secretly under dark. He stayed at Lingammama's house for a while and the conspiracy of hiding him involved many people. The police never suspected that Panditji would keep a convict in his house but all the other relatives' homes were searched for the missing soldier. Finally they decided that he must have died in the war, and informed his family that he had been lost in action, and they closed his case. After a few months, when the coast was clear Bucchi went to stay with a relative across the border. After a year the freedom of the India also gave Bucchi his personal freedom. Later he returned to Berhampur, took up a job, got married, and raised his children with dignity.

Bucchi always had a special place in Pillamma's heart. As motherless boys he and his brother had often spent their time with her. While at college the second son regularly had eaten his lunch there, along with Subbulu his classmate. Their father Balaram would make a daily visit to the house in the evenings and would stay till late. He had always been close to his Vadina and for him she was like his mother.

Bucchi had been more inclined to adventure than studies like his younger brother. So one fine day he had left home to join the army. But on every leave, he would go to spend his time with Pillamma. He had been pampered by his cousin Komalam. To the annoyance of her own children she would shower more affection on her brother Bucchi.

Bucchi had a style of his own. The first time that he had come home on leave, he had arrived with a little pet monkey which had delighted all the children except Santa. When Santa had been a baby she had been snatched by a monkey after she had been laid on the veranda. That day Komalam as usual had placed her baby Santa on a mat and had let the infant be drenched with the morning sun, a custom often followed by many mothers to strengthen an infant's bones.

Often troops of monkeys invaded the town and would grab anything they could find from people's homes. People dried pulses, poppadums, and other foods in the sun, and so the monkeys feasted on those. Before the troops arrived, householders would safeguard their food and shut their doors. After having laid the baby on the mat, Komalam had gone into the kitchen for some water when a monkey had jumped from the roof and grabbed the baby in its arms, climbing back on to the roof. In horror, the family had tried to coax and threaten the monkey to release the baby.

After hearing the commotion Errababu had arrived on the scene. He stopped the people from trying to frighten the monkey with sticks and told them that the monkey would throw the baby down in anger if they irritated it. He sent them all inside. He fetched the large banana bunch from the storeroom and placed it on the mat where the baby was. The monkey looked at the bait and waited, but after a few seconds it left the baby on the roof and came down to gets the bananas. Meanwhile Dhano climbed the roof from Errababu's annex room and got hold of the baby and brought her down. From that day, Santa had a phobia about monkeys until she grew up. Whenever she did something silly her brothers would tease her saying that she had inherited monkey characters as she had been cared for by a monkey for a few minutes. The brother's prerogative was to tease their sisters and Santa often became their victim while she was growing up.

So Bucchi with his pet monkey had ruled the house. Komalam had attended to all monkey demands and had pampered it as she pampered her brother Bucchi. The monkey climbed on to the attic in the dining hall and found a toy grand piano that was carefully kept there away from the children. It was a good quality piano that came from England and sometimes Komalam played on it as she could play the harmonium. The monkey jumped down from the attic with the piano and began to tinkle it to the delight of all. When he left, Bucchi took the piano with him, to which all the children objected, but Komalam said nothing. Thus the precious piano saved from the children was lost to please a pet monkey. In that household there came strange phenomena: things walked out and were lost in the wide world and never returned home to delight the family.

21
The Six hundred Silver Coins: 1944

On 8 August 1942 the 'Quit India Resolution' was passed at the Bombay session of the All India Congress Committee. In his 'Quit India' speech Gandhi told Indians to follow non-violent civil disobedience. He told the masses to act as an independent nation. His call found support among a large amount of Indians.

Panditji, who led the civil disobedience at Berhampur, was duly arrested and jailed at Berhampur jail. The Government had ordered that mercy was not to be shown on any of the so-called 'criminals', hence Panditji was sentenced to hard labour—one year's Rigorous Imprisonment. Soon after his arrest one of the pro-Panditji police warned Pillamma of the imminent police raid on the house.

At once a 'security brigade' led by Errababu took action. The chain of volunteers of neighbours and friends gathered in the back garden. From there they rallied the vast amount of paperwork to the houses on either side of Panditji's bungalow. It was not an easy task since Panditji's hall contained thousands of books stacked up to the ceiling in cupboards with glass doors. Errababu shifted the relevant paperwork and Gandhian literature and left the general books on the shelves. All the paperwork was stored in gunny bags. The next day the police raided the house and took some books with them. The family was advised that there could be another raid at any time. For fear of the police the gunny bags were left with the neighbours. After one year when Panditji was released he was saddened to see that his papers had been eaten by white ants. But he never shouted at anyone, and took the loss of his work like a hero.

Both Pillamma and Panditji never shed tears at their losses. If an item was pawned or destroyed they took it as part of the sacrifice that they had to endure and the price they had to pay for the freedom cause. They never moaned about the losses nor did they blame each other for the family's mishaps.

By 1944 the Indian struggle for independence was in its final stages, the British government having agreed to independence on the condition that the two contending nationalist groups, the Muslim League and the Congress party, should resolve their differences. Gandhi stood steadfastly against the partition of India but ultimately had to agree, in the hope that internal peace would be achieved after the Muslim demand for separation had been satisfied. Fortunately, at Berhampur Panditji and his colleagues set a superb example for the people. Leaders of all religions stood together and vowed to work in unity, thus curbing any racial or religious problems in the town. They, as a unity, maintained harmony among all the citizens of the town. The Governor of the time extolled the leadership of all the freedom fighters, including Panditji. Panditji always maintained harmony with all the people of the town, so much so that the town's people organised a celebration of his sixtieth birthday on a grand scale that had never been seen before in the town.

Panditji had just been released from custody at the Aga Khan Palace in Poona after four months' imprisonment there, when his co-prisoners had been Kasturiba and many prominent leaders, who had been arrested from the meeting at Bombay. On the day Panditji had been arrested, there stood before the Bombay Provincial Congress Committee office a blackboard, on which was chalked out: "Members of the Working Committee Arrested." The Congress House itself was occupied by policemen. Unceremoniously they were all arrested and sent to different jails. For the detainees at the Aga Khan Palace this was most memorable, since Kasturiba, they said, cared for them in those strict conditions like a mother. After all, she was the wife of Gandhiji, fondly called Pitaji, 'father' of the nation by the public.

The Quit India movement was followed, nonetheless, by large-scale violence directed at railway stations, telegraph offices, government buildings, and other emblems and institutions of colonial rule. There were widespread acts of sabotage, and the Government held Gandhi responsible for these acts of violence, suggesting that they were a deliberate act of Congress policy. Sporadic small-scale violence took place around the country but the British arrested tens of thousands of leaders, and suppressed civil rights, freedom of speech, and freedom of the press. In terms of its immediate objectives Quit India failed because of this heavy-handed suppression, weak coordination, and the lack of a clear-cut programme of action.

However, the British government realised that India was proving ungovernable in the long run, and the post-war question became how to exit gracefully while protecting their lives.

Panditji was released from the Aga Khan Palace after four months. It was said that Gandhiji had insisted that the detainees be freed at once. Panditji returned to a warm welcome by his town.

Those four months were a nightmare to Pillamma. Initially she was not aware of his detention at Poona. One week after his confinement the children came home from school with immense excitement. They told her that a drummer was going through the town talking about their house. In their naivety the grandchildren failed to understand the gravity of the situation. The innocent children's excitement sent shock waves to Pillamma. The drummer was the Town Crier announcing a public auction of Panditji's bungalow the very next day. The news of the public auction had spread throughout the town in minutes.

Panditji's ardent followers came along to assist Pillamma. She had already shut the main gates, and gathered all her family into the storeroom and shut the door. Yet she could hear the Town Crier and the drums. The family huddled together in an unknown fear. The friends came by the back door and talked to Pillamma. She asked Komalam to keep all the children in the storeroom and not to let them go out.

Eventually picking up courage, she met the helpers in the hall to discuss the matter and Errababu stood by her like a son. When Panditji had been arrested at Bombay he had also been fined one thousand rupees. Because he had refused to pay the fine the Government gave orders to confiscate his property and auction it to collect the payment.

Errababu tried to convince the group, which also contained some plain-clothes policemen and off-duty government officials, that the house was in his name and thus it was not Panditji's property to confiscate. The plain-clothes police officer told him that that was a matter to be disputed in the court at a later date, but for now, because Panditji resided in the house the Government had orders to auction it if they would not pay up the one thousand rupees.

Pillamma felt humiliated to know about the auction. So far she had maintained her dignity even in dire situations, but now the forthcoming public auction was draining her life out of her. Fear and humiliation mingled with frustration at the situation and her absolute helplessness made her collapse in front of her friends. They tended her and suggested that she pay the fine before the auction commenced. In those days, one thousand rupees was a great deal of money. She had paid fines a few times, and they had amounted to a few hundred at the most.

Quickly she picked up her courage and smiled feebly. As the eldest member of the family there she had to see to everyone's safety first. She could not and would not let the public auction take place in front of her eyes. Some suggested that they walk round the town and make a collection to save the house, but her pride did not allow her to accept such charity. Immedisettigaru, a businessman and a good friend of the family, offered to loan her the money, which she refused politely. Whatever decision she would take, it was not to lower her husband's prestige. So far she had managed the family on her own strength. She had to safeguard the family's prestige and certainly never go out with a begging bowl.

She went to the iron safe and collected her jewellery and some large silver ornaments, and tied them into an old *dhoti* of Panditji. She gave the bundle to Immedisettigaru, and asked him to sell them away and pay the fine at the office before its evening shutdown. He did not open the bundle—the buyer and the seller had immense faith in each other. He went home and after an hour or so returned with the receipt and handed it to Pillamma, telling her that he had kept the bundle with him and she could have it back whenever she could pay the thousand rupees. The pawning was not new to her. Over the last two decades she had deposited her gold at the bank as security and had borrowed money. Sadly she had never recovered them, and now she realised that the bundles of gold and silver would have the same fate. Neither would ever return home.

For a couple of weeks she kept the children at home in fear of being attacked by the public. Every night she woke up with nightmares of hearing the drums going round the town. When a family is publicly insulted the effects are reflected on the entire family. She recalled the humiliation and rebuffs that she and her in-laws had faced from society the very first time; twenty years before the police had raided their house for illegal literature. Along with her, even her late mother-in-law had been heartbroken. She had had to face the constant ridicule from society for her son's frequent arrests. She had often fretted to see how her family's prestige had been diminishing day by day.

The prestige of the family swayed from one end of the spectrum to the other. Some hailed Panditji as a hero and some ridiculed him for his foolishness in letting his family live like paupers. Those who had measured him by the wealth and pomp he had once enjoyed could never come to terms with his austerity in the name of the freedom struggle. They often ridiculed him, saying that freedom was his madness and in its name he had imprisoned his family in poverty.

Pillamma regularly drifted into the sea of her past whenever she encountered a challenge. Perhaps she took inspiration from her past to swim to the shores of the future. For months she awoke with fright, having heard the drum beats of the Town Crier in her nightmares. Images of the people auctioning their house paraded before her in those nightmares. Gradually she overcame that fear of the drum beats announcing the public auction. Such an auction would have been the pinnacle of all insults that Pillamma could have borne.

Her fear was valid, although it was not physical. Society laughed behind her back and ridiculed the family for the state it had fallen to. Some said that they would rather kill themselves than face society if their own house was about to be auctioned. Although the house was not in fact auctioned, the very fact that it had been publicly announced was in itself a shame to any decent family. Pillamma wondered where she stood in the scale of decency. She had learnt to tolerate such rebuffs from people who wanted her to break down and weep bitterly in front of them due to her fate—but she never did. In her slim body she had a moral strength of Himalayan heights.

Fortunately the family had as many good friends and supporters as it had critics. Pillamma had learnt to endure her life. She sighed with relief that her children were safe. When Panditji returned after his release the town welcomed him heartily.

The town had organised an event to honour Panditji by celebrating his sixtieth birthday on a grand scale. The term *shasti* in numerology denotes 'sixty' and *purti* means 'completed'. In an individual's life, the completion of sixty years is referred to as *Shastipurti*. This term is derived from Sanskrit. The sixtieth year in everyone's life is a significant milestone.

The sages and the *Rishis* of lore have acknowledged the sanctity of the sixtieth year in one's life and have drawn out elaborate rituals to mark this special event. They look upon it as a 'rebirth' and have suggested the repetition of the rituals performed at one's birth. Hence the celebration at this point of life is a sacred part of the hallowed Vedic culture. The rituals in the former go by the norms prescribed in the *shastras*, while the latter is purely conventional in nature. As per Vedic scripture, a Human Life lasts for 120 Years. Completion of sixty years means completing half of our full life. Sanskrit years also have a sixty-year cycle and each year has a name. In this function, *poojas, japa,* and *homams* are carried out to numerous gods at home. Although Panditji was not in favour of such elaborate celebrations, he consented to them because his beloved daughter Komalam had arranged them. After the traditional celebrations a feast was arranged for all.

The evening was most memorable to everyone. In the open car, Panditji and Pillamma were paraded through the town, led by the local band party and street dancers. It was like a gala function. On his request the procession stopped by his elder sister's house, opposite to the Satyanarayana Temple. The house was unique, and it was three-quarters of a circular building with an enclosed veranda and a parapet wall. Six large pillars stood, appearing to be holding the ceiling of the veranda. Children loved to play hide and seek there. Inside, the house was large with high ceilings. Perhaps the crossroads were built around the house when the town expanded, since the old building was never altered or touched by the town planners. Panditji's eldest sister was known as Pedatta to all and she was the only other surviving member of Panditji's family. As per tradition, the couple went in and took the elderly aunt's blessings. She was chuffed to see that her brother had paid his due respect to her. She gave the couple a coconut and some sweets and blessed them. Then the procession proceeded forward and arrived at the Samajam Hall, which was already decorated with fresh flower garlands and strings of lights. It was like *Diwali,* the festival of lights in the town. Young and old packed the hall and the verandas.

With a formal welcome the chief guest opened the proceedings. One by one people paid their homage to Panditji, reading the *prasansa patralu,* the testimonials. Then each of them garlanded Panditji and gave a bouquet to his wife.

There was some entertainment of dance and song which included national songs of freedom. Then some skits were enacted by some well-known artists.

Finally the organiser brought in two silver trays covered in *Khadi* cloth. The organiser presented them to Panditji. There were three hundred silver coins in each tray together to mark six hundred—to celebrate his sixtieth birthday. The silver sovereigns glistened in the lights tempting the viewers. That large amount could have helped the family of Panditji to recover from their on-going poverty.

Panditji stood up and thanked the people for their generosity and declared his intention for the gift. Some watched him in horror as he refused to take the silver coins home, while others felt certain that Panditji considered the gift to be a charity. Panditji had donated half of it, three hundred silver sovereigns along with the silver tray, to the Principal of Khallikote College, for creating two annual merit awards for the best student in mathematics—Panditji had been a mathematics professor at the college, after all—and in alternative years for the best student in Telugu and Oriya. He donated the other half of the money to the Andhra Bhasabhi Vardhini Samajam of the town, where cultural events took place regularly.

(It is noteworthy that after many years in 1962 a young Intermediate student U. Mahalakshmi won the coveted prize for Telugu. Later after completing her medicine Dr U. Mahalakshmi became the wife of Panditji's second grandson Lakshman.)

The function concluded on a high note. After the meeting the family returned home carrying plenty of testimonials dedicated to Panditji and baskets of garlands.

The next morning the family woke up to face another day of poverty. Pillamma pawned some more of her gold jewellery to feed the umpteen people who came over to congratulate Panditji. Errababu had all the testimonials framed and displayed them on the walls of the hall.

Pillamma wanted to challenge her husband about giving away the financial gifts he had received but she did not actually broach the topic, as it was Panditji's decision and she was certain that he had his own reason for it. He understood her silence and gave his explanation to her. The couple had a unique skill of reading each other's mind easily. Panditji told her that the gift of six hundred sovereigns was the collective money of the people of the town and it was only fair that it be used for the betterment of the town. It was never theirs to keep. She agreed with him in tears.

"Sorry, my Nidhi. I never meant to hurt you," he said, holding her hands. He addressed her as *Nidhi* (meaning treasure) only when he was emotionally charged.

"No sir, these are the tears of joy. I only hope people will appreciate all you do and did for the town. People's memories tend to be short."

"My dear, Bhagavat Gita teaches us to do our duty. In Mahabharata Lord Krishna advices Arjuna to do his duty without expecting rewards. Hinduism attaches a lot of importance to Karma or Duty. The *sloka* from Bhagavad-Gita reads:

"Karmanye Vadhi Karasthe Maa Phaleshu Kadachana,

"Maa Karmaphal Hetur Bhurma, Te Sanghastva Akarmani.'

"'Expecting results creates unwanted bondage and disturbances in mind. Thinking about the fruits of our hard work restricts our actions and we may not always put our best to attain the results.' It does not mean you need not do your duty to escape from these bondages. But the foremost thing is to put our best effort possible to do our duties. Results, fruits of our hard work would follow. Leave the rest to God. We should not hold ourselves the reason for the results we attain. We should only concentrate on our duty at our hand."

"True sir, you are indeed a Karma-Yogi."

"Work as if everything depends on you, pray as if everything depended on God."

Pillamma felt humbled by his humbleness and put her head down. She regretted saying that the public might forget Panditji the devoted well-wisher of the town of Berhampur.

"Another point to be happy in life is to never expect gratitude from others whether it is your children, siblings, friends or life partner."

"Sir, don't include me in that list, I'm always with you by you and for you and I am not complete without you. I shall remain in your shadow and I feel safe in your shade."

"My Nidhi, I'm so fortunate to have your support. We have to do what is right and not worry about anything else. Let history take its own course. Neither can we stop it nor can we direct it. While we are alive we must perform our duty with our entire soul and heart, and I'm so glad you are with me."

Pillamma was delighted that he addressed her as Nidhi, as he used to address her when they first got married. She was pleased that somewhere in the ocean of freedom their love remained secure and its memories revived her dwindling spirits once again. She smiled sweetly as if to say, I understand you.

After that she never raised the topic of the six hundred silver sovereigns again. This was given by the public and it was returned to the public in a different form and that was that!

Perhaps this was the first motto of freedom: By the people and for the people!

Ramalingam & Siblings, 1944

Ramalingam with family, 1944

22
Tirupati Trip: 1945

Now, in 1945, Pillamma told Panditji that she had taken a solemn oath to God that she would visit Tirupati when Ramam joined the medical college. For her his education had always been a challenge starting from his pre-school days. As he was nearly completing his medicine course she expressed her desire to visit Tirupati, the Holy Place of Hindus in South India. Once he agreed to her travel she suggested that they perform their only son's *upanayanam* (thread ceremony) at Tirupati. Panditji as a reformer did not perform such religious rituals, but to honour the promise he had given his wife Pillamma almost two decades before, to have full freedom to make all decisions about their children, he agreed to accompany her to the holy place, Tirupati. At the same time he informed her that he did not want his son to carry out his death anniversary annually as he had done for his father.

Panditji was against all those rituals but had performed an anniversary ritual known as *taddinalu* for the peace of his parent's soul as his father expected of him. He told his own son that he had no expectations and he should not perform any taddinalu for him when he was gone. In a way, he released his son from all the traditional bondages a Hindu son was obliged to perform. As per traditions no son can execute any such ritual until he has had his *upanayanam*. Pillamma was more liberal with her thoughts. She wanted her son to make up his own mind regarding honouring the ancient traditional rituals. She left the choice for her intelligent son to make up his own mind when the time arrived. Right now her only desire was to perform all the Brahmin rituals to her only son, one of which was the 'thread' ceremony.

The family was excited about their trip to Tirupati. Errababu also wanted to perform his eldest son Veeradhi's *upanayanam* along with Ramam's. The children were thrilled that they would be going on a train for the first time. Until then none of the family had been out on a holiday. The political, economic, and family conditions were such they could not go anywhere, whereas their house was like an open house for endless guests. Strangely enough none of those guests ever invited them back to their own abodes. The strange phenomenon that ruled the family about their pawned items also applied to the guests—it remained a one-way system. They came and enjoyed the hospitality and then left. Added to that they imposed themselves on the family and invariably demanded regal treatment and expected the family to pay for their expenses during their stay.

Often the older grandsons had to go and receive them from the railway station, which they obliged in doing dutifully. When they could not go to receive their guests they took the trouble to arrive at home in a Tonga and demanded that Pillamma pay the fare for it, which she did with an apology for not being able to receive them. Now the teenage grandchildren resented the guests' audacity but Pillamma calmed them down and reminded them that the guests were like gods and that they should respect them. The boys were outraged; her words did not appeal to them. They were growing up and began to notice the atrocities carried on in the name of traditions, and resented them.

Gradually they began to show the trends of free thinking. Although Pillamma envisaged the young boy's anger, she felt obliged to maintain the same standard of hospitality to all the guests whether invited or not, as her father-in-law did in his heyday, three decades before. She had to safeguard her father-in-law's prestige in those hard times and guests often took advantage of her kindness. She was entangled in her own mesh of prestige versus poverty.

Many a time she and Komalam went without food to feed the unexpected guests. In spite of all her generosity people often complained that they had not been treated as they deserved, and complained about the traditional gifts and new clothes that the hostess gave them as a farewell gift. None of them ever brought any gifts to the family—it was all take, take, and take. The hospitality and the generosity was always moved down a one-way road, whereas very few guests appreciated Pillamma or felt sorry for the predicaments that Pillamma fell into.

The children's joy knew no bounds, and for the first time they would all be going in a train. The news of their trip to Tirupati reached every nook and cranny of the town and the children talked endlessly about the intended family trip. For four weeks their trip was the hot news in town. Every Hindu would love to visit the Holy Shrine of Tirupati at least once in their life time.

As customary, women went to Pillamma with their promised offerings to the God Venkateswara at Tirupati and requested her to deposit them at the gigantic urn in the Temple. All those packages of money, gold, hair, or anything else that they vowed to the god were carefully packed away in the trunks. People who could not travel to Tirupati often sent their vowed item with any pilgrim going to Tirupati.

Hair remained an important promised item to the god at Tirupati. It could be the first hair of a baby, or the hair of a devotee. Some offered their hair at Tirupati as a penance. Then, and even now, sacrificing hair at Tirupati remained a major event. Many devotees have their head tonsured as an offer. The daily amount of hair collected is over a ton. Even in modern India, the hair thus gathered is sold by the Temple organisation a few times a year by public auction to international buyers for use as hair extensions, or for wigs and in cosmetics, bringing over $6 million to the Temple's treasury.

The custom of tonsure is a speciality of this Temple. Many devotees go there with the intention of making a votive offering of their hair to the Lord. Performing tonsure at this place is considered praiseworthy and believed to confer great merit. Not only the men execute this tonsure but also women, married as well as unmarried, and children offer their hair by getting *Mundana* conducted here.

As Tirupati is a holy place, people prefer to conduct weddings and thread ceremonies in the presence of God. Errababu, an excellent organiser, made all the arrangements personally for the intended family trip; tickets for fifteen people including three servants were purchased well in advance. The trip was for three weeks. The family planned to visit all the holy places around Madras and also to visit the Presidency College where Ramalingam had studied. A friend of Ramalingam's made all the arrangements for their stay at Madras. The excited children broadcast the details of their holiday to one and all. The preparations continued at full speed for a whole month, and women made lots of food and snacks for the journey. Cooking utensils and kerosene stoves were packed in gunny bags. Just two days before their departure, Ramam the medic arrived from Patna.

Finally the day of their departure had come. One old servant stayed behind to look after the house. All the items necessary for the trip were packed in three large trunks. Three *Tongas* waited on the doorstep to take the family to the station. Luggage was loaded into the *Tongas*. Lots of well-wishers stood outside the gates to bid them farewell and wish them a safe journey. Even the reporters were there to record the family event as Panditji had never had a family holiday before. Errababu went out to take his elder sister's blessings and returned with a glum face. Without saying a word he removed his luggage from the Tonga and went indoors.

The bewildered Pillamma and Komalam ran after him, not knowing why he had removed his luggage. As the excited children had already climbed into the *Tongas*, the puzzled public stood around watching Errababu remove his luggage. Very calmly Errababu announced to the worried women that he wouldn't be able to go to Tirupati. After a great deal of coaxing, he told them that a priest had told his elder sister that the timing was not auspicious and if they were to get Veeradhi's thread ceremony done at that time that would bring disaster to the father of the boy and he could die. As it was an inauspicious time for the father and the son, and his sister had asked him to cancel his trip to Tirupati.

The devastated family tried to convince him that this was not true. Pillamma and the elders of the town tried to convince Errababu that the time for the journey and the ceremony was the most auspicious of the whole year. Errababu was adamant and wouldn't budge. Pillamma requested him to accompany the family but not to conduct his son's *upanayanam*. Errababu could never go against his elder sister's advice and totally rejected the offer. He did not stop Komalam going, but as his wife she was obliged to follow his rules, so the distraught Komalam went out and took the children out of the *Tongas* while they protested vehemently and wailed aloud. Pillamma, Panditji, and her two children Ramam and Subbulu got into the Tongas. Panditji did not interfere in the matter. He remained a silent witness. Amidst crying and yelling the deflated party proceeded forward. Pillamma felt helpless, but she grabbed her third grandchild Devi Kumar and climbed into the Tonga. Komalam stood on the veranda with her toddler Sunder and watched the Tongas go. She waited until they were out of sight and then went inside. In tears the reduced party reached the railway station and travelled to Tirupati.

The grandchildren of Pillamma cried for days for missing the chance to travel in the train and missing the well-planned family trip but Komalam never challenged her husband about his change of mind. She understood his predicament. His duty was to obey his elder sister, who often interfered in their family matters and imposed her authority on her youngest brother, taking a vicarious satisfaction when she ruined his plans. But the people of the town talked ill of the woman who had spoiled the family trip of her brother and they remembered how she had asked her brother not to help Pillamma staying with her at Beerakaveedhi when Panditji was in jail.

For days the resident astrologers of the town argued among themselves about the auspicious time, although the priest who was supposed to have predicted the death of Errababu if he were to perform his son's thread ceremony never came forward. As nobody could trace the priest, people began to gossip that it had all been a hoax and Errababu's sister had deliberately spoiled the family trip at the last possible minute. One of them demanded to know why she didn't tell her brother Errababu about the inauspicious time before they had made all the plans for the trip. She gave no explanation and avoided going into public, and likewise the women boycotted her and stopped inviting her for their social functions.

Whatever it was, the only family trip Pillamma had ever planned was ruined by superstition and speculation, without any evidence. After three weeks Pillamma and the group returned home, but nobody ever mentioned the past event. Once again Panditji returned to his work, and Komalam and Pillamma maintained the peace of the family without taunting Errababu. Whatever he felt he never let anybody know, but the cancellation of the trip remained a hot topic and a subject for gossip in the town for months to come.

The domestic situation remained the same. That Sunday, while the men were out, a strange man appeared on the veranda. He was a big man with a long beard and thick curly tousled hair that reached his waist. He wore a red wrap around his head. He wore red sandals with bells on it. He had a stern face with blaring red eyes. He carried a large shoulder bag made of multi-coloured cloth. He looked like a beggar but he acted as if he owned the house. The servant tried to stop him but the stranger pushed him aside and reached the top of the veranda and stood there looking around. The frightened servant ran inside yelling with fear.

Lakshman, who was at home, heard his cries and came out to see what the commotion was. As soon as the stranger saw the teenage boy he took out some ash and threw it in his face. But as if he had anticipated such an attack, Lakshman stepped aside and escaped the ashes. The stranger tried to push him aside and enter the house. Lakshman stopped him by standing in front of him with outstretched arms. His boldness enraged the stranger and he began shouting at him, swearing and cursing, with which Lakshman stared back into his face boldly. Seeing that there was a strong young man in front of him, the stranger began to recite some mantras in a loud voice and asked him to give alms. Lakshman asked him to leave the premises at once.

Meanwhile the two women, Pillamma and Komalam, arrived at the scene. Seeing the angry stranger, Komalam asked Lakshman to go inside. She was afraid to cross the angry fakir who had appeared on their doorstep since she had heard that such persons could curse and ruin the family. As they were just recovering from the trauma of a failed family holiday she was not ready to take anymore knockouts. She apologised to the stranger for her naïve son's ill behaviour and went inside to get some money. But Lakshman did not wait for his mother's return; he pushed away the stranger and then by holding his long garment dragged him down the steps to the gate.

The enraged stranger wanted to retaliate, but noticed that a large crowd had gathered by the gates. For a few minutes he stood there huffing and heaving heavily. Lakshman was about to shut the gates when the stranger took out a fistful of red powder and threw it in the boy's face, cursing that he would die within twenty-four hours, spitting blood, and then he walked away with long steps.

The stunned crowd stood there in fear and awe at the young boy. Some felt he should not have angered the *fakir* but a few extolled his bravery. Komalam had witnessed the curse and was trembling in fear. The crowd by the gates stood debating the validity of the beggar, whether he was a real or a fake *fakir,* perhaps entering the house to rob it. The crowd narrated their own experiences with fake *fakirs* and a few told the crowd how the curses of a *fakir* come true and they suggested that the young boy should go and ask for the *fakir*'s forgiveness and serve him for a month like a true disciple. They were busy telling each other their own stories, but the frightened Komalam dragged Lakshman into the house.

Within minutes some well-wishers and some curious people arrived at the house to give their support to the cursed family. Opinions about the curse echoed throughout the house. Pillamma and Komalam took Lakshman into the kitchen and said prayers to the gods in their temple. Then they told the boy not to go anywhere. They kept him in the back veranda to keep a watch on him. All night the mother, the grandmother, and a few good family friends sat around Lakshman's bed and prayed all night. They kept their vigil on him until the next evening. Lakshman came out of this ordeal like a hero. After two days, when the men returned home from a congress meeting they had been attending, the news of the fake *fakir* and the curse was hidden from them. But it did reach them from the public in small episodes. Errababu felt proud of his brave son and Panditji never expressed any views on the matter. Yet most people felt that the young boy shouldn't have upset the *fakir.*

Now after their recent popularity Lakshman and his brother Veeradhi were up to their tricks again. During the summer holidays one Monday afternoon they both went for a swim without telling anyone at home. Komalam was waiting for the boys to return home for lunch. Instead after two hours some dhobis the washer men, carried the two boys on a makeshift stretcher like a bundle of the washing they carried and they dumped them on the veranda. The boys were unconscious. The washer men told Komalam that they had seen the boys drowning in the large tank where they washed clothes and had pulled them out. Immediately Jagappa was fetched to recover the boys. After an hour the boys regained their consciousness. Fortunately for them their father Errababu was not at home, otherwise they would have been punished severely for their adventure.

The summer holidays became long and drab for all the children at home, although the two brothers were never short of ideas. They came up with an idea to make money staying at home. Their sister Jani and all her friends were recruited to collect discarded negative film clips from outside the tent cinema, which they obeyed dutifully; the little children were eager to please the 'hero' and his brother. After a week the brothers put on a show called *Dammidi* for all the children in the neighbourhood and charged one *dammidi*, the smallest denomination of a rupee coin for each. They set up their cinema in the store room away from their father's eyes. They built a periscope and projected still film clips on to the white wall. The film stills had no connection to any story, but Veeradhi with his talent in music made up songs to suit the still and sang to suit each slide, and Lakshman, the entrepreneur excelling in making up stories, filled the story line for the children. Pillamma wanted the boys not to charge the children but she could not stop them. So to compensate for their greed as she saw it, at every show she gave all the children free snacks which they relished.

Komalam was glad that the boys were at home and did not get themselves into any more trouble. Lakshman never revealed how much money he made that summer. But the child volunteers kept collecting the discarded film clips regularly for a free ticket to the show. Lakshman, the budding entrepreneur, always came up with little schemes. Sometimes secretly he loaned money to people around him and charged a small interest, whereas his partner brother Veeradhi kept himself out of such schemes and became involved in a local drama group.

After a couple of months, a *Kabuliwala* (a vendor from Kabul) appeared on their doorstep. He was a well-built man of six and a half feet. He had a short beard and wore a white turban. His long, flowing robe reached the floor. He carried a dagger on his belt. He wore sandals on his feet. He carried six or seven cotton satchels on his back and one long sling bag on his right shoulder. In an eerie manner he looked like a prince in disguise. When he saw the young boy, Devi Kumar, playing on the veranda he burst out crying. Komalam came out from the house and asked the stranger if her naughty son had hurt him, as Devi Kumar often threw anything in his hand at a person if he was angry. All the stranger said was, "My son, my son!" pointing to the young boy. Komalam quickly grabbed her son and took him inside. After the recent episode with the fake *fakir,* Komalam was not prepared to take any chances when her children were concerned; she guarded them at all times when they were at home. She became distrustful of any stranger in town. The bewildered *Kabuliwala* stood there with tears in his eyes.

Recently some *Kabuliwala* had come to the town to trade with the locals. They bought dry fruit like almonds, sultanas, raisins, and pistachios from Kabul to Indian towns and cities. The men from Kabul, leaving their families behind came to India to earn a living as dried-fruit vendors. They were profoundly homesick. They went from place to place and stayed in the country until they had sold all their dry fruit and had made good money. Dry fruit was very expensive and was not in the reach of a commoner; only the very rich could buy it. Then they would return home to Kabul with lots of goods for their families.

At Berhampur two *Kabuliwalas* had arrived and they had received the town's permission to trade. The men from Kabul were known for their honesty and bravery. Besides trading in the dry fruit they often loaned money to people, but if their loan was not paid back in time they were prepared to be violent.

People were scared of the dagger that they carried on their belt in full view. Some wondered what other weapons they had hidden under their long robes. But the men from Kabul were also known for their kindness. When they saw the poor they helped them without hesitation. Often they took shelter with the poor in their small huts outside the town.

Komalam went in and told her husband about a stranger on their doorstep who was eyeing Devi Kumar. She was afraid that he might be a child-snatcher. For a while rumours spread around town that a group of child-snatchers were lurking in and about the town. They snatched children, maimed them, and made them into beggars or sometimes sold the children to big cities.

Errababu went out and saw the *Kabuliwala*. Errababu talked to the man for a while in Urdu. The *Kabuliwala* as a Pashto speaker could understand Urdu. Then he invited him to step on to veranda and gave him some water which he drank with gratitude. They spoke for another few minutes like old friends and the *Kabuliwala* left smiling.

Errababu told Komalam that he was not a child-snatcher but a good man from Kabul. He had left his family behind and had come there to make money. His son was the same age of five as Devi Kumar. He was feeling homesick, so Errababu gave him permission to come and see his son without any hesitation. Komalam was not convinced but obeyed her husband. Errababu told her that he had given the *Kabuliwala* a photo of Devi Kumar.

Over the next four months the *Kabuliwala* visited their house two or three times a week. Komalam made sure that her son was not alone when the *Kabuliwala* came and she asked the servant to stay with her son. The man from the Kabul and the five-year-old Devi Kumar talked a lot in their own lingos; neither of them understood the other. *Kabuliwala* loved to hear the bonny boy talk; waving his hands around as if he was narrating a heroic tale while the man watched the boy and laughed. He would sit on the steps and watched the boy with tears in his eyes but never touched him. When he handed over some fruit the servant did not allow the boy to accept. Over a couple of months, Komalam warmed up to the *Kabuliwala*, and offered him some refreshments as if he was a guest, but he drank only water from her hands and never ate any food.

By the end of the year, he came to bid farewell to the family as he was returning home for the *Eid* festival. Komalam went in and fetched a small parcel and gave it to him. He opened it and found a *Khadi* shirt embroidered on the collar and cuffs. Its single front pocket was embroidered 'ADIL' in English letters, the name of the *Kabuliwala*'s son. He was touched by her kindness and burst out crying. He knelt down and prayed to Allah and then touched Komalam's feet with reverence. He hugged his adopted son, as he called Devi Kumar, and placed a large bag of dry fruit of almonds and pistachios in his hand, and then left abruptly. The family never saw him again. The *Kabuliwala* had come from a faraway place, had made his mark on the family, and left leaving a cool breeze of pleasant memories in their hearts.

Devi Kumar, 1942
(Photo given to the Kabuliwala)

23

A Memorable Year: 1946

20th January – Gandhi's last visit to Berhampur

It was a momentous day for the whole town.

Gandhiji was stopping at Berhampur. The whole town marched towards the railway station by midnight, some holding candles and some with lanterns, many carrying garlands for Mahatma Gandhi. The march was colourful and exciting and the national songs echoed in that dark night, various bands playing the popular songs to delight the parade. It was as if they were all going to attend a wedding. Slowly they marched towards the railway station. There was joy, there was eagerness, there was excitement, and there was anxiousness. None of them wanted to miss the chance of seeing the great man, Gandhiji, whom they called by various names: *Bapu* (father), *Mahatma* (the great soul), and *Jaati-Pita* (father of the nation) while some revered him as God. Everybody gathered at the station well in good time.

There was still time for the train to arrive. The atmosphere at the station platform was like a fete or an open bazaar, maybe like a festival. People talked insistently about the man they were about to meet. The train arrived in the early hours of the morning. On the platform a dais was erected for Gandhiji. Panditji and the town leaders gathered by the dais and discussed politics seriously, whereas the crowd were cheerful and noisy. The children who had no knowledge of Gandhiji wondered who this magic man was and what magic he was going to perform. They were more thrilled for being able to wander about the town in the middle of the night, and they felt grown up and having equal status like the adults to attend the gathering. The police presence was visible but they mingled with the crowds and joined their celebrations.

The train arrived exactly at 1.45 in the morning on the platform. As soon as the train stopped at the station the crowd edged forward to witness the Holy Man, to see the saviour of the country and to hear him address them. The organiser stood aside as Gandhiji descended from a third-class compartment onto the platform. At once there reigned an instant silence. Gandhiji walked up to the dais and sat down in his usual manner with folded legs. He sat there holding his two palms together as if he were praying. His assistants said that Gandhiji was on his 'silent' day.

It was a great disappointment to all. For a few seconds the silence echoed on the platform. Suddenly Gandhiji's attendant started the favourite prayer song and the crowd joined him. The crowd sang the prayer song in unison: '*Eswar Allah tero naam sabko sammati dey bhagvan*,' meaning 'God is one, call him Eswar or Allah—they're all your names, bless them all.' Then they sang national songs one after another, for a good hour. The singing continued while

Mahatma sat still in his prayer position with his eyes shut. Then Gandhiji stood up and bowed to the crowd and descended from the dais and was taken to the guesthouse by the station. The enchanted crowd dispersed in an orderly manner and in complete silence. The charm of that majestic man empowered young and old alike. They returned home carrying their experience dearly in their hearts.

Gandhiji had a charisma that was unique to him. No wonder even the sahibs were blown over by him. A simple man with simple attire had simply taken the whole nation by his presence alone. He was truly born as God's messenger. Many homes kept his photo in their temples, where they worshipped daily. That night's experience of meeting *Bapuji* (the father), *Jaati-Pita* (the father of the nation) and the *Mahatma* (the great soul) was stamped in every person's heart forever. It became their life's best memory and they talked about *Mahatma* for years to come.

The next day Gandhiji addressed the public at Barracks' grounds. Children and adults listened to him with enthusiasm. He once again inspired the public with his speeches of *Purna Swaraj* and his devotion to the unity of Indians, forgetting their caste or creed. He had inspired the new generation that was just budding into the idea of freedom. The police stood around in great strength but the orderly crowd gave them no reason to react. Fortunately there were no arrests that evening.

1946 was also a memorable year for the citizens of Berhampur. The famous singer, Surya Kumari, visited the town to give her concert. She became famous singing national songs and her records were sold out as soon as they were produced. She sang about Bharatmata, Gandhiji, national flag, and more inspiring songs, and especially about 'Telugu Talli', which later was adapted as the state song for Andhra Pradesh and was popular with all Telugu-speaking citizens. Her songs became popular in towns and villages, her records were played at weddings and festivals, and even the beggars sang them on their begging rounds. Surya Kumari's open concert was arranged at Desbehra Street by a wealthy man to commemorate his daughter's wedding.

The open stage was erected in the middle of the street and people gathered with enthusiasm. The verandas of surrounding houses and the seats in front of the stage were all occupied. Meeting such an eminent singer was an occasion nobody wanted to miss. The whole street was lit with paraffin lights and they dazzled the public. The elite settled on the chairs and others sat on the rugs that were spread on the floor.

Many women sat down on the verandas of the houses in the street. Pillamma, Komalam, and the girls sat on a friend's veranda opposite the stage. The beautiful singer, who had won the 'Miss India' title once, arrived on time, climbed onto the stage, and bowed to the public. The concert opened in full swing. At first she sang the popular national songs, followed by some classical ones. She received several requests to sing some more of people's favourite songs, which she obliged gracefully and charmed them with her melodious voice.

While the concert was in full swing, suddenly there was commotion in the crowd, and the concert came to an abrupt end. Somebody had returned from the railway station with the latest newspaper that had the results of the matriculation exams. The newspaper was published from Madras and the copies were sent to the agent at Berhampur daily. People gathered around him, wanting to know if their numbers were there or not.

Komalam noticed one woman leave the concert and run home crying and wailing loudly. Komalam ran after her and found out that the woman's daughter had committed suicide as she had failed her matriculation exam. Pillamma took the children home.

Over the next few days strong debates about girl's education became a hot topic in town. All those who were traditionally inclined revelled on the news condemned mothers who sent their girls to school instead of getting them married at a young age. This topic of girl's education took a new turn and its debate was never ending. The tragedy of the girl affected many families, and as a result few of them discontinued their daughter's education and kept them at home. People also discussed the pressures of exams. On the whole, the complete education system—especially girl's education—came into scrutiny.

Panditji and his colleagues held meetings and tried to convince the public about the values of education, whereas Pillamma and some of the female freedom fighters went from house to house convincing and assuring the mothers not to discontinue their daughter's education. Pillamma managed to impress on some of them the values of education and how it was most important to the girls as it would give them a chance to stand on their own two feet in times of need and would be their *streedhanam*. She told the women the virtues of education which would help them to educate their own children, as a mother is a child's first guru. To a great extent the group were successful but a few women were adamant and refused to change their minds about their decisions and removed their daughters from schools and college and kept them at home.

Pillamma stood by the bereaved mother and supported her. Whereas some women shamelessly threw mud on the character of the dead young girl instead of supporting the bereaved mother, Panditji put a stop to it, vouching for the dead girl's impeccable character. He also told parents not to punish children if they failed their exams. Knowledge is important but life is more precious than a certificate, and once again he reiterated the values of education.

Pillamma supported and encouraged the widow who had been educating her three girls until now by her hard work, sewing clothes for others, and never asking for anybody's help. Now the devastated woman withdrew her other two daughters from schools and wanted to leave the town. Pillamma coaxed her into allowing her other two girls to continue their schooling. In life there are more critics than helpers, but for a life to thrive all it needs is one helping hand. The town's people gave that helping hand to the bereaved girl's sisters. Over the next few months wedding mania hit the town and young girls left schools and became brides.

That year ended on a high note for the town with the celebrations of Goddess Thakurani, *Ammavari Sambaralu*, now known as the famous *Thakurani Yatra*. The town welcomed the biannual festival that lasted about a month. This carnival drew thousands of people in and around Berhampur. During this festival the reigning deity of the city goddess, Budhi Thakurani, travels to her temporary abode at Desibehera Street, where she stays for 24 days. This journey of the deity is thought to be her biennial journey to her parental abode from her main temple in the city. During this time the atmosphere is like a carnival.

As per tradition, Desibehra, the main organiser of the festival and known as the "father" of the deity, along with his wife goes to the Ammavari Temple at midnight in a grand procession to invite the goddess home. After performing rituals in the temple, they return with a garland of flowers in a basket and keep the same in a temporary thatched temple constructed for the purpose in front of the house of Desibehra. The goddess will take rest for two days. From the third day of the commencement of the ceremony, the garland will be kept inside a decorated *ghata* (earthen pot) and every evening the goddess will go on her rounds visiting different parts of the city, known as *ghata parikrama*, amid religious fanfare. The main ghata is carried by the wife of Desibehra on her head. Eight other women take position behind her with their pots on their heads. It is considered an honour to carry ghata in the procession. Several others follow with their own ghata, carrying their pot on their head during ghata parikrama.

The occasion provides the people with the opportunity to rejoice and it turns into a mega-carnival when thousands of people get themselves painted as different mythological characters and roam around the city streets. Often they collect money for charity.

Since 1922 it was Ramalingam who initiated the procession. It was believed that the goddess Ammavaru refused to move until Ramalingam arrived and paid his respects to the goddess. Then Ramalingam led the procession through the streets of the town. In every street the devotees offered gifts of kind and money to the goddess Ammavaru. In Ramalingam's presence there would be no disturbances of any kind, the procession moved in an orderly manner, women and children mingled in the procession freely, and the event ran smoothly. He maintained discipline in anything he conducted. It was said they cancelled the festival in the year when Ramalingam was in jail.

In 1946 the family sent Devi Kumar dressed as a tiger into the procession. Errababu painted his son artistically and made him look like a 'tiger'. The chubby boy caught the attention of all. The whole family attended the procession. It was a memorable event for the family.

Devi Kumar was the chubbiest, strong baby born to Komalam, weighing ten and a half pounds. As he was born during the festive season of *Durgapuja,* also known as *Devi Navaratri,* he was named Devi Kumar and his naming ceremony was celebrated on a grand scale and was one of the highlighted events in the family. His uncle, the medic Ramam, showed his favouritism to his handsome nephew overtly. While the whole family including Ramam wore *Khadi*, he bought readymade clothes for his nephew from Patna and purchased *Bata* shoes for him when the whole family wore sandals. The bossy Devi dominated other children at home.

Ramalingam had a strange medical condition annually. It all started from the year 1922 when he began to lead the *Ammavari* procession. He had measles every year in April. He could almost predict the arrival of measles. The few spots always appeared on his chest and nowhere else, and he mentioned that during the measles he felt a heavy weight on his chest. This phenomenon continued all his life. The spots lasted for four to five days and disappeared. During that period Ramalingam ate no food and lived on water alone. Pillamma gently rubbed his chest with Neem leaves and placed Neem twigs all around the room. His measles never affected the other members of the family.

The Neem tree (*Azadirachta indica*) is a tropical evergreen tree native to India and is also found in other southeast countries. In India, Neem is known as 'the village pharmacy' because of its healing versatility, and it has been used in Ayurvedic medicine for more than 4,000 years due to its medicinal properties. Neem is also called '*arista*' in Sanskrit—a word that means 'perfect, complete, and imperishable'. Its seeds, bark, and leaves contain compounds with proven antiseptic, antiviral, antipyretic, anti-inflammatory, anti-ulcer, and antifungal uses.

The following festival in the annual calendar was the Dussehra Festival. In 1946, as Ramalingam was not in jail the family decided to celebrate the festival. The name Dussehra is derived from Sanskrit *Dasha-hara*, which literally means 'removal of ten', referring to Lord Rama's victory over the ten-headed demon king Ravana. The day also marks the victory of the goddess Durga over the demons Mahishasur. The name Vijayadashami is derived from the Sanskrit words *Vijaya-dashmi* literally meaning 'the victory on the Dashmi' (*Dashmi* being the tenth lunar day of the Hindu calendar month). As the name suggests, *Vijayadashmi* or *Dussehra* are celebrated on the tenth day of the month of Ashwin according to the Hindu calendar, which corresponds to September or October of the Gregorian calendar. The first nine days are celebrated as *Maha Navaratri* (nine nights) and culminates on the tenth day as *Dussehra.*

In India, the harvest season begins at this time and therefore the Mother Goddess is invoked to start the new harvest season and reactivate the vigour and fertility of the soil. This is done through religious performances and rituals which are thought to invoke cosmic forces that rejuvenate the soil. Many people of the Hindu faith observe this festival through social gatherings and food offerings to the gods at home and in temples.

Preparations for the festival at Panditji's home began in earnest. The front hall was vacated and Panditji shifted to the annex. *Bommala Koluvu* served as one of the days for socialising. Invitations are extended to friends and relatives. Invitees visit people's homes beautifully dressed. It is also an exciting time for children during *Bommala Koluvu.* The traditional arrangement during *Bommala Koluvu* Navratri involves nine steps for the nine divine nights. It has spiritual significance. Apart from being a social event, it also conveys a spiritual thought. It represents the essence of creation with the display of dolls. The world in itself is a creation of *Durga,* the creative aspect of the Supreme Truth. The arrangement of *Koluvu* in nine levels showcases creation from gods to humans, animal species to inanimate things. It conveys the truth about the presence of a source from which creation emerges. The dolls represent the fact that when forms and figures vary, the essence or the inherent material remains the same. *Navratri Bommala Koluvu* thus conveys the purpose of the creation, existence, and truth of spiritual oneness.

Errababu organised the *'Bommala Koluvu'* assisted by the rest of the family. The *'Koluvu'* occupied half of the hall. All the *Bommalu,* dolls, and other ornaments—antique items collected from all over the years—were brought out of locked cupboards. They had been wrapped in cotton wool and muslin cloth before they were stored away. Errababu made the nine levels with different themes for the display. The top tier was for Kailash Mountain, the abode of Lord Shiva. It is believed that the river Ganges originated from there. Errababu built a waterfall that flowed down the mountain to the village at the bottom tier. The village scene looked authentic with all its village features. On the second tier he created the modern India with Gandhiji and the political situation depicted in statues and artwork. On the third tier he placed the goddess Durga sitting on a lotus that floated on water. By her side Lord Ganesh and statues of other gods were placed. On the fourth tier was a rural scene depicting national folk dances and folk art. On the fifth tier was the display of fine porcelain and china dolls of the world.

The sixth tier was reserved for the modern railway system, and trains came down the mountains through tunnels and reached the bottom tier. The working railway system attracted all. The steam engine attracted young and old alike. The carriages made of glass, mirrors and metal that came from Germany looked impressive. The railway tracks were from England. Pillamma collected all the dolls and toys from her childhood, and her rich uncle and her wealthy father-in-law helped her with her collection. Many of them were given as gifts by sahibs to her father-in-law who had entertained them frequently. Since 1920 when Ramalingam had joined the freedom movement Pillamma carefully wrapped each item of her collection in cotton wool or muslin cloth and locked them away in large cupboards. After two decades her collection came to light. Errababu took extra care to unwrap each parcel and carefully handled them, keeping all children at a distance from the collection.

The seventh tier was displayed the carpenters with working models which attracted all. The eighth tier had a model of Gandhiji spinning on *Charka*. Errababu with batteries made all models work like real people.

The waterfall finally reached the bottom tier and ended in a pond with ducks and lilies. Adjacent to the pond Errababu created a forest scene on the floor with forest animals and birds. The tigers roared at intervals, startling the visitors. Right in front of the *Koluvu,* idols of the goddesses Saraswati and Lakshmi were placed and Komalam did daily *puja* to them. On either side by the windows on large tables gifts neatly wrapped in envelopes waited to be handed over to the guests. Every day Errababu changed one scene of the display to surprise the family. Errababu came alive with the Koluvu, and Pillamma was glad to see him participate with so much enthusiasm.

Special sweets called *rasgoras* were made by the sweet vendor to order. In whatever Pillamma did she showed her generosity. As per tradition, coconuts, fruit, kumkum and *pasupu* packets were given to all the women visitors. Kumkum is made from saffron and the flower Crocus *sativus*, in the *Iridaceae* family. The plant has many names in Sanskrit: Ghusrun, Rakta, Kashmir, Balhik, Kesar, Kashmiraj, Kumkum, Agneeshekhar, Asrugvar, Shatha, Shonit, Pitaka, or Rudhir. Pasupu is turmeric. Kumkum and pasupu are given by the hostess to the guests for good luck and good health.

There was a traditional method of inviting the guests. To start with, the hostess goes from house to house inviting women personally by putting kumkum on their forehead to attend their function. Komalam and Santa went to one side of the town to invite people while Pillamma and Jani covered the other end of the town. Subbulu preferred to stay at home. She was rather timid at such functions.

On the final day of the festival, late in the evening a car driven by a chauffeur stopped outside Panditji's house. A very beautiful young lady got out and was escorted by a well-dressed gentleman as she entered the hall. He touched Pillamma's feet and took her blessings. He turned to the young lady and told her that he would come to collect her. She nodded shyly. After the initial formal chat Komalam asked the lady, Suvarna, to sing a song. Suvarna was well known for her singing.

Suvarna's widowed mother had had no finances to pay for her daughter's music lessons. But on seeing the young girl's natural talent her guru gave her free singing lessons. Suvarna had been in her final year at college when a young ICS (Imperial Civil Service) officer was invited as a chief guest. He had given the most coveted music prize to Suvarna and was smitten by her beauty, intelligence, and most of all, her melodic voice. Within months he had become married to her without any dowry. Everybody extolled Suvarna's fortunes. To start with her husband had stopped her college and wouldn't let her complete her degree course. Gradually he isolated her from her mother and friends. She was forbidden to attend any social functions and people thought that Suvarna, as the wife of an ICS officer, had become proud and did not want to mingle with common people. Her husband had become a complete control freak and Suvarna found herself locked in a 'pleasure-prison' as she termed her life with her husband. She had all the comforts one could have but she had become a recluse from everything and from everybody. She was forbidden to sing, and slowly she became mute. Even in the bathroom she was afraid to hum. Now, as this was Panditji's house her husband brought her there by himself.

As Komalam asked her to sing she hesitated but slowly started singing. One after another she sang melodies nonstop as if she were possessed but when she heard the car outside she collapsed on the floor and had a severe convulsion.

Panditji and Pillamma took her to the hospital and her husband could not stop them. Komalam went and fetched Suvarna's mother to the hospital. Suvarna stayed there for three days. Her mother told Pillamma about her daughter's miserable married life.

Later Panditji personally counselled the young ICS officer, who broke out and said that he was only protecting his wife from the public. He confessed that he could not bear anyone looking at his beautiful wife or even praising her. And as for her singing, he felt that it was her curse as her voice invited more admirers. After several sessions of counselling over a few months, the man showed some signs of improvement. He relaxed his control on his wife. He allowed his wife to visit her mother occasionally and to socialise with a selected few of his choice. To maintain the peace at home Suvarna never sang in public but her husband gave her permission to sing to herself when he was not at home!

Komalam thanked God for giving her a good husband like Errababu. He never tried to control her, and when they were together they sang to each other. Often Komalam sang at social female functions, at home, and mostly to her mother. When Pillamma was tired and worn out she would ask her daughter to sing to her. Komalam sang Pillamma's favourite songs, Jayadeva Gitalu and Asthapadulu to sooth her mother's aching soul. Music gave the mother and daughter a renewed enthusiasm to always face another day of poverty at home.

Thakurarani Festival
(Ammavari Sambaralu, 1920s)

24

The Changing Scenes of the Town: 1947

The beginning of the year had brought some hope to the town, hope of what nobody could spell out. But people felt positive about the year, as the annual predictions of the New Year promised prosperity and good health to all. At the same time the conflicting reports about freedom and a partition of areas were floating around. Communal disturbances began to sprout in some parts of the country. Panditji and his colleagues, forgetting their religious differences, maintained harmony at Berhampur by setting good examples.

In 1947, after World War II, Britain could see that it no longer could hold its power over India. It was becoming increasingly difficult and Indian freedom fighters were in no mood to give up. With the international support also coming to an end, Britain finally decided to relieve India from its power—but not before June 1948. However, the impending independence more enhanced the violence between Hindus and Muslims in the provinces of Punjab and Bengal. The communal violence grew so large that it became impossible for the new viceroy Lord Mountbatten to control it and as such, he advanced the date for the transfer of power, allowing less than six months for a mutually agreed plan for independence. Thus, India gained its independence on 15 August 1947, but not without paying a heavy price. A partition was made and a separate state for the Muslims was formed, with Muhammad Ali Jinnah being sworn in as the new Pakistan's first Governor General in Karachi. On the midnight of 15 August 1947 India was also sworn in as an independent country, with Pandit Jawaharlal Nehru as the Prime Minister. The official ceremony took place in Delhi.

Indians whether either educated or not believe in astrology. After detailed astrological calculations believers decided that midnight would be the most appropriate time for the birth of a new nation and to take charge of a new India. At that time the *lagnam* was in a most favourable position for foundations of buildings and stable independence.

Lagnam in astrological predictions is a very important calculation. *Lagnam* literally represents your soul in astrology. The amount or intensity of the light or rays of the sun at the exact minute you were born is calculated accurately and is called Lagnam. A simple explanation is: "*Lagnam* is the accurate degree at which the sun's energy falls at the time of birth, represented in a graphical way." It has been recorded by Sir Woodrow Wyatt that the time of Indian Independence was chosen on astrological considerations, but within the twenty-four hours given. The astrologers who advised the Government were Hardeoji and Suryanarain Vyas. Sir Woodrow Wyatt wrote in May 1988 an article on the central page of the Times, London: "Who Does Not Consult Stars" and he defended Ronald Reagan, the US President, for consulting astrologers. There he revealed that Indian astrologers had chosen the time of Indian Independence and that the subsequent history of India was somewhat more successful.

Prior to the independence, early in the year of 1947 Berhampur began to take a new look. Street entertainers became a common sight. The free entertainment attracted one and all and many stopped by the entertainers on their daily routes. Jani was hooked by the magicians on the roadside and often arrived late at school and was punished. Almost every evening Balaram, who was a teacher at Town School, came round to her house to complain about the young girl to Pillamma, his sister-in-law. The young girl began to absorb the magic of life around her and was intrigued by the real-life magician by the roadside across the Barracks ground. He could make a mango tree grow from a seed to a tree and produce mangoes, all in a few seconds. She went to school and asked her teacher to teach her how to grow a tree in minutes and consequently annoyed him. He was exasperated with her impertinence and gave her an imposition. She failed to differentiate between magic and real life. She felt empty, she felt cheated, and she felt frustrated. She wanted answers and nobody had any time for her 'silly questions', as they saw her curiosity. Her grandfather, who could clear all her doubts, was hardly at home.

Her mentor and her guru was Linagmmama, Pillamma's older brother. He lived a mile away from her house. Every day he walked all the way and visited them. He spoke to his sister, Pillamma, for a few minutes and if any visitors came round he left abruptly. He despised the 'two-faced people' as he called them, and walked back home. Often Jani followed him as if she were escorting him to his house. On the way she could ask him about anything and he had time to clear all her doubts. Sometimes his explanations were too philosophical for a little girl of eight, but she listened to him carefully. He often used to say that his words would guide her in her life. She was pleased that he did not dismiss her doubts as 'silly'. Sometimes she remembered his bombastic words and used them within her circle of friends, impressing them with her knowledge. Once he reached home, she stopped to talk to Buddi, his caretaker, drank some water, and then returned home, with Lingammama dutifully accompanying her home. These journeys to and fro, each escorting the other, amused Pillamma.

Once Jani complained that all the post came to her grandfather and nobody sent her any letters. So Lingammama, after escorting her home, returned to his home and wrote a postcard to Jani and posted it. Sometimes he wrote in Telugu and sometimes in English. His writing was hard to decode. He used a script known as *golusukattu* writing. This cursive writing without full stops was intriguing and hard to read. He used the same method for writing in English. Jani never understood what he wrote, but all the same she treasured the post. She wanted to save it in a safe place but in that large house Jani never had a place to call her own and all her secret dens were attacked regularly by her younger brother, Devi Kumar. When she moaned to Lingammama about this he told her that words could be wiped out but nobody could erase her memories, and he asked her to store everything in her 'memory box'. Jani absorbed his philosophy as well as she could. As her teacher once said, no knowledge ever goes to waste; it comes in handy at the right time.

There was a strong man who made a mark on the town with his remarkable feat. He was called Ellayya Sannaya of Manglavarampeta. He wrestled with a full-sized real brown bear. Some cynics claimed that the bear was his pet, so to clear their doubts he wrestled with any bear they could bring to the show. He would never hurt the bear and instead, after the fight, he would feed the bear with honey and brown sugar. He was known as the kindest person in town. His strength and his techniques impressed all. Wherever his show was organised people flocked to see the strong wrestler grapple with a real brown bear.

The face of the town was definitely changing. With some cynicism people reluctantly welcomed the changes, accepting them rather unwillingly. Now the tent cinema moved to a purpose-built cinema. The buses that had run on charcoal had become diesel buses. The *Tongas* were gradually replaced by cycle rickshaws. The changes were not planned by anyone. They appeared as if they had sprouted from nowhere and arrived as seasonal changes. Every change brought some disaster to the people. The *Tongas* were put away but the horses that had pulled them became redundant and most of them were sold away to the butchers. Pillamma said that the change was like a river. When the monsoon arrived the new water that flowed into the river pushed away the old water into the sea. Old gets replaced by new, and that is the nature of Nature.

While playing hide and seek on her way to school Jani accidently found out that one distant relative of the family lived in a horse stable behind the main road, Bank Street that led to her school. He had no family. He was a tall and thin man with a long beard grown to his waist, and had long curly stringy hair and blaring red eyes. His only friend was a thin and weak old horse. He had a small charcoal stove known as *kumpati* in a corner of the stable, with a pan and a rolled-up mat hung on the wall. The weak horse was asleep on some hay. He looked at the girl and shooed her out. Pillamma told Jani that he, known as Sonkilimama to all, was a recluse and lived on his own. He didn't like any intruders to his abode. Lingammama told her that a recluse liked to live alone but even he couldn't give her any reasons why they chose to be reclusive.

She shared her information with her friends. Now they all kept their eyes open and looked for more recluses in town. At the end of the Roman Catholic Church Road and just before the entrance to Barracks Road there was a corner house. That was a big house with high white walls. The children of the town were frightened to go by that house; they often crossed the road running quickly to avoid the madman who lived there. Selvy, their friend who lived opposite the madman's house, told them that the man came out of his house in the darkness, paced his veranda for a long time, and then went back into the house and shut the door. He always appeared in a white lungi and a long white shirt. Now that recluses were different to Sonkilimama, the friends could come to no conclusive ideas about recluses. They remained an enigma to the friends. Pillamma warned her not to go there and disturb them.

Jani and her friend Gunnu realised that there were many secrets they did not know about their town, but sadly nobody could throw any light on the secrets. Lingammama told her that all people were different and they should live as they wished. The girls should not disturb them.

There was one man called Totamama whom Jani found interesting. He had a large photo studio on the Bank Street. His beautiful teenage daughter Tota Kamala was the little girl's heroine. Kamala was a professional dancer and gave many performances in classical Bharatnatyam in town and also toured round the country performing at various functions. Often on her way to school Jani would stop by the Tota studio and watch Kamala practise her dance at home for the forthcoming performance. Totamama often gave Jani the exposed film rolls which the little girl made into trumpets.

At lunch break Jani and her friend went to the Town Hall Garden behind their school, where they washed their tiffin carriers at the taps in the garden and drank the water. The old gardener taught them how to spin round their water-filled tiffin carriers without spilling a drop of it. The old gardener had tremendous patience and answered all the girls' curiosity about the plants and the garden which he looked after. He taught them how to use a spanner and mend the leaking taps. Everything was interesting to the girls. They were ready to absorb any amount of knowledge that came their way. The girls found out that even the gardener was a recluse, as he lived on his own in a small hut in the garden. Jani told Lingammama that she had found another loner who was very nice and friendly. He roared with laughter at her discoveries. He told her that the old gardener was not a recluse, but since his wife and daughter had died he was living on his own. Now the two friends had another version of a recluse.

Lingammama realised that the little girl needed another aversion to divert her almost obsessive interest in recluses. The girl was full of energy and her mind was seeking to absorb everything around her. He had to divert her inquiring mind to the right path. He felt that her mind was like the waves of a sea. He remembered the old saying—*Egirey tarngam viragaka maanadu. Parugettey tarangam ekkado akkda aagaka tappadu*—meaning that 'the rising wave gets broken and the running wave has to stop somewhere'. Lingammama told her of the Hindi classes that were running after school at the Samajam Hall, which was not far away from her school.

In December 1927, while addressing some college students at Chatrapur, the administrative capital of the Ganjam District near Berhampur, Gandhiji had expressed his vision of a common language for all Indians. He agonised about the unhealthy competition between various Indian languages.

"I am beseeching the lettered classes of India to make Hindi their common language. There would be no reason why we should not all be knowing five or six vernaculars." (Ref: from the Photostat of the Gujarati-G.N. 4731)

Gandhi envisioned Hindi as a confluence of languages and a major contact language for Indian society. It could take on the challenges of English on its own. The language debate continued endlessly because in a country with various well-established ancient languages to choose one over the other became impossible. Some were prepared to accept Hindi as an official language rather than the National Language of India. Ever since, the validity of languages always has remained a sensitive topic to all Indians. (In the free India the states were formed on the basis of local languages.) While the common National

Language debate continued in some places they began to run Hindi classes for all people outside the school hours.

Jani and a few other friends joined the Hindi classes and Lingammama could divert her attention from her 'recluses'. She loved the classes and after a year took the first exam in Hindi and was thrilled to get her first certificate of her life. She tasted the sweetness of success and she longed for more success in the future. She began to concentrate at school and that year she won the first prize for mathematics. She treasured the compass-box and a certificate that she received as a prize.

Once when on her way to Lingammama, Janis stopped and played with some girls in the street. Suddenly they stopped playing and ran into their friend Sarojini's house when they heard Tabla playing. Jani also went in and saw Sarojini and two other girls taking dancing lessons from a teacher in her central courtyard and her mother was sitting in a chair on the veranda and was supervising the girls. Jani and the other girls stood on the veranda and watched the dance practise. After a few minutes Sarojini's mother asked all the girls to join the dance lessons. Jani and another two girls jumped at the chance whereas other shy girls ran away giggling.

The dance lessons continued for four weeks without any interruptions. On that day, Pillamma told Jani that her father was very angry and forbad her to go and learn dancing at Sarojini's house. The little girl tried to tell her grandmother that the teacher did not ask for any tuition money. Pillamma explained to her that her great aunt, Errababu's older sister, took objection to the little girl's dancing lessons as it was against their family tradition and moreover dancing is for cheap girls and not for the prestigious girls of her late father P.Venkateswarlu.

The little girl was heartbroken and wept bitterly. Lingammama explained to her that in a family it was polite to respect the elders as Errababu had no choice but to obey his older sister.

Once again his older sister, sitting in her house, had been keeping an eye on her brother's family and was interfering in his family matters. Thus another dream of Jani to become a famous dancer like Tota Kamala was aborted in its infancy. But often she went and watched Tota Kamala practise at her home. She remembered the steps and practised in the back garden with her friends. A year before that, when Komalam wanted Santa to learn violin the same older sister of Errababu put a spoke in the works, saying it was against their family tradition.

During the children's summer holidays Errababu brought home two reams of white paper for their notebooks. He let them make their own note books. The two older boys and their sister Santa made their note books by folding and cutting the paper to size and stitched them together and took them away along with the scissors. As they were in the senior school they needed more notebooks.

Komalam saw that Jani was struggling to cut the paper to size. She told her how to cut them without any scissors. She folded the paper in half, creased it, and inserting a cotton string she used for sewing she dragged the string along the crease and cut the paper to size. Komalam taught her how to sew the paper into a book with needle and thread. Now the little girl had learnt another trick which she shared with her friends.

Gunnu's Aunt Sita, who was at college, ordered her niece about. She demanded that Gunnu and Jani write down the words for songs and give them to her, so that she could sing, not in any concert but upstairs on the terrace. Gunnu said her aunt wants to be a heroine. In the cinema house the songs could be heard from a distance. Those who could not go to the cinema sat outside in the Barracks grounds and listened to the whole film with dialogues and songs.

The two friends sat outside and wrote down the words for the songs and gave it to the aunt. They often made mistakes in the lyrics and were told off by her aunt Sita. The aunt loved singing the songs, but the two girls found to be a chore to sit down writing the lyrics regularly. They would rather play without doing errands for Gunnu's aunt.

They dreaded whenever a new film was to be shown at the cinema house. There was the whole world to discover, rather than doing errands for an aunt. They had no choice but to obey the college girl. The two girls living next door to each other were both adventurous and loved to explore the whole world around them.

Once Gunnu's older sister and Jani's older sister had a big falling out over some flowers that were grown on the common hedge. They stopped talking to each other and forbad their younger sisters to play with each other. Now the two friends had no choice but to obey their elder sisters. Otherwise the older sisters warned them of severe consequences. The High School girls kept their animosity and grudges alive for well over a year.

The frustrated girls asked for Lingammama's advice. Lingammama told Jani and Gunnu not to play together at home, but it was alright to be friends outside, as that wouldn't be considered as disobeying an older sister. So the two girls left home separately and joined at the end of the street. Fortunately their older sisters were at the High School on the opposite side of the town. They followed the same method in the evenings and played happily at the open Barracks grounds. Whenever the two friends had any problems Lingammama found a safe solution for them.

That year many weddings took place in town, making the town echo with celebrations as if it were preparing for the forthcoming big day. The town was buzzing with the eminent rumours of freedom. Pillamma was thrilled to hear the news. At last her family would be out of the woods of the freedom struggle and they could have a normal life. She waited for the big day of relief. But destiny has its own mind. In life the path to a destination is always a step away.

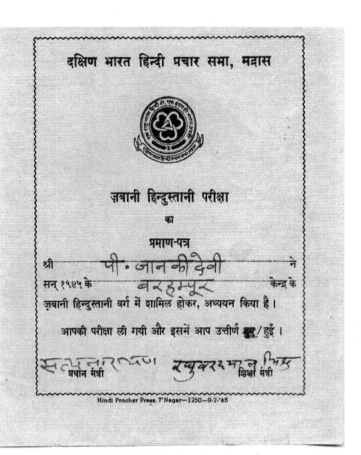

Hindi Prachar Sabha, Madras
Jani's first certificate

25

The Freedom

15 August 1947

At last the memorable day for all Indians had arrived. The long-suppressed nation was freed from the shackles of the mighty British Empire. It was the day to end the widespread movements that had boiled the nation with emotions and anger. The day brought new light and rays of new hopes for India. When the world was asleep, India woke up to new life and full freedom. A new nation was born, bringing the end of the colonial rule, suppressed agitations, and other movements to inhibit the freedom fight. For the first time in the history of India, it had become one nation. Previously India was made up of about fifty-two individual kingdoms. Fighting together against a common enemy, Indians became united and formed a single unit of India—the whole India. The day was celebrated to commemorate the birth of the world's biggest democracy. Jawaharlal Nehru, hoisting the national flag, gave a very emotional speech:

"Long years ago we made a tryst with destiny, and now the time comes when we shall redeem our pledge, not wholly or in full measure, but very substantially. At the stroke of the midnight hour, when the world sleeps, India will awake to life and freedom. A moment comes, which comes but rarely in history, when we step out from the old to the new, when an age ends, and when the soul of a nation, long suppressed, finds utterance. It is fitting that at this solemn moment we take the pledge of dedication to the service of India and her people and to the still larger cause of humanity.

At the dawn of history India started on her unending quest, and trackless centuries are filled with her striving and the grandeur of her successes and her failures. Through good and ill fortune alike she has never lost sight of that quest or forgotten the ideals which gave her strength. We end, today, a period of ill fortune and India discovers herself again.

"Freedom and power bring responsibility. That responsibility rests upon this assembly, a sovereign body representing the sovereign people of India. Before the birth of freedom we have endured all the pains of labour and our hearts are heavy with the memory of this sorrow. Some of those pains continue even now. Nevertheless, the past is over and it is the future that beckons to us now."

The whole country celebrated the day with vigour. The father of the nation, Gandhiji, abstained from any such celebrations. Gandhiji, the real hero of the New Delhi ceremony, was absent from the capital of his country in its triumphant hour. At the moment when his great dream came true—though not precisely in the form he had wished, being partitioned into two countries—

Gandhiji was in humble surroundings of his own choosing, among the Muslims of Calcutta, where he felt he was needed more. But his name was publicly praised by others at every flag-hoisting ceremony throughout the country.

Veeradhi also arrived home from Cuttack to take part in the celebrations at Berhampur. As soon as he completed his Matriculation with excellent results Errababu put him in employment, against the family's wishes. A year before that, Subbulu and Veeradhi had typing lessons from a family friend who ran a typing institute in town, and they both passed the typing exam. The family, especially Pillamma, wanted Veeradhi to go for higher studies and join the college, but only for reasons that he alone knew, Errababu chose not to send his eldest son to college. He found a clerical post at Cuttack, about 230 miles from Berhampur, and Veeradhi took up the job unwillingly. Pillamma begged Ramalingam to intervene and stop the injustice Errababu was doing to his eldest son, but as ever Panditji refused to interfere in Errababu's decision, saying that he as a father had a right to decide his son's future.

Komalam never expressed her views or said what she felt. Even though Subbulu, despite being a girl, was completing her degree, Veeradhi had to compromise with only a Matriculation certificate. Some of the family's friends asked Errababu to let his son join the college, but the father of the boy never changed his mind. Veeradhi was getting only 120 rupees as salary. He used 50 rupees for his boarding and lodging and sent 70 rupees to Pillamma. Thus Veeradhi became the first earning member of the family in decades. As some people expected, Errababu never made any claim on the boy's income. Veeradhi never moaned about his fate and accepted it as his destiny. But wherever he went, he took laughter and happiness with him. He was a welcoming guest at any gathering. He was always jovial and often entertained people with his singing. Perhaps he had inherited his father Errababu's music talent. Whatever he did, Veeradhi was methodical and kept everything neat and tidy. He was ambitious and continued to educate himself by reading books.

At Berhampur several leaders of the freedom movement hoisted national flags at different locations. Panditji hoisted the national flag at the *Khadi Bhandar*. The strange man Johnny attended the flag-hoisting ceremony. He had changed his gear from a three-piece suit to white pants and white shirt with a Gandhi-cap. Some people were about to taunt him but Panditji stopped them. When the Europeans left the town, Johnny thought they would take him with them to England, but they did not acknowledge his status as a European, in spite of his European looks with blond hair and fair skin. He was neither accepted as an Anglo-Indian by the Anglo-Indian community. It was believed that his both parents were European and he was orphaned in his infancy, an old Indian Ayah raised him and when she died he was left to fend for himself. In free India, Johnny remained without any status. Panditji made him a citizen of Berhampur since he was from there, and gave him the post of a caretaker at the *Khadi Bhandar*.

The town was united in their celebrations; all the shops and cinema houses were kept open, free for all. At schools free slates and slate-pencils, and books and pencils were distributed to all children. Sweets were given out to everyone. The transport became free for all. Suddenly everything was free in the new liberated country. People celebrated the birth of the country as they would celebrate the birth of their firstborn.

At the Town School they held their own celebrations. In the open grounds they built a stage below the high veranda where the children performed. One teacher built a gramophone box with a cardboard and painted it with the image of the HMV Dog (His Masters Voice) and attached a horn to it like in the gramophone box. Jani was chosen to be in the box to sing some national songs. She was thrilled at the privilege and honour she had been given. Dr H. Mehtab, the minister of Orissa, visited them. After the function everyone gathered for the group photo with the VIP. Totamama the photographer of the town settled them in three tiers for the group photo just below the veranda. There suddenly began the pushing and shoving by the group, each struggling to be next to the chief guest in the photo. Jani was pushed out of the frame by teachers and some stronger children; she stood aside with a long face. Totamama, the official photographer, gave her a secret clue. She quickly climbed the veranda and stood right behind the chief guest appearing prominently in the photo, and she felt triumphant.

Free cinema attracted most children. They saw the films in English, and one of them was about dancing on ice. For the children, who had never seen any ice or snow, the film made no sense and they left to seek some other free entertainment. The magic shows, dances, and sports events attracted them most. Sweet shops became popular with all children. Some sweet-vendors made tri-colour sweet watches and tied them on the children's wrists, which they licked sweetly. The vendors, the entertainers, teachers, and mothers used their skills to make everything around them in tri-colour. It was heart-warming to see all children behave well and there was no vandalism of any sort. The Police recorded that no crime, even petty, occurred in that first week of free India. Perhaps the psychologists would have found the 'free' phenomenon interesting.

Lots of prayers were held at temples and other religious places and were kept open for all without prejudice. Gandhiji would have loved to see the sight of his Harijans enter the temples freely.

That night Pillamma made a sumptuous feast for the family. Then grandfather Pandit Ramalingam asked Pillamma what would be her wish on this very special event.

Pillamma looked at everyone moving her eyes slowly from one face to the other and with tears in her eyes said, "My only wish is that nobody and none of my family should join politics for at least for seven generations."

Panditji looked at her and smiled as if he understood her agony. It was Veeradhi who stood up and blessed Pillamma as if he was a priest and said: "We grant you your wish, our Lady."

He made the atmosphere light and they all enjoyed the feast.

The celebrations lasted non-stop for one whole week. In the evenings, oil-lamps were lit at every home and in the streets. It was as if Diwali, the festival of lights, had come early with strings of *Diyas* everywhere. Every evening, firework displays at the Barracks ground attracted all. People were ecstatic to get everything free. They welcomed the new India wholeheartedly. Sadly, Panditji's European friends had left town and it was said they migrated back to

England. But his best friends sent him congratulation telegrams before their departure. All good things had to come to a halt.

The next week the town went back to its routine. Children's playtime was over and they began to attend schools to study. The freedom of freeness stopped and the town resumed its duties. The shops opened for trade, the transport charged fees, the cinemas began to sell tickets, and free entertainment ceased. The sudden alteration to their previous state was like magic, as if the town woke up from their sweet dreams to face the reality. But they woke up with a triumphant feeling in their hearts.

The new dawn brought some new changes to town. People went to work with renewed enthusiasm. They were not working as slaves, but working with self-pride to make their town a success and make their lives worthwhile in their own country. There was hope in their hearts, there was desire to reach the heights, and most of all they felt their dignity had been restored and they were ready to prove to them and to the world that they were not inferior to any nation. At Town School all children began to receive free milk and a snack called *idles* before the classes commenced, and every evening after school, teachers conducted various outdoor games which most children enjoyed. The town echoed in euphoric hope and glory. Everybody worked with inspiration and vigour in every field.

At home Pillamma felt like a fish out of water. Somehow, perhaps naively, she thought that everything would become normal and her agony of twenty-seven years in the freedom struggle would abruptly come to a full stop. On the contrary, more visitors came round increasing her workload. The financial situation at home had deteriorated to below zero. Now Panditji got more involved in building the new nation. He stood behind the politicians and advised them on every matter. A gentle struggle between people erupted to usurp important positions in the new government. Panditji worked as a mediator and calmed the situation. He often reminded them that all eyes of the world were on India and that they should not fight among themselves. He wanted people to be elected democratically.

On the home front, Komalam's health began to deteriorate. The doctors could not put a name to her condition, and she began to lose weight. Fortunately Pillamma's malaria bouts had ceased. Slowly the brass utensils at home were sold away, with every item sold had an effect on Komalam. She felt frustrated and helpless, she was very sensitive, and she took everything to heart. At home she worked harder in the garden and developed a good kitchen garden producing enough fruit and vegetables to suffice the whole family's needs. She took special care of the two banana plants that a tribal man had sold her.

It was two years previously that an old tribal man had come to their house and collapsed on the floor. Komalam gave him wiped his face with cold water and sat there fanning him gently. When he opened his, she asked the servant to carry him to the garden. There in the kitchen garden he relaxed while she went brought some food on a banana leaf. The old man ate it and dozed off under the tree.

When he woke up he took out two tiny saplings from his waist band and gave them to Komalam. He said they were rare banana plants and that she should plant them. Komalam looked at them – the saplings looked dried and dead. She thanked the old man and when he was leaving she gave him some food in a banana-leaf parcel which he refused to take and left, smiling to himself.

Duly she asked her two sons, Veeradhi and Laxman, to plant them in the kitchen garden in front of the kitchen. In no time they grew upwards but not as tall as the other banana plants in the garden, as they were a dwarf variety. They produced large bunches of bananas with red skin that reached the ground. Komalam was thrilled to see the new variety and they all enjoyed the fruit.

By the end of the year the new-born calf of the cow had died and the cowherd brought the dead calf home. He stuffed the calf and placed it in front of the cow to milk it. The tender-hearted Komalam could not bear this, she asked the cowherd not to bring the stuffed calf to show to the cow. She spent a lot of time in the cowshed with the cow and dried the cow's tears, as if it were her best friend. Her attachment to the cow was deep. Pillamma recalled the predictions, when Komalam had been born as a caul baby, that she would have more affinity with the animals. The cowherd took the calf to the forest and buried it there and the cow was never milked again. Pillamma began to buy milk from a milkman who brought two cows home and milked them in front of Pillamma. Every evening Komalam spent some time with the cow and shared its sorrow silently.

The children were all growing up and their demands began to increase. Pillamma had to manage them all to her best ability; fortunately the discipline at home was praiseworthy. There were many social functions specifically for girls, like *atla tadiya*, which all the girls in the neighbourhood celebrated every year. Pillamma had to pacify her two young granddaughters, saying that such festivities were prohibited for their family as they would be a bad omen to them. Every festival had its own expenses and the family had no finances for pleasure.

The New Year 1948 arrived, bearing the most wonderful news for the family; the son of the family, Ramam, had attained his medical degree and he was posted at a small place called Aska, about 25 miles from Berhampur. Komalam rejoiced with her brother's success more than anybody else. It was her dream to see her brother become a doctor. She told Pillamma that she couldn't wait for her daughter Santa to be a doctor like Dr Margaret Bhore.

Komalam went to Aska with her brother and stayed with him for a couple of weeks, settling him in the new place, and then returned home. Ramam was treated like a prince in the new place; he had a cook and a servant to look after him. Pillamma thanked the Almighty for having made her son a success. Like a flash, the memory of her struggle to educate her son and to admit him to Town School against his father's wishes ran like a film reel through her mind. Komalam went round the town distributing sweets and informing everybody of her brother's success and that now he was a real doctor. They smiled, knowing her affection for her only brother and congratulated the family by visiting them. It was Panditji who showed no emotions.

Dr Ramam earned 250 rupees at the government hospital. He sent regularly 150 rupees to Pillamma. For the first time the family began to have a regular income from Veeradhi and Ramam. Ramam also felt that Veeradhi should stop working and join the college, but still Errababu wouldn't agree to that, and people were surprised that Errababu had no ambitions for his firstborn. So Ramam asked Veeradhi to take a correspondence degree course. He obtained the books and the course syllabus for his nephew.

On his own steam, Veeradhi also passed a Pitman's Shorthand exam and became a regular typist come clerk in a government office at Cuttack. His future was sealed for good. With the freedom of the country Veerradhi had lost his personal freedom for Higher Education but the hope that one day his future would be as bright as his uncle's kept him going.

26
The Eclipse Year: 1948

Pillamma's family celebrated the *Sankranti* festival, which falls in the middle of January with the whole family. The three-day festival was celebrated in its traditional manner. For her two granddaughters Pillamma ordered twelve sugar pots with lids for each. They put a new *dammidi* coin, a piece of sugarcane, two dates, and a toffee in each pot. They took them to their best friends' homes and presented them and similarly they received sugar pots from their friends. Each girl collected a lot of sugar pots. Devi Kumar demanded a share of them from his sisters and complained that why boys also could not have such traditions. Pillamma solved the problem by sharing equally all the sugar pots the girls had received amongst all her children, she always gave equal shares to all in the family, including the servants.

On the third day of the festival, Sunder, the youngest toddler of the family, had the *Bhogi Pallu* ceremony. The child was seated on a chair and he was showered with fruit, called *Regi Pallu*, mixed with coins and sweets in front of many female invitees. They sang songs and blessed the child. Then the mother of the child threw away the tray of fruit and coins on the floor, where the servants were to take them away. The *Regi Pallu* were from their own garden. They are sweet berries grown on a tree. In Komalam's garden there were two such trees. The one with small berries was just outside Errababu's quarters, which were used in the ceremony. The larger tree was next door to the cowshed. The tree's bark attracted caterpillars with long white hairs. As soon as the berries appeared on the tree the caterpillars occupied the tree. The sweet juicy berries were beyond the reach of children.

Once, when Devi Kumar was five, he climbed the roof of the cowshed in spite of Pillamma's warning, and when he heard his father coming he jumped on to the berry tree and slid down its bark, and yelled with pain. He was covered by caterpillars and all their hairs adhered to his tender skin. The caterpillars were removed easily but the hairs were not simple to extract. The child fainted in pain. Four adults picked each of the caterpillar hairs from his body, one by one, with forceps made out of fine reeds called *chipuru pullalu*. His body was covered in red patches. He was laid on a banana leaf and was applied with a special herbal ointment made by Jagappa, the family physician. After three arduous weeks he was cured. The caterpillars lingered on the bark for three to four weeks and then disappeared suddenly. Then they could collect the berries. The annual appearance of that variety of caterpillars did not affect any other tree.

It is believed that the *Bhogi Pallu* ceremony will protect the child from evil eyes and keep him in good health. Komalam was concerned about her child Sunder who was born a weakling and needed all the good wishes he could get. The hostess gave generous gifts of fruit and sweets to all the guests.

On the last day of the festival the animal kingdom is remembered and in particular, the cows. Komalam bathed the cow and decorated it with turmeric and kumkum and prayed for its good health, as it had begun to deteriorate since its calf died. She fed the cow with the sweets she had made herself. For her the cow who had lost her calf was more than a friend; it was like her own child.

The *Sankranti* festival was celebrated satisfactorily. Both Pillamma and Komalam felt elated. They looked ahead for the future of the family with immense optimism. They began to make future plans for their children. Having the whole family together gave the two women moral strength.

Since the new India had been formed, the town had been buzzing with enthusiasm and people looked happy and content. They wished each other with *'Jai Hind'*. The recent independence of the country was still fresh in their minds. Plans were made for the future of the town and more concentration was given to education for all. Evening classes for adults sprouted up in town. Similarly literary classes began for labourers and the uneducated. Ramalingam and his colleagues were keen on promoting literacy and good education for all.

The town was certain that nothing would and could stop them from progressing and making their mark at an international level. They woke up every morning with renewed enthusiasm. Hopes, enthusiasm, and diligence became the key note for all youngsters. They were ready to prove their worth in the free India. But the language problem persisted. Oriya became the state language, along with English and Telugu. Minor differences between the communities were ignored by all and they began to work as one unit for the benefit of their town Berhampur. Still the discipline and respect for the elders was maintained by all.

But that evening, on the fatal evening of 30th January, the town was to draw to a standstill.

The workers returning home in the evening walked home in utter silence, and even the children returned home from the playground silently carrying an unknown fear. The whole town walked as if it were hit by a meteorite.

They had just heard the news of Gandhiji's assassination in Delhi. It wrenched the town from its roots.

Gandhiji's assassination news came as a frightful shock out of a clear sky. It was the death of a man of the highest moral prestige, and it left the nation with forebodings for the future. The people retreated to their homes and hid themselves from the disastrous news. They were afraid to believe it as true, and they spent the dark night inside their abodes, hiding away from the bad news. Still many of them refused to accept what was surely a rumour. They found it easy to deny it all. But at dawn their fears were verified when the newspapers reported the truth of the news.

Gandhiji's pictures were sprawled all over the pages. Anything written about the father of the nation was not complete. Various accounts of the assassination were reported in several papers and leaflets and were broadcast on the radio. People gathered outside the Park to listen to the radio. Many homes did not own one. Errababu had just purchased a Bush Radio to celebrate the Independence Day. He placed the radio, which was always in his room, in the Hall and people gathered to hear the broadcast from Delhi continuously.

"If I am to die by the bullet of a mad man, I must do so smiling. There must be no anger within me. God must be in my heart and on my lips," Mahatma Gandhi had said, two days prior to his assassination when a previous attempt had been made to kill him.

Mahatma Gandhi had been leaving for Bombay to hold talks with Mohammad Ali Jinnah on 9 September 1944, when Hindu activists had stopped him. The leader of the group, Nathuram Godse, was found to be in possession of a dagger.

On 30 January 1948, at around 17:10, Nathuram Godse and his accomplices, Madanlal Pahwa, Shankar Kistaiya, Digambar Badge, Vishnu Karkare, Gopal Godse, and Narayan Apte, assassinated Mahatma Gandhi.

Jawaharlal Nehru, on the gate of Birla House, delivered his emotional speech, **"The light has gone out of our lives and there is darkness everywhere."** While dying, the Mahatma uttered, **"Hey, Ram ..."** Gandhiji was shot dead—that was the last of the Nation's Father. It was then 5:12.

Gandhiji: Born 2 October 1869, Died 30 January 1948, Aged 78 years old.

Nehru orated in the parliament on 3 Feb 1948, three days after Gandhiji's assassination:

"How shall we praise him and how shall we measure him, because he was not of the common clay that all of us are made of? He came, lived a fairly long span of life and has passed away. No words of praise of ours for he has had greater praise in his life than any living man in history. And during these two or three days since his death he has had the homage of the world ... Glory has departed and the sun that warmed and brightened our lives has set and we shiver in the cold and dark ... He lives in the hearts of millions and he will live for immemorial ages."

Albert Einstein said, "Generations to come will scarcely believe such a man as this walked on earth in flesh and blood."

Lord Mountbatten said: "Gandhiji's death is truly a loss to mankind which sorely needs the living light of those ideals of love and tolerance for which he strove and died. In her hour of deep sorrow India is proud to have given to the world a man of his imperishable renown and is confident that his example will be a source of inspiration and strength in the fulfilment of her destiny. India, indeed the world, will not see the like of him again, perhaps, for centuries. Our one consolation in this hour of unparalleled grief is that his life of truth, tolerance and love towards his fellows may inspire our troubled world to save itself by following his noble example."

Rabindranath Tagore spoke: "Mahatma Gandhi came and stood at the door of India's destitute millions, clad as one of them, speaking to them in their own language ... who else has so unreservedly accepted the vast masses of the Indian people as his flesh and blood? ... Truth awakened Truth."

The astrologers made their own statement on Gandhiji's life and death and analysed his birth chart. Accordingly he was highly learned and his books were widely read and well respected. He could not earn any land, houses, or properties for his own self. He even sacrificed his earnings and own possessions. As Mars was the lord of two death-causing houses, 2nd and 7th, and Mars is in birth-lagnam, he was assassinated and he died of wounds caused by a weapon.

Such prediction did not sooth the aching souls of the people. They said that a violent ending was so strongly indicated in his birth chart. Gandhiji's last words as he collapsed were 'Hey Ram, Hey Ram', and the priests said that his soul was certain to reach the Supreme abode, the *Vaikuntham*, the eternal world of no anxiety. People generally took comfort and solace, knowing that an event was inevitable according to their birth chart. But in Gandhiji's death, nobody found comfort with those astrological analyses and priests' words.

Rage, anger, frustration, and such feelings began to multiply like mushrooms in their hearts. Revenge killings took place in many cities, especially in Bombay. Shock and sorrow mingled with anger and revenge ruled their emotions. Violent incidents took place in Pune, the hometown of Nathuram Godse. Violent incidents occurred in other parts of India as well. The Maharashtrian Brahmin community was specifically targeted, after it was known that the majority of the assassins were Chitpavan Brahmins.

The media revealed that previous attempts to kill Gandhiji had been made earlier in his life. But Gandhiji, once talking about death, had said:

"Birth and death are not two different states, but they are different aspects of the same state. There is as little reason to deplore the one as there is to be pleased over the other."

The first attempt to kill Gandhiji was on 25 June 1934.

Mohandas Karamchand Gandhi was in Pune along with his wife, Kasturba Gandhi, to deliver a speech at Corporation Auditorium. They were travelling in a motorcade of two cars. The car in which the couple were travelling was delayed and the first car reached the auditorium. Just when the first car arrived at the auditorium, a bomb was thrown, which exploded near the car. This caused grievous injury to the Chief Officer of the Pune Municipal Corporation, two policemen, and seven others. Nevertheless, no account or records can be found of the investigation or any arrests being made. Gandhi's secretary, Pyarelal Nayyar, believed that the attempt failed due to lack of planning and coordination.

The second attempt on the life of Mohandas Gandhi may not have been an attempt to assassinate, but a demonstration of anger by a young man who tried to bow down to Gandhi and was rejected. In May 1944, Gandhi was sent from Aga Khan Palace prison and soon after he contracted malaria. On the advice of doctors, he took a holiday to Panchgani, a hill station near Pune. During his stay at Panchgani, Gandhi was staying at Dilkush Bungalow.

A group of 15–21 young men came to Panchgani after realising that Gandhi was staying there. This young crowd was led by Nathuram Godse. By evening, during the prayer meeting, Nathuram Godse rushed towards Gandhi with a dagger, shouting anti-Gandhi slogans. He was unable to reach Gandhi as he was overpowered by Mani Shankar Purohit (the proprietor of Surti Lodge, Pune) and D. Bhilare Guruji of Satara (who later became a Congress legislator from Mahabaleshwar). The documentary evidence of this attack can be found in the depositions made by Mani Shankar Purohit and D. Bhilare Guruji before the

Kapur Commission set up an investigation of the assassination of Gandhi. However, the Kapur Commission rejected this theory, as many of the close associates of Gandhi were not present during that time.

The third attempt was also at a demonstration. However, people who testified before the Kapur Commission referred to it as an attempt at violence. Mohandas Gandhi began his talks with Mohammad Ali Jinnah on 9 September 1944, which lasted for 14 days. While leaving for Mumbai from Sevagram Ashram, a group of Hindu activists stopped him. They did not want him to go to Bombay to hold talks with Jinnah, but these protesters were stopped by volunteers of the Ashram. The leader of this group, Nathuram Godse, was again found in possession of a dagger. (This incident has also been portrayed in the film Gandhi by Sir Richard Attenborough. In this, it is not portrayed as an attempt to murder but as a peaceful demonstration in which the demonstrators were waving black flags.)

Fourth attempt: On 20 January 1948, Madanlal Pahwa, Shankar Kistaiya, Digambar Badge, Vishnu Karkare, Gopal Godse, Nathuram Godse, and Narayan Apte came to *Birla Bhavan* (aka Birla House) in Delhi to carry out another attack on Mahatma Gandhi and Huseyn Shaheed Suhrawardy. Apart from Madanlal Pahwa and Vishnu Karkare, everyone else reached the venue through the rear entrance in a cab. Madanlal Pahwa tried to bribe Choturam, the driver at Birla Bhavan, to let him go behind the podium to take pictures of Gandhi. However, Choturam became suspicious and asked Madanlal Pahwa why he needed photographs from behind, and inquired about the absence of a camera. Madanlal Pahwa instead left, making Choturam think he was going back to the taxi. However, he placed a cotton ball enclosing a bomb on the wall behind the podium and ignited it. The bomb went off without creating any panic (Ref: The Assassination of Mahatma Gandhi, Wikipedia.)

At Berhampur, Ramalingam called for a dawn meeting with all his friends and politicians. He discussed with them that they should not allow any communal riots in their town. They all agreed to conduct a public mourning ceremony. By sunrise they had all gathered at the Barracks ground, and there was one stage constructed for the speakers. They waited there for people to arrive, as there were no demonstrations or any earlier publicity. They hoped that the public would get there.

That night was a silent night for all. Next morning the town woke up in silence. They felt betrayed, they felt angry, and they felt frustrated at the sudden death of the man who had given them the freedom. They feared that as their guardian was not anymore, the foreigners might again take over their country and enslave them.

To quell their mixed-up emotions they walked slowly in a silent procession. The grieving men, women, and children led by a man carrying a life-like portrait of the Mahatma reached the Barracks ground. The bewildered children were told that Bapu was no more. They saw the leaders of the town waiting for them.

Then Ramalingam, with tears in his eyes said, "Our Bapu belongs to us all, let us all share our sorrow." When they saw their Panditji, their Masterji, in tears, they began to sob.

Panditji went to escort an old lady onto the stage. She sat down on the stage and wept bitterly. "No mother would like to see her son go before her." There was a lot of crying from the crowd. One volunteer escorted her back to her family. Several people climbed onto the stage and talked, but what they said was not important. The language was not important; it was their genuine feeling for their Bapu that remained most important. The public grieving continued all day long. At the Barracks ground the vendors and some people in the neighbourhood provided snacks and water for the mourners. It became a public affair not organised by anyone. The public stood in unity to the delight of the law and order units.

Emotional validation is something we all seek and crave, far more than we realise. When we are upset, angry, frustrated, disappointed, or hurt, our tendency is to want to discuss our feelings with others so that we can get things off our chest. Many more climbed up the stage and spoke ardently about Gandhiji. Their words were not political speeches but their feelings were genuine and their words were from their hearts.

However, getting things off of our chests by telling others about our feelings is not always satisfying. Experiencing anger, the emotion is usually attributed to external factors that are beyond our control. It can be a result of blocking motivated behaviour. An individual may react in several different ways. Anger is an emotion related to one's psychological interpretation of having been offended, wronged, or denied and a tendency to react through retaliation. Anger is like a pressure cooker, which could explode if not controlled.

Fear is an emotion induced by a perceived threat which causes entities to quickly pull away from it and to usually hide. Fear is the ability to recognise danger leading to an urge to confront it or flee from it. But in extreme cases of fear (horror and terror) a freeze or paralysis response is possible.

Fear is frequently related to the specific behaviours of escape and avoidance, whereas anxiety is the result of threats that are perceived to be uncontrollable or unavoidable. It is worth noting that fear almost always relates to future events, such as the worsening of a situation, or the continuing of a situation that is unacceptable. Fear can also be an instant reaction to something happening at the time.

It was a death that touched everyone instantly and directly. Few were the people who did not cry that long weekend. People talked about what Gandhiji had said in his lifetime. They wanted to take revenge.

Immediately, another man stood up and reminded people what Gandhiji had said about revenge:

"An eye for eye only ends up making the whole world blind."

Then various people repeated Gandhiji's sayings:

"Man should forget his anger before he lies down to sleep."

"A man is but the product of his thoughts. What he thinks, he becomes."

"Always aim at complete harmony of thought and word and deed. Always aim at purifying our thoughts and everything will be well."

"Anger and intolerance are the enemies of correct understanding."

"As human beings, our greatness lies not so much in being able to remake the world—that is the myth of the atomic age—as in being able to remake ourselves."

"Men often become what they believe themselves to be. If I believe I cannot do something, it makes me incapable of doing it. But when I believe I can, then I acquire the ability to do it even if I didn't have it in the beginning."

"Happiness is when what you think, what you say, and what you do are in harmony."

"It is the law of love that rules mankind. Had violence, or hate, ruled us we would have become extinct long ago. And yet, the tragedy of it is that the so-called civilised men and nations conduct themselves as if the basis of society was violence."

"Hatred ever kills, love never dies; such is the vast difference between the two. What is ordained by love is retained for all time."

"Where there is love there is life."

"It may be long before the law of love will be recognised in international affairs. The machineries of government stand between and hide the hearts of one people from those of another."

"To forgive is not to forget. The merit lies in loving in spite of the vivid knowledge that the one to be loved is not a friend. There is no merit in loving an enemy when you forget him for a friend."

People narrated what they remembered of Gandhi's sayings. They listened to every word as if they had come from the mouth of a saint. They elevated Gandhiji to sainthood. Whatever they said, people cheered and cried at the same time. Nobody had ever seen such public grief.

The town declared a week's holiday, a week that had no resemblance to the week of celebrations a few months before. Every day and in the evenings the public mourning continued at Barracks ground. People carried the photos of Gandhiji and paraded in the streets, some crying and some singing national songs. The lyricist wrote songs about Gandhiji and his love for the country. In their own way people expressed their sorrow; there were no restrictions or prohibitions.

(Gandhiji's funeral from newspaper cuttings)

The police had no role in controlling public anger. By sharing and expressing their grief in their individual manner they mourned together and consoled each other. The temples were kept open to all, and all the differences of creed and caste were forgotten in communal mourning. Gandhiji would have loved to have seen his people united as one in his death. The public went to temples and prayed for the soul of their Bapu.

The public grieving continued for four days and on the fourth day the town performed the last rites to the image of their Bapu and they concluded it with communal feasting. Their unity in grieving calmed the frustration of the people, it lessened their anger, it comforted their aching hearts, and as a result the town escaped any communal riots.

Liingaammama, 1948

27
The Curtain Drops: 1949

Gandhiji's death had a severe effect on Komalam. She became anxious. She feared an unknown danger was about to hit the family. She felt that the death of father of the Nation was a sure sign of forthcoming disaster. It was like a premonition of disaster that was going to descend upon them. Gandhiji was more than a political leader for the family; he was the reason why the family had left everything behind and had got involved with the freedom movement. Gandhiji was part of the family, his views enveloped the family's existence, and their lives were tied down with him and his lifestyle. She felt that destiny was sending them some warning signals. Panditji never revealed his feelings in front of his family, and Pillamma feared for the future. The family became anxious and the family dreaded their future. The void that Gandhiji had left in their family could never be fulfilled by anything else or anybody else. Pillamma was more concerned of what the effect of Gandhiji's loss would be on Panditji. She had looked forward to having a 'normal' life, but now with Gandhiji's sudden death she also felt that some impending danger lurked around the corner.

"Amma, I'm afraid," said Komalam, hugging her mother. Pillamma was surprised as it was a long time since her daughter had last hugged her.

"What are you afraid of, Komalam?"

"Amma, I think happiness is not written in our lives."

"Don't worry, Komalam. All will be right soon."

"No, Amma … try to understand. We celebrated the Independence Day with so much happiness but within months Gandhiji's death wiped out all our happiness. Father is so upset. He walks around as if he is looking for something he has lost. I'm afraid for my father too. If anything happens to him, I can't live without him, Amma." She cried, hiding her face in her Amma's lap.

Pillamma watched her daughter's agony with great concern. Komalam's fears were genuine she was frightened of losing her father. Komalam had tender heart; Pillamma remembered how much she was upset when the calf died. Pillamma understood Komalam's worry, and tried to console her.

"Komalam, nothing will happen to your father. He has faced many tragedies over the years. He is tough. He will not leave us now in the middle of the ocean. He knows we swim with him, we walk behind him, and we follow him blindly and obey his rules. So how could he leave us now? Tell me Komalam, can your father leave us in lurch? I promise you, your father will not die. He promised you that he would make your daughter a doctor. He is a man of his word.

"Even during three decades of struggle for freedom he never neglected his duties. He cared for his mother, he loved his brothers, and he loves you more than his life. I promise you Komalam he will never die on us."

With some frankness, with some warmth and love, and with further assurances about her father's promises, Pillamma managed to reduce Komalam's worries for the time being. At the same time similar worries niggled in her heart and soul. She had no one to share her worries. She gulped her tears and put up a brave face for Komalam and the family.

But in her heart she also felt that happiness was not written in her life. As soon as she rejoiced about anything, a disaster followed straight away. Pillamma became a cynic and cursed her destiny. She recalled how much her father-in-law had loved her and had given her the education she had longed for. Then again, he died young, leaving her to her fate, resulting in an abrupt halt to her education. She recalled many more disasters that had followed her happy moments as if the happiness carried the disaster as its shadow, so much so that Pillamma often dreaded any happy moments in her life. She enjoyed those happy moments but always looked over her shoulder for the evil shadow that lurked behind her.

Komalam's health began to concern Pillamma, but Komalam did not want her brother to know about her illness. She began to bleed a lot and she put it down to heavy periods. Pillamma consulted Jagappa; his treatment gave some temporary relief to Komalam. Those were the days when women felt shy to discuss their vaginal problems openly. Her vaginal bleeding continued for months before easing off. First she had put it down to a miscarriage, but she was relieved to know that it wasn't related to pregnancy. Komalam had her sixth child a couple of years earlier and she wanted no more children. After a brief pause Komalam's bleeding started once again. As it could not be controlled, Dr Venkatarao admitted her to the women's hospital. There a lady doctor conducted a minor surgery on her, but it had no effect and there was no improvement. Both Pillamma and Komalam missed their friend and physician, Dr Margaret Bhore, who sadly passed away a couple of years before c. Pillamma felt that Dr Bhore, who had given life to Komalam when she was born, could have solved her medical condition now.

Once Komalam returned from the hospital she became very active. She wanted to celebrate Diwali, as they used to do when she was a child. Ramalingam and Errababu began to prepare for the celebration with immense enthusiasm. That summer the two men got out their coveted family recipes for making fireworks for the Diwali festival. In town many families made their own fireworks for Diwali and often there was a friendly competition between the families to see who made the best. The ingredients were purchased and dried in the sun for days, so that not a drop of moisture remained in them. That was the first step to making good quality fireworks. The whole family took part in the preparations. The women ground the raw ingredients with a pestle and mortar. Then the servants sieved them with a muslin cloth. Pillamma ordered earthen pots to make flowerpots and fountain fireworks. The older boys made paper tubes to make Roman candles.

When the time had come for stuffing the mixed ingredients in pots and tubes, all the children were dismissed from the back veranda and the four adults took charge of completing the fireworks. It was a tricky and dangerous job.

If the stuffing was not done tight enough, the firework would not burn, but if it were packed too tight, it could burst in your hands. It needed patience and dexterity. Errababu, Komalam, and Pillamma took charge of it and Panditji supervised the task. Panditji prohibited having any bombs or rockets made at home, to safeguard the children. Pillamma placed an order with the potter for nine hundred divas—the oil-lamps. Fresh turmeric was pounded from the turmeric pods and kumkum was made at home. Gifts of kumkum and turmeric packets were to be distributed to married women, along with coconut, sweets, and fruit. Children made paper bags for the gifts.

Preparations for Diwali were in full swing. The house was decorated with whitewash, or lime wash made of shells. Whitewash, or calcimine, or lime paint, is made from slaked lime (calcium hydroxide) and chalk (whiting). It is made from limestone which has been crushed, burned, and slaked with water to make lime putty. The lime putty is matured for several months before being thinned with water to make lime wash. Lime putty was available to purchase. After the lime wash, the house gleamed bright

On the Diwali day, early in the morning Pillamma conducted prayers at home. Then Komalam and Pillamma went round to their friends and distributed the bags of kumkum, turmeric, coconut, sweets, and fruit gifts to the married women. In the evening soon after sunset, Komalam took her two daughters and went to Ranganathaswami Temple in the vicinity, carrying ghee and divas. The three of them arranged four hundred lit-divas all around the compound walls of the temple and in the temple. It was customary for volunteers from different families to take it upon themselves to decorate the temple with Diwali divas. Meanwhile the rest of the family decorated the compound wall and the house with the divas. All the houses in town were decorated with divas, and the town began to look pretty, like a bride. Later the whole family celebrated, lighting the fireworks. That particular family celebration had been the happiest day for the family in three decades. In her happiness Pillamma failed to see the dark shadow of happiness lurking behind.

Once Diwali was over, Komalam began to make preparations for the Sankranti festival that comes in January. She did not rest for a minute. She continued to work as if she were possessed. She made three sets of clothes for all her children to celebrate the three-day festival. Now the *Khadi* material was available with prints and colours. She purchased printed *Khadi* with purple and pink flowers and another material with blue motifs. Using her talent she stitched three maxi skirts and blouses for Santa and three dresses for her second daughter, Jani, and on Jani's request she put three pockets on each dress, two to the sides and one hidden pocket on the waist line. Jani liked to store her precious possessions in her pockets, safe from her younger brother Devi Kumar.

For the older boys the tailor made two striped shirts and one blue one each. For the young boys Komalam stitched checked shirts and shorts. One evening a vendor came to the house with a new stock of materials. Komalam purchased two mini-saris made of parachute material printed with bright coloured flowers. It was the latest trend and the material looked like silk. Although it was not *Khadi*, she bought the mini-saris for the girls, who loved dressing up. She stored them away as a surprise for the girls, and only Pillamma was aware of them. The

Sankranti festival was celebrated by the whole family with gusto and vigour. Joy and happiness drenched the family with its gentle shower and each and everyone was happy.

After a month, Komalam developed a large abscess on the right-hand side of her abdomen and along with it she continually had a high fever of 104 degrees and above. After several tests and discussions all the doctors gave the name of ascites to Komalam's condition. Her congenital liver problem had relapsed.

Ascites is the accumulation of fluid (usually a serous fluid which is pale yellow and clear) in the abdominal (peritoneal) cavity. Ascetic fluid can have many sources, such as liver disease, cancers, congestive heart failure, or kidney failure. Such a clear diagnosis was not available at Berhampur in those days. The most common cause of ascites is advanced liver disease or cirrhosis. For patients who do not respond well to medication, frequent therapeutic paracentesis is performed to remove large amounts of fluid (a needle is carefully placed into the abdominal area, under sterile conditions). Some complications of ascites can be related to its size. The accumulation of fluid may cause breathing difficulties by compressing the diaphragm and the formation of pleural effusion.

Komalam had swollen feet and her stomach bulged as if she were pregnant. She accumulated fluid in her stomach. The doctors said that it was a typical symptom of her condition. She stayed in the hospital for ten days and then Komalam insisted on going home and begged her brother Dr Ramam to take her home. At home, daily, the fluids were syringed out but within hours it had refilled. She needed blood transfusion and some special medicines that were not available in town. So Panditji travelled by train to Calcutta for medicines and blood.

Pillamma watched her daughter going downhill, but she could do nothing. She ran to the well, her secret place to shed her tears. The well absorbed all her tears as a mother would take in all the pain of her child. She sat there by the well recalling Komalam's childhood. To start with, she had agonised over her baby's birth with caul, but that hurdle had been crossed over in a fortnight's time with the help of Dr Margaret Bhore and Jagappa. The public labelled her baby as cursed but wise doctor Margaret Bhore put their minds at rest saying the caul babies are born with a boon and bring good luck to the family and the people around her.

At six months of age Komalam had developed an eye problem. She had a cataract in her right eye, and the doctor suggested surgery but Pillamma had been afraid that her infant might lose her eyesight altogether. Then one elderly woman called Taayaramma, who lived opposite their house in Temple Street, had come forward to treat Komalam. Taayaramma was a Lord Vishnu devotee and she treated eye problems freely in the name of God. At first she applied some ointment called *kaatuka* in the right eye. After an hour she carried the infant to her house and bathed her and put some ointment in the eye. She repeated the process four times a day. After three weeks the cataract was dissolved without any surgery. Jagappa learned the treatment from Taayaramma.

Komalam always looked healthy and had seemed to be growing into a big girl. At one and half years she had a liver problem. Her arms and legs became thin and she looked like a skeleton. The doctors tried their best to treat her. Her temperature both fell and rose like the tides of a sea, the child began to grow week, and finally they gave up on her. Then Pillamma's Atta heard of a Telugu physician who lived in a village called Chompapuram. The physician came and lived in the house for fifteen days. He had his own cook with him who prepared the meals for the physician in the garden. He wanted to be away from the family, so he camped in a hut in the garden.

Although the infant was having high fever, he gave her a bath every day and in the evenings after sunset he scrubbed the patient's whole body with turmeric and then bathed her again. Jagappa looked after the physician. After a fortnight the physician returned home and visited this little patient once a week. Jagappa took charge of the physician's travelling to and fro. The physician continued with his treatment, and after six months Komalam had fully recovered. On the physician's advice, Pillamma carried on the medicine he had given her for another year. Komalam had recovered completely form her liver problem and it had never relapsed until recently. Pillamma sent for the previous physician, but sadly he had passed away. Pillamma cursed her misfortune, as Dr Bhore, the physician who treated Komalam in the past sadly passed away in 1945 and she felt that the Almighty had closed all openings to save her precious daughter. But suddenly Komalam perked up a bit and spent a lot of time reading and writing. Once Pillamma saw her making an astrological chart on a piece of paper, and made no remarks.

The treatment continued daily and the fluid in Komalam's stomach was being drained but the fluid would return by the following day and the bulging stomach made her breathing difficult. She failed to urinate and all her systems began to shut down. The elders of the town asked Errababu to remove her from the four-poster bed and place her on a mat, as per tradition, as the bed on which a person would die had to be given away to a *dhobiwala*, the washer man.

Enraged at their insensitiveness, Errababu dismissed all of them from the room and sat next to Komalam on the four-poster bed. He brushed her long luscious hair and plaited it in two and let it hang from the bed, reaching the floor. Pillamma sat in a corner of the room and watched her beloved daughter, her firstborn, sink slowly. But Komalam kept talking until the next day, and on 31 December 1949, Komalam refused to take an injection from Dr Venkatarao, preferring her brother Ramam to give her the injection with his own hands, which he did.

The final efforts to save her failed, and that day Komalam passed away peacefully soon after midday. The people went to collect Panditji from the railway station, and Panditji returned home with all the medicines, but the patient had already made her exit from this world.

Lingammama fetched the children from the schools. Somebody took them into the room and showed their mother's face, and then took them away to a neighbour's house. The bewildered children failed to understand the situation. Jani, who wanted an explanation to everything, kept quiet when she saw her father sitting there in a corner of the room with a handkerchief on his mouth. She was scared to see her father cry, and ran away looking for her grandmother, but she was nowhere to be found. Gunnu came round and took her to her own house.

The pubic took charge of the situation. Meanwhile the toddler became unconscious and Pillamma, forgetting her own loss and unable to mourn for her Komalam in peace, had to tend to her Komalam's last born. The toddler Sunder remained unconscious for four days, causing more agony to the family. Komalam was cremated in front of all the males of town on 1 January 1950; women were excluded from the cremation ceremony as per the traditions of those days.

The New Year arrived laden with heavy sorrow for the family. Mostly it was too heavy for Panditji to carry. He said not a word to anybody and took part silently in the funeral. The public took charge of performing all the necessary proceedings that followed the cremation.

Errababu obeyed their orders like an obedient pupil and performed his duties as the husband of Komalam. He burst out crying when he had to light the funeral pyre of his beloved with his own hands. Komalam was not just a wife to him; she was his love, his only love. For him Komalam was the reason for his existence and she was the only person who had given him the love that he had lost as a four-year-old little boy when his mother had died.

Every member of the family hid in their individual shells and failed to share their grief or cry together. Instead they retrieved into their individual sorrows, a land of no return.

Sadly, ascites, like an epidemic, took many lives both young and old in town at around the same time and many children became orphans. Jani's friend Chinnarambabu also died at the age of nine.

Komalam
1913-1949

28
The Exodus of 1950

It was only two weeks after the funeral of Komalam that people already began to bring up marriage proposals for the forty-five year old widowed Errababu. He was infuriated by their suggestions. They called themselves well-wishers, but Lingammama called them interfering pests, persistently trying to influence the heartbroken Errababu by citing his father's example and how he had remarried soon after his first wife had died and had several children with his second wife. Some explained to Errababu that his children were young and his daughters particularly needed a mother until they got married. He told each and every one of them that there was only one woman in his life and that was his Komalam, and nobody else could come into his life.

Pillamma nursed the toddler back to health, and pined for her Komalam. Now with only two of her children alive she did not want them to be out of her sight, even for a moment. She was aware that Sabbulu, who had just completed her degree, would get married and would go away. She did not want to lose her only son.

By March the whole family moved to Aska to be with their son, Dr Ramam. It was like an exodus, with their belongings, heavy hearts, and utter defeat for Pillamma, who had lost her children over the last three decades at Berhampur. The family severed its roots from Berhampur and left. The dismayed citizens of the town bid goodbye to the prominent member of their society, the beloved son of Berhampur. What Panditji felt about the move was never known; for family matters, he left it all in the capable hands of his wife Pillamma.

Aska was about 25 miles from Berhampur, a town in its infancy that was just beginning to shed its village look and was on the fringes of being a town. Most people there called it a village, but the few literate residents called Aska 'a small town'. Ramam rented two bungalows that belonged to two brothers who lived in Delhi. They twin houses had a connecting door thorough the courtyard to join the two bungalows. The small hospital, not far away from the bungalows, was fairly equipped and Ramam, the diligent doctor, soon earned the people's love and respect. In no time they treated him as a lord. Besides his popularity, the people of Aska felt honoured that Panditji had come to live in their small town. They saw him as another Gandhi. Although Ramam continued to wear *Khadi* clothes, he was different to his father. As far as work was concerned he was dedicated to it and many a time he went out of his way to help the poor. In his spare time, he volunteered to visit neighbouring villages and conducted free medical camps for the poor. Patients considered him as a godsend and praised him for having healing hands.

In the villages, having the reputation of healing-hands was more beneficial to patients than the real treatment; they were sentimental, they were prejudiced, and they existed in their beliefs irrespective of their validity. The young doctor gave the poor people free medicines that came to him as free samples from the medical representatives. Sometimes he spent his own money to buy medicines for the needy. Reputation for a doctor was vital in the society. If the patients believed in him, they went to him. But all it needed was just one mishap to wipe out his reputation and then patients would avoid him like the plague and would boycott the doctor. The young doctor was generous and he was kind to all. At the same time, he was ambitious and mingled with the elite of the town.

The two bungalows were large and roomy. Pillamma removed the connecting door and used both bungalows as one. After a week, Errababu went to show Pillamma a note that Komalam had left behind a photo of Lord Venkateswara in his room. Pillamma read it and wept bitterly. It was written in Telugu and it read:

Demudaa emi chestavo needey bharam. Naa pillala bhadyata nammeda vunchutavaa leka naa amma meeda vestavaa?

Or,

God, are you going to leave the responsibility of my children on me or are you going to burden my mother with them? It is up to you.

Pillamma was speechless; she was overwhelmed with sorrow, remembering every word Komalam had written. She envisaged the agony of Komalam before she penned those words and felt her frustration in her last hour.

Pillamma constantly questioned herself and blamed herself for not to ease her daughter Komalam's struggle before she died. *Why didn't my Komalam speak to me about her worry? Why did she keep me in the dark? My daughter was so worried and I didn't even realize. All the time I was concerned about my daughter ... why did I not see that Komalam was also concerned about her children? What kind of a mother am I? How could I be so insensitive to a mother's feelings? Komalam, why didn't you speak to me about your worry?*

With feelings of guilt and agony for her loss Pillamma hid her face in her palms and wept uncontrollably. Errababu watched her with tears in his eyes.

"Amma, please look after Komalam's children. Now they are your children. Please say that you will be their mother and grandmother now. I must go, Amma, I must."

"Errababu, don't go! Let's all live together as before. Komalam's children are now my children, I'll take care of them but they also need their father, stay here and give me your support."

"Thank you Amma, I know you will look after the children, but I need to find peace in myself. My life without Komalam is not worth living. I must go." He turned round and left for Berhampur.

Pillamma, who had always tried to keep the family together, now felt powerless to see her family disintegrate. Lakshman also returned to Berhampur to continue his degree course. Santa had just finished her Matriculation. Ramam and Pillamma wanted to fulfil Komalam's wish, so Santa joined the Parlakimidi Maharaja College to study Intermediate (ISC). She became a lodger with Errababu's cousin, P. Krishnamurthy, and his family. He was a mathematics Professor at the college and became a guardian for Santa. Devi Kumar and Sunder joined the local boy's school. Veeradhi returned to his work at Cuttack.

Now Jani and Subbulu remained at home. Unfortunately, as there was no school for girls Jani had to stay at home. Pillamma looked at her diminished family and sighed heavily. She was more concerned for Jani and she despaired that the history of her family was repeating itself. Komalam had been removed from school at the age of nine by her father as per Gandhiji's wishes to boycott all government institutions. Panditji applied the rules first at home before he carried them to the public, and now Jani was unable to go. Pillamma felt that she had no control over anything, and the family began to drift aimlessly in the hands of destiny.

The same year Lingammama, perhaps feeling lonely, became very ill. The only relative he had was his sister Pillamma, but since she had moved out of Berhampur he felt lonely and had lost the will to live. Komalam's death had its deep effect on every member of the family including Lingammama. Pillamma went to stay with her brother in his last three days. One early morning he passed away peacefully in his sister's lap. Pillamma lost her only link to her maternal family. She felt that Berhampur had deprived her of all her happiness and that she had sacrificed all the people she loved to that town.

After six months, Ramam wanted a car. Pillamma was in a very depressed state. She was prepared to give her life for her the happiness of her children and keep them together. Panditji felt that Ramam was utilizing his mother's depression to his own advantage and was making unreasonable demands. But for Pillamma nothing mattered more than her son's happiness. She sold her house at Berhampur, where Lingammama had lived until he died, and which she had inherited as *streedhanam* from her mother.

The last gram of gold and silver that she had was sold and given to Ramam for his car. Pillamma sold gold and silver to their family friend and businessman Immedisettigaru for fifty rupees per *tola*, equalling 11.5 grams. *Tola* is the weight used in India for weighing gold and silver. When she gave her son all the silver that there was, he promised to replace it all within few years, but the family never purchased any precious metal again—not even a silver spoon! Silver and gold meant nothing to Pillamma at that moment of time she was going through severe depression. All she wanted was to see her son happy and living with her. The 26-year-old doctor wanted all the luxuries of modern life. As a student at Patna he mingled with the rich and he liked their life style. He was a young man who had been brought up under strict discipline and good morals, which he maintained all his life. He never picked up any bad habits, but he longed to escape the poverty line at which the family existed.

Ramam gave all his salary to his mother and Veeradhi also continued to give a share of his salary for the family budget and with both incomes Pillamma managed the family well. Ramam went to Vijayanagaram with Baburao, a distant cousin and a family man, with a wife and two children who befriended Ramam as soon as he became a doctor. The two of them travelled to Vijayanagaram to purchase a new Vauxhall car. Ramam employed a boy called Seenu to look after the car. The boy washed and polished the car daily and kept it in top condition. Seenu, lived with the family and became an added member of the family. Baburao, who lived in Berhampur, became a frequent visitor to Aska; he used the car more than Ramam did.

After purchasing the car, with the remaining money Ramam bought an HMV Gramophone and twelve long-playing vinyl records for his sister Subbulu, who would normally have been given the money from the sale of the Lingammama's house as her *streedhanam,* but she made no fuss about it.

The house had vinyl discs to entertain them. Occasionally Baburao arranged family outings in the car for the whole family. He was the main driver but he shared it with Ramam. Pillamma felt that Baburao was taking undue advantage of her son but she could do nothing about it as Ramam trusted his middle aged cousin as a good friend. By owning a car Ramam became more popular in the town. He made friends with the elite of the town and had frequent parties with them; sometimes he took his sister Subbulu to one good friend called Pandas and his family. His wife Kunni befriended Subbulu and their daughter of the same age as Jani, studying at a boarding school in Shimla made friends with Jani when she came home on her school vacation.

In the evenings the young men played tennis. Anything Ramam did was looked upon by the locals as being great. They would gather outside the tennis court to watch the men play. They felt that the young doctor had brought 'city' to their small town. He inspired some young boys to get educated and become doctors like him. In spite of his modern outlook, Ramam never discarded wearing *Khadi* clothes and remained a vegetarian all his life.

Panditji continued to go on his daily walks around the village and wherever he went the people stood up in reverence. He would enquire about their welfare and when necessary asked his son to look into their health problems. As a doctor, Ramam was kind and considerate to all his patients. There the traditions of the place were as that of a village, where women were not to allowed to wander on their own. A young girl like Jani was not even allowed to play out with her brothers and their friends. She was cut off from the world. The free-spirited young girl felt that her wings were severed and she was imprisoned. She began to hide in her depressed world.

Subbulu spent a lot of time reading or dreaming. The two brothers of Jani went to school. Ramam worked at the hospital and Pillamma spent her time in the kitchen or on the steps that led to the garden and cried silently in memory of her Komalam when nobody was watching her. The household was running like a silent movie, all doing their duty and nobody speaking. The servants and the gardener worked silently. There was no running water in those bungalows, so the servants fetched and carried water from the two wells. Sometimes Jani went to talk to the old gardener, who was a nice man but was afraid to talk to her openly in case the master of the house should get cross with him. The girls had a lot of restrictions that Jani had never heard of at Berhampur. She was confined to four walls, and she roamed from room to room, from one backyard to another like a lost soul. She waited for her brothers to come home from school and play with her, but sadly they made their own friends and she was excluded from their group. When Ramam came home for meals the atmosphere changed as if they all received a cue for action, when Pillamma talked, and Panditji would come out of his room to dine with the family. Ramam always talked and teased Jani, which she liked. He would have his lunch, and then after taking a few minutes' nap he would return to his duty at the hospital. At once the household would return to its silent mode.

Jani waited for summer holidays for her sister to come home. When she finally arrived, then she was a different girl; she hardly spoke to Jani. Pillamma perked up and she paid all the attention to Santa. Ramam discussed with her about her studies and everybody was eager to talk to her. After a week, a group of ten girls, her classmates, arrived to spend two weeks at Aska. It was Ramam's idea that Santa should socialise more. Those bubbly girls loved Jani and talked to her about their college life and the fun they were all having there. Jani cringed with shame and embarrassment when they all pitied her for not being clever like her sister. Like others they too came to the conclusion that she was at home because she was not interested in studies. Jani cried in her heart but said nothing and gave no explanations to them by then she was tired of justifying her situation, she found it easy to remain silent. She remembered what Lingammama told her once- once an opinion is opined there is no use to try and change it, opinions are as strong as the roots of a Banyan tree easily spreads it's roots but to budge it is hard more you try more it spreads.

Those two weeks were memorable for Jani. The cheerful girls' company was refreshing, and their laughter was like a monsoon shower. Their friendship towards her was warm. They treated her like their little sister. Ramam took all the family on many outings. They visited the surrounding hills, historical places, and to Russellkonda. Russellkonda town is in the Goosur taluk, Ganjam District, 50 miles north-west of Berhampur on the Loharkandi River. It is named after George Russell, who was appointed Special Commissioner in 1835 to put down the disturbances in that area.

Another exciting trip was to a spa called Taptapani. Located at a distance of 55 miles from Aska, Taptapani, as the name suggests (*Tapta* meaning 'warm' and *Pani* meaning 'water') is a hot water sulphur spring in Orissa. Set amidst the greenery of a lush forest, the sulphur spring of Taptapani is situated on the top of a hill. The hot waters erupt in bubbles in two specific places and the temperature of this hot water varies between 90 to 100 degrees Fahrenheit. The water from the hot spring of Taptapani is channelled into a nearby pond, which is open to the public for bathing. The water of the Taptapani spring is believed to have medicinal properties that can cure diseases of the skin and body. The spring is attributed with religious virtues and therefore a temple has also been built near it. The shy girls washed their feet and face in the pond and nobody bathed there in public view.

In the evenings the girls gathered in the courtyard, sang songs, and danced to amuse the family. While resting under the blue sky they talked all evening about their dreams and their future. Jani loved their dreams and she wanted to tell them of her own, but she restrained herself in case they made fun of her. None of them felt necessary to ask Jani about her dreams as they had concluded that her fate was sealed and because she was staying at home without much education Jani would soon simply get married and settle down. One of them commented, 'I wish I was like Jani, a free bird doing nothing, but my father wants me to go to college and get a degree.' Jani heard her loud and clear. She looked at her sister for support but Santa was paying no attention to her little sister. Jani gulped her tears and choked. She ran into the kitchen and Pillamma hugged her silently. There was no need for any words; the grandmother and the granddaughter understood the agony very well.

After the two week's holiday the girls, along with Santa, left for Parlakimidi. Once again the house fell back into its silent mode. Ramam's duties extended to the neighbouring villages. He travelled daily and would return home tired and late.

Sometimes Jani would curse her mother for having died so suddenly and putting her in her present predicament. She felt like crying aloud, but knowing that it would hurt her grandmother, she held her sorrow in her heart. She remembered what a neighbouring woman had told her when she cried for Komalam's death. "Jani, remember one thing, never cry in front of your grandmother. Then she will also cry and she will die."

From that time Jani had never cried aloud. She held her sorrow within her heart and often its weight weighed her down. Then she went and sat by the well as she used to at home in Berhampur, the only difference being that there she had sat with Pillamma, whereas here they both sat separately at the two wells, although their sorrow was in unison.

Jani longed to have Lingammama with her, who understood her feelings, however naïve they could be and always listened to her and advised her. While shifting to Aska she had lost all the letters Lingammama had posted to her. Then she remembered his words: "Store them in your memory, Jani. Then you will never lose them."

She sat on the steps of the second garden by herself and mused over his words. He once had said, "It's good to have attachment with detachment." She pondered over that. Could it refer to her attachment to her life at Berhampur and was Lingammama asking her to detach herself from it? If that is true did he know that I would end up in this prison at Aska? How could that be possible? Lingammama was clever but did he see my future? Then why didn't save me? Over the last two years Jani had been maturing rapidly in both body and mind, but more doubts and thoughts became muddled up in her head and made her confused.

She ran to Pillamma and hid her face in her lap and shut her eyes. She did not let her grandmother see her cry. But her quivering body gave away her distress. Pillamma understood the agony of the young girl. Komalam had felt the same frustration when she was removed from school although fortunately she found an excellent tutor who educated her in all subjects. Komalam accepted her destiny, whereas Jani was not yet prepared to accept her situation. To top it all, the visitors invariably commented on Jani as not being clever as her sister. What Jani hated most was their pity. Pillamma noticed how Jani would retreat to her room as soon as any visitors came into the house and abstained from their company.

Pillamma was more concerned about Jani hiding away from people. This was unlike Jani's character. She held her in her arms and wiped her tears. She explained the family's position.

"Jani, even your uncle is tired of this place. He is trying to get a transfer to a city. Have patience my dear girl. Success follows patience and patience precedes success. I promise, you will go to a nice school in the city, and you will be successful. We know you are the brightest in the family. But right now I'm helpless, Jani. Your mother has done us all an injustice and has died on us, but we've no choice but to be with Ramam. Have patience, my dear. The egg becomes a chick only when it is hatched, but if you break it, there is no chick."

Jani wanted to challenge her grandmother and demand that she be sent to Parlakimidi along with her sister Santa. As if Pillamma knew what went on inside her head she explained,

"Jani, Santa is at college, and she is staying with the family of your father's cousin. They cannot take another girl. We cannot burden them. Please, Jani. Have patience! Soon we will be going to live in a big city. Your uncle is trying for a transfer."

Pillamma pacified the distort girl, but in her heart she knew that she was not giving any justice to Jani. So she asked her husband to give tuition to Jani at home. Panditji began to coach her at home in Mathematics and English. Both the tutor and the student had no enthusiasm in it and the lessons lasted for no more than a few minutes. What Jani longed for was to go out, to make friends, to go to school and be happy with her classmates. Panditji was still mourning for his daughter Komalam and had not yet recovered from the shock of losing her.

The congress committee kept in touch with Panditji, but because of the 25 miles distance from Berhampur the visitors were not frequented as before. People wanted him to return to Berhampur. At Aska he rested his oars and the Orissa Congress leaders who worked with their guru, shoulder to shoulder, requested him to stand as the Berhampur M.P. (Member of Parliament.) Panditji—their guru, friend, and philosopher, refused to stand for any election but chose to work with the party. Even after elections, Nityananda Kanungo, Biswanath Das, and Hari Krishna Mehtab—the prominent political leaders were determined to make Panditji a minister working for the Government. Panditji politely refused their offer, saying that it was for the young to form the Government and serve the people. He said that no elder congressman should be greedy to become a minister, as per Gandhian principles.

It was two years since the family settled at Aska. Once again, for the 1952 General Elections the Congress Party requested Panditji to contest for the first Parliament from the Ganjam District. But one senior member, an advocate Ayyagari Subba Rao, expressed his desire to contest for the same seat as he was senior to Panditji. Panditji, listening to his fervent appeal, withdrew his candidature in favour of the man and to the annoyance of the Party. But the congress party gave the seat to another person and not to Ayyagari SubbaRao.

He often remembered what Gandhiji had said: **"The day the power of love overrules the love of power, the world will know peace."** Ramalingam never craved for positions or power.

As the president of the Railway Trade Union, Panditji went to Nagpur to attend a meeting and Subbulu accompanied him. Jani felt left out of everything. She began to spend more time thinking, just mulling over Lingammama's words.

She felt that she had become inconspicuous at home. She took everything that was literally thrown at her without dispute. Once, Lingammama told her not to be so meek. He said:

"Don't be too soft my child. That will get you nowhere. Kindness doesn't mean that you be soft and succumb to everyone. Learn to differentiate between duty and obligation. In life you are not obliged to anyone. You must know you are responsible for your own actions. At the same time, do not forget your duties you are expected to do either morally or socially. Especially in an Indian society people force you to do what you need not do. They pressurise you with moral and emotional blackmail, so never succumb to that. Sympathy and empathy are good terms to remember, do practise them, but never at your own cost."

Jani tried to understand his every word, but his philosophy went over her head. She went to Pillamma and demanded her right to go to school and asked her to send her to Parlakimidi where her sister was going to college. Pillamma cried and sympathised with the young girl's agony. She explained to her that Santa would soon be returning home after her final exams. Jani remembered: sympathy and empathy are good terms to remember—but never at your own cost.

In a huff Jani stood up and complained that she was discriminated by her own family. Pillamma cried silently as she felt the agony of the girl, but under the circumstances she was helpless to help her.

Jani retreated to her room and wept and also felt guilty to have made her grandmother cry. She could never bear to see her cry. Lingammama had asked her not to be influenced by emotional blackmail. Jani, at Berhampur, had run errands for Pillamma, going to bank and pawning items. She had been aware of the family's financial position from a young age of seven. She was certain that her grandmother would never 'use' her. She felt that Lingammama's words did not make any sense in her present situation.

More confused and frustrated and with more agony she ran to her grandmother, hid her head in her lap again, and wept for a long time. She fell asleep in her grandmother's lap. Silently, with tears in her eyes, Pillamma comforted the young girl and sat there without moving until dawn.

Another dawn and another weary day stood in front of Jani.

Santa's friends at Russelkonda, 1951

29
The Mega Decision

Santa returned from Parlakimidi after obtaining an Intermediate certificate in science. Her two years absence from the house was over and serious discussions took place about her future.

Ramam was keen to honour his beloved sister Komalam's dream and to send Santa to study medicine. Pillamma gave her consent, as even she was aware of Komalam's dream to see Santa be a doctor like Dr Margaret Bhore. But Panditji wanted them to find out what Santa wanted to do in future. He stood one against the two, but to respect him the family called for a meeting. So that day, when the boys were at school the family got together to have a conference with Santa in the living room. Jani waited for all to settle down on the floor, while Panditji sat in a chair. Before she entered the room, Pillamma was about to ask Jani to leave as the young girl went to sit by her grandfather's feet. He smiled at her and touched her head fondly, so Pillamma couldn't dismiss Jani from the serious discussion. She was afraid that Jani might ruin the serious matter with her usual moaning. She warned Jani by her glances, which the young girl understood clearly and sat quietly.

Santa sat next to Pillamma. Ramam was about to make the opening comment that her mother Komalam wanted her to study medicine but Panditji intervened and asked Santa what she would like to do for her future, as she had finished the two-year course at Parlakimidi. Santa said nothing, but her face reddened and she shed tears.

"Santa, don't get upset my child. We want to know what your wishes are. It's your future and you must have a say in it," said Panditji to her with assurance.

Jani sitting there patiently, thought in her mind, "Why they don't ask me what I want? If they ask me I won't miss the chance. I'll tell them loudly and clearly that I want to go to school." But she kept mum, as she knew that if her uncle got angry he would throw her out.

"Don't cry, Santa," said Pillamma, wiping her tears tenderly with her sari.

'It's not fair ... I never find such tenderness when I cry," Jani silently told an imaginary friend, Mitra.

"Santa, why are you crying? Crying never solves anything. You can speak your mind. But you must tell me exactly what you want to do with your future," said Ramam, showing his frustration. He never had patience. He dealt with every situation as if it were black or white. There never was any place for emotions and he never exhibited any tenderness. Perhaps he felt that showing emotions openly was not manly enough. If his father were not present there, he would have walked out in a huff. Pillamma remembered those days when she had suggested that Ramam should go for medicine and how he had accepted it willingly. But now she was not sure about Santa … she hesitated to make any decision about the young woman. She wished there could have been Komalam there to make the choices for her dream daughter.

Jani looked at her grandmother with pleading looks. Pillamma was talking to Jani silently, "I know what you want to say Jani, but please don't speak now. I haven't forgotten you. If you must know, your worry is mine and your concern is also my concern. I want you to have everything best, but right now I'm helpless. But soon, all will be well. I will not let Komalam's education disaster be repeated in your life. You will also go to college—that's a promise. Be patient, my Jani. Don't look at me with those bright eyes. I see pleading in your eyes; I see your frustration. If you must know, we all feel guilty to keep you at home without any schooling."

There was a strange bondage between Jani and Pillamma. As if they had some psychic connection, it was as if they had been best friends in their previous birth. Although there were other children older than Jani, Pillamma had always trusted her to do important errands like pawning gold at the Bank and carrying notes to the relevant people during the freedom struggle. As if she had sent her a telepathic message, Jani witnessed the agony in her grandmother's eyes and slowly lowered her eyes and laid her head in her grandfather's lap. Pillamma sighed to see Jani compromise on the situation with diffidence as she used to compromise on her position at home all those years before. "I hope Jani has a better life than me" she said to herself.

"Come on, Santa—I haven't got all day. Speak, do you want to continue your studies or do you want to get married? Your father is coming soon. I'll ask him to find a suitable groom for you," said Ramam, teasing her in his jovial manner. When Grandfather looked at him Rahman lowered his head.

At last Santa opened her mouth, "I want to be a graduate—no marriage please."

"Good. Then that's settled. I will look into the matter, then…"

But Panditji stopped him abruptly.

"Son, 'then' comes then. Let her complete her degree first. Then she will be more matured to tell us what she really wants in her life," he said, ending his statement. He stood up and left for his room, and Jani followed him, carrying the two cushions on which he had been resting, and the conference ended peacefully.

Ramam found a good college at Kakinada for her degree course. He made all arrangements for her stay at the women's hostel. Preparations began in earnest, new clothes were purchased for Santa, and Pillamma made several snacks for her to carry. Ramam purchased necessary books, and all was packed as if she were going to her in-laws. Ramam felt that his niece should not be short of anything in a new place. For him, she was his sister Komalam's daughter, and it was his mission to fulfil his sister's dream. He got her admitted to the science college at Kakinada and returned home feeling that he was a step nearer to fulfilling Komalam's dream.

Out of the two hundred and fifty rupees of the family income, one hundred rupees were sent to Santa at Kakinada for her to cover her hostel and tuition fees. Pillamma, who had years of experience in managing the family with minimum finances, coped with the new situation very well. The kitchen gardens of the two bungalows provided more than enough to suffice for the family needs. With the excess fruit and vegetables Pillamma made pickles, jams, fritters, and poppadum's and stored them away. The dairy products like milk and butter were very cheap in the town of Aska.

The very next month, Errababu came over to Aska and told Pillamma that he would like to take Sunder, his youngest son, to Tirupati to honour his wife's wish to carry out his Mundan ceremony there.

There are many traditional rituals that surround the birth of a child in a typical Indian family. These traditions and rituals are aimed at blessing the child to have a long, fulfilling life. One of these sacred ceremonies is known as *Mundan Sanskar*, the first haircut of the baby. The *Mundan* ceremony is an important tradition in India, and relatives and friends are invited to bless the child. This first haircut of a child in India has an important significance, which is discussed in the following lines.

The child usually receives his/her first *Mundan* in either the first or the third year of age. A priest is called to conduct the rituals according to the traditions and a barber is called to shave off the hair. The priest recites sacred hymns and chants and shaves a part of the head. The barber then shaves the entire head, sometimes leaving a clump of hair at the back of the head. Some of this hair is offered in the sacred rivers of holy cities like Haridwar and Varanasi. To cool down the head and to cure nicks and cuts, a paste of turmeric and sandalwood is sometimes applied on the entire head. Thereafter, a child may be shaved now and then or never, depending on the desire of that particular family.

There is a significant reason as to why the head is shaved in such an elaborate ritualistic way. According to the Hindu beliefs, the hair present at birth is supposed to represent unwanted traits from past lives. In order to make sure that the child has no undesirable qualities of the past birth in this life, the head is shaved to ensure a new beginning and a fresh start. Medically, it is said that shaving off the hair stimulates the cells and improves blood circulation to the brain. Some also believe that this gives the child a long life.

Different people have different traditions associated with *Mundan* ceremony. Some people celebrate it at their home, amidst their friends and family in a religious ceremony. Some families travel to some holy place along with their friends and relatives. Ceremonies are generally conducted amongst the people they love and each can be performed as the family desires, making it a mega ceremony or dwarfing it as minute, all depending on the individual family and their finances. Whether big or small, the basis of a ceremony is to bless the recipient. Sunder was born weak, so Komalam took an oath to the god, Venkateswara, that she would cut the infant's birth hair at the holy place of Tirupati.

Now at the age of six, with his long curly hair Sunder looked like a beautiful girl. At school in Aska the boys teased him, saying that he was a girl. They dared not tease Sunder when his strong brother Devi Kumar was around, since he protected his younger brother with his life. Once when Sunder could no longer bear their teasing, in the middle of the playground he dropped down his shorts and stood in front of them, yelling, "Look, I'm a boy just like you all!"

That had shocked the boys and they stopped teasing him. The Headmaster told Panditji about the incident and the family laughed to hear it.

Three years after Komalam's demise, Errababu remembered his wife's wish and wanted to honour her oath to God at Tirupati. Pillamma told him that Santa had joined Kakinada College. All he said was, "I know, Amma. Panditji writes to me regularly about the children's progress. There is no need for that—they are all your children. You take care of them."

The next day he took Sunder and travelled to Tirupati on a train, it was Sunder's first train journey. After the hair-removing ceremony was performed in Tirupati, Errababu stopped at Madras with a friend called Nyapati Raghava Rao, who conducted the most popular children's programme live every Sunday afternoon on All India Radio. He was fondly known as Radio Annayya, meaning brother for all children, and he was the pioneer for a children's programme called Balanandam in the South of India. That Sunday, Radio Annayya took Errababu and his son into the studio. He asked Sunder on the live broadcast to sing a song and without any hesitation Sunder sang an Oriya song that was broadcast on All India Radio to all. Sunder became the first radio artist in the family.

Errababu was thrilled to see that his son also had music in him. If only he had known that his eldest son Veeradhi was also an accomplished singer, he would have been much happier. It's hard to say if Errababu was aware of Veeradhi's talents or not. He never disclosed his inner feelings to anyone, not even to his good friends. For two weeks, Errababu became close to his youngest son Sunder and showed his fatherly affection towards him in a way that he could never show to his five other children. Sunder was the only child who was not afraid of his father, whereas the other five avoided him and kept their distance.

After two weeks Errababu brought Sunder back to Aska, stayed for the night, and then left for Berhampur. Pillamma begged him to stay with his children but he refused, gently saying that his life and his thoughts were with his wife in the house where she had lived. He had not yet overcome his sorrow. In his bedroom he used a single string bed after having given away the four-poster bed to the washer-man as per tradition. There was a portrait of Komalam on the wall and plenty of books. He read a lot and lived in Komalam's thoughts, surviving with her sweet memories. Nobody, not even the mighty Lord Time, could fill the gap that Komalam had left in his life. He travelled through the country aimlessly searching for his inner peace. He could feel only darkness all around him, and he failed to reach the new dawn of his life. He became a recluse, a loner, and he became a cynic. When he closed his eyes tightly he could see nothing around him, but his thoughts almost glowed in the darkness, constantly reminding him of his loss. He pined for his beloved, his only love in his life, and he failed to compromise on the present situation. He could never escape his grief. He often recited the Sanskrit Sloka:

Asatoma Ma Sadgamaya from Upanisahd:
Asato ma sadgamaya
Tamaso ma jyotirgamaya
Mrtyorma amrtam gamaya

Lead me from the *Asat* (untruth) to the *Sat* (the truth)
Lead me from darkness to light
Lead me from death to immortality.
(Brhadaranyaka Upanishad — I.iii.28)

This is a true prayer—the seeker's admission of his sense of limitedness and his heartfelt cry for assistance in transcendence. It is not a prayer for the things of the world. It is not a prayer for material things. The essence of each of these three mantras is the same: "O, Guru, help me free myself from my sundry misunderstandings regarding myself, the universe, and God and bless me with true knowledge." Whatever he did and however much he prayed, his life with his beloved glistened like mercury in the darkness of his mind. He visited many ashrams to find peace. Once, one guru told him about nature and destiny:

"Everything has its own nature. Air's nature is to blow. Fire's nature is to burn. Water's nature is to flow. To jump, to cry, to wish, to feel sorrow, try for what is not yours anymore is the nature of the mind. Son, you have to come to terms with your beloved's loss. She is no more and nobody can return her to you. Clouds come and go, and then all that is left is the blue sky. Losses come and go but only their sweet memories live forever. You loved your wife, so cherish them, son, and live on those sweet memories."

All those soothing words from the saints, *fakirs,* or gurus gave him some temporary relief, but once he had returned back to his room those comforting thoughts vaporised in the heat of his sorrow. He led a solitary life in and around Berhampur. It's easy to bear the tiredness of body but the tiredness of mind is unbearable. Exhausted, both in body and mind, he continued to travel all around the country to find his peace.

Subbulu had a good proposal from a son of a good family. He was an army doctor and Subbulu liked him. Ramam was delighted that his brother-in-law would also be a doctor. Panditji was glad that the groom did not demand any dowry and respected his principles, and Pillamma thought how happy Komalam would have been to see her sister marry a doctor, since Komalam adored doctors. For her a doctor was no less than an incarnation of the Almighty on earth to heal the people, to save them from their suffering, and to cure them. Her thoughts all stemmed from her adoration for Dr Margaret Bhore, who had given her life to medicine.

At Subbulu's wedding, Errababu recalled his own marriage scenes and how Panditji had given him a *Charka* as a gift. Panditji gave his doctor son-in-law a *bhagvadgita* and a set of books on *Ayurveda* (life-knowledge). Ayurvedic medicine is a system of traditional medicine native to the Indian subcontinent and a form of alternative medicine. The oldest known Ayurvedic texts are the *Suśruta Saṃhitā* and the *Charaka Saṃhitā.* These classical Sanskrit encyclopaedias of medicine are among the foundational and formally compiled works of Ayurveda. Panditji believed that knowledge should be gained and valued wherever it comes from, just as the ancient scholars travelled on foot from place to place and country to country seeking the wisdom of the local wise men; learned the local language and then wrote many books on the ancient knowledge of the world.

So Subbulu got married and left home with her husband, while Jani became a loner at home. She spent her time in self-imposed solitary confinement. Her childish thoughts went haywire. She could not put a name or give a shape to them but they were little different from those of her father Errababu, who pined for his wife Komalam as Jani pined for schooling.

Dr Ramam at London, 1954

Sunder, 1953
(Tirupati Trip)

30
The Nagpur trip

Panditji had to attend a Railway Trade Union meeting at Nagpur. He took Jani along with him and she was over the moon. At last, a relief from her solitary life within the four walls. They set off on a train and for Jani it was her first ever train ride. Panditji was a volunteer and took no salary for being the President of the Trade Union. He was given first-class coupé tickets for travelling to attend the meetings.

The two-day journey was the most memorable for the granddaughter and the grandfather. Jani talked nonstop about Berhampur. Even after three years she remembered every minute detail of her life there. Her innocent talk and her excitement of recalling her friends, her enthusiasm about Berhampur, brought smiles to Panditji's face. Jani had always been close to him. She had followed him like a shadow when he was at Berhampur and had attended public meetings he addressed. She, with her chatter, always brought happiness around. He remembered how once she had climbed onto the stage and insisted that her name be enrolled when the leaders called for women volunteers. He laughed when she told him how she and her friend had gone looking for recluses in town. Once again Panditji and Jani came alive.

Suddenly she cried for Lingammama. Then they both talked about Lingammama, who had eased out her cluttered feelings about death and losing nice people. She wanted to talk about her mother's death but stopped abruptly, remembering what an elderly neighbour had said to her: "Jani, if you cry in front of your grandmother she will cry to death. You don't want to lose your grandmother too, do you?"

Her grandfather understood her agony. He noticed how she avoided talking about her mother. Now as the opportunity had come for him to share his sorrow with his granddaughter he wanted her to express her feelings first. But Jani restrained herself from crying for her mother. Instead she made an odd comment, "Grandfather, do you think the cow is still crying?"

He recalled how the cow Komalam had cared for had mooed day and night when Komalam died. Not even Pillamma was able to console the strange animal. She had cried for her best carer, and she grieved, shedding tears and mooing continuously. Eventually the cow was given to the milkman, who promised to look after the bereaved animal. But soon after Errababu returned after immersing Komalam's ashes in the River Ganges, the cow had died. He did not want to tell Jani about the cow's death as she had not yet come to terms with her mother's death.

"I think the milkman is kind and looks after it," he said, and Jani said no more about it, but he noticed that her eyes had filled with tears. She stood up and went to the window, watching the scenery from the running train. In the family nobody openly talked about Komalam's death, as if they were trying to protect each other from the sorrow. It was indeed a strange situation. Panditji was afraid that the volcano of their grief would one day erupt and consume them all.

Throughout the two-day journey Jani loved the meals her grandfather ordered for them. When the train stopped at major stations, a butler brought meals on silver plates covered in a round dome, and water in a large jug and two glasses. The meals were sumptuous and had a sweet dish too. Jani took charge of serving the meals on the folded table that was in the carriage. At the next station, the butler collected the plates and left. Jani found his disappearing acts funny. When she laughed, grandfather wanted to know what was so funny.

"Grandfather, the man is like a genie. He looks like a genie with his white and red turban, his white and blue baggy pyjamas, and his red waistcoat. He comes with meals on a silver plate and vanishes like a genie. After a while he suddenly appears again and vanishes with the empty plates. Wait until I tell my friends at Berhampur—sorry, not friends—I will tell my brothers. Devi Kumar and Sunder won't believe that I have seen a real genie!"

Whenever the train stopped at a major station, as if they were expecting Panditji's arrival some men entered the compartment with files in their hands and talked to Panditji about the work. While they talked, she opened the rear door of the coupé and sat on the floor, dangling her feet outside and holding tightly on to the rail. It was a dangerous thing to do but Panditji knew that Jani was a very sensible girl and she needed to release her adventurous spirit that had been kept in a corked bottle for well over two years.

At intervals, grandfather purchased from the station vendors Jani's favourite snack samosas for her. He pampered her throughout the journey. He wanted her to be happy. For Jani the whole trip was an experience she cherished. She loved taking a shower in a cubicle. The train had all the facilities that she had not seen before. She enjoyed climbing up and down from the upper berth and loved to sleep on it. Throughout the journey she felt like a free bird released from a cage.

When they reached Nagpur, a group of officials came to receive them. They were taken to a friend's house first. Panditji talked to them briefly and left Jani there while he went away with the officials. It was a beautiful house, but quiet. Before Jani could say anything the lady told her that all her children were at school but they would be coming home soon. Jani had a shower, ate some food, and wandered round the house.

When the five girls returned home in their smart uniforms they surrounded Jani and bombarded her with questions. They all spoke in perfect English. Jani could understand but was unable to reply, and they looked at each other in surprise. Their mother said something to them and they retired to their rooms to do their homework. Once again Jani felt left out.

That evening when Panditji returned they all surrounded him and talked about politics, finances, and many other subjects, but they conversed entirely in English. Panditji took keen interest in their studies; two of them were at college and three at school. Then he turned to Jani and told her in Telugu that all the girls said she was beautiful. Such a compliment had no effect on her young mind; she wanted to be like those smart, clever sisters. Their parents also participated in discussions, leaving Jani to play with their three-year-old granddaughter. Again Jani felt out of place and she agonised over how they had looked at her with pity when grandfather had said something to them about her. Later she found them giggling at her.

The next day they got ready, took their lunch boxes, and left to school and college. Jani was left alone again. The toddler loved her new playmate. She wouldn't leave her for a minute. Jani entertained the toddler with dances and songs.

That weekend the whole family went on an outing. They were shown nice places in Nagpur. Jani loved the zoo best, but she compared herself to those caged animals. The family played games and had a good picnic in the park but meanwhile, Panditji was tied down with work. The sisters were very nice to Jani and she enjoyed their company. The toddler was also learning to speak two languages, English and Tamil, her mother tongue. While playing hide and seek the toddler called out to Jani, 'Dummy catch me, dummy catch me.'

Quickly the older sister came over and shut the toddler's mouth, but Jani had heard her loud and clear. She felt embarrassed. She felt hurt and humiliated to know what the sisters thought of her. She felt like crying but she held her tears back. She was not one to shed tears in front of anybody. But she pretended not to have heard those words.

The next morning Panditji bid goodbye to the family. They gave Jani a nice gift of ribbons and bangles, and to Panditji a box of satsumas called '*santras*', famous in Nagpur. The toddler wouldn't let go of Jani. She did not want to lose her playmate. Jani stayed quiet throughout the return train journey.

Just before they reached home, Jani looked at her grandfather and asked him, 'Am I a dummy, grandfather?'

He understood the reason for her silence, and said nothing to her.

Pillamma was surprised to see her bubbly girl return home so demure. Jani went into her room and shut the door behind her. For two days she would not emerge from her room and she ate no food and starved.

Ramam tried to make her laugh. "Jani! We've already got independence, so don't go on a hunger strike like Gandhiji," he teased her.

Jani burst open the door, came out, and stood in front of him with folded arms. "Uncle, I haven't got my freedom. I'm in a prison!" She retreated to her room and shut the door behind her again. He was flabbergasted to see her reaction, and he felt that she was being unreasonably difficult. He was about to retaliate, but Pillamma stopped him.

"Son, do something if this continues. We might lose Jani. Either she would go mad or she would die."

"Amma, I'm trying my best for a transfer to the city. Believe me, I can also see her agony," he cried, and then walked out and slammed the door behind himself too. Now with each one trying to avoid the other, the atmosphere became more strained at home.

The next day Pillamma stood in front of Jani and wept bitterly. Jani had never seen her grandmother cry. She ran to her and hugged her, crying herself, saying, "I'm not a dummy! I'm not a dummy! I'm not a dummy!" and with that she passed out in Pillamma's arms.

Pillamma understood her distress; she nursed her for three days. Slowly Jani recovered but she was like a flattened balloon, and she became dumb. Pillamma tried to boost her confidence, often reminding her of the prizes she had won at the Town School of Berhampur and her coveted school prize for mathematics. Unfortunately her prize, the compass-box, had been lost in transition from one place to another. Jani was beginning to lose weight. Although she was eating food again, it made no difference to her depressed mind.

Jani spent a lot of time either alone in the backyard by the well, on the steps to the garden, or alone in her room. It appeared as if the grandmother and granddaughter had chosen the two wells to shed their grief. Jani longed to have her Lingammama with her. She knew the whole family was feeling sorry for her, and she saw pity in her uncle's eyes. But what she despised most was pity.

"I am not a pitiable thing," she often reminded herself. She mused over her past life at Berhampur. She remembered Lingammama's words:

"Jani, we cannot compare the past with the yardstick of today. Surely we should learn from our past but not judge the present with the yardstick of the past. Time changes, places change, and attitudes change—that is natural. We should cherish and use our past to make our life better, but we cannot live in our past after alone.

In her mind she raced up the path of her future. She began to string her wishes into a beautiful garland, with scented flowers. "My future will be nothing but beautiful if only they let me have a future," she assured herself. She shook herself out of her gloom and made plans for her future.

She listed her priorities for her future.

1. *I would like to go back to school.*
2. *If possible to a boarding school, far away from the grips of the family.*
3. *Then ...*

She paused when she heard a knock on the door; it was Pillamma who came to call her for lunch. Jani was afraid that others may snoop into her dream world, so she shut the door to her dream world and went into the dining room to eat with the family, just the three of them, her grandparents and herself. Ramam was on duty at another village. Jani returned to her room and wrote her thoughts to that imaginary friend called *Mitra* (*'Mitra'* meaning friend).

Dear Mitra,

What shall I call you? Yesterday grandfather gave me some sheets of white paper and asked me to write my dreams in it. I know he was trying to cheer me up. Like me he is also sad but he never shows it like I show my feelings so shamelessly. My idea is that unless you tell people how you feel, how can they understand your agony? How can they realise that you are hurt and how can they see your deep thoughts hidden within you?

I think honesty is the best policy, but I am not sure if it is the right way to go through life. All the same I strongly feel I have a right to say my feelings openly to my family, even if it's shameful. It's my right that I like to use the most; it's my human right that I cling on to so much. Sometimes I wonder, what good does it do? Yet I often feel I must.

I get urges to shout my feelings to my family so that.. 'So that what,' you may ask? 'What' I don't know myself, so how can I explain to you?

One thing is certain, that I'm very sure that somehow recently in between what's happened to our family, they have forgotten me. Not sure if they did it on purpose or if it was just what happened to the family because we left our town and moved to this horrible place. Whatever it was, that's what happened to me, my family has forgotten that I still exist, that's a fact. I can say that for sure, a hundred per cent sure! Well, that's just a different thing for the time being.

Do you know what my sister said to me before she left to her hostel? She said the family loves me and that's why they kept me with them and are sending her away? I quickly said, well then, let's swap places, sister. Then you will find out what it's like to live with the name of Stupid written on your forehead. She didn't reply but gave me a hug, and she left. If only she realised how lucky she's been. But I don't blame her, Mitra. It's all due to my mother's fault if you ask me.

From the time she was born she wanted her first girl to be a doctor, so why didn't she think anything about me too? Don't you think it's my birthright that my mother should have some dreams for me too? Why didn't she have any dreams for me? Never mind, I will make my own dreams, because nobody can stop me from dreaming.

Dreams, I have plenty, Mitra, I hope they come true one day. But right now what I want is to have just a friend, a friend to play with that I like, to tell what I don't like, and say what I think in my head, and not be worried about it. I need a friend who likes me just the way I am. I know I have to change a lot to my new life, perhaps to call it my NEW CAGE is better. I'm trying to get used to it. My grandmother tells me of how she had to get used to things she didn't like. I don't deny it, but do I have too? I don't know, I have no control on my life, not at all, and I've never felt so helpless, so sad, and so miserable like I do now.

What I need now and deserve and wish is to have a friend. Will you be my friend? I want you to be my friend for life, that is the life I have to put up with and the life I have to live, and also for the life I dream to have. Right now my life is in a cage, yes I am caged, and my wings are cut short so that I can never fly away into the sky! Maybe you don't want to be friends with such a miserable girl like me.

My dearest friend, Mitra, only if you saw me three years ago you would never have said I was a miserable girl. I wish we met a couple of years before then I would have showed you what I really am! Dear friend, I plead with you, now, just bear with me and please do be my friend, that's all I ask of you. I call you Mitra because I know that in Sanskrit, 'Mitra' means friend. See, I'm not all that bad, I can think cleverly too. How do you like your name? Sweet! Don't you agree? You are as sweet as all my friends I left behind.

Perhaps one day you may meet them somewhere, sometime in this wide world, and realise that I have not told lies about how they are. Of course you don't know them yet so I shall tell you about them to you, one by one as time goes. I am certain that you too will love them as much as I do. They are just good friends. They are truly wonderful friends just as you are now, my dearest friend Mitra.

Her thoughts began to choke her. She decided to run away from home, where to go, but she wasn't sure. First she considered going back to Berhampur, but then she remembered that her father was there. For all she knew he would send her back to Aska or would get her married off. For him, all problems could be resolved with marriage. She pondered about running away to obtain her freedom. She had heard that freedom was everybody's birth right. She had heard such emotional words loudly pronounced at public meetings, and even her grandfather often talked about freedom. She paused and put a stop to her thoughts and halted the spate of it.

Suddenly she recalled another thing that Lingammama had told her once:

"Remember Jani, your freedom to do as you wish should not become a restraint to the rest of the girls in the society. Freedom comes with a great burden and responsibility. You should set good examples to other girls in what you do. As you know, many of your cousins are not allowed to go to schools and many get married very young. Your grandfather is a reformer and your grandmother wants all girls to have education. All eyes are on you two sisters—they are waiting for a chance to prove that education for girls is bad, so anything you do without thinking not only ruins you but also jeopardises the future of many girls in town.

Nothing remains the same forever, and changes are inevitable. If you want changes, work hard for it and eventually you will get it. I'm sure you'll get whatever you want, even if it comes a bit late. Don't despair when things don't go as you expected. Sometimes none of us can go against the tidal wave of destiny. You're destined to help others, you are destined to make people around you happy, and you're destined to achieve dreams you never knew you had. Just be patient. Life is long, life is beautiful, and life is fascinating. Experience life as it comes. You may not understand what I'm saying now, but store my words in your memory-box—they will come of use when the right time comes."

Jani contemplated over her situation. She considered the consequences of her running away from home. Grandmother would cry forever more. As yet, she hadn't stopped crying for Komalam. Her father's sister at Berhampur would blame Pillamma for not being able to look after her brother's children.

Jani remembered how once her father's sister had stopped her when she was about to go on an errand, soon after Komalam's death, and asked her a strange question: "Come here Jani. Is your grandmother looking after you properly?"

Jani gave her the standard reply, "I don't know" and ran away. Two years before she had failed to understand the connotation of those words. Now she realised that the woman was trying to create trouble between her and her grandmother.

I will never hear the end of it. Everybody, family and people will say how selfish I have been. Lingammama would be so disappointed with my stupidity.

Jani analysed the consequences her running away would bring and abandoned the idea for the time being. Her heart kept calling her a coward, but her brain assured her that she had been very sensible, as running away from a problem was not an answer.

She invited her friend Mitra's opinion:

My Dearest Mitra,

From this very moment you and I have created a special bond, a bond of friendship and secrecy. You should never reveal anything I tell you to anybody, especially my two little brothers. They snoop around my things without any shame, I'm warning you, just be careful when they are around and keep mum.

Mitra, I want to tell you so many things, but I don't know where to begin. Let me think! Well, today is the day our country got freedom, five long years ago, (yes, I mean the word L...O...N...G, for me these three years have been the longest and they drag on and on), and sadly this day means a tragic note in my life. Exactly two and a half years ago to this day I've lost my FREEDOM. How horrid it is. Can you believe that I who had all the freedom of life until then had lost it all at one stroke? I don't know who to blame for it. Grandfather fought for the freedom of the country for over 30 years but he didn't notice that my freedom was snatched away from under my feet forever, even though I'm his favourite granddaughter. I very much want to hate him for it, yet to be honest he's my only well-wisher, That stops me hating him now or ever.

What about Grandmother, you may ask? I'll tell you. She too has changed her tune a lot ever since we came over to this horrible place. Without any worry she has put a nasty curfew on me, and holds me inside the four walls of this vast house. Sometimes like a guardian angel my uncle comes to my rescue and lifts my curfew from time to time, but only now and then, I suppose that's a sort of blessing and I should be thankful for little mercies in my life. Not really, instead why shouldn't I protest against any curfew which is just for me and not for my brothers? Why should they pick on me, and only me, in my own family?

The biggest culprit in all this is my own mother. Just imagine your fate, if your own mother goes away and leaves you in this mess. What else can anyone do? Maybe I was born as an unlucky girl in this whole world, maybe born with a horrible future, or maybe just born to suffer. Don't get me wrong, Mitra. I don't want any sympathy from you, sympathy is something I simply hate. I'm a brave girl and I'm sure I shall sail through this mess sooner or later. Sail I will and certainly I shall sail, but where to go I really don't know. Where will I end up or what kind of shore will I reach? Right now, at this very moment my life, my future, is as dark as can be. Mitra my dearest friend, I am so sorry we had to meet at this troubled hour of my life! I hope you don't have second thoughts of becoming my friend, my soul mate and my sincere well-wisher!

Sorry I can't talk you right now, I must go, and someone is calling me. Bye for now. See you later!

In his room Panditji was equally lost in his own musing.

I know the whole family depended on Pillamma and she conducted her duties as such with greatest precision like the knife of a surgeon. She knew exactly where to cut, what to remove, and how to sew the wounds and made the surgery perfect.

I'm aware of the hardships the family had to endure during the three decades of my absence from the family matters. Pillamma never complained when I appeared or disappeared from the family scene frequently, leaving her to cope with everything and the young family, which she did with immense love and sacrifice. All material goods have been lost forever and yet she nurtured and nourished her young brood with love and care. She was their only support and she protected them as any mother does with strict discipline and strict behavioural codes. She weighed and valued each of her children and tried her best to guide them into their own paths. She knew they were different and had different needs and values to survive and succeed in the world. She took every step with precise calculation and let each one of them to grow up with their own natural personalities. She never compared nor contrasted them with each other. Instead she appreciated the variety of their characters and cherished them. She would often say, "Look, all the fingers of a hand are different, but at the same time each finger is valuable."

That was then, and now she is altogether a different person. She has become restless, irritable, helpless, and weepy. She is extremely careful not to shed a tear before anyone, especially in front of her children and has remained strong to continue to raise her children to adulthood. Some are on the threshold of adulthood and some are at the infancy of their lives.

I noticed that she has lost lust for life itself but continues diligently to fulfil the responsibility Komalam put on her. Responsibilities when imposed become are a burden, when volunteered they become a challenge. Like Jani, her grandmother loves challenges, or maybe it's the other way round. Perhaps they were the peas of the same pod, one matured and one tender and young! They reflect and complement each other in every possible way. Jani's emotional outbursts are killing her.

I must do something or else I might lose both of them. I must take charge of Jani's education and guide her through her future.

Panditji made up his mind and waited for dawn to break, while in her room Jani called her friend Mitra again.

Mitra, listen to me ... The 'freedom movement' took away the basic freedom of the whole family. Grandfather saw himself as a drop in the ocean of 'freedom fighters', and all those drops flowed together down to their final fate. Mitra— you tell me ... what should I do? All I want is to go to school like my sister and rub out the name of Dummy from my forehead. I want nothing else. Am I being difficult when I ask for such a small thing? Everybody is angry with me ...
That night the young girl dreamt of a solution to her problem. Next morning she woke up with enthusiasm. Pillamma was glad to see her so cheerful. Jani got ready and ran to her grandfather and laid her bright idea in front of him.

"It's the best idea, Jani," he said. "I will contact the authorities. A school for girls is the best thing here." Jani twirled and danced as if the girl's school was going to appear like magic. When Ramam heard of her idea he was glad.

"Amma, there is another reformer in the family. Jani is going to walk in her grandfather's footsteps, and you will see the future leader."

"No son, we don't need another leader in the family. You all promised me that none of you will ever join politics, at least for seven generations. Our family has already paid a big price in politics, so no more politics please. Just have a normal life. There is nothing more left to be sacrificed."

She cried without stopping. Jani stepped over to wipe her tears.

Five weeks passed by, but no school was open for girls. Grandfather gave Jani a daily report of the progress. One day Ramam came home cheerfully. He picked Jani up by her arms and twirled her round and round, and all gathered around them.

"Jani, we're going to a city! Amma—I got a transfer to Cuttack. And there, Jani, there are many schools for you."

Those words worked like an elixir to them all, and Pillamma prepared a feast for the family.

"Now you don't have to pester your grandfather to start a girl's school here," teased Ramam. Panditji waited to see how she reacted.

"No, Uncle, I will go to school at Cuttack—but what about so many girls here?"

Panditji smiled at her and Pillamma felt very proud of her. Her Jani was not selfish and just like her, she wanted to promote girl's education.

That night, Jani talked to Mitra:
Mitra, you are truly my best friend, see nobody will call me Dummy anymore. I'll prove that I'm as good as others. Mitra, you and I are going to Cuttack. I can't leave you behind! Get ready for a new venture in a city!

Jani (centre) with Nagpur children, 1952

31
City Life

Cuttack is located at the apex of the Mahanadi Delta, and the city is surrounded by the River Mahanadi and its tributaries from almost all sides. The tributaries include the Kathjori, the Kuakhai, and the Birupa. Mahanadi provides much of the drinking water to the city. Until 1947 it was the capital of Orissa. The next year, the capital moved to Bhubaneswar.

Cuttack was familiar to Pillamma. She remembered the few months they had lived there when Panditji was an advisor to the Government. Lakshman came over to help with the move, while Veeradhi had arranged a decent-sized house on rent in the locality of Pottapol Sahi. The move was smooth and quick. The forest like surroundings had many large trees, one of which was a drumstick tree, the drumsticks hung from it like snakes and frightened the children.

Moringa Oleifera (*Moringa pterygosperma*) is the most widely cultivated species of the genus Moringa, which is the only genus in the family *Moringaceae.* English common names include moringa, and drumstick tree, from the appearance of the long, slender, triangular seed pods. The tree itself is rather slender, with drooping branches that grow to approximately 10m in height.

Laksman told his younger siblings about a Greek princess called Medusa, who was cursed by Athena turning her beautiful tresses into snakes and giving her the destructive power to turn anyone who looked directly at her into a stone. He warned the children not to go there after dark as the drumstick turn into snakes.

Jani looked out of the window and saw blue sky. Her heart leapt with joy and revived her spirits at the sight of girls going to school. Veeradhi took the two boys, Devi Kumar and Sunder, and got them admitted at the Ranihat High School. The next day Panditji took Jani to the local girl's school and as she waited outside he went in to talk to the Headmistress, but came out disappointed.

Jani had crossed the school age to go to school. But he did not tell her the bad news. All he told her was that she could not be admitted in the middle of the year. But before she could ask him he told her that because the boys had transfer certificates they were to be admitted at school.

Jani returned home and talked excitedly about her new school where she would soon be going, and Pillamma sighed at her excitement as she had been told the truth. By summer Ramam got his brother Lakshman admitted at the prestigious VJTI College, the Victoria Jubilee Technical Institute, founded in 1887. It is a premier engineering and technological institute, located in Bombay, and one of the oldest engineering colleges in Asia. Veeradhi made all the arrangements for his brother, who went along with Ramam to Bombay and got his brother settled in the hostel. He was proud of his clever brother.

Pillamma and Panditji were amazed at Verradhi's generosity and his support to his beloved brother Lakshman. He never grumbled that he did not get such an opportunity in his life. And then as he was living at home, Veeradhi gave all his salary to Pillamma. She was so pleased to have her first grandson live with them because he spread joy and laughter around with his company. Next to Ramam, Veeradhi was her most favourite.

Within two months, once again Ramam moved the family to another house at Hazra Bhavan in the Ranihat area of Cuttack. It was close to the hospital he worked and nearer to schools and colleges. He told the family that Santa had written to him expressing her wish to join the medical college after her degree was completed.

Hazra Bhavan was an enclosed area with five houses within it. The landlord had a large house in the complex and the four houses belonged to his sons who rented them. The main gate opened to the main road and the small lane at the rear of the main house led to the hospital and medical college. Hazra Bhavan had vast open grounds at the front, leaving it well away from the main road, and children of all ages, both boys and girls, played there. They all spoke Bengali, and the tenants were of Telugu, Punjabi, and Bengali families. Jani looked out of the front window, and Pillamma told her that she was allowed to go out. The young girls came running to her, and soon the two older girls, Abha and Khuku, became her friends. They communicated in a language of friendship.

Jani felt like a bird just released from her cage; she loved her new abode. The boys and girls played badminton, tying a string between two coconut trees to act as net. They played cricket, drawing three lines on the wall as stumps. Invariably the boys made the girls fielders and never allowed them a batting. Every evening they all played together. The boys and girls had constant quibbles and each group tried to dominate the other. It was such a relief for Jani, and for Pillamma too, as she watched her granddaughter come alive again.

The house itself was like a doll's house, very small, but that did not bother Jani as she had found new friends, and Pillamma was so accommodative because all the family was together. For her, wherever her son was—that was her heaven.

The house was built in an L-shape. The three small rooms in a row had an open veranda and along the shorter arm of the L-shape there was a small kitchen and a small store room. In the centre, the open courtyard was fairly large. It had a well in the centre and behind it were the bathroom and toilets. The back entrance led to a narrow lane. Except for a mature Guava tree there was no other vegetation or any place to grow a garden. It was all concreted.

Pillamma smiled to see how her life had diminished with their every move since they had left Berhampur. She noticed that Ramam had not brought his car from Aska; he informed her that he had sold it.

After five weeks Ramam told his father Panditji that he intended to move to England for specialisation in surgery, and his father gave his consent to the thought without any hesitation. But he had to break the news to Pillamma, and she was heartbroken.

"How could he desert us in this strange place and sail away across the seas?"

"I understand your concern, but it's his life! Let him have the freedom to live as he wants," said Panditji in an attempt to reason with her.

"What about the children then? He loves them so much, so how can he leave us?" she cried, weeping uncontrollably.

"Let's understand one thing: we took the responsibility of Komalam's children. If you remember, in her last note she expressed her wish that you should be the mother for her children."

"I know ... I remember her every last word."

"But we can't land our responsibility on a young man. Your son has been supporting the family with his salary. True, he loves all of Komalam's children, but that does not mean we have to burden him with responsibility for them. He is still young, and he is a bachelor. He will indeed get married and will have his own family. But he is ambitious and he looks forward in life. Let us not hinder his progress."

"It's easy for you to let him go. But aren't you going to miss him?"

"Yes I will—I certainly will. You always wanted a bright son, so you are proud of him and his achievements. But let him chase after his dreams. He wants to be a surgeon, and if he ever is, then you will be the proudest mother."

"I can't lose him too. I have lost my Komalam, now Ramam is deserting me."

"He will return soon, maybe in a couple of years. He is going there for important studies—so let him go."

"I can't live without him! Let him be in this country. Let him go to any other city to study. I can take that, but to go away cross the seas ... I can't bear it. I know that he will never come back."

"My dear, you are worrying unnecessarily. I know what you are thinking. When your great-uncle went to England in 1820, things were very different. Now the times have changed. Your great-uncle was not accepted by the family because he married an English woman; he was outcast by the family. I'll ask Ramam to meet his cousin in England."

"Oh no! Please don't do that ... he might ..."

"Don't you be afraid. He won't follow his great-great-uncle. Your son is sensible. Has he ever crossed his limits? You should be proud of him. He lived most of his life away from home but he did not pick up any bad habits. He's got good discipline, and it's all thanks to your upbringing, my wife." She blushed at his compliments.

"Well, he is your son too—disciplined and stubborn," she remarked sharply.

They talked for a long time about Ramam's trip to England. Panditji tried his best to reason with his wife, but without any success. Pillamma was completely broken down with the news. She could never come to terms with her son going away from her and from the country. After two weeks, in the middle of the night Ramam left home and went to Bombay to catch the plane to England.

The next morning the Sun rose in the sky as usual, but Pillamma's sunshine was not there. From then onwards her life became mechanical. She did her domestic duties and sat down pondering over her life. She remembered what Komalam had said when Gandhiji had died: "Amma—perhaps happiness is not written in our lives. As soon as we celebrate, the dark shadow of our happiness lurks behind and leaps on us."

Just for a couple of months in that small house she had enjoyed having all her children together. Suddenly one of them left her. She became melancholic and she dreaded to be happy again. Now she existed with only one mission in her life: to see that Komalam's children would reach the shores of their destiny safely.

Often she wondered how Panditji had come to know about Ramam's plans before her. Ramam had taken his father into his confidence and discussed all his plans and his travel arrangements with him. He had applied from Aska for a post at a London Hospital. He had sold his car to pay for his airfare, and he shifted the family to Hazra Bhavan so that the medical college was near. He remembered his promise to his sister Komalam and he wanted Santa close to the medical college and the family. Pillamma was hurt that her son, for whom she had gone against her husband's wishes and had admitted him to school and then had sent him to study medicine, had failed to share his plans with her. She sighed, thinking that he too was a brood of patriarchal society. For Ramam, she was a mother and nothing more. She recalled how Panditji always gave her equal status in his life.

Her days began to drag, but Veeradhi cheered her up with his antics. She learnt to compromise with her destiny once again. She wondered if she had ever made a mistake by leaving her roots, the town of Berhampur; she knew there was no turning back now. The river flows ahead and not the other way round. Her flow of life had to flow towards her destination. After all, Cuttack was a delta area, and perhaps her life would flow into the sea.

Panditji went out on his daily walks and sometimes Jani accompanied him. She walked besides her grandfather with her head held high. There were no restrictions in Cuttack for girls wanting to walk in the streets, as it was in Aska. That day they both went to attend a meeting at Ravenshaw College to listen to Vinoba Bhave.

Vinoba Bhave was widely regarded as the spiritual heir of Mahatma Gandhi in India. He was born on 11 September 1895 to a devout Brahmin family near Bombay. As a youth he felt torn between the desire to spend his life as a spiritual seeker in the Himalayas or to join in a violent revolution against the opposition to British rule. It was said that Gandhiji had two successors; one was Pandit Jawaharlal Nehru, his political successor, and one was Vinoba Bhave, his spiritual successor.

Vinoba Bhave created a very great movement. He walked all over the country for almost thirteen years, and he created the idea in the mind of the people that this was real revolution, because he was asking for land from the landlords. Eighty per cent of India is in the villages, and eighty per cent of its poor people are in the villages. So Vinoba Bhave would approach the village, sing devotional songs, and his disciples would too. Consequently he was considered to be Mahatma Gandhi's spiritual successor, almost a 'mini-mahatma'.

He would wait until people gathered, including the landlords, and then he would talk about *Vedas* and *upanishads*—ancient Hindu scriptures—which appealed to the people. He would talk about *Ramayana,* and that too was appealing to the people. Then he would plead, "Those who have land, if you have five children let me be your sixth child. Give me the sixth part of your land and I will distribute it to the poor." Perhaps due to his charisma, and his wealth of knowledge, landlords donated land generously, and he collected millions of acres of land and distributed it to the poor tillers of the land.

In 1951 Vinoba Bhave started his land donation movement. He took the donated land from land-owning Indians and gave it to the poor, free of cost, for cultivation. He gathered more than 1000 villages in the form of donation. Out of these, he obtained 175 donated villages just in Tamil Nadu alone. This was called the Gramdaan movement. He walked everywhere without sandals as the poor did. He became one of them, to feel and realise the poverty of the poor farmers.

The meeting was held at the Ravenshaw College. Jani's eyes nearly popped out upon seeing the majestic building. Her heart throbbed with excitement to see so many boys and girls at the meeting. After Vinoba Bhave's speech, he requested Panditji to say a few words to the young people there. As congress workers, Vinoba Bhave and Paniditji knew about each other. Panditji talked to the audience—not about land donations, but about education and the role of students in building up the new nation. As ever, his inspiring oration attracted the people, and after the meeting they gathered around Panditji and discussed politics and education with him. Later, one of the girls looked at Jani and asked her if she was going to join the college. Jani felt embarrassed. Panditji intervened and told them that soon she would be a student there.

The grandfather and the granddaughter returned home in silence, but he remembered Jani's frustration, and her protest with fasting after her return from Nagpur. He realised that if anybody talked about her education then Jani would return into her shell; as she was of college-going age the girls at the meeting had asked her about her admission.

Nothing more was said about the meeting at home. One week passed by in silence. Once again the household had adopted its silence mode. As soon as the boys left for school in the morning and Veradhi left for work, then the house became silent. Pillamma would spend her time in remembering the good old days she used to have when she first got married and how her father-in-law had given her the gift of literacy and her life partner had educated her, providing good literature and encouraging her to take an equal role in his life.

On the eighth day following the Vinobha Bhave meeting at the college, Panditji asked Jani to come to the front room. Jani walked in slowly, where both her grandparents were waiting for her.

"Jani, from today we are going to start your matriculation course." The young girl looked puzzled.

"You do want to go to Ravenshaw College, don't you?" Her face brightened up.

"Yes," she mumbled.

"Then let's begin today. I have got the syllabus for Utkal University. I'm going to teach you, and as soon as you are ready you can sit for the matriculation exam."

"School? Am I not going to school?"

"No, Jani. You have passed the possible school age. But don't worry; you can take matriculation as a private candidate."

"I know it, I know it! You don't want me to go to school. Uncle promised me school," she wept wildly. Pillamma took her in her arms and first consoled her. Then she explained the situation and the rules of the schools.

"But uncle promised me."

"Yes, your uncle promised me too that he would never leave me, but now he is across the seas." Panditji realised then that the situation would get out of hand if Pillamma slumped back into her melancholy mood. There would be no stopping her if she did, so he quickly took charge of the situation.

"Jani, I've tried all schools, but the rules are all the same. Surely you don't want to go and sit with little girls in a classroom, do you? So here now here is a real solution: you can jump school and go to college like a young woman."

"Jani, you have two options. Either sit and cry or use the opportunity that is available. Go for matriculation. The faster you learn, the faster you can take the exam. There is no age limit for matriculation. Don't miss this chance Jani! You are a clever girl and you can do it." Pillamma told her with all her persuasive skills.

Jani walked out without saying a word. Panditji looked at his wife and sighed.

"Give her time. She has endured a lot. I know my Jani—she is not going to give up now. She will come round. Once she is determined, she will do it," assured Pillamma.

The next day Santa arrived from Kakinada, and Veeradhi went to collect her from the station. She received a grand welcoming. Everybody talked about her medicine course. Relatives and friends visited the house to see the young medic in the making. Congratulations and encouragement poured in from all. Jani could not fail to see their pitiful looks at her, the 'dummy' of the house. She gulped her tears and smiled feebly at them. Fortunately, as grandfather was present the visitors made no snide remarks at Jani, but their eyes revealed their thoughts more than words could say.

After four weeks, Santa joined the medical college. Panditji accompanied her and got her admitted. Ramam wrote to his father that all the help Santa needed should be given to her. He was determined to honour his beloved sister's last wish and desire and to make Santa an accomplished doctor like Komalam's idol, Dr Margaret Bhore.

Jani pondered over her situation; once again she was in a limbo. She made up her mind to face the facts, to face the reality of her situation. She had no option but to compromise with her present situation. She went and talked to her grandfather for a long time. On the day when Santa took admission at the medical college, Jani enrolled with her grandfather to have private tuition to study for her matriculation.

Pillamma was happy for both Santa and Jani, and she assured Jani that she would also be going to college soon.

**Opening of Co-op Bank
Cuttack, 1953**

Ramalingham at Cuttack Co-op Bank, 1954

32
The Shadow Follows

Just after two months at Bombay, Lakshman became very ill and had to discontinue his engineering course at VJTI and return home. Pillamma was heartbroken, and likewise Ramam was so disappointed. He wanted his sister Komalam's children to achieve well in their lives. Even from across the seas he was concerned for them and never neglected his duties and his promise to his beloved sister Komalam. Lakshman was treated at the local hospital and slowly recovered from his pleurisy but couldn't go back to study at Bombay. Pillamma cursed her luck, as any happiness seemed to be invariably followed by Lady Luck's dark shadow. She pined over her life which had become a vast shadow and she labelled herself as the 'Woman in Shadow'.

Lakshman was not the one to give up. He bounced back and took a clerical post at the A.G. (Accountant General Office) at Bhubaneswar and joined the evening classes to study Law.

Panditji continued his involvement with the Congress Party. He was not forgotten at Berhampur. Often the Congress workers visited him and took his advice on political matters.

The two younger boys at Ranihat School were doing well. Panditji made a comprehensive timetable for Jani to follow. She had to study almost from scratch to cope with the heavy syllabus, and prepare to take exams in nine subjects. She chose extra mathematics as her optional subject. Pillamma was glad to see her diligent Jani and she knew that the girl would eventually reach her goals.

After a year, Ramam gave her another surprise. He wrote to his father to say that he had fallen in love with an Indian doctor from Bombay. He said he would like to wait to get married to her when he returned home.

When Panditji gave her the news about her son, Pillamma was most upset that Ramam had not told her himself about his love. Panditji gradually informed her that he had given his consent to Ramam to marry the girl there in England and when they had returned home they could have another wedding ceremony here in India.

Pillamma was dumbfounded, but Ramam duly married Tara, a gynaecologist, in London by civil marriage and sent their wedding photos. Pillamma had to accept yet another change of course in her life. Even after marriage, Ramam continued to send 250 rupees home every month to his family at Cuttack. He never neglected his duties. Pillamma had dreams about her son's wedding but once again her dreams remained only dreams.

Veeradhi passed his Law examination and also his Master's degree in English literature, joining the evening classes. He left his clerical job and took a senior position at Rourkela Steel Plant, of the Steel Authority of India Limited

(SAIL). Rourkela is located in the north-western tip of the Indian state of Orissa at the heart of a rich mineral belt. It is the third-largest city of Orissa. One of the largest steel plants of SAIL is situated there. It is surrounded by a range of hills and encircled by rivers. It is situated in an area with the richest deposit of mineral wealth in Orissa. It came into prominence in 1955, with the establishment of the Rourkela Steel Plant. The city's name is derived from the famous 'Ruhr' iron and steel belt of Germany, with whose collaboration the Rourkela Steel Plant was set up. With his increased salary Veeradhi contributed 150 rupees to the family.

After two years, Jani was ready to take her matriculation exam. With her grandfather she went to her test centre at the same girl's high school that she previously could not join. To her surprise there were more than a hundred girls taking the exam. At lunch break Jani met two girls of her age, one Oriya girl and one Bengali girl, who came to her with a smile. Over the last two years Jani had learnt to speak Oriya and also managed in Bengali. The girls introduced themselves. The Bengali girl was named Deepali and the Oriya girl was Mitra. Jani had jumped with glee when she'd met a real-life Mitra; she felt that it was a good omen. Over the next two weeks the girls became good friends and they talked about their future and their dreams, exchanging their identity passport-size photos with sentimental messages.

Jani went home and told Pillamma about her new friends. Waiting for the results, Jani told the whole family that she was going to be an engineer. Pillamma suggested that perhaps she might be a doctor if she so desired. Jani was single-minded about being the first woman engineer in the family.

Two days before her results were received, Errababu arrived at Cuttack. Panditji told him about Jani's exams and her wanting to join the Science College to take her intermediate course first and later join the Engineering College. Errababu categorically refused to let Jani be an engineer. He suggested that it was not suitable for girls and suggested that Jani be sent to the Art College for women at Cuttack. The results were then sent and Jani had passed with a high second class, but her delight was washed out. Panditji could not and would not go against Errababu's wishes. As he often said, although he and Pillamma were looking after his children, their father had the final say in their future.

Jani's fate was sealed forever by her absent father who had suddenly appeared, made his pronouncement, and then had left. She was admitted to Sailabala Women's College to study arts. She opted for two languages, economics, and mathematics. She hung on to mathematics, hoping that some miracle would occur and she would become an engineer one day.

Sailabala College started as an intermediate college for women in the year 1913. It was raised to the status of a First-Degree College for Women in Orissa State in the year 1946. Since 1952, it has been functioning in its present premises, the residential building of Utkal Gourava Late Madhusudan Das, which had been gifted to the Government of Orissa by his daughter Sailabala Das. The college was named after her.

In the same year, Ramam's wife Tara returned to Bombay for her baby's birth. She had a beautiful baby girl and they called her Komal after Ramam's sister Komalam. Panditji, Pillamma, and Jani travelled to see the baby and spent three days in Bombay. Tara returned to London with her baby. Pillamma was pleased to see that her son had settled well in life with a beautiful wife and a lovely child.

On his return from Bombay, Panditji was offered a Congress ticket to contest for the second Lok Sabha Elections. The Lok Sabha or House of the People is the lower house of the Parliament of India. Members of the Lok Sabha are elected by direct election under universal adult franchise. Each Lok Sabha is formed for a five-year term. Once again Panditji withdrew in favour of V. V. Giri, his former pupil, who had requested his guru to give him a chance to contest from Ganjam District. Later Giri had to change his constituency at the last moment, due to political developments in the area. Ramalingam refused to take any ministerial post offered to him, saying, "It is for the young to form a government and serve the people." He said that no elder congressman should be greedy to become a minister, as per Gandhian principles.

1957 was a memorable year for the whole of Hazra Bhavan. For over a month the police had become active in the area. Plain-clothed police kept an eye on every person, young and old, men and women of all the residents. Children let their imagination go wild and thought that a criminal or a spy was in the area. They composed weird stories and frightened each other. They brought to life all the characters of their adventure books that they read. For four weeks they had both fun and fear. According to their vivid imagination they were witnessing a live crime story.

Jani tried to get some clues by interrogating Panditji and Pillamma. All Panditji said was to let the police do their duty and Pillamma denied all knowledge of the police presence. But Jani noticed her grandparents look at each other and smile. She concluded that the criminal or the spy must be in their house.

She watched every person carefully ... she was determined to catch the spy all by herself and become famous. After three weeks, a group of workers came round to Hazra Bhavan and cleared all the bushes near the lane that led to the hospital. That lane over the years had become a public path to the Ranihat people. A uniformed policeman supervised the clearance work. After clearing they put a barricade on the lane. The owner of Hazra Bhavan protested with them and made a written complaint that they were trespassing on his land. Soon a senior officer went and talked to him, and the owner, Mr Hazra, withdrew his complaint.

In the following two days, the police became more active. They approached Panditji and talked with him for hours together. The police's presence at home frightened the servant, Dhano, who used to be with the family at Berhampur and was now living with them, and hid himself in the kitchen. After the police had left, he said that he wanted to return to Berhampur. Pillamma convinced him that the police were not after him.

Children's games switched from badminton and cricket, to spy games, to cops and robbers. Finally, on that Tuesday morning all traffic on the main road of Ranihat was diverted and a caravan of police cars arrived at Hazra Bhavan. A car flashing a red light following behind the caravan came into the close and stopped outside Panditji's house. All of the Hazra Bhavan residents stood outside and watched the VIP Governor of U.P. step out of the car. He entered Panditji's house, followed by two security guards in smart uniforms. While the Governor of U.P., V. V. Giri, entered and prostrated himself in front of Panditji and then Pillamma, the two security men stood outside the door.

The three grandchildren stood outside the sitting room and watched the VIP. The guru and the pupil talked for two hours in the presence of Pillamma, their political conversation making no sense to Jani and her two younger brothers. They tried to slip out of the house and narrate the story to their friends, but they were stopped by the police outside. Quietly they returned to the veranda and sat down on the floor.

Pillamma came out and gave a tray of snacks and a yoghurt drink called *lassi* to Jani to carry in. She felt honoured and served the snacks to the VIP. Giri ate the snacks and drank the *lassi.*

Again the three of them resumed their talk. Then Pillamma beckoned the three children waiting outside and introduced them to the VIP as Komalam's children. They greeted, *"Namaste,"* and stood in front of him, like children of perfection. He blessed them, touching their heads. Giri touched his guru's and Pillamma's feet and bid goodbye to them.

The Governor got back into the car and the cavalcade of vehicles drove off with a blaring siren. Panditji's acquaintance with Giri went back to when he was his pupil at Berhampur. Giri's acquaintance with his guru, Pandit Ramalingam, went back to his student days at Berhampur. Pandit Ramalingam had organised a trade union for the railway men called the B.N. Railway Men's Union with headquarters at Kharagpur. He had encouraged V.V. Giri to join the union on his return from Ireland.

In 1937, with his guru Pandit Ramalingam's blessings, V.V. Giri had shifted to the wider level of Congress activities and was contesting the Raja Sahib of Bobbili and his Justice Party. The Justice Party contested the 1937 provincial assembly elections, the first according to the Government of India Act 1935. Raja Sahib was the then Chief Minister of Madras presidency. At this election Ramalingam's brigade of volunteers had canvassed for V.V. Giri in the Congress and he had won with a thumping majority of 6,000 votes and 197 of the 215 assembly seats.

Pandit Ramalingam was the mentor, guide, and philosopher to V. V. Giri and used to advise him in many matters when he became the Minister at the Centre, High Commissioner at Ceylon, and a Governor of Uttar Pradesh. Their guru and pupil relationship was unique. Panditji was proud of all his pupil's achievements and they respected and regarded their guru as their well-wisher and called upon him for his advice and guidance, whenever they needed it.

Over the next few weeks, Devi Kumar boasted and broadcast the visit of the Governor of U.P. to meet his grandfather. The residents of Hazra Bhavan knew that Panditji was an eminent freedom fighter but now they realised his importance, as his ex-pupil, the Governor of Uttar Pradesh, had personally come down all the way to pay his respects to his guru. It was almost beyond their imagination. Suddenly the two grandsons became popular at their school. Jani was glad that the VIP did not ask her about her education. She would cringe if anybody mentioned the subject.

Ten days after the amazing incident of the Governor's visit to the house, another incident caused concern for the family. One night, a thief dug a large hole in the backyard wall by the bathroom and entered the house. He gathered clothes and kitchen utensils and transferred them to the lane. When he entered the bedroom where Pillamma was sleeping he tried to drag a heavy trunk from under her bed. She awoke and chased after him crying, 'Thief, thief!' and woke up the entire Hazra Bhavan residents.

They caught the thief who was none other than the husband of the daily maid who came to wash the dishes and mop the floor. What amused Pillamma was his lame excuse for the theft. He said that all the people near his huts thought that Panditji's family must be wealthy since the Governor had visited them.

When a neighbour was about to call the police, Pillamma stopped him. Before the thief could run away she asked him to open the unlocked trunk in front of all, which he did rather nervously. Pillamma showed its contents to the surprised spectators. The trunk contained some rocks that Veeradhi had collected over the years. As a hobby Veeradhi collected small and large rocks that looked interesting. Pillamma told the thief that he could take some rocks if he wanted, and the spectators burst out laughing. The thief stood there shivering and begged for forgiveness. Pillamma asked him to leave, and the thief ran out as quickly as he could cry and apologising.

"Amma! Why did you let him go?" asked the children.

"Think about it ... people have begun to think that we are wealthy. Now he has gone, but later another thief might raid us and he could be carrying a knife or he could hurt my children. To remove their misconception of the wealth that we don't have it was necessary for the thief to see what was in the trunk. He can stop another thief from coming to look for the non-existent treasures, those treasures we are supposed to have. Now the thief will go and tell his mates that our house was not worth robbing." She laughed as well, and others joined in. That night the Hazra Bhavan residents held a night-time picnic in the yard. Panditji looked at his wise wife with a smile, in appreciation of her forward thinking.

Dr Tara & Dr W. G. Rama Rao, London, 1956

33
Ravenshaw College

Jani enjoyed her college life. It was like a dream come true, and at last she was among friends. To her delight, both Deepali and Mitra, whom she met at the matriculation examination centre, had also joined the same women's college.

Sailbala Women's College is the premier educational institute of its kind for women's education in the State of Orissa.

Sailabala Art College was of good size, and there were about 200 girls studying there. Jani looked at the fashionable girls, all from wealthy families, mingling around in their fineries. It was more like an arena for a beauty contest. They all looked so beautiful. Jani arrived there dressed in a white *Khadi* long skirt and a white blouse, with two pigtails and ordinary sandals. Now she cringed that she would become an outcast among all the wealthy girls. Undeterred, Jani decided to utilise the opportunity she had been given for further education, and faced it. Grandfather admitted her to the college and left.

The Principal of the College, Dr Roy, noticed that this new student stood out among the crowd and she called her to her office and asked her to stand for the College Union elections. To her surprise, Jani got the majority of votes against the most popular senior student, Sushma Das. It gave Jani a new life and with confidence she took part in all college activities with immense enthusiasm. Dr Roy was a forward-looking Principal. She encouraged her students to reach their potential.

Before the end of the term her friend Mitra came to college with her wedding cards, and invited all her classmates to her wedding. Jani was surprised that Mitra was getting married so soon. In the common room, Mitra told the girls that she hated books and would love to have a romantic life with her husband. She talked about romance, sex, and love with excitement.

All the girls attended the wedding, and since Mitra was the only daughter of a very wealthy businessman, the wedding arrangements were those of a royal wedding. The band party came from Bombay, and the groom was received at the station and was paraded on an elephant through the city. Two days before and three days after the wedding the fireworks flared across the skyline of the city. The wedding ceremony lasted for three days and the whole city was fed. The lavish feast was served to the guest in the wedding hall and the poor were fed the same lavish feast in the garden.

Mitra looked stunning in her wedding gear and was drowned in diamonds and rubies. She told her friends that she could not wait to go away with her husband to Delhi and then on to their honeymoon in Paris.

But after three weeks the whole college was surprised to see Mitra back amidst them. She looked like a deflated balloon. With tears she told the girls that her husband had wanted her to complete her degree before they could start their married life. He told her that as a businessman he travelled frequently abroad and he wanted his wife to be smart and educated and able to mingle with the elite. She cried aloud, saying again that she hated books. Some girls laughed at her predicament and few felt sorry for her, but Jani and Deepali said that they would help her with the studies. As some girls had predicted, Mitra's husband had not deserted her, and he wrote to her, regularly encouraging her to complete her degree course and sending her rich gifts every month.

As a Student Union's secretary, Jani wanted to do something special for the college. She heard that her youngest brother Sunder had joined the National Cadet Corps (NCC) at his school and would parade in a smart uniform. She went to Dr Roy with her own request to start an NCC in their college. Dr Roy discouraged her saying that the girls were rather conservative and always refused to use the swimming pool in the college and consequently it had been left unused and she had to drain all the water out and keep it dry.

A bit disappointed but not disheartened Jani talked to the girls in the common room about the swimming pool but they complained that the pool was open to the view of all the surrounding buildings and there was no privacy. She carried back the news to Dr Roy, who understood the girls' objection to swimming in almost public view. Dr Roy said that when the funds were available she would have an indoor swimming pool. Jani once again requested an NCC at the college.

"Alright then—get me 75 girls' signatures that they would like to join the NCC and you will get your NCC," said Dr Roy.

Jani campaigned in the college, in the grounds, and in the common room and convinced the girls that they had to be as brave as the boys. She cited the bravery of Indian women of the Freedom Movement. All that she had learnt, all that she had heard, and all that she had witnessed while going about with her grandfather at Berhampur had now come of use to her. As she was the only girl that wore *Khadi*, the girls felt that she really was a follower of Gandhiji. She often narrated her experience of meeting Gandhiji at Berhampur. All in all, she converted the shy and demure girls to joining the NCC and she managed to get 150 signatures in favour of it and took them to the Principal. Dr Roy was pleased with her progress.

By the next academic term, when Jani was in the second year of her intermediate course, The First Orissa Women's Battalion Unit was born at Sailabala College. All the girls enjoyed wearing the uniform. Every Saturday, the girls attended the NCC parade at the college grounds. It was a strict regime and at the end of the session they were all given snacks and a cold drink.

The aim of the NCC (Senior Division) is to develop character, leadership qualities, and attitude for service. Training in the NCC consists of squad drill, physical training, weapon training, signal training, hygiene and sanitation, first aid and home nursing, and map-reading. The selected cadets go to Delhi for attending Republic Day Parade. In addition to this, cadets attend mountaineering and advanced leadership-training camps. Cadets can appear for 'B' and 'C' Certificate Examinations, and if they clear these exams they can apply for different jobs in defence services. The complete training took over four years.

Certified that Cadet P. JANAKI DEVI (Cadet No.54)of Sailabala Women's College Cuttack was a Cadet of IST ORISSA GIRLS TROOP NCC from 25th January,1955 to 30th June,1956.

As a Cadet she was very active and keen.

11TH SEPTEMBER, 1961
CUTTACK - 2.

OFFICER COMMANDING
IST ORISSA GIRLS TROOP NCC
(B.R. DEWAN)

The women's college was famous in the city for its Annual Charity function, the highlight of which was Dance Drama by the girls. Only trained dancers were selected, and most of the girls at the college were proficient in the classical dance of Orissa, called *Odisi*. The professional artists from the music and drama college trained the girls over two months for the show.

All the elite of the city attended the charity show. Jani was selected to take part in an English play, along with her friend Mable. Mable was an Anglo-Indian girl, smart and elegant. She often complained that her mother did not like her as she was different from her fair-skinned and blue-eyed older sisters. The play, Poets of Isfahan, was an Iranian legend, a land of poets and poetry. The two main characters, the princess and the poet, were played by Jani and Mable. Jani was more excited in the play as her grandfather would, for the first time, see her on stage.

The academic year was about to end, but in spite of all the activities at the college, Jani's heart was set on being a pupil at the famous Ravenshaw College that she first saw when she attend a meeting of Vinoba Bhave.

She made a few enquiries with her friends and decided to study Psychology there. Her dream of studying science had now all been wiped out, so she chose Psychology as a second option. She reminded her grandfather that he had promised to send her to Ravenshaw College. During the summer holidays she had accompanied Panditji to attend the Railway Trade Union meeting at Kharagpur. Now as she was a college student she would not hesitate to accompany him, but after the Nagpur episode she had never been there again, and Panditji had gone alone to attend the meetings.

On their return the train stopped for fifteen minutes at Berhampur, and her heart sank when she saw her father Errababu there. He came in with a parcel of food and gave it to Panditji. Jani looked at her grandfather with pleading eyes. After a casual conversation with Errababu, Panditji said, "Jani wants to do Psychology. It seems a good choice."

"Yes sir," he replied. Jani was happy to see her father humbled in front of his guru and father-in-law. Errababu did not say a word to his daughter, but as the train pulled out he waved at Jani with a smile.

No more was said about her education. There had always been a strange bond between the two men; if Panditji ever said anything, Errababu never went against his wishes, or if Errababu decided on anything, Panditji would respect that. Much later Jani deducted from her logical thinking that the two men had mutual respect and the one who spoke first always got his way. She wondered why she hadn't thought before about their strategy to get her into an engineering course.

Women's College had been a stepping stone for her further education. Carrying a lot of pleasant memories, she bid goodbye to the women's college and stepped into Ravenshaw College.

Ravenshaw College is located in Cuttack, in the state of Orissa, India. The college was established in 1868 for Thomas Edward Ravenshaw, a descendant of William Withers. Thomas and his wife, Mary Susannah Symonds Ravenshaw, were residents of India and were successful in the Indian Political Service.

After the great famine of 1866, the people of Orissa and a few liberal Britons wanted to start a college at Cuttack. Thomas Edward Ravenshaw, Officiating Commissioner of the Orissa Division, finally made the Government of Bengal realise about the difficulties of Oriya students in getting college education. He succeeded in obtaining permission to start collegiate classes in Cuttack. Thus the first college in Orissa was born in January 1868 with only intermediate classes and having six students on roll.

In January 1875 Commissioner Ravenshaw proposed to convert the Ravenshaw Collegiate School into a full-fledged degree college. The Government of Bengal accepted the demand upon the condition that a public contribution of 30,000 rupees be deposited for the proposed college. Ravenshaw took up the matter as an object of personal interest and guaranteed the collection of the required amount. Mr H. Woodrow, the DPI of Bengal, supported Ravenshaw. Mr H. J. Reynolds, Secretary to the Government of Bengal, requested that the Government of India sanction the incidental charges and the post of Principal on the additional condition of meeting half the monthly expenses by public donation.

Due to Mr Ravenshaw's efforts and the support of the Maharaja of Mayurbhanj, H. H. Shree Krushna Chandra Bhanjdeo, by means of financial help, the College department of the Collegiate School was finally converted in 1876 to a full-fledged Government Degree College, bearing the name 'Cuttack College', affiliated to the University of Calcutta. Mr Samuel Ager was appointed as the first Principal. The college then had only 19 students on roll.

The Maharaja of Mayurbhanj donated 20,000 rupees as a permanent endowment for the college, which almost fulfilled the condition imposed by the Government for public contribution. On his insistence, the name of the college was changed to Ravenshaw College in 1878 after Thomas Edward Ravenshaw to commemorate his services to the cause of education in Orissa. The college was granted permanent status by 1881.

Growth of the college in the initial days was slow. Altogether 94 graduates were produced by the closing year of the 19th century and the student strength had increased to 97. The college has seen 55 Principals. It has been accorded autonomous status since 1989. It stands today on a sprawling campus of 87.4 acres (354,000 m2). The magnificent red brick building of Gothic architecture impressed Jani. It is said that it was modelled on Cambridge University in England.

Jani took admission in the degree course of Psychology as her main subject and also the two compulsory languages, English and Telugu, and economics. She avoided opting for mathematics as one of her father's cousins was a Professor of Mathematics there. She remembered how her great-uncle Balaram, who was a teacher at Town School, complained about her to her grandmother on a daily basis. She wanted to have a good start at the college without any relative bossing her around, and she decided to make her mark on her strength.

The college, with nearly three thousand students, was somewhat daunting for the girl. There were only three hundred girls in the whole college, doing various courses in Arts, Science, and Commerce. The ambience was totally different to that of the Women's College. Here, all students wore simple clothes and there was an underlying competition between the girls and the boys to exceed each other in their studies. The discipline and dress code was strict, even to the Anglo-Indian girls wearing skirts was prohibited, the girls could wear a sari or a *shalwar-kameeze* covering their legs, and nobody dared to misbehave. The Professor of Economics Mr Misra kept a watch on all.

Jani made friends easily, and on the girls' requests she stood for the Union Elections and was elected unanimously as the girl's representative. In her *Khadi* clothes she made impression on students and staff alike, and gained their confidence.

She took part in all college activities and sports and won a few medals. Every evening she narrated the life at the college to her ardent audience, her grandparents. She was allowed to go on annual college excursions to see India. The four-week trips organised by the staff of each department were thrilling and educational, experiences that most students would cherish forever.

After graduating with honours in Psychology, she continued with her two-year Masters course in Psychology. In her final year, in early 1962, an All India Science Congress was held in Ravenshaw College Quadrangle. Sixteen post-graduate students, eight girls including Jani and eight boys under the supervision of senior staff, organised the conference.

The five-day conference was attended by all eminent scientists of India and a few from abroad. Jani mingled with the delegates and collected their autographs. She approached the eminent scientist, Janaki Ammal, who smiled at the young girl and commented, "You will make a good scientist—keep going ... you'll succeed," while Jani gulped her tears and gave a feeble smile to that modest-looking lady in a *Khadi* sari. She became sensitive to the topic of her science studies. It became a replica of her non-schooling experience at Aska. Whenever anybody talked about science studies, Jani quickly hid in a shell to hide her frustration.

That night Jani told her grandfather about the scientist, Dr Janaki Ammal, and how the scientist thought she would be a good science student. Panditji looked at his granddaughter and understood her agony.

"Jani, there is science in every subject—even in Arts," he said, trying to console her aching heart.

"But, grandfather, it's not the same is it?"

"Jani, there are only two ways for you: one is to make the most of what you have or instead to pine for what you do not have."

"At college I noticed students proudly say, 'I'm a science student' as if ..."

"You can't change their minds. People feel good about themselves by belittling others."

"But it's not fair!"

"True, your dreams have not materialised. But I think we are destined for a certain thing, and once you realise that you are led by the hands of Destiny towards your goal, you will understand that you are born to achieve only certain goals in your life."

"You are talking like Lingammama!" laughed Jani.

"He was a great man."

"I loved him ... I wish he were here now. Grandfather, what is my destination?"

"That is for you to find out by yourself. It's not handed to you on a plate."

"Hm! Do you know Dr Janaki Ammal?"

"She is a great woman dedicated to her work." He told her all about the woman scientist.

Dr. E.K. Janaki Ammal

Janaki Ammal was born in 1897, in Tellichery, Kerala. Ammal chose to study botany. She obtained an honours degree in botany from Presidency College in 1921. During the years of 1939–1950 that she spent in England, she did chromosome studies of a wide range of garden plants. The Chromosome Atlas of Cultivated Plants, which she wrote jointly with C. D. Darlington in 1945, was a compilation that incorporated much of her own work

Dr E. K. Janaki is a giant in the world of science. She obtained her Doctorate in Science from Michigan University and was also awarded the LLD at the same university for her brilliant contributions to research. She was a shining light in the field of research in India and England. On her return she was appointed as Professor at the University College, Trivandrum, at the age of 34. She presented her achievements at the Edinburgh Geneticist Conference in 1939.

Nehru met her in England and invited her to come to India. She agreed to it and was appointed as a special officer in the Botanical Survey of India. The Chromosomal Atlas of Cultivated Plants authored by her and Dr Darlington is still a reference book for the PhD Students.

The Indian Science Congress Association (ISCA) owes its origin to the foresight and initiative of two British Chemists, namely, Professor J. L. Simonsen and Professor P. S. MacMahon. The first meeting of the Congress was held from 15–17 January 1914 at the premises of the Asiatic Society, Calcutta, with the Honourable Justice Sir Asutosh Mukherjee, the then Vice-Chancellor of the Calcutta University, as President. 105 scientists from different parts of India and abroad attended and the papers numbering 35 were divided into 6 sections:

Botany, Chemistry, Ethnography, Geology, Physics, and Zoology under 6 Sectional Presidents.

Once the great event of All India Science Congress was over, all the students got back to some serious studies for the approaching final exams. Soon they would be leaving the college with their Masters certificates. Two years hard work was about to be finalised and would seal their future.

**Some delegates at All India Science Congress
Ravenshaw College, 1961**

**Ravenshaw College
Jani & Jaya, 1958**

34

The Dusk

1961 happened to be an eventful year for the family. Veeradhi got married to a beautiful girl called Beena and settled down at Rourkela. Pillamma asked Veeradhi not to send any more money for the family funds but to take care of his young bride instead and make his own family.

Pillamma cried silently in her heart. "Komalam, look, your eldest son is a married man; he has grown into a fine young man and is now very responsible. What should have been your proudest moment you are not there to enjoy it. Bless them, Komalam ... it is said that a parent's good deeds reflect on the fate of their children. Your good deeds are helping your children to succeed in their lives. We all miss you, Komalam."

In 1961, Ramalingam, who had been a Director of the Central Cooperative Bank over the last ten years since he had been living in Cuttack, decided to resign from his directorship. He was given a good send-off and they extolled his voluntary work as a director. He was the pioneer of the Cooperative Bank at Berhampur and later many of its branches opened in the Orissa State. Remembering how he had donated his sixtieth birthday gift of six hundred sliver sovereigns at Berhampur, the bank employees presented him with a modest pocket watch, which he could not refuse.

Pillamma watched him with suspicion and deep concern when he also resigned from the BNR, The Bengal Nagpur Railway Trade Union. Pillamma was concerned for his health and she felt that he was winding up his life to put a full stop to it. Santa, the doctor, arranged for a thorough medical check-up for her grandfather by all the top doctors at the hospital and Ramalingam was given a clean bill. That eased Pillamma's mind. Ramalingam assured his wife that nothing was wrong with him but the time had come to hand over responsibilities to the next generation, and moreover, his eyes were not the same as before. Over the last two years he had needed two cataract operations. Knowing that his father read all the time, Ramam wanted him to go to London to receive his cataract operations there. Panditji refused to go abroad for his eye treatment.

"Son, there are efficient doctors at Cuttack and the ones you have trained. I have faith in our doctors."

From London, Ramam assigned responsibility for his father's eye operation to his brilliant ex-student (and a good friend) Dr Rajguru. The ophthalmic surgeon, Rajguru, took the responsibility of operating on Panditji, knowing it to be a challenge because Ramalingam had the so-called 'ACHOO' syndrome. This syndrome is considered to be a genetically inherited condition. While most of us sneeze once or twice individuals who suffer from ACHOO syndrome commonly will sneeze excessively.

Physiologically, it is believed the sneezing mechanism is linked directly to the nasal allergy pathway or to an involuntary defence system. The photic sneeze reflex manifests itself in the form of uncontrollable sneezing in response to a stimulus which would not produce a sneeze in people without the disorder. The sneezes generally occur in bursts of 1 to 15 sneezes at a time. Ramalingam had those sneezing bouts occasionally. Dr Rajguru worked on the problem for two months, but as soon as he thought that he had controlled the sneezing it appeared again. Under those conditions, to operate on the eye would have been dangerous and the patient could have lost his eyesight permanently. After two months of treatment Rajguru managed to control his patient's sneezing.

On the day when he operated on Ramalingam, Jani wanted to be there to hold her grandfather's hand. Santa took her into the operating theatre against the hospital rules. As soon as Rajguru was giving an injection into Ramalingam's eye, Jani passed out and was shifted to a berth in the anteroom. By the time Jani had regained her consciousness the eye surgery was finished and completed successfully.

The 'brave' Jani turned out to have a faint heart and her two younger brothers took it upon themselves to broadcast the news of Jani's faint-hearted bravery to one and all, including her college. Jani never lived it down! The only person who never teased her about it was her grandfather, Ramalingam.

After another month, Ramalingam had the cataract removed from his second eye.

Over the two years since he had developed cataracts, Jani read to Ramalingam every day. She wrote his correspondence on postcards as he dictated, loving to be her grandfather's secretary. When she read to her grandfather, mostly in the evenings after dusk, Pillamma joined them and sat on the veranda, close to the armchair in which Panditji relaxed and listened to Jani's voice. Sometimes the reading was from a magazine and sometimes from any classical or religious books. Whatever her grandfather wanted, Jani would read it out to him. She often amused her grandparents with her anecdotes of the college life. She loved to entertain her grandparents and make them smile.

Santa came home occasionally to be with the family. As her brother commented, she came home to do her laundry. Twice a day the meals were sent to her in a tiffin-carrier and the loyal servant Dhano took it to her Hostel. Dhano, who had been in the family since he was a little orphan boy, had a mild trait of effeminacy in him. His walking and talking had the mannerisms of a woman. At the medical college the boys often teased him and finally he refused to take the tiffin-carrier to Santa. And one fine day he returned to Berhampur and Pillamma had lost a loyal servant. Another maid servant took the tiffin-carrier to Santa.

Ramam wanted no disturbances to come into Santa's studies. He wanted her to stay in the hostel if that was what she wanted. His only mission was to see that Santa became a doctor as her mother wanted.

By the summer the family celebrated the success of their two granddaughters. Santa had completed her medicinal studies and became a fully-fledged doctor. P. Santa Kumariand was placed at the hospital while Jani had attained her Master's Degree in Psychology.

Jani wanted to go to Bangalore to take a two-year diploma course in Psychiatry, but Pillamma told her that her father Errababu would not give his permission for her to study away from home. Jani laughed aloud and shook her head in disgust. She had become an ace in compromising with her destiny.

But Jani was not beaten. She went around the city looking for jobs, and aimed to be financially independent as soon as possible. She registered her name at the Job Centre. Her best friend Shirin was already employed at the Convent School where she was an ex-pupil. Jani went to meet her at lunch break and on her return she noticed a new school across the road.

She picked up her courage and crossed the road, entering the school to meet the Principal, the Reverend Father Pascal. Obviously she impressed him and he gave her a teaching post at the Cambridge School. Perhaps it was a matter of simply being in the right place at the right time.

Cambridge School was in its infancy, and Father Pascal had forward-looking views of education. He appointed all post-graduates for the co-educational High School and Anglo-Indian women in the Primary School to provide sound foundations in English to all children. His brother was in charge of the primary section.

As soon as Jani got a post at the Cambridge School, Shirin left the Convent School and joined the Cambridge School to be with her best friend. All the young post-graduates in different subjects brought their expertise and the school stood above all others in the city in terms of academics, sports, and cultural events. Father Pascal was proud of his dedicated young staff.

Cambridge School, Cuttack, was established in 1961 by the Rev. Father J. P. Singh, the then Rector of the Catholic Church at Cuttack, to provide good education to the children of the locality. Both Father Pascal and his brother were visionaries and had dreams of building up many good institutions for the benefit of the children in spite of many hurdles and limitations. Pillamma, who always told Jani that financial independence for girls was most essential in Indian society, felt proud of her granddaughter who had crossed so many hurdles in her life and had beyond doubt reached the goalpost.

At the end of the first month, both the girls came home with their pay packets and gave Pillamma 250 rupees each for the family funds.

Pillamma became very emotional and cried, "Komalam, can you see your Santa is a doctor now as you always wanted? And your Jani also has become an earning woman—she has become a teacher. Komalam, your goodness has made them successful. I wish you were here to see your clever girls." She collapsed on the floor crying for her Komalam. Her emotional outburst was most pitiable. To console her, Ramalingam put his arms round her and picked her up from the floor, telling her that it was the time to celebrate and not to weep. The proud grandfather presented both the girls with a set of filigree silver necklace, earrings, and a ring. Cuttack was famous for its silver filigree work.

Both the sisters wrote to their Uncle Ramam in England to stop him sending 250 rupees for the family as they had now become earning members and the family was getting a double income amounting to 500 rupees. Ramam stopped sending money to the family and was thrilled to know that his little nieces had become mature and responsible young ladies. He was more delighted that he could see the fulfilment of his sister Komalam's last wish, to make Santa a doctor. But he wanted Santa to not be content with a simple MBBS but to search for some area of specialisation of her choice in England and then become the best of doctors as her mother, his sister Komalam, had wanted.

By December of 1961, Panditji decided to donate his vast library to Utkal University when Shri Prana Krushna Parija was the Vice-Chancellor of the University. The Utkal University Library was established in 1946. Dr Pranakrishna Parija, the first Vice-Chancellor of the University and a scientist of international repute, gratefully welcomed the gift from Panditji. The library of Panditji included rare manuscripts in Sanskrit and many Vedas and scholarly books on various subjects, some ancient scriptures written on dry palm-leaves and many Telugu classics. Jani and Panditji took the books in rickshaws and delivered them to the Vice-Chancellor.

It had been four months from the girls' finding their employment and Pillamma was still very happy, yet at the same time she dreaded the results of being happy. As Komalam used to say, the dark shadow of happiness always lurked in the corner of their lives.

The New Year of 1962 came in, bringing joy and happiness to the family. Pillamma told her husband, Ramalingam, that the last two boys of Komalam should settle down and relieve her from her responsibilities and the promises made to Komalam. Panditji reminded her that the two youngest boys were still at school. Pillamma wondered what they would like to be in their lives. Whatever they were to be doing, she was certain that Komalam was watching her sons from above and would guide them.

For the last four months her life had become pleasant and gradually the family had recovered from poverty. On her uncle's advice Santa began to make plans for higher studies in the UK. She needed her matriculation certificate and the school insisted that she should come down to Berhampur with proof of identity. In those days children did not have birth certificates and their school records were considered to be the official records. That evening Santa set off to Berhampur to obtain her school certificate. Her father promised to meet her at the bus terminus.

After she had gone, Jani was about to go out to meet her friends, when her grandfather asked her not to go. A young boy named Raghav, whom Panditji had been tutoring to take his matriculation exam, had come to tell his guru that he had done very well in the exams. Panditji blessed the boy and said that his future would be bright. Panditji assured him that he would get a scholarship to continue his studies at the Ravenshaw College. The boy touched his guru's feet and took leave.

Raghav was fifteen and the eldest son of many children of his father's two wives. They lived in utter poverty and survived on people's charity. Raghav, a proud boy, wanted no charity. He did some odd jobs for a few rupees to support his siblings and he sent them to schools and in the evenings came to Panditji for studies.

Jani read a while from a Telugu magazine. Pillamma sat on the veranda and listened to the story. It was a tragic story of a young bride. For a few minutes utter silence ruled the veranda. To release the tension Pillamma said, "Jani, did you find any more frogs in your bag?"

"Oh no—not that again. Now I'm a responsible teacher I'm not afraid of frogs or anything else."

"Oh really?" Pillamma continued to tease her.

"Grandfather, is it fair? I tell you, I'm no more frightened," she pouted her lips and looked at her grandfather with pleading eyes. He saw her childish face and laughed. Then all three of them were laughing loudly together, to the delight of Pillamma.

The frog episode had further tainted Jani's 'brave-girl' reputation for good. It had been her first day at Cambridge School, and she had entered the classroom of ten-year olds and sat down at the teacher's desk. She was tickled by the idea that she who had sat on the other side of the table until fairly recently was now taking the teacher's place. A pupil had become a teacher. She looked at her class and smiled. The sixty-four eyes kept watching her seriously. She opened her bag to get out a pen and take register first.

That was the moment when all hell broke out. Out of her bag a large frog leapt on to the table and jumped on to the children. All the class, including their new teacher, jumped in cohesion with frog-yelling and crying. Father Pascal entered the classroom and soon realised their panic. He shoved the frog out of the classroom and left without any comment.

Later that evening, Jani identified the culprit who had placed the frog in her bag. It was her youngest brother Sunder, who was an ace at practical jokes. That evening Jani told her grandfather that she would surely be sacked by Father Pascal. He assured her that Father Pascal was an intelligent man and told her to go to school the next day. Fortunately nothing bad happened at school and Father Pascal greeted his staff with a smile, and retired to his office. From that day on, everybody, including her grandmother, teased her about the frog episode except for two people—her grandfather and Father Pascal.

That was until this evening when her grandfather could not help laughing when Pillamma mentioned the frog story. Jani did not feel too bad that her grandfather was laughing at her; she was glad that she could make him laugh and laughed with him. Their laughter echoed in that dusky evening, the cool breeze of the spring relaxing their aching souls.

Pillamma was still concerned about her husband's health. Ramalingam seemed to hide his real thoughts behind his beard and Jani wondered how come her grandfather was laughing so much, as he never had before. An invisible dark cloud was looming over them.

At dusk, Ramalingam asked Jani what the time was and she replied that it was seven.

"Well, I will never see Ramam again," he commented, looking at Pillamma. She watched him in surprise. Her wide eyes questioned him silently to which he responded a gentle smile. He knew what her question would be and she knew that when he had no answer his reply was only a gentle smile. Then he looked at Jani and said, "It's time to go."

He stood up and walked to his room a few steps away. Jani carried his cushions and walked behind him. He crossed the threshold of his room and collapsed. Jani shouted out saying that her grandfather had fallen down. Pillamma rushed in and soon told Jani that her grandfather was no more. In fright and fear Jani shouted for help. Her brothers playing in front of the house fetched the doctor from next door and when he had come, the young doctor immediately pronounced that Panditji was dead. The time of his death was noted as being two minutes past seven on 7 April 1962.

Jani & Dr Santa, 1961

35
The Epilogue

Jani was always frightened of death and darkness, yet all night she sat beside her grandfather without any fear, while he lay peacefully on his bed.

She was confused and bewildered by the sudden exit of her beloved grandfather. Many doubts about existence and death puzzled her. Whenever she was troubled Jani had always gone straight to her grandfather for answers. Now the blatant truth was that she had to sail solo in the future, and that was daunting to her.

She sat in silence without shedding a tear. She was still coming to terms with the situation as it was her first experience of facing death in its reality. Pillamma, sitting on the floor in the corner of the room, watched Jani with concern. She wanted her to cry. She wanted her to share her sorrow overtly but the silence of her granddaughter worried her. Until the next morning, both of them kept vigil on Panditji, hiding their feelings from each other. The scene of Komalam's death was being re-enacted there sadly, and it seemed that as a family they could never share their sorrow with each other and preferred to suffer alone.

Before Santa could reach Berhampur, the sad news had reached Errababu. He went to receive Santa at the bus-terminus and they both returned on the next bus to Cuttack.

The next morning, men of the town took over the situation. The priests came and chanted mantras while a few men bathed the body in the courtyard and dressed him in his usual attire. They prepared the body for its final destination. As they lifted the body to take it away, Jani burst out crying and yelled for her grandfather. The funeral procession marched to the graveyard and Jani ran after them. She wanted to be there to bid her final farewell to her beloved grandfather.

Some women grabbed her tightly and held her back. Nobody listened to her cries of her rights and that her grandfather would never have stopped her following him. Her pleas and her protests meant nothing to the women gathered there; she stood a prisoner in their hands. Jani, who always fought for her rights, had to succumb to the age-old traditions with which women were not allowed to attend funerals or witness the cremations. Her younger brothers certainly attended the funeral but she, being a girl, was left behind. Once again she was defeated and had to compromise to the established Hindu traditions of the day.

Like a true son Errababu lit the funeral fire and later performed all of the religious rights that a son must do for his father. Their mutual respect and their bondage exceeded their father-in-law and son-in-law connections and developed into a father and son relationship which stood the tides and trials of Time. Later Errababu, with his two eldest sons, Veeradhi and Lakshman, travelled to Benares to perform the last rites to Ramalingam, his guru, his father-in-law, his father image, and the grandfather and guardian of his children, but most of all the proud father of his wife, Komalam. As a son, Errababu immersed Ramalingam's ashes in the holy River Ganges and returned home carrying a huge load of memories.

After a month, when Veeradhi was clearing his grandfather's room he found his grandfather's diary, and the last entry was on 6 April 1962. It read, "According to my astrological calculations, tomorrow at 19.02 is my last breath on earth." Ramalingam had drawn his astrological chart beneath it.

Whenever Pillamma had pined for her only son, it was Ramalingam who used to console her saying, "Ramam got married to a girl he loves. He has a lovely daughter and has settled well in his life. We should be happy for him."

Pillamma recollected that fatal evening before he passed away. His last words echoed in her head like a broken record: "I will never see Ramam again."

If he were there she would have challenged him for hiding his true feelings about their son's absence to her, he too pined for his only son like she did. Her feelings fluctuated from anger to agony, from sorrow to soul-searching. She questioned herself many times.

"Did I ever understand him? We shared everything, yet he remained a mystery to me. Did I really know him? If he knew that he was going to die that evening why didn't he tell me anything? Why didn't he give me the assurances to lead life without him forever as he always did?"

She questioned herself several times but Panditji was no longer there to reply. When the girls were at work and the boys at school, she faced the silent house without her husband. She pondered about their relationship.

I knew him since I was five, even before we got married. I realised that nobody could force him to do anything against his will. His father wanted him to be a wrestler like he had been.

She recalled how they both would hide in a tree with a book whenever the wrestler came to train him. She mused about their time together.

He read to me softly and I listened to his every word. He got me interested in books. It was my father-in-law who made me literate but it's Ramalingam who educated me, bringing books from Madras and always encouraging me, narrating how ancient women of our country excelled in knowledge. He often referred to Leelvati, the great Mathematician.

When vendors or visitors came in she paused her musing but soon continued when they had left.

Even after marriage, he being thirteen and I as an eight-year-old girl, we fought like siblings, we quarrelled regularly, to the amusement of Ramalingam's father. All the same, Ramalingam never tried to dominate me, saying that he was a man and I had to obey him.

She sighed and put a pause to the flow of her thoughts as the boys came home from school. She got back to her domestic duties.

He was a treasure house for knowledge, and he encouraged me to enjoy reading for pleasure. He indulged in our siblings like jealousy whenever his father complimented me for beating him in chess or cards. Fortunately his competitiveness was short-lived.

When Jani came in she noticed that her grandmother had been crying. She sat next to her and asked to know more about Ramalingam as a boy, realising that it would do good for her grandmother to let off steam. Pillamma perked up a bit and talked about her beloved with enthusiasm. Their grieving continued separately. Jani was afraid to cry in front of her grandmother, and to upset her; similarly Pillamma was careful not to upset her children.

"Jani, as children we used to quarrel like you and your brother, Devi Kumar. Gradually our friendship passed the threshold of sibling competition and evolved into deep friendship. Like true friends we shared our thoughts without any inhibitions. I was never afraid that I could make an error and he would make fun of me. He never laughed at my faults. He explained to me where I went wrong by giving examples of life in general. He had tremendous patience. You know what, Jani? Your grandfather had a streak of a poet in him and used to compose short poems for me and about me. Some of them were so funny." Perhaps those sweet memories made her blush. She tried to hide it under her giggle.

Jani changed the topic and saved her from embarrassment. "He published a few Telugu stories in magazines, didn't he?"

Pillamma had yet to come out of her euphoria of his memories. "He was my guru and guided me through my teen years. He led me and I followed him with utter faith. He often told me never to follow him blindly but to make my own choices in life. He used to quote the famous saying "Don't walk behind me; I may not lead. Don't walk in front of me; I may not follow. Just walk beside me and be my friend." With him I read Albert Camus poems.

"Yet I remained his shadow, and Ramalingam was my sunshine. We were tied more in the bondage of friendship than in marriage." Tears rolled down her cheeks and she did not try to hide them. Jani watched her agony and did not know how to console her grandmother.

"You know what happened at school?" she said, trying to change the topic.

"I hope not another frog episode," smiled Pillamma, easing the sombre atmosphere. The two of them consoled each other in their own way and at the same time were aware of their sorrow—they both missed Ramalingam in their lives.

The next day, Jani asked, "Was my grandfather a strict man? Did he ever get cross with you?"

"Cross—never, but strict—very much so. He was a man of principles and he practised what he preached, if preaching was the apt word for his work. I still remember how he made me come out of my obedient wife syndrome waiting for his permission for every step I took. Although he was a liberal thinker he respected family traditions and did not interfere with his mother's decisions in family matters."

She paused and looked thoughtful as if she were trying to recollect her memory. "No, that is not true. Although he gave his mother her due respect and understood her attitudes, when it came to the crunch he did not hesitate to break from the protocols of the family traditions. When he took the decision to resign from his job, he made his choice on his own with no pressure from his mother or any family or friends making him change his mind. His strength was in his indomitable will."

Daily the two of them talked about Ramalingam and found comfort in it. It was therapeutic for both of them. Pillamma recalled an incident of how her mother-in-law, Atta, had refused to let Pillamma's mother dine with the family, because as a widow Pillamma's mother had not shaved her head. In Atta's eyes, that was a grave sin against Hindu womanhood. Ramalingam could not change his mother's opinion. His mother had set ideas about 'womanhood'; the age-old ideas and ideals were deeply rooted in her, and she followed them meticulously. Hence he suggested that his wife Pillamma go to visit her mother and asked her not to invite her mother to any family functions.

"Surely he was the eldest son in the family? He could have changed the old ideas."

"He loved his mother and gave her the due respect she deserved. He realised that breaking age-old traditions was not all that easy for everyone. Hence in some matters he compromised to keep the harmony of the family. But he gave me an equal status with him, not that I never felt that I could be his equal. But he made me feel that I was a woman of substance and I should never obey him like a demure wife. I remember how he used to tell me about smart and intelligent women at his college, both natives and European memsahibs. He valued and respected women in every field."

She choked on her memories and shook her head to shake off the memories of her husband crowded in her head, and failed. His memories, his thoughts, his presence of nonentity haunted her and followed her like a shadow that she could not shake off.

She remembered a saying- if you stand facing the sun, you don't see your shadow. But for Pillamma her Sun had set and only darkness stood in front of her.

Jani began to see that her grandmother would never stop grieving for her beloved. She hoped that the magic of time alone would heal Pillamma's broken heart. She often wondered what made her husband so special. Pillamma could not stop thinking about him.

Ramalingam's personality was so different from his father's. The only, single trace of his father that he had in him was a sharing of physical features. What made him so unique in his traits, which he never wavered from during his mission? I know he told me several times that our birth is not a coincidence—it is programmed to make worthwhile of a human life. Some fail to see their destination and sadly go astray. I remember asking him:

"Sir, how do we know what our path is?"

He replied with a gentle smile, "My dear, all will be revealed as you start advancing in life but nothing will appear if you don't make any moves."

"But sir, what if there are several paths open for you? How can I choose what the right path for me is?"

"My dear wife, that is a challenge for you to face alone. Sometimes destiny throws many challenges in front of us. Always rely on your intuition. As long as your intentions are fair every path leads to your destination like all rivers mingle in the ocean."

"Sir, I feel confident to stay in your shadow, walking behind you. You lead and I follow—that seems fair to me."

He broke into laughter, "Don't you remember the saying ... if you shed tears when you miss the sun, you also miss the stars?" His thoughts were like the rustle of dry leaves whispering in her ears, sometimes tickling her and a few times weighing her down.

"Sir, it is easier to follow in your shadow as I know you are taking the right path. Now whom shall I follow?" Pillamma cried in her heart. Her heart erupted like lava threatening to burst out like a volcano. She found it difficult to submerge the bubbling lava ready to erupt at any time.

"Sir, don't trample my heart with your memories. In the desert of my life your memories only raise the cloud of dust and blind me while I choke, unable to breathe." Pillamma pleaded to the unseen image of her husband.

"Sir, you are great. People hail you as their leader and they extol your sacrifices for freedom. You brought freedom for all and took away mine. My friend, my lover, my sunshine, I'm nothing without you. I know what you would say ... that I've raised our family single-handed and it's a credit to me. That's not true, sir. I was physically alone but the umbrella of your love and your warmth protected me and in your shadow we survived. The best in any person never comes alone, and it comes out in good company. I need you to fulfil our responsibility to settle Komalam's children. They are still young, and the girls need to get married. You cannot leave it all to me alone and disappear! I need you now, more than ever."

She cried in silence, sitting by the well, which absorbed her tears. Jani noticed her grandmother crying by the well as she had done in Aska when Komalam was gone. She wondered, *does history always repeat itself?*

Pillamma composed herself and took care of her Komalam's children. She had no choice but to sail solo with the mission to settle them in their lives.

Often Jani also wondered why her grandfather failed to give her any last message. She asked her grandmother, had her grandfather forgotten her in his last final moment?

"No Jani," Pillamma assured her. "Jani, remember that he wanted you to be with him in his last hour, didn't he? When you were ready to go out to meet your friends he asked you to stop with him. What does that say? He loved you more than you can envisage; never doubt his affection for you. For him you had been a very special girl ever since your childhood. He had educated you and made you stand on your own two feet. What more could he say to you? Your grandfather's blessings are always with you."

"But he could have told me that it was his last hour with us all."

"Perhaps he realised your brave heart—remember his eye operation?" she smiled. "He wanted you by his side in his last hour. He loved your reading, and in his last moments didn't you make him laugh with your frog experience? He left us with a smile."

Pillamma laughed, thinking of that frog episode. Jani was pleased to see her grandmother laugh and decided not to weep for her grandfather in front of her and make her sad.

Pillamma consoled Jani, but she could not come to terms with her sudden loss. She wished that he had said a few words before he passed away so that she would be able to remember and cherish them for the rest of her life and use his last words like torchlight to guide her in the dark path she had to tread alone. Like mercury, her past constantly glowed for her in the darkness of her mind and when she tried to hang on to it, it slipped further away from her fingers. Memories of him were playing hide and seek in her mind and weighed her down gradually.

Seven decades of their friendship had come to a sudden halt and now she stood alone. In her heart's perspective, their distance could never be bridged again. Now they were travelling on either side of the river of life. Perhaps they would never meet again unless she reached the ocean of destiny. Would he be waiting for her with the same mischievous smile on his face? Their spiritual relationship was precious for her. She knew she had to face the life on her own and find her inner peace by herself.

Her duty to Komalam's children took priority over her eternal grief. Her Sun had set and there was no shadow for her to hide in and take shelter.

Pillamma came to terms thinking that time flies over us, but leaves its shadow behind. Ramalingam often told her not to be frightened of shadows. They simply mean that there is light shining somewhere nearby. Pillamma decided to bring light into her Komalam's children. She made up her mind not to dwell in the past and concentrate her mind on the present moment. It was easy to make decisions but was not all that easy to perform them. She told herself – one day at a time and assured herself. She reminded herself – I have obligations towards my Komalam's children.

Her mind was restless and difficult to restrain. She was determined to overcome her troubled mind. She realised her thoughts were the shadows of her mind darker and emptier. She recalled Ramalingam's favourite statement.

"Pillamma, to love and to *be* loved is to feel the sun from both sides."

Pillamma shook herself free of her melancholy and raised her grandchildren with love and received their undivided love and affection from each and every one of Komalam's children.

Until now she had been the woman in his shadow; now without any shadow of her husband she remained just Pillamma!

Ramalingam had led his life until the last moment in the service of people. He was a leader who got along with people not by muscle but by maintaining harmony of words and deeds.

His legacy of the co-operative movement at Berhampur and his selfless dedication to Gandhian principles, a Satyagrahi to the core, became his trademark. He was a true son of Berhampur doing his best for the Town of Berhampur as a Congress worker and as a Chairman of the Municipality.

Ramalingam sought no political gains, and always remained a seasoned worker sharing his vast experience in varied fields of activities with others who sought it. Until his death Pandit Ramalingam remained a true 'Congress Four Anna Member'. (Four *Annas*, a quarter of a Rupee, was the membership fee for the Congress Party.)

You cry with your first breath.
Make others cry with your last breath.
The time you live in-between is your life.
Make it worthwhile and live, and laugh.

Jani at Cambridge School, 1962

Jani, Pillamma, Santa , at Cuttack, March 1962
(Two weeks before Ramalingam died)

Appendix I –

THE FAMILY

W. Mahalakshmi (Atta / Amma)

Ayyagari Subhadra (Pedatta)

W.V.V.B.Ramalingam; B.A.L.T. (Masterji/ Pandit Ramalingam/ Ramalingam Pantulu)

W. Mahalakshmi (Pillamma/ Vadina)

W. Jaganath Rao (Jagappa)

W. Balaram Murty F.A. (Balaram)

Taratarini Rama Subbamma (Komalam)

Dr. W. Gandhi Rama Rao (Ramam)

M.B.B.S; M.S; F.I.M.S.A; F.R.C.S (Edin); F.I.A.M.S; F.R.C.S (England); F.I C.S. (U.S.A)
The Dr.B.C. Roy National award in 1985

W. Subhadra; B.Sc (Subbulu)

P. Raguveer ; M.A.; LLB; M.S.W (Veeradhi)
Personnel Manager at Bhilai Refractories Plant. Regular sports columnist at the local newspaper.

Dr. P. Laxman Rao (Lakshman)
PG DIRW(XLRI); L.L.B; Ph. D; FISTD.
FNIPM- National award in National Institute of Personal Management in2001

Dr. P. Santa Kumari (Santa)

B.Sc; M.B.B.S.; D.Fp; F.F.A.R.C.S.I (U.K.); D. Ac (China); D. Music (AU)
Dr. Rukhmani Pandit Award at the National Anaesthetic Conference in 1975.

P. Janaki Devi M.A. (Psychology); B.Ed.; M.A. (Linguistics, UK) (Jani)

P. Dev Kumar D. Jr. (Journalism, Bombay, 1964) (Devi Kumar)
The first qualified 'Ranji Trophy' Umpire of Orissa; 1961 (Calcutta); Twice elected Chairman of Press Gallery Advisory Committee of Loksabha,(Parliament) Delhi, 1999- 2001.

P. Sunder Eswar D. M. E .Mechanical Engineer (Sunder)
CQMS in NCC; Presented the paper on BULLOCK-CART AMBULANCE at All India Agricultural Conference in 1981

P. Lakshmi Narasimha Rao; B. A. (Errababu)

Lingam Pantulu ; B.A; L.L.B (Lingammama)

Ramalingam's Family

Jagappa's Family

Balaram's Family

Appendix II

Remembering Ramalingam

W.V.V.B. Ramalingham
(23rd October 1884 – 7th April 1962)

From V. V. Giri's biography – "My life & Times"

The 4th President of Republic of India

had a population of about 40,000 and almost every house contributed to this praiseworthy cause. We evolved a novel method of collection; we kept a little bamboo basket in every house and requested the housewife to place in it at least a handful of rice every day. We could thus collect a substantial quantity. We also raised funds from rich officials and others, which we utilised for the purchase of vegetables and condiments. Our object was that we should provide good, wholesome food to the needy and poor. Nearly 2,000 people were served with food once a week. This scheme was very popular among the public, it served to emphasise the responsibility of the better-off sections of society towards the less fortunate. We cooked the food ourselves and took pride in doing manual labour. Our efforts were frowned upon by many but the Association continued to work successfully until the death of my uncle in 1911.

The members of the Association also collected financial contributions every year for the National Fund Association of India inaugurated by Gopal Krishna Gokhale, on lines similar to the Paisa Fund started by Tilak in Maharashtra. The objective was to assist people engaged in indigenous industries and the Swadeshi Movement financially. It also had a political content—to make the country economically free of Britain. We felt that Britain exploited us by taking away our valuable raw materials at low prices and exporting, in return, the finished products at exorbitant rates. This background was immensely useful in preparing many of us to take a plunge into the freedom struggle.

The Andhra Mahila Samaj was also established to enable women to come together. My mother, Subhadramma, Shrimati Raghava Rao, wife of one of the leaders of the Bar, and other enlightened women became regular members.

During my school career at the Khallikote College High School, many of us were influenced by the ideals of service, sacrifice and loyalty to the nation set before us by our great teacher Pandit W. V. V. B. Ramalingam. Ramalingam was a preceptor of the highest order, he regarded it as his supreme duty to guide the students not merely within school precincts but outside as well. He used to visit students at night to find out whether they were studying or not. He would often sit with students who were not diligent and advise them to rectify and improve themselves. The very fact that he made surprise visits was a compelling reason for students to be at their books after dusk. He would try to know the merits and demerits of each student, and, by his loving care and inspiring guidance would put them on the right path. Many of them rose to high positions such as Governors, Ministers, Supreme Court Judges and High Court Judges in different States. When he gave up teaching and joined the Non-Cooperation Movement he was obliged to sell whatever property he had to maintain his family. Even though he was in straitened circumstances he would not look to anyone for help. While he was in jail, friends and students like myself tried to keep the family free from want, but we did it without his knowledge. Had he known it he would have refused our assistance. Later, in 1922, we worked closely together in the trade union movement. He was a selfless worker, he never sought any reward for his services. According to him it was a call to duty and he was just discharging a debt to society. He was never harsh, even to those with whom he differed fundamentally. His sense of

Ch.Amritalingam
Assistant Chief Officer (Retd.)
Reserve Bank of India,
Bhubaneswar

Pandit Ramalingam Pantulu Garu

I came in personal contact Pandit Ramalingam Pantulu Garu when he was Director of the Orissa State Co-operative Bank Ltd., in early 1960s as a Government of Orissa nominee. At that time I was in Orissa State Co-operative Bank. Despite his elderly age, he was keeping himself fit and fine addicted to co-operative principles through Gandhian way of life. He gave unto Co-operative Principles of life with the blend of Gandhian way life. His dedication to Co-operative principles for the uplift of the poor and down-trodden is enormous. He realized that Gandhian way of life can be best achieved only through co-operative principles. His belief was that the ills of the society at large would atone only through co-operative principles through self-sacrifice and adopting "Each for All and All for Each" dictum in letter and spirit. His contribution to the co-operative movement through "self-help" principles is unforgettable particularly for bringing economic support to the down-trodden in Orissa. He was a true Gandhian wedded to the Gandhian principles and way of life.

May His Soul Rest in Peace.

My Grandparents

Pandit Ramalingam & Pillamma

The telegram of Granny's death was delivered at Rourkela when I was in at Ranchi.

The tower of affection has fallen in Granny's death. While Tatagaru, our grandfather sacrificed his life for the country; Pillamma, our grandmother sacrificed her wealth and life for the sake of her children. She gave us interminable love and boldly crossed all the hurdles and criticism in this behalf.

Not knowing that granny bade goodbye to this planet, I wrote her a letter from Ranchi. We were the last to reach Bombay and the last to leave that place with a heavy heart. Death is a most inevitable event in one's life and we have to bow down to the power of death. We faced the inevitable and with a heavy heart witnessed the end of a glorious life.

When Tatagaru, our grandfather passed away we still had the tower of strength in our grandmother, Pillamma. The tree fell down but the strong roots of our family tree held us together under the care of Pillamma. Now without the both grandparents, we have truly become orphans.

Pillamma's long life of toil and love for the children is over now. We are now left with her memories. She had been the connecting line and now we are all scattered. It was her wish that we should remain "one" family in spite of her not being there with us. She is with us spiritually now and ever.

I feel we have been blessed by having nurtured by two great people like Ramalingam & Pillamma. I pray and pay my homage to them.

P. Raghuveer

(Eldest grandson of Ramalingam & Pillamma)

23rd May 1975

Rourkela

ఇ. గౌతు లచ్చన్న,

Dr. వెంకటరావుగారికి,

నమస్కారములు.

నం.:- 407
రాయట వీర్స్
ఎ.సి.గార్డెన్స్
హైదరాబాదు-4
Dr 11-6-96

¹-------------------------------

"బిరంపురంకక్క కోట నారణ్ణ(ద్రి)న్న పాలు దివంగత
రాయుంరంగం వంటుబుదాన, నాకే కొబ స్ట్రీ యు.ఎ.ఐ.ఐ
గార్కితోను, ఉన్న ఇప్పుడ రాను రాష్ట్రంయం ఆంధ్ర
కాంగ్రెసు నాయకుల ఎంరతో సుందపు గారా. 'స్త్రీ యు
నాభార్య మకొిరూ పొి ఎ నాకు జ0RA (MRACH 1948)
సర్వ్రాయికూర స్రవారిని 'ప్రీ ' రొ రాంఖి0రంగంప రతుల
గొరు 'పరొిఇఇఎౌ లి బిరుపావచ్చ అలి ర్వ దిందడు
యుక్తం0నెను మల్లిహిహొో!"

ఇతిభాండ్
(Sd) నౌరు లచ్చన్న
ి ర్గ్గ
ఇ ఇిఇయెూ

(ఎురుబ్బ: డాక్టర్ వెంకటరాష్ట్రదివంగత రాయురంగ0వంటుబుగారు ఇ)
ఉట్టు రో ఆయనభార్య ఇ.శ్రీ మాయ్యవంటుబుగారు డ్డ)
శ్రీ ా డి0—(పురుపుర్మ)

Dr. W. G. RAMA RAO
M.B., M.S., F.R.C.S.E., F.R.C.S.,
F.I.C.S., F.I.M.S.A., F.I.M.A.

My Father

Born at Chatrapur(Ganjam District)

23rd October – 7th April 1962

As an enlightened political leader he organised the party activities, created grass root workers, and led a committed band of workers who distinguished themselves in the service of the Country in both pre and post independent India.

A brilliant academic, an ideal teacher who identified himself with the taught, revered and loved, Pandit Ramalingam's contributions to Khallikote culminate din his donating the monies collected by the citizens of Berhampur on his 60th Birthday celebrations.

As a social worker, labour leader, his contributions in the political field had no parallel. He sought no political gains, always remained a seasoned worker sharing his vast experience in varied fields of activity with others who sought it. Except to his brief appointment as an adviser to the government of Orissa, on Cooperative movement, under the Chief Minister of that great son of the soil Late Biswanath Das, he accepted no jobs in his long career.

As an elected representative of the citizens of Berhampur, he headed the Berhampur Municipality Corporation as its Chairman for a decade, to lay the foundations of the then developing city.

Dr. W. G. Rama Rao.

Discovering my Great-grandfather

It was early in the year 2009, when my aunt (Janaki Sastry) contacted me about setting up a website, penned by her and devoted to my great-grandfather who was a freedom fighter. I remember seeing some of his pictures with my dad. Once I created his portal we sent emails to others and asked them to contribute.

We continued to grope in the darkness of the lost history diligently. Every bit of information had given us a ray of hope and to pursue further.

My aunt found out from the British Archives of an incident "A man was arrested and two were shot dead for protesting his arrest." It wasn't of much use as there was no name on the records. The Madras Presidency records were transferred to Madras, at the time of Indian Independence and were not available.

Mahatma Gandhi's letter to Ramalingam led to further resources. The first person who responded to the website was Mr. Amritalingam, who worked with Ramalingam at Cuttack. He wrote *"I was personally associated with him when he was the Director of the Orissa State Co-operative Bank Ltd. He was not accepting any 'honorarium' payable to a Director. He was a leader in co-operatives as well as in educational field and management of civic life through Berhampur Municipality.*

During 1959-1962, he was on the Board of OSCB Ltd, as a Director nominated by the Government of Orissa. I was personally associated with him to bring him from his home at Ranihut to the Bank at Chowdhury Bazar, there after take his quivering left hand with his pen to get his long signature on the Board meeting Attendance register and take him back home after the meeting. The ailing ex-secretary of the Orissa State co-operative Union informed that Ramalingam also served as Director on the Board of the Berhampur Co-operative Land Mortgage Bank and also Orissa State co-operative Land Mortgage Bank Ltd during 1950-1960."

I directed Mr. Amritalingam to correspond with my aunt who was compiling the biography of Ramalingam.

Ramalingam rendered his pioneering self-less services through co-operative philosophy to weaker section of the community in helping them availing financial assistance to purchase their cottage industry, small trade/enterprises, home repairs, agricultural activities, handloom weaving etc; and saved them from the clutches of money lenders. The biography of Ramalingam would certainly connect us with the philosophy of his life.

Ramesh Pothapragada
(Second son of P.Raghuveer)
(Great- grandson of Pandit W.V.V.B. Ramalingam)

February 2009

271

A Gandhian to the core

PRESENT-DAY politicians, who are ready to go to any tent to remain in the saddle, could take a leaf from the life Pandit Wunnava Venkata raha Butchi Ramalingam, a ndhian to the core, who had fused to contest elections d turned down the pleas of s contemporaries saying, "It for the young to form the Government and serve the people d no older Congressman, to is a true Gandhian should come a minister".

Pandit WVVB Ramalingam, pularly known as dastaru", was born to Ranga to and Mahalaxmi in 1884 at atrapur in Ganjam district Orissa in the erstwhile Mad-s Presidency. He did his BA d B.Ed in 1905 at the Preside-y College, Madras, and later ined the Khallikote College, rhampur, as a lecturer.

Ramalingam, right from his rudent days, was attracted to-ards the nationalist movem-t and developed keen inter-t in the cooperative movem-t and the welfare of railway bour. He had great sympathy r the working classes and rmed unions for their elfare.

Responding to the call of ahatma Gandhi in 1921, Ram-ingam quit his job and burnt l foreign clothes and then on-ards wore khadi only. In 22, Ramalingam along with V Giri and Malladi Krishna-urthy was arrested for orga-ising a meeting to call upon he people to join the non-coop-ration movement, in defiance f the prohibitory orders issued by the Ganjam district collector. The trio along with Pullela Sitaramayya from Icha-pur were sentenced to one year rigorous imprisonment.

In 1930, Ramalingam gave a call for conducting a salt satya-graha coinciding with the Mah-atma's Dandi March. The saty-agrahis marched to Gopalpur on Sea and to Balacheruvu in Vizag. Ramalingam was impri-soned at the Vellore jail along with NG Ranga, Tenneti Viswa-natham and VV Giri.

Ramalingam's house was a beehive of activity of the Cong-ress. Mahatma Gandhi visited his house during his Orissa tour in 1933. Ramalingam started the Berhampur Urban Cooperative Bank and as the chairman of the Berhampur municipality, he launched a housing scheme for slum-dwe-llers.

The Bengal Nagpur Railway (BNR) workers looked upon Ramalingam as a father-figure and elected him as their union's central council vice-president, while he was in jail in 1932.

"When the Railway workers were on strike, the union used to raise donations by selling his photographs and the amo-unt used to be spent for the mai-ntenance of the workers dur-ing the strike period", recalls his daughter B Sobha Devi (72), who had also participated in the Quit India Movement.

Ramalingam remained a true Gandhian and a Congress worker till his death on April 7, 1964.

—B Madhu Gopal
—Visakhapatnam

Prof. W. V. V. B. Ramalingam
Vice President, Central Counc..
B. N. RY INDIAN LABOUR UNION.
(Sentenced to 1 year R. I. on 5—2—12

A Profile of a forgotten Hero

After Independence of India, thousands of freedom fighters went into oblivion without seeking power or perks. One such person was Pandit W.V.V. B. Ramalingam of Berhampur. He came from a Zamindar family. After obtaining his degree at the prestigious Presidency College of Madras, he took up teaching at Khallikote College as a Mathematics Professor and soon was promoted to the position of Vice-Principal of the College. He established a new style of student counselling, and used to give feed back to their guardians. Many of his students remembered him fondly and were grateful to their guru for moulding their characters early in their lives.

In 1920 he resigned from his teaching career and plunged into the National Movement initiated by Gandhiji. His luxurious life style overnight turned into Khadi Dhoti and Chappals to wear. Until then he had rich immovable and movable property, and when he joined the National Movement, the British government, as an act of punishment confiscated his rich immovable property like farms and land. His wife Pillamma had to sell her movable property to fend her children when her husband was mostly engaged in organising meetings, demonstrations, leading processions and getting frequently imprisoned in jails. During his absence, his wife Pillamma raised the family by high moral values preached and practiced by Pandit Ramalingam.

Along with the National Movement he also had active role in the Trade Union Movement. During his tenure as the elected Chairman of Berhampur Municipality, he personally supervised the health, sanitation, roads and education.

On 15th August 1947, Indian Independence Day, as a high school boy I vividly remember the proud moment, when my grandfather Pandit Ramalingam unfurled the Free Indian flag with Charka at the Khadi Bhandar of Berhampur. For me he was my guru, friend and philosopher for life. Till his last moment he led a life of sacrifice following true Gandhian Principles, and was a Satyagrahi to the core; and he firmly remained a "Congress Four ANNA Member."

With reverence I pay my homage to that Great man Pandit Ramalingam, my grandfather.

Laxman.

Dr P.Laxman Rao

1st May, 1997

Visakhapatnam.

273

నేతలను తీర్చిదిద్దిన మహామనిషి

విశాఖపట్నం, ఆగస్టు 14 (న్యూస్‌టుడే). ఎందరెందరో మహానుభావులు ఎన్నో త్యాగాలను చేసి మనదేశానికి స్వాతంత్ర్యాన్ని దీపాందిరచేసిన మహానుభావుల నిస్వార్థ సేవ. దేశంలో వివిధ ప్రాంతాలను తమ నేతృత్వం వహించి ఎదుగుదలకి ఎందరెందరో పాటుపడ్డారు. స్వాతంత్ర్యానంతరం మననేతల్లో కొందరు పదవులను చేపట్టి భవిష్యత్తరాలకు ఆదర్శంగా ఏ విధమైన పదవిని ఆశించకుండా నిస్వార్థ సేవకోసం నిలిచారు. మరికొందరు స్వాతంత్ర్య పోరాటే లక్ష్యంగా ఏ పదవులను ఆశించక నిస్వార్థ సేవలోనే కాలం గడిపారు.

అలాంటి వారిలో వెండివెండు వెండిన ప్రఖ్యాత ప్రొఫెసర్ డాక్టర్ వి.వి.వి. రామలింగం ఉన్నవ విలువలు వెండిన భవిష్యత్తరాలను కానివి నిర్దేశించగలిగేలా యువతరాన్ని తీర్చిదిద్దటానికే పరిశ్రమించారు.

ఉపాధ్యాయునిగా

వండిట్ ఉన్నవ రామలింగంగా ప్రసిద్ధి పొందిన ప్రొఫెసర్ డాక్టర్ వి.వి.వి. రామలింగం 1884లో జమీందారుల కుటుంబంలో జన్మించారు. మద్రాసులోని ప్రిన్సిపెస్ కళాశాలలో విద్యాభ్యాసం పూర్తి చేసుకుని విజయవాడ ఎస్.పి.ఎస్‌లో కళెక్టర్ కళాశాల పేదరుగా లెక్చరర్‌గా జీవితాన్ని ప్రారంభించారు.

స్వాతంత్ర సమరయోధునిగా

గాంధీజీ పిలుపు మేరకు 1920లో ఉప్పు సత్యాగ్రహంలో ఉప్పు సత్యాగ్రహంలో ఆయన పాల్గొన్నారు. స్వాతంత్ర సమరయోధునిగా పేరు పొందిన స్థూల గొప్పవారు. 1930 ఏప్రిల్ 18న శ్రీకాకుళం డివిజన్ సబ్ కలెక్టరు ఆఫీస్ వండిట్ రామలింగంను అరెస్టుచేసి రెండోసారి జైలుకు తరలించారు.

వండిట్ ఉన్నవ రామలింగం

వ్యాపారశీలి వండిట్

స్వాతంత్ర్యం వచ్చిన తరువాత కాంగ్రెస్ పార్టీ 1952, 1957లో లోక్‌సభ ఎన్నికలలో పార్టీపాలను నేతుగా ఉన్నవ రామలింగానికి వచ్చింది. ఎమ్మెల్యే పార్టీకి అవకాశం ఇవ్వాలని కోరించిన ఆయన 1952లో స్వాతంత్ర్యవాద ఆయనగారి సుబ్బారావు, 1957లో వి.వి.గిరీ అవకాశం తప్పివేందుకు పోటీ నుంచి విరమించుకుంటున్నారు. 1961లో రైల్వే బ్రీడ్ యూనియన్ ఉద్యోగులకు మధ్య యువను ప్రైవేటు ప్రొఫెసర్‌గా ప్రొఫెసర్ పాలు సాయంలో తన విలువైన గ్రంథాలయాన్ని ఉత్కర్ యూనివర్సిటీకి ధారాదత్తం చేసిన ఉన్నవ రామలింగం తన 78వ ఏట ఆగస్ట 1962లో స్వాతంత్ర్య స్వర్ణోత్సవాల సందర్భంగా జాతి నివాళులర్పిస్తోంది.

VOLCONIC HEAD OF FREEDOM MOVEMENT IN GANJAM DISTRICT

The British Government had decided to auction the excise revenue collections in 1922 in Orissa. It was decided to carry out the auction at BALIAPADAR, ICCHAPUR & BERHAMPUR of Ganjam District. The freedom fighters, who were opposed to this idea, had decided to launch demonstrations, picketing and sit-in-strikes during this period.

Among others, master Ramalingam, were arrested and put behind bars (jailed) in connection with the above demonstration.

Five years later in 1927, Mahatma Gandhi had visited Ganjam for the second time (first time was in March 1921) and addressed public meetings at Berhampur, Asika, Gobara, Bhanjanagar, Kodala, Boirani. Polsara, Khellikot & Rambha calling upon the people to join freedom movement.

Volunteers of "SALT Satyagraha" at Huma, engaged in salt extraction, were being supplied rice and vegetables from "UDYOG MANDIR" at Berhampur.

For effective coordination of this Saytagraha, "UDYOG MANDIR" was opened at Berhampur. To feed the camps of "Satyagrahis" at Huma, engaged in salt extraction, rice and vegetables were being supplied from Udyog Mandir.

Simultaneously, the Telugu Satyagrahis of Berhampur, led by the then chairman of Berhampur Municipality Ramalingam Pantulu, moved towards south and called collected salt from the sea near BARUA. They carried it to Berhampur to be auctioned in the main market.

For disobeying the government ban on collecting salt from sea, these Satyagrahis were rounded up and imprisoned some were even tortured by the British Police. Those volunteers were nicknamed "vanara Sena" (monkey brigade).

Pandit W.V.V.B. Ramalingam's name will be written in golden letters in connection with the cooperative urban bank movement at Berhampur.

His farsightedness in helping locals' in house building loans reflects in choosing the central place of the town for Berhampur Urban Co-operative Bank building. It was the first permanent structure.

Even after 96 years, the structure stands erect. Pandit Ramalingam had worked as administrator of the Bank for 24 years and secretary for 13 years.

Ref: Udyog Mandir. Berhampur, Orissa

ప్రజాసేవలో చెరగని సంతకాలు / ఉన్నవ సోదరులు

(మునగవలస-బరంపురం)

మన్నెం మన్నెం బరంపురం

City High School

Thursday, February 7, 2013 Source: The Hindu (Posted by Ram Prasad Tripathy at 7:41 PM)
Ramlingam Pantulu Block opened at City High School

Pandit Ramlingam Pantulu, who was chairman of Berhampur Municipality in British era, was also involved in the development of City High School which was established in 1930. A statue of his was also established on the school campus which was garlanded by his descendants of new generation. His grandchildren and great grandchildren have come forward to build Pandit Ramalingam block on the premises of City High School. Several of them were former students of this school. Now members of this extended family are also scattered in different parts of the country and abroad. The main donors for the project are his granddaughter Janaki Sastry, who lives in UK, and Dr P. Santa Kumari & Dr P Mahalakshmi of Visakhapatnam. This year is Ramalingam's 50th death anniversary.

"We requested them to construct these rooms, as the school did not have enough space to conduct classes," said P Satya Narayana, President of student-teacher association (PTA) of City High School. The present school building was also constructed with the efforts of Ramalingam, who was also the chairman of the then Berhampur Municipal Corporation, and his cousin Contractor Ramalingam," he said.

Several dignitaries of the city attached to this school attended the inaugural function of this new block which has three class rooms. According to head master of the school, Subash Chandra Pradhan, new class rooms were an extreme need of the historic institution.

P. Satya Narayana (Babu) & Lakshmi

Chief Coordinators of the project

Ramlingam Pantulu block opened at City High School

Staff Reporter

BERHAMPUR: Descendants of eminent Gandhian Pandit Ramlingam Pantulu have come together to build a new block for City High School in the city. The new block was inaugurated on Sunday.

Pandit Ramlingam Pantulu, who was chairman of Berhampur Municipality in British era, was also involved in the development of City High School which was established in 1930. A statue of his was also established on the school campus which was garlanded by his descendants of new generation.

His grandchildren and great grandchildren have come forward to build Pandit Ramlingam block on the premises of City High School. Several of them were former students of this school. Now members of this extended family are also scattered in different parts of the country and abroad. But all of them extended their hands of support to take up this project for development of their old school. The main donors for the project were Janaki Sastry, who lives in UK, and P.Santa Kumari of Visakhapatnam.

During the inauguration ceremony Ms Santa Kumari announced two awards for meritorious students of the school in memory of her grandfather. Several dignitaries of the city attached to this school attended the inaugural function of this new block which has three class rooms.

According to head master of the school, Subash Chandra Pradhan, new class rooms were an extreme need of the institution.

City High School gets Rs 10 lakh worth building and furniture.

Berhampur, March3 , 2013: (Bureau)

They have not forgotten their sweet old home town nor the institution built by their ancestors, even though residing overseas. In the memory of their forefathers, their descendants have built three rooms within the premises of the City's oldest City High School.

Pandit WVVB Ramalingam was a former chairman of Berhampur and had taken a leading role in building the city high school. Along with him his cousin Contractor Ramalingam took charge of building the school.

This school has been imparting education to children of Berhampur continuously with dedication. Today Rs. 10, Lakhs was donated to the school by one of his granddaughter, who has settled in England, Mrs Janaki Sastry. Dr P. Santa Kumari & Dr P. Mahalkshmi from Vizag and others have also contributed in building these three rooms.

Today, the rooms Pandit Ramalingam Block was officially opened and Ramalingam's extended family attended the function. Speaking on the occasion, head Master of the school Mr Subash Chandra Pradhan said they were compelled to run two shifts due to shortage of classrooms. With the completion of these additional rooms, the problem of imparting education will be overcome.

It was worth mentioning that Pandit WVVB Ramalingam was an educationist and a freedom fighter, and he has served as an advisor to Orissa's first Premier Minister Biswanath Das. He had educated many a students and important personalities in his life time. They included former President of India Sri V V Giri and Sri Biswanath Das, former Chief justice of India and Justice Sri Lingaraj Panigrahi .

Dr P. Venugopal Rao& Dr P. Suvarna

Chief coordinators of the project

The legendary Pandit Ramalingam Garu

Pandit Ramalingam Garu was personally known to me and was famous as a versatile teacher, at the "THE KHALLIKOTE COLLEGIATE HIGH SCHOOL BERHAMPUR" on the side of the Main Road, leading to the Railway Station of Berhampur Town. He was generally known as Pandit Ramalingam Pantulu, or Mastergaru or Masterji. He was fondly called Gaddam-Tatagaru by children as he had a long beard.

His attire was simple, a white Khadi dhoti and a long 'Kanduva' draped over his shoulders. He always had the "jandhyam" thread across his chest. He carried white Khadi cloth shoulder-bag containing writing materials; his handkerchief, and other belongings besides a small snuff-box. HRamalinamis pince-nez spectacles over the bridge of his nose, the walking stick in the right hand and the Kahdi shoulder-bag on the left shoulder enhanced his majestic personality as he walked with his head held high. He wore "Chappals" made by the local cobbler.

Pandit Ramalingam was a staunch follower of Mahatma Gandhi and took active part in Indian freedom movement and was jailed frequently. He was in those days, especially during the first half of the 20th Century was heading a trade Union as the Vice-President then as President of the then Bengal Nagpur Railways (BNR) worker's union and amicably resolving the employer and employee relations, leading tension free work culture, thus help inspiring their efficiency. While he was the Chairman of the Municipality, the Berhampur Municipality during 1926-1930, won a prize as the Best Urban Municipality in Eastern India.

After independence when he was offered a ticket for Berhampur, in the first Lok-Sabha on behalf of the Congress by no less a person than Pandit Jawaharlal Nehru, the first Indian prime Minister designate, he did not enter into Indian politics and the first Independent Indian Parliament, but recommended the name of his ex-pupil V.V. Giri for M.P. Ticket, who was then practicing Advocate at Berhampur Bar, who later rose to the gubernatorial position of the President of Indian Republic as a resident of Orissa bringing thus laurels to Berhampur a Bi-lingual Town brought on to the Indian Political Map.

He was one of the important founder members of Berhampur Co-operative Urban bank. Pandit Ramalingam Garu, a doyen in many fields including teaching, administering the local Self Government, setting and running of financial institutions like a Co-operative Urban BaRamalinamnk etc. I salute the great Soul from the depth of my heart.

(Er.Pochiraju Surya Narayana Rao)
Former Addl.Director of Industries
& Technical Educational
Government of ODISHA
POCHIRAJU HOUSE
Gadevari street
Berhampur 760002
Ganjam District. Odisha

ଅଞ୍ଚଳ କଥା

ପୂର୍ବ-ପୁରୁଷଙ୍କ ସ୍ମୃତିରେ

ସିଟି ହାଇସ୍କୁଲକୁ ୧୦ଲକ୍ଷ ଟଙ୍କାର ଗୃହ ଓ ଆସବାବପତ୍ର ପ୍ରଦାନ

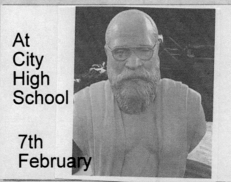

At
City
High
School

7th
February

2
0
1
3

Sri.Wunnam Ramalingam the Master Garu popularly known as GADDAM Ramalingam master garu's name sounded in my ears during my student's life and it is still the same sound that repeatedly flashes in my mind and heart.

Ramalingam Garu was a rare combination of godly person and a social reformer with an excellent teaching qualities , he use to take care of the students who were not succeeded in their examinations to conduct special classes for them .Students will never ever forget him as a teacher through generations. He was very active in public life and was elected as the chairman of Berhampur municipality; he was a very regular visitor and use to take personalized care of the wards of the municipality.

Even this date his way of functioning is admired by various officers and most of them feel and try to follow his foot prints. During tenure as a Chairman Berhampur municipality he set everything right in the municipality specially the drainage, road and transport system of the city.

It was his commitment and excellence that Berhampur municipality was awarded very first time and his work was appreciated from all corners of the society. He was the founder member of Berhampur Co-operative urban bank and also the Director of Berhampur cooperative central bank Ltd ,it is on the record that his regime was the golden era of Berhampur municipality and all other organizations those were headed by this great freedom fighter who spent his important time in the jails to save the sovereignty of this great nation, I salute the late legend and expect we all will remember his advices and will fulfill his dreams by making our Berhampur municipality as a model for the state and nation.

(M. Jagannadha Rao

Memories of my Great-grandfather

I recall my faint memories of discussions with my father and grandfather (Jagappa). Both used to revere Pedda Tatagru (Ramalingam Tatagaru) and hold him in high esteem.

Jagappa Tatagaru revered his elder brother, Ramalingam Tatagaru like his own father/parental figure. As a child when I inquired, Jagappa Tatagaru told me that the age difference between himself and his elder brother (Ramalingam Tatagaru) was considerable. I faintly remember from my grandmother that their two sisters of Ramalingam were married even before he (Jagappa) and Balaram were born. Their father Rangarao passed away when they were kids. Hence to Jagappa, his eldest brother, Ramalingam was a father figure and he respected him as such.

My father Ranga Rao(named after his grandfather Ranga Rao) used to revere his Peddananna (Ramalingam Tatagaru). He used to always remember him as *purshottamudu"*. The very first highly educated person and *gyani* in the family and was an honest person of truth and integrity.

Further, my father saw his Peddananna in his dreams on several occasions during Pedda Tatagaru's lifetime and there after too. Father on each such occasion on waking up used to say that appearance of Peddananna in his dreams was a sign of a good omen and indication of a forthcoming good event in his life.

It is now a very difficult and strenuous to piece together bits of data and information about our ancestors. But we must endeavour to do what best we could to collect and pass on this valuable information and stories to posterity.

Kanna

(W.V.G.Venkata Ramana)

26th December 2010

New Delhi

India

283

I was pleased to learn that a statue of Pandit W.V.V.B. Ramalingam Garu is being installed in the City High School, Berhampur. It is a fitting tribute to the most outstanding citizen of the City of Berhampur.

Pandit Ramalingam Garu had left behind a rich legacy of honesty, integrity, spotless character, hard work, efficiency and selfless service to the citizens of Berhampur, especially as Chairman of the Municipality, when Berhampur was considered the cleanest city in the Madras Presidency. This was no trivial achievement.

He was an erudite scholar, a wise teacher and administrator at Khallikote College.

His services, as a political leader, to Berhampur, to the state of Odisha (nee Orissa) and to the nation, most importantly to the Bengal Nagpur Railway labour movement are all well known.

Pandit Ramalingam Garu had left behind a legacy which the students and staff of the City High School, as well as the citizens of Berhampur could and should follow.

Dr. Pothapragada Venkateswarlu, D.Sc., Ph.D
(Grandson of W. Jaganadham Garu, brother of Pandit Ramalingam Garu)
January 30, 2013.
6330 Humboldt Ave South
Richfield. MN 55423.
USA

Remembering MR. Ramalingam -

SMT. Komalam and Yerrababu my parents brought me to this world. My mothers' parents SMT. PILLAMMA and Pandit RAMALINGAM broughtup me with care to become a doctor. Ramalingam garu participated in Independant struggle and used to go to Jail When he suddenly goes to Jail Pillamma garu took over the responsibility of the family management with dignity and courage. Seeing this I learned to face the hurdles in my life with calmness, courage and dignity. Ramalingam garu taught us the dignity of labour. This concept helped me doing all work for myself till to-day Ramalingam garu when give advice to a problem it would be the same for family members or outsiders Grand parents never enforced their views on us. By watching them we learned what is right and what is wrong. Great grandparents they are who influenced my life so much that every-day I remember them and I miss them a lot.

Santakumari

(DR. P. SANTH KUMARI

రామలింగం తాతగారు

"పిల్లలు, పెద్దలు రామలింగం తాతగారు వచ్చారు అందరు రండి" అని మార్కండేయ తాతగారి గొంతు వినబడగానే ఎక్కడెక్కడ వున్న పిల్లలు పెద్దలు అందరూ హాలులోకి వచ్చారు. అక్కడ పెద్ద కుర్చీలో బాపూజీలా, దేవదూతలాగా, రవీంద్రనాద్ ఠాగూర్‌లాగా కనిపిస్తున్న స్పురద్రూపి గెడ్డం తాతగారు కుర్చీని ఉన్నారు. అందరం వరుసగా వెళ్ళి ఆయన కాళ్ళకు నమస్కరించి ఒక ప్రక్కగా నిల్లున్నాం. ఒక్కొక్కరిని పిలిచి నాలుక, కళ్ళు పరీక్షించి "ఒరే మర్కండేయులు, వీరందరికి ఎవరా, వికాంప్లైట్లు టాబ్లెట్లు ఇవ్వరా" అని చెప్పేరు తాతగారి వద్ద చాలా అప్యాయత, ప్రేమ, వాత్సల్యం, అభిమానం పొందేవారము. తర్వాత మాకు తెలిసింది ఏమిటంటే రామలింగం తాతగారు బరంపురం మున్సిపాలిటికి చైర్మన్‌గా పుండేవారనన్న ఆ గ్రామపెద్దగా వ్యవహారించేవారనన్న బరంపురం కో-ఆపరేటివ్ బ్యాంకును. సెంట్రల్ కో-ఆపరేటివ్ బ్యాంకుకు చైర్మన్‌గాను, కల్లికోట కాలేజికి వైస్ ప్రిన్సిపాల్‌గా చేసారని ఆ ఊరందరికి ఆయన నడిచివచ్చే దైవమని అందరి కష్టనష్టాలు తీర్చేవారని, దేశం కోసం చాలా త్యాగాలు చేసారని తెలిసింది రామలింగం తాతగారు మార్కండేయ తాతగారికి మేనబావ మరియు మామగారు కూడాను. కాలేజిలో పిల్లలు సరిగ్గా చదవకపోయిన కాలేజికి రాకపోయిన ఇంటికి వెళ్ళి వాళ్ళపెద్దవారికి తెలియజేసేవారు రామలింగం తాతగారు తన షష్టిపూర్తి 1944లోని జరిగినప్పుడు తనకొచ్చిన అమౌంట్ అంతయు కల్లికోట కాలేజికి ఇంటర్‌మీడియెటల్లో అవుట్ గోయింగ్ మెరిట్ స్టూడెంట్‌స్కి (మేధమెటిక్స్, తెలుగు) స్టూడెంట్స్కి మొదటి బహుమతిగా పెట్టరు. అదృష్టవశాతు 1961 లో తెలుగు నుండి మొదటి బహుమతి నాకు వచ్చినందుకు నేను గర్విస్తున్నాను.

నేను రామలింగం తాతగారి పెద్ద కుమార్తె కోమలం గారి రెండవ కుమారుడు పొత్తాప్రగడ లక్ష్మణరావు గారి భార్యను. మా వారి ద్వారా తెలిసిన కొన్ని సంగతులు. రామలింగం తాతగారి ఎక్కగానొక్క కుమారుడు రామారావు చదువులకని బయటకి వెళ్ళినప్పుడు ఒక కట్ట పోస్టుకార్డుల మీద "రామం - క్షేమం" అని వ్రాసి తన సొంత అడ్రస్ వ్రాసి నెలకి ఎక్కటి పోష్టుచేయమని ఇచ్చారు. ఆయన ముందు చూపుకి జోహార్లు. రామలింగం తాతగారికి ప్రతి చైత్రమాసంలో చిన్న అమ్మవారు ఎంటిమీద వచ్చేది దానికి అమ్మమ్మగారు తెలగపిండి కూర భోజనంలో వేద్దించటం వేపమండలతో విసిరేవారట దానితో ఆయనికి పూర్తిగా నయమయ్యేదట. రామలింగంతాతగారు ఒక మహోన్నత వ్యక్తిత్వం గల ఉత్తమ పురుషుడు. అమ్మమ్మగారు కూడా చాలా ఉన్నతమైన భావాలగల స్త్రీమూర్తి.

డా|| పి. మహాలక్ష్మి
W/o. డా|| పి.యల్. రావు
కనకమహాలక్ష్మి నర్సింగ్ హోమ్,
విశాఖపట్నం 530 002. ఆంధ్రప్రదేశ్, ఇండియా

ABOUT MY GRAND FATHER

My illustrious grandfather was present at my birth. A cherished possession is an early photo taken of me, with his handwritten note of my name on the back. Growing up, we'd call him "gaddam tatagaru". This was very befitting his long, flowing, sage-like beard (and mien). He would relate many stories, some from mythology and others from his life. He was very playful and patient, and would sometimes put me to sleep. All of us loved and respected him immensely.

After I left Cuttack (where I was born), I'd be enraptured by my mother's (who was also inspired by her father in the freedom struggle) accounts of his escapades during the Independence movement.

However, it would take me many more years to understand the magnitude of his influence on the movement, his peers, and his famous students. It will take me a lifetime to fully comprehend the immensity of his patriotic sacrifice, and how his family stood with him in
strength and dignity for the higher ideals of a nation's right to independence and self-determination.

To me, he will live in memory as a paragon, a rare man of the highest expressions of selflessness and scholarship.

A true gentleman and patriot. And I am proud he was my own Grandfather.

B.K.Anand

Anand. B.K
Sr GM--Project
B.Sc(Engg), MIE, Dpl in MBA,C.Engg
Dangote Industries(Zambia)Ltd.,

Remembering Ramalingam.

Thoughts by Angela Wunnam.

On 18th August 2013 something truly magical happened in my life. I received a letter from a hitherto unknown cousin, Janaki Sastry. She had been trying to find me for a long time. We have since been in correspondence and she has introduced me to the amazing man, Wunnava Venkata Varaha Buchi Ramalingam. I am astounded and deeply honoured to find that I am related to him through my paternal grandfather, Eswara Venkata Sitapati Rao Wunnam. Sitapati came over to England in the early 1900's to study law in order to help run the family estate. Sadly, for the family back in India, he fell in love with and married an English lady, Annie Hiles. His father gave him the dreadful choice of abandoning my grandmother or being disowned. He chose to stay with my grandmother, which meant losing his father and being cut off from the family. His father stopped his generous financial stipend and they were plunged into immediate, dire poverty but with great effort and difficulty they survived. He passed his exams and they had one son, Ramon Rao Wunnam – my father. Sitapati never went back to India although there is evidence of some correspondence between him and his father after many years had passed. Tragically both my paternal grandparents died prematurely at the end of 1949, in their early 50's, depriving my father and myself of that vital link to India. I do not remember my grandfather as I was only seven months old when he died. However, my parents told me that he loved me very much and that we had connected closely.

The terrible rift in the family caused by my grandfather's marriage has meant that I have never had access to my Indian ancestry, despite a life-long yearning interest. I do vividly remember my 'Uncle' Ramon and 'Aunty' Tara, who visited us when I was about six years old. I have some letters and documents but otherwise have little knowledge of my Indian family.

So, at very long last, I am now connected. I am in touch with one lovely cousin and she is helping me to work out where my grandfather fitted into the family of Wunnam/Wunnava. When I married, I decided to keep the name of Wunnam as it meant so much to me. My husband, Joe, fully supported and encouraged me to do this and is as excited as I am about my magical connection to Ramalingam and Janaki Sastry. Janaki is doing the family a great service by writing the biography of Ramalingam. Ramalingam was clearly an incredible and amazing man and deserves to have his story told and for more people to know about him. He has also done something wonderful for me in connecting me to my Indian family.

Angela Joy Wunnam

My memories of Tatagaru

My Mum, the second daughter of Pandit Ramalingam told us children about our Tatagaru (grandfather) how she used to travel with him when he attend the meetings of BNR (Bengal Nagpur Railways). Our Tatagaru was fondly known as Gaddam-Tata to young and old. He had radiance and commanded respect from every one by his grace and personality. She said he would put up his hand first for any sacrifice or work that was called upon Gandhians at that time.

My mum used to tell everybody how Tatagaru continued his selfless service to the community and always thought about others and put others interests first. My mum said that when Sri V V Giri wanted to contest for the Parliament, where the Congress natural choice was our Tatagaru , Pandit Ramalingam blessed his pupil and stood down and said the country should be in the hands of youngsters like him. Sri V.V. Giri has acknowledged this in his autobiography which speaks of volumes about what my Grandfather stood for.

Education was always a priority for Tatgaru and as per mum he made his wife (our Ammamma) responsible for the 8 kids that were left in her and Komalam's care. On my visit to the Khallikote college in 1992 the Principal had informed me that an annual award is given in Pandit Ramalingam's name to the best Mathematics P.G. student at the Khallikote college.

From what I heard about him he is no less that the great Mahatma who did not want a position or a place of authority in Independent India and always supported the young to grow and care for this country and the community. We are all proud to be his descendants.

Vinod Siva Bommireddipalli

(Grand Son of Late Sri W. V. V. B. Ramalingam)
Sydney NSW
Austrlia

My grand father, Pandit Ramalingam, was a staunch nationalist. And had undergone imprisonment several times during the freedom struggle of India.

His nationalist ideology got reflected when the question of formation of separate state of Orissa cropped up. The southern districts of Ganjam and Koraput were to be given to the then Madras Presidency.

But my grand father, opposed to the idea, fought tooth & nail and stood steadfast with the Maharaja of Parlakhemundi to ensure that these two districts remained with Orissa. And they succeeded in their endevour.

May be his love for Orissa made him to force my father to get me admitted to a Municipal Primary school with oriya medium after the first linguistic state of Orissa was formed (in 1936). I had Oriya as an optional subject till my Intermediate, which helped me to get into journalism. I began my career with a Oriya news paper as a reporter at Cuttack.

Ramalingam Tatagaru as I remember him in awe:

From childhood I used to hear about Ramalingam Tatagaru from my own grandfather Pothapragada Krishna Murthy garu and my father Narasinga Rao garu who himself was a Mathematics Faculty in Parlakemidi. It was in 1954 that I came closer to Ramalingam Tatagaru and know more about him. That was the year we shifted from Parlakemidi to Cuttack as my father was transferred to Ravenshaw College, Cuttack.

Whenever I visited Ramalingam Tatagaru's house in Ranihat in Cuttack I was always awe-struck by the large shelves full of books amidst which he would sit in an arm-chair and read. His stylish reading glasses and flowing beard used to draw me into a trance. While my father would be discussing so many things with him, I used to play with my cousin Devi (Devkumar), also a class-mate at Ranihat High School.

The two incidents etched deeply in my memory of Ramalingam Tatagaru were;
(i) He convinced my father to agree that I should write my Matriculation examinations in English rather than Oriya, at which I was not very proficient having started learning the language just two years before. Probably it was only Ramalingam Tatagaru alone, who could make my father change his mind, my own grandfather having expired a couple of years before.
(ii) Second was his advice, a turning point in my life in 1959. My father died in an accident while I had just completed my first year Engineering. Utkal University offered a job under humanitarian consideration of an administrative job; Ramalingam Tatagaru insisted that whatever be the consequences, I must continue my Engineering studies and not take up that job. Against many pressures of near and far relatives, I took Tatagaru's advice and continued my professional studies.

Out of his own children Subhadra (atta) was one of my favourites. I always thought she and Baburao Mamayya made such a handsome pair, so affectionate to me and my family. I would always carry his fond pat on the back as a push into the future for bigger achievements. That we are born into such ancestry and lineage is a boon in itself.

Pothapragada V B R K Brahmam
b 1941
Adviser, Quality Systems
Achrya Instutes, Bangalore

సమాధానం తెలియని (ప్రశ్న)

చిన్నతనం నుంచి రామలింగం మేష్టారి గురించి తెలిసినా వారిని వ్యక్తిగతంగా కలుసుకొనే అవకాశం చాలా చాలా కాలం వరకూ రాలేదు. కో కాలేజీ చదువుమూర్తి క్లాస్ నెలలో అయిపోతుందనగా ఎవడోపని మీద కటకం వెళ్ళి వెళ్ళి వచ్చింది. అది అయ్యేక వారింటికి వెళ్ళి—కటకంలో ఆ అయలు తెలియన వారెవరు? — తలుపు కొట్టేసాను. లోనుండి "ఎవరు?" అని ప్రేమలతో కూడిన గర్జన విన బడింది.

ఏమని సమాధానం చెప్పాలో తెలియక "నేనే నండి" అన్నాను. తికమక పడుతూ. మరో అయదు నిమషాలకి తలుపు తెరుచుకుంది. ఏమి గంభీరమైన విక్రమం రావాలుయూ! "నేనంటే ఎవరు?" రవంత చికాకుగాసే! నేను గుటక మింగి జవాబు చెప్పేలో నే "ఎవరు కావాలి?"

ఒకనాటి సమాధ్నాని, వారి మనుమరాలి పేరు చెప్పేసు. "ఎవరూ ఇంట్లో లేరు. రేపే పోదికిరా" తరువాతి కథ అప్రస్తుత మనుకొండి కాని ఆ (ప్రశ్న) 'ఎవరు నువ్వు?" నన్ను యీనాటికి వదల్లేదు. చిత్రమేమం టే భగవాన్ రమణ మహర్షి పరిధిలోకి వచ్చిన తరవాత అదే (ప్రశ్న)! సమాధానం గురించి యింకా ఆలా చెప్పస్తునే వున్నాను...

— రామకృష్ణ శాస్త్రి

My Inspirational Grandfather

On his 129th Birthday today when I reflect about my late maternal grandfather Wunnava Venkata Varaha Buchhi Ramalingam, I feel humbled in myself.

The charisma of Gandhiji was so contagious and his influence was so profound it not only mesmerised his countrymen but the whole world; and my grandfather was no exception. Coming from a well to do Zamindar family he let himself become an ardent follower of Gandhiji's philosophy and thought and gave up everything he had on Gandhiji's call for Independence through TRUTH and non-violence (the Two powerful weapons Mahatma gave to world) and thus Ramalingam was nick-named as 'Orissa Gandhi'.

WVVB Ramalingam was unbiased with anyone -- family or outsiders; and delivered his opinion/advise/judgement alike.

Ramalingam could sign with both hands, but he always signed with his left hand on official documents. Clad in Khadi dhoti and a cotton sling-bag on his shoulder and the walking stick he imbibed Mahatma's simplicity and sacrifice to the world, adhering to the two other potent weapons -- TRUTH and non-violence. Just like his very high thinking and ACTIONS on any issue and the hold Ramalingam had on the subject was a bit difficult for any ordinary person to understand him unless they lifted themselves higher. Fortunate was Ramalingam to live and work along and during Mahatma's lifetime.

As the only one among his grandchildren to have Ramalingam as my middle name, I feel blessed. Like him I am also a left-hander. I am truly influenced by my late grandfather's traits and try to live up to them.

I sincerely pay my homage to my grandfather W.V.V.B. Ramalingam.

(Dr. Bommireddipalii Ramalingam Santosh)

Visakhapatnam. Andhra Pradesh. India

23rd October 2013

I am filled with awe and admiration when I think of my great grandfather Late W.V.V.B. Ramalingam. His patriotism for the nation and the unconditional love he showered to the family inspire us even today.

On his 50th death anniversary we all pay homage to our great grandfather. We at home in our humble way paid our homage to him with a kind remembrance and lit for 24x7 a big mud oil-lamp in front of his photo. We try to complete the ellipsis of Wunnava-family and hope that all his descendants will cherish his achievements, his dignity, his dedication to the cause he believed in and his contributions for the welfare of his home town and his personal sacrifices. For me my great grandfather remains my role model and I am personally proud to be a small part of his family. I am filled with awe and admiration when I think of my great grandfather Late W.V.V.B. Ramalingam. His patriotism for the nation and the unconditional love he showered to the family inspire us even today.

On his 50th death anniversary we all pay homage to our great grandfather. We at home in our humble way paid our homage to him with a kind remembrance and lit for 24x7 a big mud oil-lamp in front of his photo. We try to complete the ellipsis of Wunnava-family and hope that all his descendants will cherish his achievements, his dignity, his dedication to the cause he believed in and his contributions for the welfare of his home town and his personal sacrifices. For me my great grandfather remains my role model and I am personally proud to be a small part of his family.

Jai Hind!!

Sign _Narasimha Rajesh_ 21/07/2013
Pothapragada Narasimha Rajesh
s/o Late P.Raguhveer

ANECDOTES OF PANDIT RAMALINGAM

Pandit Wunnava Ramalingam Garu, a scholar par excellence, a revered teacher, an inspiring leader and a great human being was a pillar of Berhampur town in Ganjam district of the state of Orissa in the early twentieth century.

A lot has been said and written about him and I have come to know many anecdotes about him from my father, Late Dr. P. L. Rao; but two of these anecdotes stand out in my memory. First, during his student days, he was so well versed in his subjects, especially mathematics, that he would first chew some betel leaves and nuts (paan) before starting to write the exam. While all the other students were busy writing he would slowly prepare the paan and chew it. He would then turn his attention to the question paper and in a jiffy he would complete answering the entire paper. This uncanny ability of his to identify solutions to problems / questions in very quick time stood him in good stead in his later life.

Second, during his stint as the Chairman of Berhampur Municipality almost a hundred years ago, he used to go on early morning rounds to verify whether the municipal sanitation employees were doing their job properly or not. He also used these early morning rounds to resolve any complaints that the residents of the town had. So a sense of discipline was inculcated in the municipal staff by setting an example and grievance redressal was done on the spot without putting the residents in a bother. These modern management principles elucidated by Management Gurus like Peter F. Drucker were practiced by Pandit Ramalingam almost a hundred years ago. My congratulations and best wishes to the author, Janaki Sastry, for having painstakingly brought out an informative tome on the great man, Pandit Ramalingam.

Ravi Tez Pothapragada, B.E., PGDTD
Son of Dr. P. L. Rao, Ph.D., Grandson of Pandit Ramalingam
e-mail: ravitez2006@yahoo.co.in

ପଣ୍ଡିତ ରାମଲିଙ୍ଗମ୍ ଙ୍କ ସୁନ୍ଦର ଇଶ୍ୱର ଙ୍କ ଉପରେ ପ୍ରଭାବ

[Odia handwritten text]

Master Ramalingam's impact on Sunder Eswar's life

Pandit Ramalingam with his life style made a great impact on the lives of his grand children. I being one of them too acquired the discipline, punctuality, long hours of reading and keeping regular contacts with friends and relations. He encouraged in learning different languages and he himself was a linguist. His passion for state language Oriya was such that he put his two grand children in Oriya medium schools for studies and chandamama the monthly magazine oriya edition was promptly subscribed at the earliest.

Pandit Ramalingam was an voracious reader and had a large number of books on different subjects and in different languages. He had donated all his collection to utkal university library when it was a cuttack as mr. G.C. Rath, its registrar. The books were around one truck load.

His love to meet friends and relations was so great that on his last day of innings he has his usual rounds of visits on return home in the evening, retired to his room and breathed his last.

WE MISS HIM –

(Sunder)

My Great-grandfather

As a child I remember listening with awe and wonder at many remarkable episodes of my great-grandfather's involvement in the acquisition of India's freedom. He was guided by the philosophy of 'Bhagvat Gita', which he was allowed to carry while he was in jail. He would often quote:

Karmanye Vadhikaraste

Ma Phaleshu Kadachana;

Ma Karma phala hetur bhuh

Ma te sangostv akarmani.

(chapter2, verse Verse47)

Meaning:

"Do your duty and be detached from its outcome, do not be driven by the end product, enjoy the process of getting there."

He had photographic memory and hence mastered several Indian and European languages. He had an exceptional sense of purpose and often said that a strong motivational sense is essential for achievement together with the correct attitude driving an appropriate action. This was very much the motto of his life.

The way he led his life has always inspired and guided me throughout my life in numerous ways. I am fortunate to have known about this mighty personality who will always remain a living legend in my heart.

Mahita

(great-granddaughter of Pandit W.V.V.B.Ramalingam)

Tribute to Pandit Ramalingam

I would like to cordially greet everyone who came to this inauguration function to show our appreciation and gratitude to a noble man; both in birth and in dedication to the cause he believed in. In his work Pandit Ramalingam sowed intelligence and creativity, boldness and prudence, and always strived for justice, he had a heart sensitive and valiant, a soul austere.

He was well respected and highly successful provost, known to his contemporaries for his judgement and was regarded as the leading light of the Non-cooperation Movement of Ganjam district prior to Independence of India. He was generous and genuine convener who listened as much as he spoke, identifying common ground, defining shared purpose, and driving progress.

Today, in the year of Pandit Ramalingam's 50th death Anniversary, we are gathered to celebrate his life, his devotion to the City of Berhampur and his devotion to education.

Pandit Ramalingam resides in the heart of every member of his family as loving person both as a parent and as a grandparent along with his wife Pillamma.

On a personal level I would like to pay my profound and heartfelt tribute to my grandfather who I believe has made me what I am today.

I sincerely wish to pay my immense gratitude to Dr. P. Venugopal Rao, the stalwart of this mammoth task he undertook, and thank him for his undivided support, dedication form the outset. He was supported in this task by Sri P. Satyanarayana alis Babu in fixing and conduction, co-ordinating all the activities in this project . As Dr P. Venugopal Rao says **"Babu was a pillar of strength to the project and without his full support the construction of the Ramalingam Block classrooms would not have been materialized."**

(An extract from the Inauguration speech)

Janaki Sastry

Janaki Sastry

3rd February 2010

U.K.

Appendix III

Documents

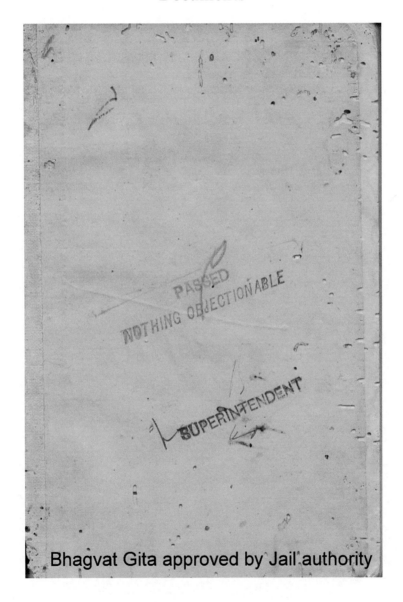

PASSED
NOTHING OBJECTIONABLE

SUPERINTENDENT

Bhagvat Gita approved by Jail authority

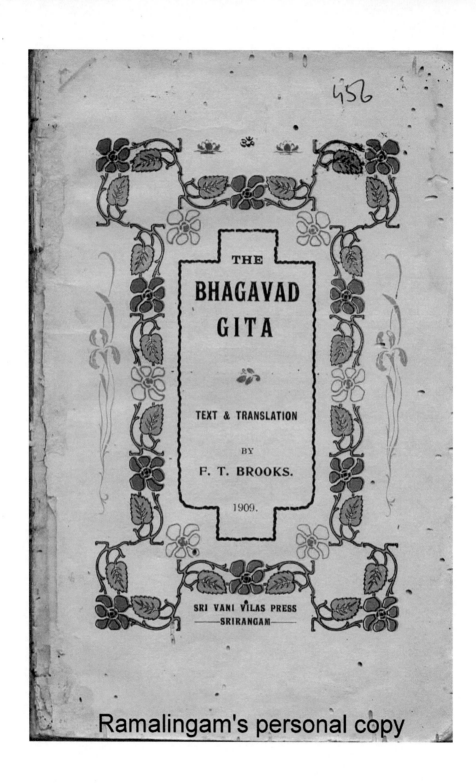

THE
BHAGAVAD GITA

TEXT & TRANSLATION

BY

F. T. BROOKS.

1909.

SRI VANI VILAS PRESS
—SRIRANGAM—

राजन्संस्मृत्य संस्मृत्य संवादमिममद्भुतम् ।
केशवार्जुनयो: पुण्यं हृष्यामि च मुहुर्मुहु: ॥ ७६

तच्च संस्मृत्य संस्मृत्य रूपमत्यद्भुतं हरे: ।
विस्मयो मे महान्राजन्हृष्यामि च पुन: पुन: ॥

यत्र योगेश्वर: कृष्णो यत्र पार्थो धनुर्धर: ।
यत्र श्रीर्विजयो भूतिर्ध्रुवा नीतिर्मतिर्मम ॥

इति मोक्षसंन्यासयोगो ना
अष्टादशोऽध्याय: ॥

इति श्रीमद्भगवद्गीता समाप्ता ॥

The last page of Bhagvad Gita

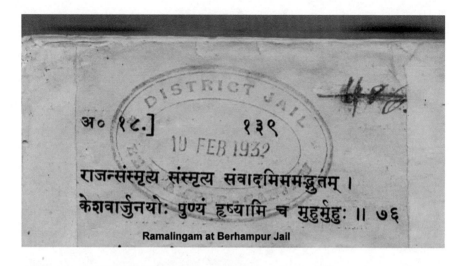

राजन्संस्मृत्य संस्मृत्य संवादमिममद्भुतम् ।
केशवार्जुनयोः पुण्यं हृष्यामि च मुहुर्मुहुः ॥ ७६

Ramalingam at Berhampur Jail

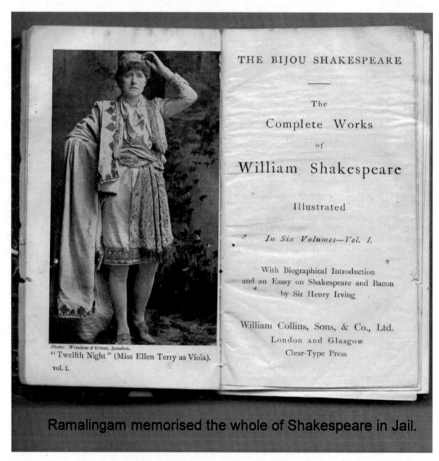

THE BIJOU SHAKESPEARE

The

Complete Works

of

William Shakespeare

Illustrated

In Six Volumes—Vol. I.

With Biographical Introduction
and an Essay on Shakespeare and Bacon
by Sir Henry Irving

William Collins, Sons, & Co., Ltd.
London and Glasgow
Clear-Type Press

Photo: Window & Grove, London.
"Twelfth Night" (Miss Ellen Terry as Viola).
vol. I.

Ramalingam memorised the whole of Shakespeare in Jail.

THE PILGRIM'S PROGRESS FROM THIS WORLD TO THAT WHICH IS TO COME DELIVERED UNDER THE SIMILITUDE OF A DREAM BY JOHN BUNYAN

WITH EIGHT COLOURED
AND OTHER FULL PAGE
ILLUSTRATIONS BY
HAROLD COPPING

"I have used similitudes."—Hosea xii. 10

FIFTH IMPRESSION

London
THE RELIGIOUS TRACT SOCIETY
4 Bouverie Street and 65 St Paul's Churchyard
1907

Another book he was allowed in Jail

Arjuna's Questions

1. What is my duty? — II 7

2. What is the mark of the man of steadfast wisdom? — II 54

3. If true insight is superior to work why do you urge me to do this horrible work? — III 1

4. What impels a man to commit sin in spite of himself? — III 36

5. How didst thou teach Vivasvat born long before you? — IV 4

6. Which is better renunciation of works or their selfless performance? — V 1

7. As mind is fickle, how can there be yoga of evenness of mind? — VI 33

8. What way does a man go who has faith but is not steadfast + fallen away from yoga? — VI 37

9. What is absolute?
   „ Soul?
   „ Work?
   „ underlying all created things?
   „ gods?
   „ Sacrifices here in the body?
   How art these to be known at the time of death by the disciplined? — VIII 1+2

10. What are all thy divine forms?
    How am I to know thee by constant meditation?
    In what aspects art thou to be contemplated? — X 16, 17

11. I have learnt from thee the origin of beings
    „ dissolution „
    thine inexhaustible greatness.
    Show me thy divine form — XI 3

12. Tell me who thou art — with form so terrible — XI 31

13. Show me thy other form 4-armed — XI 45-6

14. Having seen thy human form I am composed — XI 51

15. Which are better versed in yoga —
    those that worship thee
    or „ „ „ the unmanifested?
    + imperishable — XII 1

16. What are the marks of those who have risen above 3 dispositions — XIV 21

17. What is the state of those who leave aside the ordinances of scriptures, but offer sacrifices with faith — is it Sattva or Rajas: or Tamas? — XVII 1

18. What is the true nature of —
    1. Renunciation
    2. Resignation? — XVIII 1

Ramalingam's righthand writing

304

Chapter IV

1) $a \times (b \times c) + b \times (c \times a) + c \times (a \times b)$
$= a \cdot cb - a \cdot bc + b \cdot ac - b \cdot ca + c \cdot ba - c \cdot ab$
$= b a \cdot c - c a \cdot b + c b \cdot a - a b \cdot c + a c \cdot b - b c \cdot a$
$= a(-bc + cb) + b(a \cdot c - c \cdot a) + c(-ab + ba)$
$= a \cdot 0 + b \cdot 0 + c \cdot 0 = 0$

2) $a \times \{b \times (c \times d)\} = a \times (b \cdot dc - b \cdot cd)$
$= a \times (c \, b \cdot d - d \, b \cdot c)$
$= a \times c \, b \cdot d - a \times d \, b \cdot c$
$= b \cdot d \, a \times c - b \cdot c \, a \times d$

$a \times (b \times \{c \times (d \times \varepsilon)\})$
$= a \times (c \cdot \varepsilon \, b \times d - c \cdot d \, b \times \varepsilon)$
$= a \times (b \times d \, c \cdot \varepsilon - b \times \varepsilon \, c \cdot d)$
$= a \times (b \times d) \, c \cdot \varepsilon - a \times (b \times \varepsilon) \, c \cdot d$
$= (a \cdot d \, b - a \cdot b \, d) c \cdot \varepsilon - (a \cdot \varepsilon \, b - a \cdot b \, \varepsilon) c \cdot d$
$= (b \, a \cdot d - a \cdot b \, d) c \varepsilon - (b a \cdot \varepsilon - a \cdot b \, \varepsilon) c \cdot d$
$= b \, a \cdot d \, c \cdot \varepsilon - a \cdot b \, d \, c \cdot \varepsilon - b \, a \cdot \varepsilon \, c \cdot d + a \cdot b \, \varepsilon \, c \, d$
$= b(a \cdot d \, c \cdot \varepsilon - a \cdot \varepsilon \, c \cdot d) - a \cdot b(d \, c \cdot \varepsilon - \varepsilon \, c \, d)$
$= (a \cdot d \, c \cdot \varepsilon - a \cdot \varepsilon \, c \cdot d) b - a \cdot b(c \cdot d \, \varepsilon - c \cdot \varepsilon \, d)$

$(a \times a) \cdot b = a \cdot (a \times b)$
$a \cdot b = b \cdot a$

Ramalingam's lefthand writing

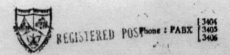

REGISTERED POST Phone : PABX 3404 3405 3406

BERHAMPUR UNIVERSITY
BHANJA BIHAR
BERHAMPUR - 760 007 (ORISSA)   Regd. Post.

No. 6524/33 /Welfare/gu/91   DATED 13-6-91

From:

The Deputy Registrar, SC/ST Cell,
Berhampur University.

To

Dr. W.G.Rama Rao,
M.B.,M.S.,F.R.C.S.E.,F.R.C.S.,F.I.C.S.,
F.I.M.S.A.,F.I.M.A.,
Urvashi Building,
Flat 602, Off Sayani Road,
Prabhadevi,
B O M B A Y - 400025.

Sub:-   Pandit W.V.V.B. Ramalingam Award.

Ref:-   This office letter No.1496 dated 18.2.91
        Your letter dated 22.3.91.

thousand) only for creation of an endowment be accepted from

you with thanks and a Gold Medal and certificate of merit

in memory of your father late Pandit M.V.V.B.Ramlingam be

awarded to a meritorious M.Phil (Mathematics) student of

this University each year and the draft rules prepared in

this regard has been approved and attached herewith.

With regards.

Yours faithfully,

13/6/91

DEPUTY REGISTRAR

Enclosures:

Ramalingam award for best M.Phil (Maths)

306

Office of Collector, Ganjam.

Dated, Chatrapur, 16th Aug. 45.

Sir,

Your presence is requested at the Barracks Maidan, Berhampore, at 9·00 A. M. on the 20th August, 1945 to participate in the Victory Parade and the Celebrations marking the end of the War with Japan. Please be in your seat by 8-45 A. M.

Yours sincerely,

C. L. Bryson.

To ....

Invitation to Errababu

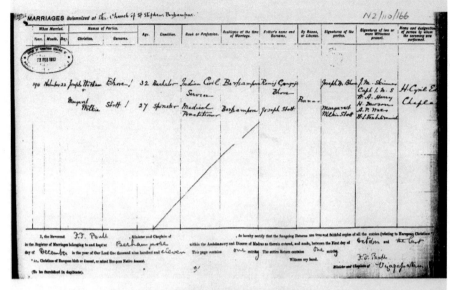

Dr Margaret Stott got married at Berhampur

NOTICE

A Public Meeting under the auspicies of THE GANJAM DISTRICT WAR COMMITTEE, will be held at THE MUNICIPAL HALL, BERHAMPUR, at 6 P. M. on SATURDAY the 6th JANUARY 1945 and will be presided over by I. H. MACDONALD ESQ., I. C. S, Collector and President, The Ganjam District War Committee to inaugurate THE SAVINGS DRIVE FORTNIGHT.

You are cordially invited to attend.

F. R. Steele,

BERHAMPUR,

1st. January 1945.

Secretary,
The Ganjam District
War Committee.

To Ramalingam

P.L-N.Rao
c/o P.L. RAO.
P.W.O.

A.C.C. Limited
WADI - 585 225
INDIA.

My Dear Jani,

You are all now doubly orphaned with the demise of your Grand old Mother. She was more than a Mother to you all. She left you all in great sorry and indebtedness. What all she did you children and we could not be redeemed in our life. May God rest her kind Soul in Peace.

Obituary of W. Gandhi Rama Rao

Stop Press

Dr WG Rama Rao
1915-2010

It would be hard to find a postgraduate in PMR who would not have been amazed at the zeal with which Dr WG Rama Rao used to come in smiling and talking with them, teaching, asking questions, telling them how to study, demonstrate signs, refer to what came up recently in the literature and the least to tell them the importance of the speciality. I was taken aback the first time I was reading a paper on 'Gait Analysis in Hemiplegia' at NIRTAR in 1982. Dr Rama Rao had remarked, if a person with hemiplegia can walk is good enough, it does not matter how he walks. At that time being young and over enthusiastic and new to the speciality, I was eager to come out with an anecdote that won't it be nice if he could walk better. Now with years gone into rehabilitation, I realized, how true and practical he was. He was not pulling my leg that I thought at that time but teaching me the realities of rehabilitaton.

Everytime Dr Rama Rao entered our department, he would carry a load of journals, he used to be the editor of two, and requested us to please have those delivered to the persons nearby. I used to wonder why does he have to carry such a load all the way from Mumbai, now I realize after being into this how much effort and money is saved which is always short to publish and post a journal. He had showed me his room filled with journals, papers, old envelopes he used to keep to be used for rough work not very different from Mahatma Gandhi's ideologies of not to waste a thing. True to have the great man's name "Gandhi" in his own.

Even though he came into PMR much later in his life, he devoted more than his full attention to it in addition to being an active member of the IOA and founder member of IAPMR. Formulations of rules and regulations of IAPMR to the memorandum of association was all a gift of Dr Rama Rao. He was the know all person for any dispute or a dilemma and would be able to cite the rule straight out of his memories. That is the reason he was always looked up to for any constitutional matter in the association.

How many of us write to fellow members or to any governmental or other organizations about what we feel strongly about. Dr Rama Rao never ever missed an opportunity he had or any thing that he felt needed to be changed or brought about. He would seek an appointment with any conceivable person and say what needed to be done for the speciality, for the association or a member of the association. Earlier days, his famous Inland Letters were a treasure. In the recent years, changing with times, he moved over to the modern method of communication over the emails. Not many even younger to him could adapt to that change though with great humility he would say that he just knows how to press a button and reply.

Love for the young ones and any one was ample right from his heart. We hardly offer to drop our seniors or friends off to a place if they are visiting us. The last time I visited his place a couple of years ago, he came down from his building to say good bye to me but instead ended up dropping me off to the Railway Station in his car while saying that his dear wife does not allow him to drive during the night but it is all right once in a while since it was getting late for me and the station far off. He himself used to walk over two kilometers to Dadar Station from his home and encouraged me to do that a few years ago while I was about to hail a taxi.

We stick on to the worldly things and never ever think of sharing. His love of traveling to various centres and love for those new to the speciality to learn more did not make him think twice before traveling himself to all the corners of the country on his own and interact with everyone but also made others go around at his cost by initiating such a novel fellowship, Dr WG Rama Rao's Fellowship, to enable young physiatrists to go around and gain knowledge and spread knowledge. Most of us have availed that. Donating a huge amount of money, more than a hundred times the salary of a PG at that time was donated by him to the association. How many can ever think of doing that leave aside even setting aside a month's salary for this kind of purpose or any philanthropic cause..

Such a great human being did not wish to bother even his family running around the hospital knowing very well that his time had come, he had to suffer any way but he did not wish anyone in his family to suffer along with him. He chose his right to be at home and right to not being investigated or treated against his will. He wanted to be at home, at peace, with his family. Prayers poured in from all corners of the world for his recovery. He did recover fully, from his pains and sufferings and had a wonderful end to his most wonderfully fulfilling life people only dream of having. Rightly called the 'Bhishma Pitamah' of IAPMR. The 'Physiatrist of the Century' would be remembered not only for centuries but probably for ever. IAPMR salutes this great personality with a heavy heart..

Dr U Singh
Editor

Pandit.W.V.V.B.Ramalingam,   Hazra Bhavan, Ranihat,
         B.A;L.T.   Cuttack-1. 9.2.62.

My dear Veeradhi,

                  Yours of the 3rd. inst.
The theaves dug a hole
in the compound wall by the side of the bath room
and entered. Only a few brass vessels were lost,
as they didnot come this side of the well since
there was a light on the varandah on which Dev &
Sunder were sleeping.

                 I am glad your mother-in-
law lives very near you. She will be helpful
to chy. sow. Vani.   What did you do on the
annual Sradh day of your mother! You are were
perhaps in the train.   We are all well here
and hope the same with you both there.

               Yours affectionately,

Ramalingam's last letter

Appendix IV

References

1. Pillamma's tape recording of 1963
2. The Berhampur Co-operative Urban Bank Ltd
   Golden jubilee Souvenir
3. The Berhampur Co-operative Urban Bank Ltd
   Diamond Jubilee Souvenir
4. History of Andhra Bhashabhivardhani Samaj, Berhampur
5. Salt Satyagraha in the Coastal Andhra by Dr CH.M. Naidu (1986)
6. V. V. Giri by G.S. Bhargva, (1969) Page 14
7. Alumni of Presidency College, Student No.40
8. My Life & Time- V.V.Giri (Macmillan Co of INDIA 1976) Pages 10 & 121
9. Glimpses of the History of Co-operative movement in Orissa by M.K. Purkait (2000)
10. The Orissa Co-operative Journal. Volume 15-16 (published by Orissa State Co-operative Union) Page 116& 117 Obituary
11. History of the working-class movement in Bengal (People's publishing House, New Delhi, 1978) page 42
12. Jail Manual (volume1, 1928) prison Act by W.W. Hunter
13. W.W Hunter Director General of Statistics to the Govt. of India Volume V-Ganjam.
14 .Madras Presidency records 1920-1947
15. Orissa Ganjam District records 1932-1947
16. Studies in National Movement in India by Himansu S. Patnaik & Prasanna Kumar Misra, Utkal University, P.G. Dept. of History
   Pages 39-41
17. Indian National Congress & Orissa, 1885-1936, by Purushotam Kar published by Kitab Mahal, 1987.
18. COLONIALISM in Orissa by R.N. Bhattacharya, (January 2006) page 109
19. Mehatab, Harekrishna (1960) The History of Orissa Vol. II
20. H.K. Mehatab – History of Freedom Movement in Orissa, Cuttack, 1954.
21. British Collectors of Barampur by C.C. Bryson (Now Ganjam District)
22. Orissa Review(highlights of Freedom struggle in Orissa) by K.S.Buhera (p.35)
23. Udyog Mandir of Berhampur
24. The Collected Works of Mahatama (in public domain)= i.e no copy right
25. The story of My Experiment with the Truth by M.K. Gandhi.
26. India office Records at British Library, London
27. APAC Reference Services at the British Library, London
28. W.W.W. World History
29. Beginning of organised Trade-Union Movement in Bengal
30. V.V.Giri letter (16.6.1975)
31. Information collected from friends & family.
32. Several photos contributed by friends & family.

33. Satyagrahis led by Ramalingam Pantulu, Chairman, Berhampur Municipality
 Personal dairy of G.Sivakanthamma (freedom fighters from Giri family)
34. Information from few free websites & Internet contributors.
35. Wikipedia sites.
36. Photos & Information from friends & family.

Appendix V

Photo Gallery

Dr Rajeswar Rao & Mangamma

Dev Kumar interviewing Prince Charles
1975, India

Angela Wunnam, granddaughter of Wunnam Sitapati

Dr.Ramam, Mahita, Jani

Anne & Ramon J. Wunnam, (cousins of Dr. W.G Rama Rao)

Wunnam Sitapati & Annie Hiles
1905

Late Dr. P.Uday Tez
Great-grandson of Ramalingam

P. Markendeya Rao

Anne, Dr Ramam, Jani, Mahita, Ramon Wunnam, 1976

Appendix VI

Great-grandchildren

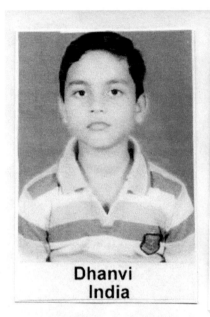

**Dhanvi
India**

Sindhu
India

Nikhil , USA

**Rahul
India**

**Shobana & Venkata
Australia**

Shashank
India

Divya
India

Vikram
India

Amulya

USA

ROHAN & SHAUN

Australia

Deepti USA

Nikhil & Tara
U.S.A.

Veer &
Rhea

India

Rohit & Pallavi, INDIA